THE MONTGOLFIER BROTHERS

AND THE

INVENTION OF

AVIATION

1783-1784

THE MONTGOLFIER BROTHERS

AND THE INVENTION OF AVIATION

1783-1784

With a Word on
the Importance of Ballooning
for the Science of Heat and
the Art of Building Railroads

⌐ *by* ⌐

Charles Coulston Gillispie

Princeton University Press
Princeton, New Jersey

To
*Jean and
Michèle Darde*

CONTENTS

PREFACE

THE OPPORTUNITY to write this book arose through my good fortune in meeting Monsieur and Madame Charles de Montgolfier, who have since become fast friends. They invited my wife and me to spend as much time in their house, Mauvent, on the outskirts of Annonay, as we needed in order to go over papers pertaining to the history of their family. There, through the extraordinary kindness and generosity of many of their relatives, we were able to assemble from different households hundreds of letters and technical documents and to photograph the most important. I have thus been able to study the contents of these family records in conjunction with other records, published and unpublished, that taken together permit reconstituting the circumstances that attended the birth of aviation. Detail concerning those materials will be found in the bibliographical note at the conclusion of this work. Let me here just mark out its boundaries.

The events themselves defined those limits. The book treats mainly of aviation so long as Joseph and Etienne de Montgolfier were directly involved. That was true for little more than the opening year of flight. Thereafter, the subject becomes the contribution of the Montgolfier brothers and of their great-nephew and Joseph's intellectual heir, Marc Seguin, to comprehension of the properties of heat as a form of motive power. As will appear, the invention of the balloon was an early episode in a sequence of developments that culminated in the design of the first French locomotive and construction of the first French railway. The general interest lies in the inventiveness, the science, and the technology, and the particular interest in the start of aviation. In larger matters, the Montgolfiers shared the preoccupations of many of their kind, early industrialists and civil engineers concerned with power in many

countries. Their collective legacy is manifest in the science of thermodynamics no less than in modern systems of transportation.

Seldom has the author of a small book had the pleasure of expressing gratitude as extensive as I feel to so large a number of people, whose cordiality and collaboration have enabled me to bring it off. In addition to Charles de Montgolfier, others of the family in Annonay confided papers to my perusal, notably the late Madame Jean de Montgolfier and her granddaughter Madame Patrick Bodard. Monsieur Régis de Montgolfier was equally generous with the important materials in his possession, especially the archives of Jean-Pierre de Montgolfier, brother of the inventors. Monsieur Stanislas Seguin and his mother, Madame Roger Seguin, allowed me to pass many days in the library of their house, Le Colombier, among the papers descended from Camille Seguin. Madame Amédée Seguin received my wife and me at Varagnes, where we visited the library and laboratory in which Marc Seguin spent his last years.

The abbey of Fontenay, which Marc Seguin also owned for a time, is still the property of a branch of the Montgolfier family. It is also officially a *Monument Historique*, where we were guests of Monsieur and Madame Bernard de Montgolfier. Bernard de Montgolfier is curator of the Musée Carnavalet in Paris, and I am further beholden to him for the photograph of the windmills that the first manned aircraft barely cleared in landing on the Butte-aux-Cailles. Finally, Monsieur Xavier Frachon, who retired recently as director of the Canson and Montgolfier paper mill at Vidalon, took me on a tour and opened to me his personal knowledge of its history. He also welcomed the researches in the archives of the plant of Leonard S. Rosenband, whose thesis on the relationship between management and labor in the factory is the initial source of my knowledge of the industrial background.

As for public archives, I am indebted as in other writings to the courtesy of the personnel of the Archives de l'Académie des Sciences, and in this case equally so to the responsible officials in the Musée de l'Air, the Institut National de la Propriété Industrielle, and the Conservatoire National des Arts et Métiers, all in Paris. In the home territory of the Montgolfiers, the staff of the Archives Départementales de l'Ardèche in Privas were helpful beyond the call of duty or even of professionalism. My demands on the Bibliothèque Municipale de la Ville d'Annonay and on the archives of the Académie des Sciences, des Belles-Lettres, et des Arts de Lyon were less unreasonable, but their forthcoming responses are no less appreciated.

Others have assisted in various ways. Foremost and first is my wife, Emily Gillispie, who in ascending order has been typist, research associate, enthusiast, critic, and fellow passenger in a flight of experimental fancy. We owe our chance to see and feel for ourselves to Malcolm Forbes, who invited us for a ride in a latter-day *montgolfière* on a still August morning in central New Jersey. He has also kindly provided one of the illustrations from among the materials in the balloon museum he has installed in the chateau of Balleroy in Normandy. Alain Dubois took a week from his own work to come from Paris to Annonay to photograph the documents and to develop and print the film. Two of my former students, David Allison of the Naval Research Laboratory, and James Secord of Churchill College, Cambridge, procured photographs respectively of the Meusnier Atlas in the Library of Congress and of Joseph de Montgolfier's *pyro-bélier* from the British patent records conserved in the Science Museum, Kensington. In regard to Joseph's ideas on heat and to the career of Marc Seguin, I have benefited greatly from frequent conversations with Pietro Redondi, who was a member of my seminar at the Ecole des Hautes Etudes en Sciences Sociales in Paris from 1980 through 1982.

A number of illustrations are drawn from the Harold Fowler McCormick Collection in Firestone Library of Princeton University, and I should like to express my gratitude for the interest and courtesy of the staffs of the Rare Book Room and of the Division of Photographic Services, and my special thanks to John C. Leypoldt, who directs the latter. The largest number of pictures, however, comes from the library of the United States Air Force Academy at Colorado Springs. Donald J. Barrett, the Assistant Director, responded to our request for access with a largesse worthy of the splendid aeronautical collection given to the Academy by the late Colonel Richard Gimbel. My research was supported in part by two summer grants from the National Science Foundation.

In observing that good fortune permitted me to come to know the Montgolfiers, living and departed, I do not mean to suggest that a lucky accident was responsible. The meeting was arranged, or so I have strong reason to suspect, by the fine friends to whom this book is dedicated. Michel Darde, Jean's brother, has undertaken to translate the work. May it serve as a small recognition of how the Darde welcome, which grows all the warmer with the passage of time, enlarges our lives and the lives of the many who are their friends.

Paris
June, 1982

A NOTE ON UNITS

THERE IS frequent occasion in this book to mention sizes, weights, and costs. They are given in the units of the period.

Before the definition of the metric system in the Revolution, the basic linear unit in France was the foot. It was divided into twelve *pouces* (thumbs), or inches, and each inch into twelve *lignes* or lines. The next larger unit was the *toise* of six feet, corresponding to the English fathom. The actual lengths varied in different regions, but for scientific work the *pied du roi* of Paris was the standard. It measured 30.5 centimeters or approximately 1.07 English feet.

The basic unit of weight was the *livre* or pound of sixteen ounces. It was equivalent to 489.5 grams or approximately 1.08 English pounds.

The major unit of currency was also called the *livre*. Like English currency, it was divided into twenty sous (corresponding to shillings) and each sou into twelve *deniers* (or pennies). The rate of exchange in the 1780s was approximately twenty-four *livres* to the English pound. In the Revolution the franc, divided decimally into 100 centimes, replaced the *livre*. The value of the franc was equivalent to start with, but inflation was drastic in the 1790s. Comparisons of purchasing power across two centuries are probably meaningless, and social and economic historians often adopt the earnings of a skilled journeyman as an index of value. In the 1780s such a man could expect to earn thirty sous a day, or approximately 400 *livres* a year.

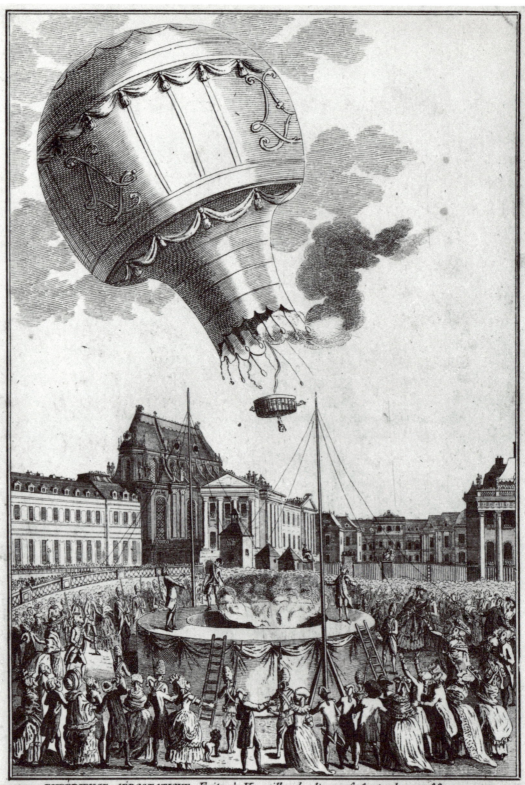

EXPERIENCE AEROSTATIQUE Faite à Versailles le dix neuf Septembre 1783.
En présence de leurs Majestés, de la Famille Royale et de plus de 130.milles Spectateurs. Par M.rs de Montgolfier
avec un Ballon de 57.Pieds de hauteur, sur 41.de Diamètre.
Cette Superbe machine a fond d'Azur, avec le Chiffre du Roi et divers ornements en couleurs d'Or, déplaçoit 37500 pieds
cubes d'Air Atmosphorique, pésant 3192 livres mais la vapeur dont on la remplißoit pésant moitié moin que l'Air commun il restoit
une rupture d'équilibre de 1596 livres sur quoi la machine et la Cage ou étoit un Mouton un Coq et un Canard, pésant ensemble
900 et ce poid devant être soustrait, le Ballon auroit pû enlever encore 696 livres A une heure un Coup de Canon annonça
qu'on alloit remplir la machine, onze minutte après, un second coup apprit quelle étoit pleine et un 3.e quelle alloit partir, elle s'eleva
alors majestuesement à une grande hauteur, a la surprise des Spectateurs et au bruit des aclamations publie. Elle se soutint
quelque tems en Equilibre et descendit lentement 8 minuttes aprés, à 1700 toises de distance du point de son départ dans
le bois de Vaucreßon Carrefour Maréchal. le Mouton le Coq et le Canard n'éprouverent aucune incommodité

Aerostatical Experiment at Versailles, 19 September 1783

THE MONTGOLFIER BROTHERS AND THE INVENTION OF AVIATION

1783-1784

1. To Fix the Date

On Wednesday, 4 June 1783, rain marred the day in Annonay, a small city in the northern tip of the region called the Vivarais. Even so, people began gathering late in the morning in the Place des Cordeliers, the lower square from which a single-arched bridge traversed the river Deûme, a swift little stream that rushes into the slightly larger and slower Cance a short way further down (Fig. 1). In the middle of the square a pair of brothers directed four husky laborers in the construction of a wooden scaffold. Joseph and Etienne Montgolfier, forty-three and thirty-eight years old respectively, were dressed in the fashion of the prosperous provincial bourgeoisie, Joseph carelessly, Etienne neatly. Their men set up two masts stayed with cords, one on either side of the platform, both fitted with a pulley inside at the top. Two detachable ropes, one running over each wheel, were fastened to an eye sewn onto the center of a pile of fabric collapsed on the platform. Drawing on the cords, the workmen hauled the mass into position so that it hung shapelessly between the poles, an enormous bag of sackcloth lined with three thin layers of paper, though the spectators could not see that.

The spectators could see that the bottom gaped open. Stretched on a frame of scantling, the mouth was eight feet square. Under it the brothers slid a brazier in which they had kindled a fire of shredded wool and dry straw, started with the aid of alcohol. They had awaited the emergence from an official doorway of some two dozen witnesses whose presence in Annonay was the reason for proceeding in the face of inclement weather. The diocesan assembly—*Etats particuliers*—of the Vivarais was in the next-to-last day of its annual week-long session. Interest among the deputies

and other observers rose with the swelling of the great balloon from limpness into form. Like a live thing it began bucking and tugging at the ropes as it filled with hot air. The quartet of peasants reined down with all their weight. Etienne ordered them to let go, and the great globe leaped almost straight up to a height of 3,000 feet (500 *toises*), whereupon air currents carried it a good half-league (over a mile and a half), before it settled to earth, lighting on a rough stone fence between sections of a vineyard. At the last moment the brothers had decided to suspend the brazier below the mouth of the balloon in order to counter the cooling of the rain. After landing, the iron basket tipped over and spilled embers onto the fabric, setting it afire. Country folk working among the vines were too frightened to put out the flames, and in a few minutes the great envelope was consumed.

No eyewitness said whether this progenitor of all balloons was decorated with the gaiety that has enhanced the appeal of its descendants, but we do know its physical characteristics from a letter written by a brother of the inventors, the abbé Alexandre-Charles Montgolfier.[1] It weighed 500 pounds. It was slightly elongated with a lateral diameter of thirty-five feet and a displacement near 28,000 cubic feet. The bag was pieced together out of four fitted segments, consisting of a dome and three lateral bands, the middle being the longest, all fastened by 1,800 buttons sewn in three rings along the upper edge and one end of each band. The assembly was reinforced vertically by a kind of fishnet of strong cords covering the outside surface (Fig. 2). Loss of hot air through the buttonholes was the main reason for the limitation of flight time to about ten minutes. The next day Joseph and Etienne petitioned their lordships of the Estates to record

1. Annonay, Place des Cordeliers as it appeared in the early 19th century

a formal approbation of the experiment, and thus to establish their priority—"donner une datte certaine"—in this first public trial of flight (Fig. 3). For their "machine diöstatique" had performed according to the theory that had guided them in its construction; they meant to improve the design and make it useful; they feared lest others benefit from their discovery and appropriate the glory. The deputies obliged on 5 June and adjourned.[2]

The body whose minutes officially recorded the start of the age of flight was itself something of an anomaly. First convoked in 1381, the Estates of the Vivarais were unique among comparable assemblies of the French monarchy in representing only two orders, the nobility and the third estate. The bishop of Viviers sat only as baron of Largentière, and the clergy sent no deputies. The Vivarais combined a local identity going back to the Helvii of Roman Gaul with a transitional geography. Part of Languedoc, its territory constituted a wedge of that great province pressing north along the west bank of the Rhône into the mass of central France. Annonay

was and remains a market town and an industrial town in the commercial and cultural orbit of Lyons. A mere 120 kilometers to the south, Aubenas belongs to the Midi, as do the riverside communities below Viviers. On the west the low granitic ranges that divide the region from the upper Loire hint of proximity to Auvergne. Give or take a dozen-odd communes along the southern and western fringes, the Ardèche of today (named in the Revolution for the river that flows from the Cévennes by Aubenas into the Rhône) virtually coincides with the Vivarais of old. The modern department thus has the distinction of more nearly corresponding to an ancient province than does any other.

Among the privileges of the local assembly was that of sending deputies to the Estates of Languedoc sitting in Montpellier, by far the most vital and enterprising of the representative institutions that had survived from the Middle Ages in peripheral regions of France. The Estates of Vivarais apportioned the taxes levied by the Estates of Languedoc and had oversight of diocesan civil funds, of public works, and of police and public order. They acted as a combined chamber of commerce and agricultural society and expended small sums in promoting economic initiatives on the part of farmers, tradesmen, and manufacturers.

Local worthies rather than august personages made up the membership. The nobility was represented by thirteen barons, among ten of whom (three did not have the right) rotated the annual duty of sitting for their order in the Estates of Languedoc. The nobleman whose year it was would come on to preside over the Estates of Vivarais. Those sessions alternated between An-

2. Imaginary sketch of Annonay and the first balloon, by the chevalier de Lorimier

DEDIER A MM. DE MONTGOLFIER Freres.

nonay, Viviers, and Aubenas, always in the week following adjournment in Montpellier. Except for the presiding *baron de tour*, the great lords who held these fiefs—the duc de Bourbon for Annonay, the bishop of Viviers, the comte de Vogüé, the baron de Montlaur, etc.—rarely appeared in person. Their place was normally taken by a bailiff, usually a member of the judicial nobility.

As for the third estate, thirteen cities had the right of representation in the Estates of Vivarais, and eight of them rotated in sitting for the diocese in Montpellier. In the intervals of the formal sessions, the powers of the Estates were exercised by three commissioners, a delegate of the Estates of Languedoc, a royal judge, and the consul of Viviers. Finally, a syndic or administrator, a clerk-of-court, a tax collector, and several inspectors comprised the local bureaucracy. In form, they were named annually by the Estates. In fact, these offices had become virtually hereditary in certain families of notables, people of the level of the Montgolfiers, who were leaders in the paper industry.[3]

An unlikelier setting than Annonay for the birth of aviation would be hard to imagine. The north bank of the Cance is precipitous where the small river skirts the town, and the Deûme pours into it through a deep, narrow cleft in the last kilometer of its independent course after flowing through a hilly countryside. Much of Annonay was built into the shelter of these declivities. The main road from Le Puy followed the Cance and that from Saint-Etienne the Deûme. They joined above the Place des Cordeliers, and the combined route there came together with the highway to Lyons. Around about the time of the trial of the balloon, the population consisted of 7,000 to 8,000 inhabitants (today it is about 22,000).

Etienne Montgolfier left a brief sketch of the local economy. At a weekly market people of the mountains to the west exchanged commodities with agricultural producers from the plains of Dauphiny and the banks of the Rhône. The immediate countryside yielded wine and beans, the latter of high quality and much in demand in Provence and Languedoc. Silkworms flourished.

à Nos seigneurs des Etats particuliers
du Vivarais

Supplient humblement Jh. Michel et
Etienne jq. Montgolfier Représentant.
que le 4 juin 1783 il plut a nos seigneurs
d'être témoins de l'essay d'une Machine
Diostatique qui s'éleva a plus de 800
toises d'hauteur que les supliants encouragés
par le succés des diverses experiences qu'ils ont faites
toutes conformes a la théorie qui les a conduit
a cette decouverte Et reflechis les avantages
qui en peuvent resulter de sa perfection
s'occupent de la perfectionner et rendre
utile mais comme ils ont a craindre que
profitant de leur decouverte d'autres
ne s'en approprient la gloire ils suplient
nos seigneurs de vouloir bien par leur
approbation donner une datte certaine
a ce premier essay public Et qu'il plaise
autoriser les suppliants à invoquer
leur témoignage et en outre
ordoner qu'il en soit délivré extrait au suppliant
et les autoriser a invoquer le témoignage de nos
seigneurs

3. Petition by Joseph and Etienne Montgolfier addressed to the *Etats particuliers du Vivarais*, 4 June 1783, in Etienne's hand. The document establishes that the date of the flight was 4 June, not 5 June as is often stated. In the original, the last six lines are on the verso of a sheet of notepaper

A few enterprising cultivators were succeeding with the delicate, temperamental white variety. Tawing leather for the luxury trade in gloves, tanning skins, shearing sheep, preparing and dyeing woolens, a new ribbon factory—all that along with paper, the most important industry by far, made up the manufacturing sector.[4]

2. THE PAPER INDUSTRY

In the 1780s four paper mills were dotted along the Deûme in locations that are still the sites of modern factories: at Faya on the edge of town; at Marmaty upstream a little; and finally at Vidalon-le-bas and Vidalon-le-haut, both deep in the ravine of the parish of Davézieux. The Deûme has a steep pitch and turned the mill wheels strongly except during a few months in summer. Its water is clear and soft, good for washing the rags and holding the pulp in a clean suspension. Annonay had ready access to the markets of Orléans and Paris by way of Saint-Etienne and the Loire and even more so to Marseilles and abroad by the Rhône. The Saône and upper Rhône made the supply of raw material convenient, since the best rags came from Burgundy. The climate was dry and mild enough for sizing paper the year around. Marmaty and Faya belonged to the Johannots and the two Vidalon mills to the Montgolfiers.[5]

The rival families were much alike except in being respectively Protestant and Catholic. In one respect Annonay was thoroughly Languedocian. The city had been grievously split in the religious wars of the 16th century. Early in the 20th century, properly brought up Catholic children were still not allowed to make friends with the offspring of Protestants. Thus divided, and in fierce competition commercially, the Johannots and the Montgolfiers nevertheless had common interests in improving the conditions for trade and manufacturing in the region, in the maintenance of discipline among the labor force, and in the state of the art of making paper. Of the two firms, the Montgolfiers were somewhat better known throughout the industry.[6]

Family tradition has it that the Montgolfiers were already papermakers in the 14th century, when they migrated from Bavaria to Auvergne, settling in Ambert. Their ancestors are said to have brought the art from Damascus to Frankenthal on returning from the Second Crusade in the mid-12th century. It may have been so. There is, at any rate, little doubt that, after many vicissitudes, including several generations in which the Montgolfiers were Protestant and a further migration to Beaujeu in Beaujolais, two sons of Jean Montgolfier, Michel and Raymond, born in 1669 and 1673, came to Annonay as suitors for the hands of two daughters of Antoine Chelles, proprietor of the paper mill at Vidalon and one of their father's associates in business. Michel, an artist, chose the prettier sister; Raymond, an artisan, preferred the sturdier. The brothers gave the bridal pair gowns they had stopped in Lyons to buy, and the two couples were married in a joint ceremony on 14 January 1693. Michel's lovely Françoise died soon after giving birth. Antoine Chelles's own sons proved feckless, and their father turned to his capable son-in-law. Thus Raymond, twenty at the time of the double marriage, came into control of the mill, and through his wife's inheritance Vidalon became home to the Montgolfiers.[7]

Raymond Montgolfier and his wife, the robust Marguerite, had nineteen children. The fifth, and the oldest boy to survive infancy, Pierre, was born with the century in 1700 (Plate I). In 1727, he married Anne Duret. In eighteen years, she gave birth to sixteen children, the twelfth and fifteenth, Joseph and Etienne, being our inventors of aviation (Plate II). Their grandfather, Raymond, died in 1743. He had built up the mill from artisanal to industrial dimensions, forming his heir, Pierre, in the business and confiding the companion mill, Vidalon-le-bas, to his second son, Antoine. Raymond was employing over one hundred laborers by 1735, when he petitioned the archbishop of Vienne to allow consecration of a chapel on the property so that his dependents might have the consolations of religion without leaving the premises, even on Sundays. For discipline extended from the work to the lives and morals of the employees, man, woman, and child, most of whom were lodged and fed as part of their livelihood.

Vidalon was home and workplace, nursery and church, to the working families and to the ruling family. A formal set of "Rules to be observed in the Montgolfier paper factory at Annonay" opens with this preamble:

> Since the Master cares for the workers as if they were his children, it is only just that for their part those who work in his household should watch over his interests and should live in peace and harmony with one another. Since, further, there may be some among their number who out of weakness would allow harm to be done the Master, and others who may neglect his interests, it is also just that the guilty should incur the penalties and not the innocent.[8]

And the document goes into detail on the use to be made of the tools, on the accommodations, on the sanitary facilities, on the arrangements for board and lodging, and on the precise fines to be paid for infractions of every sort. Parents were responsible for the conduct of their offspring, who were brought up in the factory and put to work at an early age. If through "ill-controlled tenderness," the children were allowed to have their way, fathers and mothers were responsible for the damage.

A visitor to the Ardèche today is at first astonished at the size of the compounds that once housed the rural population. Too rude ever to have been dwellings of nobility, they may contain seventy or eighty rooms. Such originally was the "mas" of Vidalon, deep down on the floor of the narrow valley of the Deûme. Many years later, Adélaïde de Montgolfier, a daughter of Etienne and a minor writer in the 1840s, recalled the factory of her childhood, which had been constructed shop by shop in a series of additions to this ancient farmhouse. With the ear of memory she could still hear the thundering of the mill wheels and stamping mill; the splashing of the torrent on the oaken blades; the groaning of gigantic joists and axletrees; the sighing of the breeze

in the drying racks; the peremptory whistles of the foreman in the shop where the new Dutch cylinders were making pulp; the patois of the workers; the nursery songs of women and children cutting and sorting rags. All that mingled in her recollection with the sound of the wind in the willows and poplars and the singing of nightingales upstream and down.

To the passerby on the highway above, however, Vidalon seemed a deserted structure. Not a human figure was in view, for the laborers were shut up inside all week long and crossed the courtyard only twice a day on their way to the refectory. Nothing could be seen of this hive humming with industry but the tiles of the roof, the masonry of the outside walls (in a virtually perpendicular perspective), the gray blue granite of the cliff face opposite, and the kitchen garden adjoining the northern facade of the original house. Its careful cultivation was the only outward sign of life.[9]

In that upper portion of the complex the Montgolfiers resided. The family historian uses the Fourierist word "phalanstery," half-seriously.[10] In families of this size, only a few of the children could earn their keep through management of the business. Unmarried daughters were expected to enter religious orders, and younger sons to branch off commercially or to become priests. Of Pierre's juniors, Augustin was a Carthusian under the name of Dom Thomas in the entourage of the archbishop of Toulouse; Etienne was a Sulpician priest in Montréal, a sweet and gentle man who even spoke well of British rule after 1763; and Jacques was a financier in Paris, married, childless, and the source of avuncular aid and comfort to many a nephew passing through the capital.

Not everyone thus made a place for himself in the cloister or the world. The successive heads of the family in the three generations of the 18th century—Raymond, his son Pierre, and finally Etienne—each combined an austere ethic of work and duty for himself with a sense of responsibility for less virtuous or fortunate dependents. No relations were ever turned away from Vidalon. The artistic and ne'er-do-well Uncle Michel, who married again twice; the idling Chelles brothers-in-law, their wives and children; widowed aunts; discouraged nuns; canons without a living; dejected cousins—a place was found for everyone, no matter how cavalierly some had eaten up their share of the substance that gave them all a start in life. An older sister of Joseph and Etienne, Marianne, born in 1733, remembered all these kin, who together with her brothers and sisters must have brought the number in the household to forty or fifty.[11]

In the parlance of the trade, an overseer in a paper mill was a "governor." Pierre fitted the appelation even more fully than the father who had built up the business for him to take over. Succeeding to the inheritance when he was forty-three (and when Anne was already fourteen times a mother), Pierre graduated in the fifty years remaining to him to the status of a patriarch. No one of the third generation could imagine that he had ever been young and unsure enough of his purposes to think of entering the priesthood, though so he had. In his governing of himself he combined a Catholic authoritarianism with a puritanism that may have been a throwback to the generations when the Montgolfiers adhered to the Reformed church.[12]

Whatever the season, Pierre rose every morning at four o'clock and washed his face and hands out of doors in the millrace. During the day, he saw to everything: the supply, sorting and fermenting of the rags; their maceration and the preparation of the pulp; dipping, couching, pressing, drying, sizing, and finishing the sheets; sale and shipping of the product; the cost of every operation; the price of every grade; the commissary and kitchen that fed the work force and the family; the conduct, skill, and productivity of every laborer from the most unskilled female ragpicker to the foremen in charge of vats, stamping mill, and press. Nothing escaped his implacable attention. He even heard the catechism of the factory children. Since imparting religious instruction was the primary obligation of parenthood, all the fathers and mothers were expected to bring their offspring before the Master on Sunday morning. If youngsters in apprenticeship failed to appear on their own, they were returned to parental supervision.[13]

Dinner was taken every day at noon. In the evening Pierre went to bed after supper, on the stroke of seven. Thereafter, he was not to be disturbed no matter what happened in the establishment. So long as he was in the salon, light conversation was not tolerated, least of all anything that verged on levity or skepticism with respect to religion or the monarchy. After he retired, the family relaxed and passed what was often an agreeable soirée, sometimes with music and dancing. A great-grandson, Marc Seguin, seven years old at the time of his formidable forebear's death, always remembered how "a glance from his narrow, grey eyes, keen and quick, inspired in everyone around him a fear beyond anyone's power to overcome."[14] Although Pierre delegated active direction of the factory to Etienne when he was in his seventies, he kept his faculties and vigor to the end in 1793. In his eighty-ninth year he stood godfather to another great-grandson. A member of the congregation was impressed that, perfectly erect and without assistance, the old man carried the baby in his arms down the awkward flight of steps from the door of the church to the baptismal font.[15]

Characteristics of the life at Vidalon survive in attenuated form in the French family of more recent times. Apart from a few friendships usually begun at school, relations among its members seem to have fulfilled their capacity, or their desire, for intimacy, or even sociability. Affection was truly felt among the Montgolfiers, but the ties that bound were moral, civic, and economic, not sentimental. They harbored no illusions about one another's qualities, respected one another's individuality, and made no pretenses about personalities to themselves or others. Taking each other as they were, they in effect avoided that unkindness of the idealistic or romantic temperament that requires more of people than it is reasonable and realistic to expect. Ability, chance, and the judgment of elders (rather than mere primogeniture) gave greater weight and influence to some than to others, but worldly success or its absence was never a factor in the legitimacy of everyone's place in the circle of the family. Only once were ranks broken in the 18th century, by the disloyalty of a grandson-in-law, a certain Colonjon, of whom more later.

What has not survived the old regime is the overwhelming authority of a paterfamilias like Pierre Montgolfier. No doubt cultural and economic developments would have eroded such dominance even without the political limitations imposed in the Revolution. Indeed, the process had already begun. Its seeds were sown in the provision that he and many another father of his generation made for the schooling of their boys. Pierre, a man of the 18th century, sent his sons away from home to be educated formally. The experience of the world, of science, and of letters—in a word, of the Enlightenment—blurred the pattern in which he had been formed himself, his father Raymond having bred him up to life and business in the operation of the mill. As will appear, Pierre's children remained closely knit, nonetheless, exercising family solidarity in commission, so to say. Indeed, the brothers and sisters used the old phrase "en petit comité" for the conclave they formed in support of Etienne and Joseph, who were spending all their attention and energy on exploiting and extending the success of the "montgolfières" that gave their name to the first aircraft.

3. The Inventors

Within the global unity of family, Joseph and Etienne were polar opposites in temperament. They shared an aptitude for mechanics and science and little else. Joseph was a dreamer and a maverick, the very type of the inventor, imaginative with objects and processes, impractical in business and affairs. Large of frame and powerfully muscled, he was indifferent to his dress and appearance and shy with other people. They somehow felt in him a diffuse benevolence, even though he showed little interest in themselves individually. The La Fontaine of physics, Biot called him in Napoleonic times, when Joseph had become a venerable figure. His absent-minded-

ness was extraordinary, even by the standards of the notably creative (Fig. 4). On one occasion he went off from a hostelry without his horse, and on another without his wife. In 1771 he wedded a first cousin, Thérèse Filhol, a beauty, much against the wishes of his father, who thought the consanguinity indecent. Early in what proved to be a very congenial marriage, Joseph was to take his bride for a visit to Lyons. En route they put up for the night in Vienne. Arising at dawn for a constitutional, Joseph so lost himself in thought that he walked straight through to his destination, remembering that he had left Thérèse asleep in the inn only when their hosts asked after her.

He was thus less discommoded than most young husbands would have been by his bride's stipulation that she remain at home in Annonay in order to help her father with his faltering business. Joseph was trying his hand all the while at various schemes, insulated by a certain distance from his own father's dismay at his rash borrowing and lending. For he was always having to be

4.

J. Montgolfier.

rescued from creditors by his father, by his Uncle Jacques in Paris, or by his brothers. He had little of what normally passes for self-discipline, but little anger either, and though he might and did rebel, he never lost his temper. He learned by ear and eye, by hand and thought. He was always trying the tools in the factory, taking machines apart and putting them together better, making his own furnaces, "and torturing various substances with fire in order to acquire knowledge of them." So says Matthieu Duret, the cousin who wrote down memoirs of many of the family, and who married Joseph's niece.[16]

Joseph had a fine memory. After two or three hearings or readings, he would repeat entire songs and recite long poems by Voltaire. He was hopeless, however, in a conversation or discussion, following his fancy wherever it strayed instead of sticking to the point. His father tried, nevertheless, to do right by this wayward son, and put him into school, first in Annonay, and when that failed, in the Jesuit college at Tournon. The establishment was a famous one, and all its rules and priestly ways drove the boy to active rebellion. When he was twelve or thirteen, he ran off down the Rhône to the Mediterranean and freedom. For a time he wandered through Languedoc, finding shelter where he might and earning a few sous by picking leaves for silkworm feed.

The long arm of the family soon plucked him out of the mulberry trees and dropped him back in school. There he resumed suffering through lessons in theology while furtively devouring elementary texts of arithmetic, chemistry, and mechanics, forbidden books smuggled to him by a clerk in the bookstore. Among the earliest of his surviving papers are folders in which he systematized for himself elements of basic science: the principles of the seven simple machines of statics; the nature and quantity of variable forces (*vis viva*, motive force, action, etc.); the essentials of astronomy with the methods for navigational reckoning; the structure of matter, with respect notably to considerations of density (Fig. 5). These compositions include an essay against the Leibnizian concept of monads and an abstract of Buffon's *Epoques de la nature*. In a square, almost

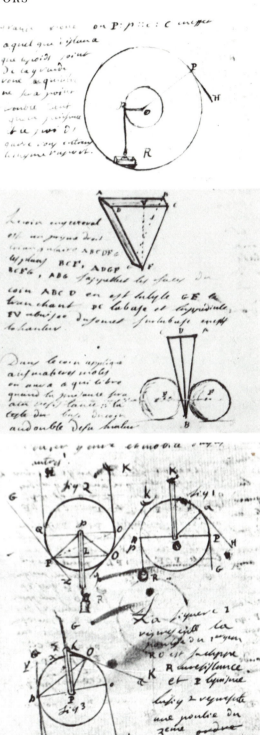

5. The wedge, the winch, and the pulley from Joseph's notebooks

childish handwriting, they exhibit the non-academic record of an autodidact. Of this self-education, which Joseph fortified with experimental verification of the various propositions wherever possible, he later regretted only that he had received no formal training in mathematics. He had to evolve his own methods of calculation as he wrestled his problems to the ground. They amounted to a kind of clumsy and continuing reinvention of the calculus.[17]

Etienne, by contrast, was well educated in mathematics, mechanics, and much else, including self-discipline. Less romantic than Joseph, he may have been more passionate, with the passion under pressure. For it has to be admitted that he did lose his temper on occasion, not in a cool and calculated way, but when anger or scorn escaped control. He could then be thought a little mean. The potential being there and felt, it may explain why, except among a very few intimates, Etienne inspired rather esteem for his reliability and capacity than the generalized affection that surrounded Joseph, despite the latter's relative indifference to the individual needs of others. Joseph is recognizably the same man in all surviving portraits, appearing merely younger or older, more or less remote (compare Fig. 4 and Plate III). Etienne looks different from one picture to another. One extraordinary rendering of an almost hairless, spritelike figure might have been an Ariel or some wise child of William Blake's imagining (Fig. 6). In all the other likenesses, he is the strait-laced pillar of respectability, whatever the expression he has assumed to mask his feelings (Plate III).

Originally there was no thought that Etienne, the youngest boy, would be needed in the business. Pierre idolized the oldest of his sons, Raymond, and conveyed succession to the factory to him as a marriage portion in 1761. Besides Joseph, four other brothers were ahead of Etienne, though to be sure one was paralytic and defective mentally, and another, Alexandre, was in holy orders. Accordingly Etienne was sent off very early to learn a profession under the eye of his Uncle Jacques in Paris. There he enrolled in the college of Sainte-Barbe. Architecture was the most

6. Etienne de Montgolfier. After a portrait painted by a daughter.

eligible outlet for talents of the kind that might later lead an industrious young man of bourgeois background into civil or mechanical engineering. Etienne commended himself to the notice of the famous J.-G. Soufflot, and was given various of the great man's commissions to execute in the capital and the suburbs.

Of these the most important was the wallpaper establishment of Jean-Baptiste Réveillon in the faubourg Saint-Antoine. Réveillon, a self-made man, was the first French manufacturer to contest successfully the domination of that art by English competitors. He became one of the few friends to share real intimacy with Etienne, who was a little younger. Two other important friendships dated from student days in the capital. One comrade was Antoine Boissy d'Anglas, a fellow countryman who during the Revolution was the most influential deputy sent by the Ardèche to the national assemblies. Another close companion was

I. Pierre Montgolfier

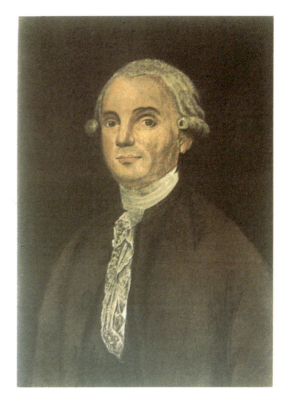

III. Etienne de Montgolfier

II. Anne Duret Montgolfier holding (it is said in the family) Joseph in her arms

IV. Panic at Gonesse

LE GLOBE AEROSTATIQUE construit à Versailles a été placé dans la 1ère Cour du Château, dite Cour des Ministres, sur un échafaut de 60 pieds quarré et 8 de hauteur. Environ 100 Ouvriers travailloient aux preparatifs, et le tout étoit enfermé d'une toile pour empêcher le Public de voir ce qui se passoit intérieurement. Ce Globe de la capacité de 60 pieds de haut et 40 de diamétre, fond d'azur, son pavillon et ses ornemens couleur d'or, contenant 4000 pieds cubes de Gaze, pouvoit enlever deux cent livres pésant, cependant il n'a été chargé que de six cent, sans compter son poids qui étoit de 7 à 8 cent, on y a attaché une Cage dans laquelle étoit enfermé un mouton, et le 19 7bre 1783 à 1 heure aprèe midi, ayant été rempli d'air inflamable, il s'est enlevé en présence du Roi et de la Famille Royale. Sa direction formoit avec la méridienne vers le couchant un angle de 87 degrés 40 min. l'angle au dessus de l'horison étoit d'un deg 55 m 58 sec ce qui donne une hauteur de 243 toises au dessus du rez-de-chaussée de l'Observatoire; le diamétre apparent étoit d'environ 6 min ce qui indiquoit que la machine s'approchoit de l'Observatoire, et en effet elle a été porté sur Paris à 1800 toises du point de son départ au Carrefour Marechal, dans le Bois de Vaucresson près le chemin aux Boufs où il est tombé.

A Paris chez Esnauts et Rapilly, Rue St Jacques à la Ville de Coutances.

V. The balloon at Versailles near to capsizing, 19 September 1783

Dessiné par le Ch. de Lorimier.   Gravé par N. De Launay.

Premier Voyage Aërien   *En présence de M. le Dauphin,*
Experience faite   *dans le Jardin de la Muette,*
Sous la Direction   *de M. Montgolfier,*
Par M. le Marquis d'Arlandes   *et M. Pilatre du Rosier, le 21. 9.bre 1783*
Vue de la Terrasse de M. Franklin à Passi.

VI. The Pilatre-d'Arlandes flight seen from Benjamin Franklin's terrace at Passy

FIGURE EXACTE   ET PROPORTIONS

DU GLOBE   AËROSTATIQUE,

Qui, le premier,   a enlevé

des Hommes   dans les Airs.

Hauteur du Globe	70. pieds.	Poids du Globe	1600. Liv.
Diametre	46. pieds	Poids qu'il a enlevé 16. à 1700 Liv.	
Capacité	60000. pieds cubes	La Gallerie avoit 3. pieds de largeur.	

La partie superieure étoit entourée de Fleurs-de-lys; au-dessous les 12 Signes du Zodiaque.
Au milieu les Chiffres du Roi, entremêlés de Soleils.
Le bas, étoit garni de Mascarons et de Guirlandes; plusieurs Aigles à ailes éployées
paroissoient suporter en l'air cette puissante Machine.
Tous ces ornemens étoient de couleur d'or sur un beau fond bleu, ensorte que ce su-
perbe Globe paroissoit être d'or et d'azur.
La Gallerie circulaire, dans laquelle on voyoit M. le Marquis D'ARLANDES et
M. PILATRE DE ROZIER, étoit peinte en Draperies cramoisi à franges d'or.

VII.   The first manned aircraft, dimensions and characteristics

Aux Amateurs de Physique.

Representant les Murs de la Terrasse des Thuilleries du côté de l'eau au desous, le Globe Aérostatique de M.ᶜˢ Charles et Robert enlevé le 1.ᵉʳ Decemb. 1783.
La manière dont se sont servi plusieurs personnes pour entrer sans billet.
Se Vend Presentement chez Basset rue S.ᵗ Jacques pres les Mathurins.

VIII. Gate-crashing at the Tuileries. The telescope, however, is trained on an object other than a balloon

ELEVATION DU GLOBE AÉROSTATIQUE DE M.M. CHARLES ET ROBERT, au Jardin des Thuileries,
le 1er Décembre 1783

Le même jour à 3 heures 3 quarts après midi la Machine Aérostatique est descendue dans une prairie entre Nesle et Nelouville, à 9 lieues de Paris. Le Procès Verbal
en a été fait par M. Charles, et signé de M.M. Charles, Robert le jeune, Jean Burgat Curé de Nesle, Charles Philippet Curé de Frenay, Thomas Hutin Syndic de cette Paroisse,
et L'Heureux Curé L'Helonville. M.gr le Duc de Chartres et M.r de Fitz James qui sont arrivés un quart d'heure après, ont honoré ce Procès Verbal de leur signature. A quatre heures
un quart, M.r Charles a remonté seul dans la Machine et a continué sa route environ une lieue et demie dans l'espace de 30 minutes; il prétend qu'il s'est élevé à 1524 toises dans
ce second voyage, mais le calcul qu'on en a fait depuis prouve qu'il est monté à 1700. Ensuite il est descendu dans des friches du bois de la tour du lai, d'où ayant été apperçu par
un Gentilhomme Anglois, il s'engagea à passer la nuit chez lui; il revint le lendemain à Paris.
Il a rapporté que la Machine Aérostatique n'avoit souffert aucun accident.
A Paris chez Renauts et Rapilly rue Saint Jacques à la Ville de Coutances.

IX. The takeoff from the Tuileries

Extrait du Procès Verbal.

Ce Globe fut enlevé le 1ᵉʳ Decembre 1783 à une heure 40 min. dans le Jardin du Palais des Thuilleries et est descendus à 3 heures 3 quarts dans une plaine entre Nesle et Hedouville près Beaumont Mᵍʳ le Duc de Chartres et plusieurs Seigneurs arriverent a l'instant de sa descente ou se trouverent les Curés de Nesle d'Hedouvilles et dautres personnes qui ont signés le Procès Verbal. Mʳ Charles est reparti a 4 heures et un quart dans la même Machine en présence des mêmes témoins.

Descente de la Machine Aérostatique, des Sᵗˢ Charles et Robert.

X. The landing of Charles and Robert at Nesle

XI. The *Marie-Antoinette*

Ami Argand, a Genevan inventor of, among many other things, a chimney lamp.[18]

Etienne made acquaintances of others, among them Nicolas Desmarest, a mineralogist and manufacturing inspector for the Bureau of Commerce; the comte d'Antraigues, whose family was of Vivarais; and Lamoignon de Malesherbes, the liberal and enlightened nobleman who was a familiar in scientific circles. In such company he was enjoying the sophistication of the capital, and was well started in a cosmopolitan career when in 1772 the Montgolfier heir apparent, Raymond, died, and the aging Pierre, a realistic judge of the capacities of his children, sent for the youngest son to take the place left vacant by the oldest. Such was the strength of family discipline that Etienne never demurred abandoning architecture for the paper business; and the three older brothers, Jean-Pierre, Joseph, and Augustin, never exhibited the least resentment at being passed over for its inheritance. On the contrary, they joined in their father's preference. Only the widowed daughter-in-law later caused trouble, abetted by Gilbert de Colonjon, who married the second of her three daughters. Colonjon contested the settlement Pierre made on revoking the legacy of Vidalon to his late father-in-law. Lawsuits shadowed the clarity of Etienne's title, which was conveyed to him as a lease on the occasion of his marriage in 1774.[19]

The marriage of Etienne partook of the passionate quality that somehow kept breaking in on the rationality of the conduct of his life. An older sister, Marguerite-Thérèse was an Ursuline, more from realism about her homeliness (she was darkly bearded) than devotion to her calling. She divided her time and managerial competence between Vidalon, where she supervised the commissary, and the convent at nearby Boulieu, where her aunt had been prioress. There in the cloister Thérèse befriended one Adélaïde Bron, a novice of good family in Vienne. Her parents had prevailed on her to take the veil in order that they might concentrate their resources on their son. Deeply unhappy, Adélaïde confided in the strong and sensible Thérèse, who enlisted the sympathy of her worldly, witty, and humane brother Al-

exandre. The abbé was well connected and pulled the levers in Rome to have the girl released from her involuntary vows. The reverend brother and sister prevailed on their father to shelter Adélaïde at Vidalon while the papal machinery turned. Etienne was then just back from Paris, and the young patron promptly fell in love with the new ward. As soon as she was free, he married her and they lived harmoniously ever after. Four of their six children, all daughters, survived infancy.

When Etienne took charge of Vidalon in 1772, he was twenty-seven. He spent the next ten years modernizing the techniques and rationalizing the production in the factory in concert with a leading technologist, Nicolas Desmarest, whom he had known in Paris, and who was now a member of the Academy of Science. To the latter's influence we shall return. In running the company, Etienne was loyally seconded by his brothers and sisters, who in effect constituted the management. The abbé we have just met. A favorite in the benign capacities of uncle and godfather, he had a career in the Church unmarked by devotion, success, or chagrin. Some minor sinecure, a judicial post in the Seneschal's Court, brought him a few hundred livres a year, but no real living. The abbé was affable and gregarious and much in Lyons, where he often represented the firm commercially. Like all Pierre's children, he knew the paper business and could and did lend a hand when needed in overseeing operations and negotiating sales (Fig. 7).[20]

Marianne, the oldest daughter, born in 1733, married one Jean-Laurent Desruol. He left her after a few months, returning only to take possession of their boy at the moment of the baby's birth. Marianne never saw her son again until 1798, when he was forty-five years old. Back home in Vidalon, she became mistress of the household after her mother's death in 1760. She had the force and brains to run a business herself, and (like her sister Thérèse in the food department) Marianne took charge of the shop where the women and children picked and sorted the rags.[21]

Jean-Pierre, one year her senior, became Montgolfier l'aîné, the oldest son, after Ray-

7. The abbé Alexandre Charles Montgolfier

mond's death. Extroverted, combative, as a boy pugilistic, Jean-Pierre teased and fought with his older brother all through their college days in Annonay, and was then put to work alongside the laborers in the factory. Pierre judged that this boy was the toughest of the lot, and let him go off like any apprentice on his *tour de France*, the itinerant practice through which youngsters moved from one shop to another all over the country, learning their trade. Jean-Pierre lodged with his Uncle Jacques in Paris and took over the business there when Jacques obtained the office of tax collector in the archbishopric of Paris. Just married, the nephew had his wife's dowry to defray the cost. Alas, domestic strife undid the newlyweds. Their firstborn was a deaf-mute, and the young parents blamed each other. Jean-Pierre took to the fleshpots and the taverns, neglecting his wife and ruining his business. The two were never again happy together and had no choice but to fall back on Vidalon. There Jean-Pierre threw himself into farming various family prop-

erties. He also knew paper, however, and Etienne drew him into the mill, where he was plant manager. Assisted by Jean-Baptiste, his second son, he freed Etienne for policy, technology, and overall development of the business. Whenever Etienne was absent in Montpellier, Lyons, or Paris, whether for reasons of commerce, the balloon, or (later) politics, Jean-Pierre replaced him as the boss.[22]

As for Joseph, whom we left educating himself in the teeth of his schooling, he escaped his teachers a second time and headed over the mountains to Saint-Etienne. There he drew upon the practical chemistry he had acquired, and, not yet twenty, set up in a one-boy business fabricating dyestuffs, particularly Prussian blue. When he had a good stock, he would take to the road and sell his product at fairs and markets in the Vivarais and Forez. In 1760, Pierre thought to find occupation for Joseph at home together with his next younger brother, Augustin. At fourteen, Augustin had hied off to Paris for his turn with Uncle Jacques. He scraped a living as a public scribe and accountant for illiterate market-women in Les Halles. Next he ventured out to India, where he made and lost a fortune, and still in his teens roamed on to try his luck in Santo Domingo. Pierre's idea was to set up the nineteen-year-old Augustin and the twenty-year-old Joseph, steadied by their older sister Marianne, in the companion mill of Vidalon-le-bas, where their Uncle Antoine, Pierre's younger brother, had just foundered financially.[23]

Independence proved unattainable so close to home, and the lower mill was soon returned to the cadet branch. Augustin went off to the West Indies again, while Joseph experimented with life in Paris for a time, frequenting the café Procope. On their return the brothers resolved to try again the only trade they really knew. There were paper mills in Dauphiny, and Joseph and Augustin formed a partnership that took a lease on two mills, one to be run by Augustin at Rives and one by Joseph at nearby Voiron. Joseph was inattentive, and Augustin was highhanded with his workers. Neither venture was a success commercially, although Rives, in which the government took an interest, became technologically a pilot plant in the province. Little is known of Joseph's business, except that Voiron carried papermaking only through the formation of the sheets, which Joseph sent to Vidalon to be sized and sold. A portion of the unfinished product he distributed himself. Toilet paper is still called "papier de Joseph" in the Montgolfier family. The details of his life are unrecorded, however, though evidently it was peripatetic. He would turn up now in Montpellier, now in Avignon, now in Lyons, and ever and again in Annonay, especially after his marriage in 1771.

4. THE INVENTION

When did Joseph begin imagining aviation? For there can be no doubt that the idea of the balloon was his, not Etienne's. Legends abound, naturally enough. The most egregious has Joseph, in one of the picaresque moments of his youth, coming on a barefoot orphan girl blowing soap bubbles to waft her sighs and kisses to her mother's soul on high. She begged the godlike passerby to build her a little boat with wings to carry her to paradise like the butterflies and angels. Over twenty years later, when everyone else dubbed the globe Joseph had invented a "*montgolfière*," he secretly thought of it as "La Séraphine," for that was the peasant faery's name and he had kept it in his heart. The story has at least the merit of reminding us that, at the time of the demonstration in Annonay, Joseph was already a middle-aged man.[24]

A slightly more credible story has Joseph drying lingerie—some have said his wife's chemise—over a blaze. The fabric billows and lifts with the heat. Could not a large sack be filled "with the same gas" and sent aloft? According to a cousin, Matthieu Duret, Joseph had been musing in this manner as early as 1777. In that year the young man's father persuaded Joseph to accompany his son to Montpellier, where Matthieu was to take his medical degree, having followed the public courses in the appropriate sciences in Paris. In their time together, Joseph pumped the fledgling

doctor to find what he had been told of the new chemistry of gases in the lectures and demonstrations of Bucquet and Fourcroy, of Rouelle, Macquer, and Darcet, the leading expositors of the science in the capital. Word of English pneumatic chemistry was just then reaching Paris. Joseph Priestley had discovered dephlogisticated air (oxygen) in 1774, and Henry Cavendish had isolated inflammable air (hydrogen) in 1766. The latter gas was notable for its relative lightness, a sample weighing one-eleventh as much as an equal volume of common air.[25] Joseph listened closely to all that Duret could convey at second hand about these phenomena. In response he shared ruminations that he had long been meditating on methods for traveling in the air and for raising water above its own level. Duret thought these notions chimerical, and said so forcibly. "All that you have taught me of chemistry," Joseph replied, "only confirms me more fully in my ideas. I must make some experiments."[26]

In its general outlines, this account rings true, the more convincingly since the impetus is credited to chemistry while the hydraulic allusion is to winning mechanical advantage. The earliest pertinent remarks written down in Joseph's own hand occur in letters addressed to Etienne in the summer and early autumn of 1783.[27] The correspondence follows directly out of the successful demonstration in Annonay in June, and we may thus be confident that Joseph was expressing his mind as he knew it at the time. A close reading of those letters, in the perspective of all his later work and of contemporary preoccupations in technology generally, suggests that the basic problems in Joseph's eyes concerned heat and mechanical work. Flight appears to have been a byproduct and not the object of the search, a tail that wagged the dog and even pretty wildly for a while, but not the beast itself. On 16 May 1783, only three weeks before the Annonay experiment, Joseph wrote to Etienne from Nîmes about a steam engine—he calls it a pump—being used there to drive flour mills.[28] At moments of discouragement during the development of the balloon, he complains that he and Etienne were misguided in interrupting work on the "heat pump"—

"pompe à feu"—that they had been perfecting together.

To put ourselves in Joseph's place, we must also appreciate that the action of heat was for him, as for most of his contemporaries, as much a chemical as a physical process. "The most expansive and elastic of known fluids" he calls it in one of these letters, apropos of the explosion of gunpowder.[29] Inflation of a balloon consists of combining atmospheric air with heat, and the dilated gas is not merely rarefied air. It is a different substance (note the reference to the "gas" that rippled his wife's chemise). As will appear, the competition between the Montgolfier hot-air balloons and the hydrogen balloons invented by J.-A.-C. Charles dominated the first year of the history of flight. But the contrast we might strike between chemically and physically filled balloons would have been nothing like so categorical in the eyes of the inventors. The combination of heat with air was as chemical a reaction as ever the production of inflammable air. Heat and hydrogen were not altogether different, and might even reduce to the same principle at bottom. Such, at all events, were the implications of Joseph's telling young Duret that the chemistry lectures reported from Paris confirmed his thinking.[30]

A good deal is known about the circumstances in which Joseph thought to apply the expansive power of heat to an actual flying device. Among his refuges from the chronic failure of his business, Avignon was a favorite retreat. In 1780 he and his brother, the abbé Alexandre, both in their forties, took the improbable step of enrolling there in the faculty of law. To be sure, legal competence might often have stood Joseph in good stead. Early in 1782, he spent several days in debtors' prison in Lyons, having imprudently mortgaged his shaky credit to the vindictiveness of the Johannot clan, the rival papermakers in Annonay.[31] It is hardly to be supposed that either brother was serious in his studies, however. The University of Avignon was something of a diploma mill, and the attractions of the community were other than academic. The city and the surrounding Comtat Venaissin were still ruled distantly by the pope. Equivalent intellectually to a modern tax haven and exempt from French censorship, the area was an enclave where books and ideas might circulate freely. Late in 1783 a committee of the Academy of Science in Paris reported on the Montgolfier balloons. Its spokesman made much of the appearance in Avignon in 1755 of a piece of science fiction, or science fantasy, *L'Art de naviger dans les airs*, by a Dominican, Father Joseph Galien, professor of theology and philosophy at the university.[32]

Joseph never alluded to that work, however, or to other items in the literary prehistory of flight. One evening in November 1782, by his own account, he was idly contemplating a print on the wall of his sitting room depicting the long siege of Gibraltar. From the time of the Spanish entry into the war of American independence in 1779 until the peace negotiations of 1783, the fortress was invested by Spanish forces. In vain. Impregnable by land, impregnable by sea—might not Gibraltar be taken from the air? The evenings were growing cool in Avignon. A fire burned in the grate. Surely the force that carried particles of smoke up the flue could be confined and harnessed to lift conveyances and float men above the surface of the earth.

Such was the story told by Joseph in much later years to a friend, the philosopher Joseph Degérando, who incorporated it in a funeral oration.[33] It is not inherently implausible, and there is independent and contemporary evidence. On 11 July 1783, five weeks after the Annonay balloon, Etienne departed for Paris to exploit the sensation the news had created. Left in charge of Vidalon, Jean-Pierre the next day sent a letter chasing after him. He, Jean-Pierre, had just remembered that the family knew the father of the ambassador to Constantinople, Emmanuel Guignard, comte de Saint-Priest. Saint-Priest *père* was influential and might prove useful. Etienne could say that "in principle" the attempted conquest of Gibraltar had motivated the machine, and that furnishing the Sublime Porte with a model could be a way of providing military assistance without seeming to intrude upon Turkish affairs.[34] The naiveté of the suggestion measured the distance from Annonay to Paris, and also confirms the story of what triggered the invention.

Thus galvanized by the draft up the flue, Joseph set to work there in his rooms in Avignon to build a model of a machine that would be made lighter than the air it displaced by the expansive power of heat. The house where he lodged on the third floor still exists at 18, rue Saint-Etienne. He took a bolt of fine taffeta and stretched the cloth around a frame that he pieced together of the thinnest possible wood in the form of a paralleliped, three feet on a side at the base and four feet high with a foot-square opening in the bottom. He rested the construction on a support, inserted a few twists of paper through the opening, and ignited them. In a few moments the contrivance floated right off the stand and bumped against the ceiling. All excitement, he dashed off a note to the brother who counted most, to Etienne: "Get in a supply of taffeta and of cordage, quickly, and you will see one of the most astonishing sights in the world."[35]

Joseph hastened home, and within two weeks the brothers were collaborating on larger models there in the semi-secrecy of Vidalon. For the skeptical and rational Etienne immediately put aside the cares of the paper business to join with his fantast of a brother in what might seem a characteristically harebrained venture. In order to understand how that came to pass, we shall need to turn back and consider what Etienne had accomplished in the ten years since he had taken over direction of the company, and where its affairs stood at just the moment when Joseph's neglect of his own factory issued in the invention of aircraft.

5. CRISIS AT VIDALON

Even before Etienne assumed responsibility, there were intimations that the family model for relations between employer and employee was producing something other than perfect industrial harmony. In 1769 the Bureau of Commerce, the agency within the Ministry of Finance that hovered over the health of manufacturing and trade, made a survey of the paper industry. The intendant in charge, André de Bacalan, addressed a questionnaire to leading manufacturers, among them Pierre Montgolfier. Precipitating the inquiry was the recognition that Dutch paper was of better quality than French, which was beginning to lose out in competition. Pierre responded, casting some blame upon the central government for the burden of taxes, tolls, and internal customs duties that all French commerce had to bear. What specially incited his ire, however, was the conduct of the labor force.

"Nothing," he told Bacalan, "is more revolting than the tyrannical power that the worker wields with respect to his master, nothing more degenerate or insolent than this wretched bunch of rascals, and by the same token nothing so urgently requires the attention of the Council as these seditious upstarts."[36] Wages were set by custom and were not the issue. The issue was custom itself, the set of practices (called "modes" in the paper trade) through which working men, joined in *compagnonnages* (journeymen's associations), had acquired the right to determine their own output, to collect dues on hiring and promotion of apprentices, and to celebrate certain rites and fooleries at times of festival. The effect was to put the employees in a position to resist all attempts at technical innovation, and that was the source of Pierre's frustration. In the 1750s he and fellow papermakers, notably Matthieu Johannot, had experimented with one of the elements of the Dutch system. They had tried substituting horizontal rollers studded with spikes for the stamping mills consisting of great mallets, four to a trough, where the rags were chewed up for pulping. No one in France had succeeded with these "hollanders," and the failure was generally attributed to inadequacy of maintenance by unskilled mechanics and to resistance amounting to sabotage among workers at large. The burning of the famous Montargis mill, chosen by Diderot to illustrate the trade in the *Encyclopédie*, was widely believed to have been arson.[37]

With his outburst against the modes off his chest, Pierre acknowledged the excellence of Dutch paper, and asked for a governmental subsidy to send one of his sons to Holland in order to learn all the reasons for it. The Bureau of Commerce had already thought of that, Bacalan replied. One of its inspectors of manufacturing, Nicolas Desmarest, had just returned from precisely such a mission. He would visit the Montgolfier mill on his next tour of the region.[38] In Paris all this while, Etienne (it will be recalled) had already met Desmarest, a person of middling importance in the technical bureaucracy and twenty years his senior. They would have had no reason as yet to talk of paper. Etienne was a fledgling architect. Desmarest is known to the history of science mainly as a mineralogist who convinced scientists of the volcanic origin of the basalts occurring in the peaks of Auvergne, where he often traveled in the discharge of his official duties.[39] Only after Etienne's return to Vidalon did these early encounters ripen into a close collaboration between a manufacturer and an expert.

Desmarest made his trip to Holland in 1768. There he learned that other, less dramatic features of Dutch technology were more fundamental than the hollanders, and that all differences derived from the preparation given the raw material. The French eased the disintegration of the rags by rotting the cloth for up to two months before pulping under the mallets. The Dutch fed clean, fresh rags directly to their rollers. The reason was the dependence of Dutch mills on windpower. Huguenots had brought the trade to Holland in the 1690s. Too often the weather calmed just when rags had soured to the point that they had to be macerated or spoil. Accordingly, a technique had to be devised for using sound rags directly. Other variations in the later stages of papermaking followed out of this necessity. As the sheets were dipped out of the vat—that operation was much the same in the two processes—they were tipped onto a pile or post, consisting of half a ream—in which layers of felt alternated with layers of sopping paper. The post was pressed first with and then without the felt blotters. Thereupon, the Dutch product, being grainier, required additional operations that were the secret of its eventual superiority. The posts were disassembled and reassembled in random

order, and pressed again, the purpose being to compact the fibers and to smooth surfaces against each other. Like the shuffling of a deck of cards, this "exchange" was repeated several times over. Since the sheets were less porous, Dutch millowners had to size their paper while it was moist. The finest grades would then undergo several more exchanges and pressings before drying.

Desmarest reported his findings in a pair of memoirs delivered before the Academy of Science and published in 1774 and 1778 respectively.[40] In them he summoned the paper industry to mend its ways. For the role of a manufacturing inspector in the Bureau of Commerce was more than a matter of analyzing processes and verifying the observance of standards. Acting with the authority of government and in the name of science or reason, the Corps of Manufacturing Inspectors took the lead in developing progressive technologies and in emboldening entrepreneurs to adopt them.[41] In 1771 Desmarest was reassigned to Chalons-sur-Saône, an easy journey from Annonay. Etienne Montgolfier returned to run Vidalon in the following year. This fortunate conjunction greatly favored the relation that developed between them, that of mentor and disciple, of scientist and producer, of cosmopolitan and provincial. The family is always hoping that Desmarest will make a visit to Vidalon part of his official itinerary. The ladies of the house will never forgive Etienne and the abbé when they return from a meeting in Avignon without having prevailed on Desmarest to come along. After one too brief stopover, they send after him two cases containing sixty bottles of Côte Roti. They recognize his natal prejudice in favor of the wines of Champagne, but he had had no more than a taste in passing, and "messieurs les académiciens" are supposed to reach a decision only after "ripe reflection."[42]

The deference the Montgolfiers felt for Desmarest, reciprocally with the condescension (in the 18th-century sense) he showed to them, were signs of how loftily the structure of officialdom and society towered above the level of a country manufacturer, only two generations removed from the status of artisans. In the eyes of Annonay,

Desmarest was the personification of reasoned influence with authority. In actuality, he was a fairly minor figure in the Academy of Science, to which he was elected only in 1771 at the relatively late age of forty-six. He represented the humblest of the sciences in a body dominated by the mathematical éclat of a d'Alembert and later a Laplace, by the literary elegance of a Buffon, and by the intellectual and financial eminence of a Lavoisier. But the Academy itself, even in these higher reaches, was subordinate in its consulting responsibilities to great agencies of state, notably to the Bureau of Commerce, to the royal household, and to the Ministries of Finance, War, and the Navy. Normally the members of the Academy answered to officials of the bureaucracy, the *grands commis d'état*, or civil service. Over them were set the ministers or secretaries of state heading the major departments of government, formally responsible for policy and serving at the pleasure of the king. Around the king, finally, swarmed the court in the intricacy and extravagance of Versailles, intermingling in mood and taste with the world of fashion in the capital. Those were the altitudes to which the balloon soon bore Etienne. He was, of course, aware of their existence from his young days in Paris, but he had regressed far from all that back home in the paper mill on the banks of the Deûme.

In the earlier (1774) of his reforming memoirs, Desmarest expounded the virtues of the Dutch process of exchange in finishing the sheets, and in the second (1778) he expressed his gratification that the enlightened manufacturers in Annonay had adopted these procedures. He did not there identify the Montgolfiers, and in fact the Johannots were also practicing the exchange. It required no new equipment, and no doubt they wished to please the inspector and to keep up with their competitors. Desmarest's second memoir goes on to address the more fundamental question, the vicious effect of using rotted rags. Here, the Johannots played no part, whether for lack of interest or lack of opportunity there is no way of knowing. Apparently, Etienne diverted one of the stamping mills and vats at Vidalon to experimental purposes for a time, and he and

Desmarest conducted a series of tests. They found that sound fabric could be pulped by mallets, but only when the choice of rags was restricted to the finest and softest linen. The cost would have been prohibitive, and using fresh cloths at reasonable expense would require converting to hollanders.[43]

The introduction of hollanders was more than a question of changing one machine for another. The entire system of production would have to be transformed. In Desmarest's view, which Etienne adopted early on, the superiority of the Dutch lay, not just in their cylinders and healthy rags, but in their management. Entrepreneurs in Holland had learned to dominate their machinery and to substitute it wherever possible for labor instead of being dominated by custom and letting their laborers impede the efficient use of their machines. Ignorance and routine were the enemy in France, exhibited in inertia among manufacturers no less than resistance among laborers. The most effective possible measure of reform

> would be the creation of a workshop wherein all the processes and machines would be in operation, and which would be open for the observation and research of those who would like to inform themselves more or less thoroughly. Such a workshop, designed according to a rational plan, would show the order and connection of the operations, their sequence and progression. It would exhibit, in short, a general system for manufacturing every type of paper, in accordance with which manufacturers could adopt the features best suited to their ideas and their business. They would find there only those processes tested and verified by results.[44]

Money would be needed, as well as resolution, and no private manufacturer could reasonably be expected to risk investment in a scheme intended to benefit an entire industry. What with the worsening deficits of the central government, Desmarest had more hope of funds from the provincial authorities. He proposed to the Estates of Languedoc that they offer a subsidy of 18,000 to 20,000 livres to any entrepreneur in their jurisdiction who would undertake to install holland-ers. Conditions were attached. A candidate must complete the installation in eighteen months, ac-quire or construct related machinery, and follow every step of the Dutch process from rags to fin-ished sheets, for all grades of paper. Most im-portant, he must keep his plant open to visitors and competitors so that they could study the de-signs and observe the operations, and he must hire an experienced foreman whom Desmarest would recommend to supervise the construction of the hollanders and the training of personnel. Desmarest thought there was little chance that laborers set in their ways could be made to adapt themselves to the new technology. A millowner thinking to try the venture had better be willing to change his work force for a new one.[45]

Clearly this was one of those applications tai-lor-made for a particular applicant. Although Desmarest kept up the appearance of referring to all the manufacturers of Annonay as a pro-gressive group, the stipulations were so drawn that only the elder branch of the Montgolfiers would qualify. Vidalon would thus become the model workshop of Desmarest's program, the revolutionary cell within the paper industry. Des-marest put in a word with the archbishops of Narbonne and Toulouse, the highest dignitaries of the province. Etienne paid calls in Montpellier, and was warmly received by the presiding officer of the Estates, who warned him lightly not to overdo the estimate. The Estates accepted Des-marest's recommendation on 3 January 1780.[46] Matthieu Johannot made no bid, and later com-plained that he was never notified of the availa-bility of the award. Antoine Montgolfier, Etienne's cousin at Vidalon-le-bas, felt similarly slighted.[47] The money was not the important thing. Only in the next session of the Estates, in January 1781, was the appropriation actually voted, and three years later half of it had still to be paid out of the provincial treasury.[48] No, what mattered was official recognition and prestige.

The overseer Desmarest had in mind was a Dutchman of Huguenot extraction called (of all things) Ecrevisse—"Crayfish." The Montgolf-iers installed him at Vidalon in the late spring of

1780, before they had received a sou. Through-out the summer Desmarest was often there, con-sulting with Etienne on the design and disposi-tion of the new machines. Contracts for their construction were let with carpenters, black-smiths, and suppliers there in Annonay, in Lyons, and in Flanders. By the end of the year, the hol-landers were in place and operating successfully in conjunction with one of the four vats. The old and new processes were then run concurrently until in later years the entire production was con-verted to the Dutch process.[49]

In providing Vidalon with the sanction of the provincial authorities, Etienne was certainly an-ticipating trouble with the laborers. Indeed, it might well be thought that he provoked it. Nerved by Desmarest, and by the spirit of rational tech-nology emanating from the Bureau of Commerce, he and Jean-Pierre were if anything more deter-mined than their father about overriding obstruc-tions deriving from the workers' modes. They were fortified in their resolve by the example of Augustin in his government-encouraged factory at Rives, which made progress technically though it never made money. In converting his work force from *compagnons* into employees with no recourse beyond their employer, Augustin had encountered threats of arson and acts of vandal-ism. So far he had prevailed—though his plant burned down five years later, in 1786. His advice reinforced Desmarest's premonitions. Let his brothers not suppose that long-term workers could be retrained for new tasks. If any were to be kept on, it must be for jobs they knew.[50]

At Vidalon grumbling attended construction of the new equipment in the summer of 1780, and sulky insubordination accompanied its breaking in by Ecrevisse and his team late in the year and into 1781. What precipitated matters was not the new technology in itself, but the refusal of the trainees brought in by Ecrevisse to pay the dues exacted from apprentices according to the modes of traditional employment. Old hands insulted Pierre and others of the family for ap-proving the attitude of the new men. In October 1781 leaders among the malcontents persuaded the veteran workers to down tools in protest and to leave the premises. Unfortunately for the Montgolfiers, Matthieu Johannot was then *maître-garde* of the municipality. His halfhearted mediation produced a breathing space of six weeks, but at the end of November the whole body of long-term employees went out on strike. Etienne converted the walkout into a lockout and refused further negotiation, although he did gradually take back some former workers who renounced the modes.[51]

These highhanded tactics naturally alienated laboring people, while at the same time Etienne had aroused the resentment of fellow manufacturers and competitors by his preemption of patronage from the Estates. Success with the hollanders, in short, had created hostilities that precluded opening Vidalon as a temple of rational technology and a model to be emulated throughout the industry. A scientifically progressive management had produced a problem in public relations, and that was the situation of the firm in November 1782 when Etienne had word from Joseph to lay in a supply of taffeta and cordage. There is nothing to prove that he turned his energies from managing the mill to capitalizing on his brother's initiative with a view to repairing reputations, but he need have acted no differently if that had been among his motives at the outset.

6. The First Demonstration

At the same time, Etienne was truly intrigued, for the sight that Joseph showed him was indeed astonishing. Early in December Joseph repeated the Avignon experiment in the seclusion of the "New Garden" just north of the house at Vidalon with the family all gathered around. The buoyant little box leaped up to a height of seventy feet and floated in the air for a full minute. Etienne was as enthusiastic as ever his impetuous brother could have wished. The two immediately set to work to build a model three times the size, nine feet on a side, and nine times the capacity. They tried it on 14 December 1782, a calm and sunny day. They had underestimated the force it would develop. Even before they had given it all the

"activity" it could acquire (to use Etienne's language), it broke the retaining cord and floated right out of the ravine, coming to ground at the edge of a field a quarter of a league distant. There it was demolished by what Etienne calls the "indiscretion" of passersby. It cannot be said that the cat was out of the bag, since no one knew what the animal was, but word was now about that the Montgolfier brothers were up to something, deep in the recesses of Vidalon.

Apprehensive lest they be done out of whatever advantages the invention might be made to yield, Etienne decided to confide their news, even if prematurely, in the highest quarters to which he had access. On 16 December he wrote a long letter to Desmarest in Paris. It opens with a slightly artificial mixture of newsiness and jocularity, in a tone not at all like the Etienne of business. He and his brothers find themselves involved in a "novel speculation." It was less useful, perhaps, than what they were accomplishing in the industry, but was something much more brilliant and sure to create a greater sensation than all their experiments with paper. Etienne then alluded to a daredevil in Paris who had just broken an arm soaring off a vantage point on Montmartre with a pair of artificial wings. Of course, they had no thought of following that example. Still, in chatting about it, analyzing it, amplifying it, all in the bosom of the family, they had thought—thus Etienne—that it should be possible to make a machine rise in the atmosphere by taking advantage of the weight and spring of the air. Joseph had even tried that idea three weeks ago in Avignon. And now they had had success with a further contrivance that weighed fifteen to sixteen pounds and that broke a cord with a force equivalent to a weight of twenty to twenty-five pounds.

Despite all their precautions, the thing has unfortunately made a certain stir. "We are surrounded by hornets," wrote Etienne, "and they will not hesitate to steal our work and appropriate the credit." That is why he writes, begging Desmarest to announce the construction of such a machine to the Academy of Science. Since the device could lift weights at very little cost, it might prove useful for passing signals, for sending messages into cities under siege, and for making experiments on the electricity in clouds, etc., etc. But the urgent thing now is to fix the date.

Etienne was ten years removed from the sophistication of life in Paris. He was without direct experience of the world of science. It would stretch matters to call their little flier an invention at this embryonic stage. Nevertheless, his instinct was that priority was what counted. He keeps recurring to that. Desmarest will probably think the whole thing a dream. He, Etienne, would suppose the story an exaggeration if he had not actually seen it. He will refrain from sending anything about the really big machine they plan until they have tried it. Next, however, they are going to fly the same model again and make more careful observations. These he will communicate along with precise calculations of the load it can carry, the altitude it can reach, its speed of rise and fall, and all other variables and characteristics. "But so that no one poaches on our preserve in the meantime, I beg you to announce it in our name to the Academy, or if that cannot be done, in some journal, so that a fixed date may result." As if to fortify their claim to innovativeness, Etienne goes on to tell Desmarest of another invention that Joseph has just made. He has imagined a new method of printing, so that plates containing expensive typography can be preserved from one edition to another and revisions made around them. Joseph means to ask for a subvention from the government, or at least an exclusive privilege. How do we go about that? Please don't dismiss us as dreamers.[52]

Clearly, Desmarest was nonplussed by this uncharacteristically frantic appeal from his steady and controlled collaborator in the reformation of the paper industry. "Since I do not yet understand your ascending machine," he replied curtly, "I have been unable to use what you tell me of it. . . . In order to make the use and effects known, a good drawing and a detailed description are essential."[53] Desmarest evidently decided to keep this strange letter to himself throughout the winter and spring of 1783. No one else in Paris heard anything about the affair until word of the public demonstration of 4 June reached the capital.

The documentation thins out for that six-month interval, perhaps because Joseph and Etienne were working too hard to write down much about what they were doing. The main lines are marked, however. All the family were drawn in—Jean-Pierre together with his son, Jean-Baptiste, the abbé Alexandre, Marianne, and the wives of Joseph and Etienne, Thérèse and Adélaïde. Augustin came on from Rives, at least for a time. They all went about their duties by day while Joseph and Etienne worked on the machine, and talked of nothing else at mealtime and in the evening. Pierre was eighty-three by now, and (as old age would have it) had become more difficult for his children to manage than was the business. Although he no longer took an active part in operations of the plant, he loomed over it. Whatever was done either had to have his assent or to be concealed from him. To go against him was unthinkable, and the aerostats could scarcely be concealed. Grudgingly, he shrugged along with these follies of his sons, although on one express condition: if ever that machine lifted men into the air—not that it ever would, for clearly the whole thing was a mania with which Joseph had somehow infected Etienne—still, if ever it did, they must swear a filial oath not to fly themselves.

The old man was right in suspecting that manned flight was in their minds. Drafting a further letter to Desmarest, Etienne lets his imagination go. His calculations show that the aerostat might lift 50,000 to 100,000 pounds, that it could carry "a considerable number of men." Since there was a war on during these natal-stage experiments, military applications were what first came to mind, even to the possibility of carrying bombs over fortifications. With peace, however, trade will revive, and no end of opportunities will suggest themselves, especially for the transportation of goods at very low cost. He and his brother now wish to assign their invention to the government or to the nation. The expense of developing it will exceed their means. Again Etienne bespeaks Desmarest's intercession with the Academy, this time with a request to arrange the naming of commissioners before whom he can demonstrate the machine "during my visit to Paris." This letter is undated, but it must have been written in 1783 either just before or immediately after the demonstration of 4 June.[54] In either case, it is clear that Etienne was already planning a campaign for recognition in the capital.

The second stage in the development of the balloon consisted in modifying the rigid, box-kite form of Joseph's first invention to that of a flexible bubble and calculating the optimal dimensions. In a memoir written four or five years later, Etienne recalled that they had explored the possibility of obtaining a light gas more "permanent" than hot air, and had examined Joseph Priestley's work in search of information on specific gravities. There they learned that "inflammable air" is ten times lighter than common air. They tried experiments, but no sooner was the idea formed than they abandoned it because of the expense of procuring the substance (hydrogen) in sufficient quantity. Other alternatives appeared to be no more feasible, and the brothers fell back on perfecting the original device.[55]

For the first balloon was no mere random bag. The mathematical analysis fell largely to Etienne. Unfortunately, the most coherent series of calculations in his hand survives from a time some eight months later, when he was making computations on the tacking of sailboats pertinent to the project for a dirigible. Only scattered jottings remain from this early period, but at least they make clear how he saw the problem and how he attacked it. The weight of an approximately spherical balloon is proportional to the surface and thus increases as the square of the diameter. The lifting force is proportional to the difference between the weights of the enclosed gas and of the displaced air. It is a function of the volume and hence of the cube of the radius. Thus, the levity increases exponentially with size. The limits to observe are determined by considerations of cost and maneuverability. The upward acceleration varies directly as the lifting force and is diminished by a factor deriving from air resistance. The duration of flight and speed of descent

depend on the rate of cooling.[56]

In the absence of data on the temperature of the enclosed gas, on the variation of its density with temperature and pressure, or on the decrease of atmospheric temperature and density with altitude, none of these factors could be determined numerically ahead of time. Nevertheless, Etienne and Joseph made a start. They made many measurements relating the consumption of fuel to the lifting force generated in aerostats of varying size, exploiting the accident that had cost them secrecy. When a model acquired the levity to break loose under controlled conditions, they measured the breaking strength of the cord by hanging weights on a further length of it. Extrapolation from these figures led them to the dimensions of the Annonay balloon, which they calculated to be the largest they could reasonably expect to manage. That is what Etienne meant in observing to the *Etats particuliers* that the performance they witnessed had answered to theory. Construction of the balloon presented practical problems. According to the abbé Alexandre, his brothers saw immediately that the taffeta of the first model was a heat sieve. Given their business, it was natural to think of backing cloth with paper. Shaping the pieces and lining the fabric was something no tailor or seamstress had ever yet attempted, and we can only imagine what cutting and fitting that required, what matching of buttons on one strip with buttonholes on the overlapping edge of the next.

How often Joseph and Etienne tried the 4 June model before the public demonstration is uncertain, but there were at least two or three preparatory launchings. Repairs to the fabric and modification of the techniques of filling and launching followed each. On the first attempt, probably on 3 April, a wind was blowing, and Etienne let the balloon, held captive by its cords, rise only about three or four feet above the platform constructed for it. At the second trial, on 25 April, again in the privacy of Vidalon, the day was still. Four laborers grasped the cords for what was intended to be another captive flight. Despite all the calculations and experimentation with small-scale models, no one was prepared for the rapid increase in lifting force. Startled, two of the anchormen let the ropes run through their hands. Even more startled, the other two were lifted off their feet. Unready to be the first aviators, they let go and fell back upon the launching pad. The trial balloon soared out of the ravine, the second model thus to slip its leash, and settled on the property of one Gratet, who farmed the *mas* of Déomas just beyond Davézieux.[57] This time the Montgolfiers recovered their flying machine virtually undamaged. In a remaining trial or two before the public demonstration, the tether held. According to the romantic tale told half a century later by Etienne's daughter, Adélaïde, one such test in the seclusion of the abandoned monastery of Colombier terrified passing peasants who had thought to take shelter.[58] Another story by the family historian has Etienne and Joseph attending a convivial dinner given by a local notable, Boullioud de Brogieux, and surprising their host with a preprandial demonstration. The company at table then had the idea of springing the balloon on the Estates in their forthcoming session.[59] A more plausible remark by the abbé has several of the deputies hearing of the Montgolfier experiments and asking to see a repetition.[60]

With priority assured by success in public, family councils were unanimous that Etienne must be the one to go to Paris to make their fame and fortune. Joseph entirely concurred in the opinion that he himself was altogether too shy and unworldly to think of taking on that mission. Before Etienne could depart, the pieces of the new balloon that he would somehow assemble in the capital had to be fabricated. They were ready by the second week in July. Jean-Pierre saw to the packing and dispatched the crates under the care of two trusty couriers on 12 July. Etienne had departed by diligence the day before. We have already mentioned the reminder about the embassy in Turkey in the letter Jean-Pierre sent on his brother's heels, bearing the advice and good wishes of all the clan. It opens with word of their father. In the midst of his sons' success, enthusiasm, and hopes, the old man finally could not bear to stand aside. He now wanted Etienne to know that he remembered his father's telling him of a stunt. An egg might be emptied of its contents through a very small hole carefully punched in the shell. If the aperture was then sealed with wax and the shell heated over the kitchen stove, it would float up to the ceiling.

1. ARRIVAL IN PARIS

On 10 July, the day before Etienne departed Vidalon, the first published word of the balloon appeared in Paris. The *Feuille Hebdomadaire* printed an extract from a letter written by a land-owner near Annonay. It was neither good-natured nor accurate, and allowed only that the Montgolfiers had put on a truly curious show. They had fabricated a contrivance of cloth and paper shaped like a shed 36 × 16 × 16 feet, and lifted it off the ground by means of heat. When the thing filled with smoke, it went up like a rocket. The apparition terrified his peasants and caught fire on landing. Luckily so, for one of those Montgolfiers talked of riding in it. They might still try that, even though the stunt had cost them 900 livres. People said they would give up only when one of them broke his neck. Their colleague, Matthieu Johannot, spent his time more usefully. He had just built a new paper mill, the roomiest and possibly the most handsome in France. Johannot had shown the author of this communication samples of his product. It was very beautiful.[1]

Over two weeks later, the *Journal de Paris* included a more objective and informative piece under the rubric "Physique" in the issue for 27 July. The author had the physical characteristics of the balloon right, and attributed the motivation of the experiment to the discovery several years previously of "inflammable air or gas." Mont-golfier (he uses the singular) could have obtained it by burning damp straw. Only if the modern reader is incautious enough to identify this sub-stance too categorically with hydrogen will the guess appear ignorant. For the journalist goes on to say that, if it had been possible to procure inflammable air drawn from the action of iron,

the levity would have been eight to ten times greater, but the experiment would have cost much more.[2]

Evidently the reporter for the *Journal de Paris* got his information from the committee ap-pointed meanwhile by the Academy of Science to take cognizance of the prospects for aviation. The minutes of the Estates of Vivarais reached the controller general of finance, Lefèvre d'Ormesson, late in June. He it was, the principal minister of government, who learned of the An-nonay experiment before anyone else in the cap-ital. Clearly, it fired his imagination, for he wrote forthwith to the marquis de Condorcet, perma-nent secretary of the Academy, enclosing the *procès-verbal* for the information of that body and bespeaking its reaction.[3] What Desmarest must have felt may be conjectured. Through these high channels he learned that Etienne's strange letters had all along been reporting fact instead of fancy. Naturally enough, Desmarest was named to the committee, and (now that his own eyes had been opened) no doubt he convinced his colleagues that the affair was to be taken seriously.[4] Among the seven others were Condorcet himself, ex of-ficio, and (most important) Lavoisier, whose work was just then bringing the chemical revolution to its climax. The committee convened on 19 July, and reported to d'Ormesson that, since they understood that Montgolfier was coming to Paris, they would await his arrival before proceeding.[5]

Actually, Etienne was already in Paris, lodging with his uncle and aunt in their apartment at the archbishopric, and taking counsel before making his presence known. Besides his Uncle Jacques, two friends from school days were in his confi-dence. Ami Argand and Jean-Baptiste Réveillon collaborated with Etienne intimately throughout the trials that followed. Argand was beginning to be recognized for his lamp and for other inventions. Réveillon, then in the prime of his age, had become enormously successful in the manufacture of wallpaper. He conducted his business in a very great property at 9, rue de Montreuil, an improbable address since the extensive garden, sumptuous courtyard, and lavish mansion were surrounded by the warren of the faubourg Saint-Antoine. The ensemble had been created by a financier of an earlier generation, the tax farmer Maximin Titon, and was known (inevitably) as Titon's Folly.

Down home in Vidalon, the family was hanging on the mail. Etienne had left his wife, Adélaïde, seven months pregnant. (Only two of their four children, all of them daughters, had survived infancy.) Jean-Pierre, the senior in age and experience, remained in charge of the plant, and Marianne of the ménage and the work of women and children. Their brother, the abbé Alexandre, took over Etienne's oversight of orders, correspondence, and deliveries. Joseph roamed back and forth between Lyons and Annonay. Augustin kept in close touch from Rives. It had been agreed that Etienne would send general word of developments in letters containing nothing likely to disturb their father so that they could be read out in Pierre's presence. Etienne's real news he would send under covers addressed to Adélaïde, to be shared around after Pierre had gone to bed.[6] Unfortunately, we do not have his letters in July and August. They were much less frequent than the family had expected, and from their responses to what he did write, it is clear that they were worried about him. For a time, he appeared to be out of his depth.

What Etienne might reasonably have expected to do is unclear. How would a provincial businessman proceed in a great capital to usher in the age of human flight? Certain subsidiary goals he did set himself, having to do with the paper business rather than with aviation. He meant to capitalize on the publicity to win concessions from the government, foremost among which was the transformation of Vidalon into a training plant or national school of papermaking. His brothers were mainly interested in favors of a more concrete sort: further privileges and subsidies for

capital equipment; orders to supply the needs of the India Company; a decent prebend or other clerical living, preferably without duties, for the abbé. The last was Jean-Pierre's favorite proposal. As to ballooning, the only object they had clearly in view was reimbursement of their expenses from the Treasury and provision of funds for further development. What further development might entail and whether Etienne or Joseph had reckoned with the prospect of converting themselves, singly or together, into lifelong practitioners or impresarios of flight—as to those and similar questions, there is no evidence that anyone had looked further ahead than "repeating" the Annonay experiment in the capital.

Moreover, Etienne was ill-prepared to pay the personal price of getting things done in Paris. He had little stomach for the calls to be paid on courtiers, the court to be paid to ministers, the influence to be cozened from bureaucrats, the tacit understandings to be arranged with customers, the salons in which to play the lion or the lamb, the sang-froid to exhibit amidst the shrilling of mockery that deflates many an accomplishment, pretended or real, in the French capital, even if it be the first balloon.[7] Neither could he foretell that his preoccupation with lifting force would prove to be convergent with the concern of the most influential of scientists in the properties of hydrogen. The coincidence was very close. On 16 June, just before word of Annonay and the putative role of inflammable air reached Paris, Lavoisier demonstrated that water is a compound of dephlogisticated and inflammable air, or of oxygen and hydrogen.[8] Nor did Etienne then imagine how aerostatics would open a new domain of engineering to mathematical analysis and furnish rational mechanics with a novel set of problems. Least of all, finally, was he ready to deal with the enthusiasm of advocates whose impetuosity took the repetition of the Annonay experiment out of his hands before he had a chance to make any provision at all, and placed him in the position of competing for exhibition of his own invention with the most popular lecturer on physics in the capital, J.-A.-C. Charles (Fig. 8), financed by a subscription list that included most of fashionable Paris.

8. Charles

2. THE HYDROGEN COMPETITOR

The principal advocate was a well-born natural-
ist, Barthélemy Faujas de Saint-Fond, whose career was animated rather by enthusiasm than by
professionalism. We owe much of our knowledge
of the first months of flight to the book that he
got out within the year, *Description des expériences de la machine aérostatique de MM de Mont-*
*golfier et de celles auxquelles cette découverte a donné
lieu.*[9] Faujas opened the subscription that paid
for the Charles experiments before Etienne had
arrived in Paris and quite without his knowledge
or approval. Such was the interest that word of
mouth sufficed to bring subscribers to the Palais
Royal, where the list was quickly filled up at a
table set aside in the Café du Caveau (later the
Rotonde).[10] The certificate was a ticket entitling

the bearer to admission to a public experiment at a time and place to be announced.

How Faujas presumed to take it on himself to act the impresario, he never says. He was forty-three years old, and thus scarcely a young blade. Of a landowning family in Dauphiny, Faujas had renounced his father's plan that he become a lawyer. Instead, he promoted his taste for natural history into a minor geological place in the retinue of Buffon, then nearing the end of his fifty-year intendancy of the royal botanical garden, nowadays the Jardin des Plantes. Coincidences abound throughout this story, for Faujas in his claim to scientific notice complemented Desmarest's geological observations amid the peaks of Auvergne. In 1778 he published an immense folio volume of volcanology, much of it second-hand and much of it travelogue. The principle of selection was the same that he observed in his book on ballooning: he put in everything. The only scientifically original aspect consisted in a demonstration that the *puys* of Vivarais and Velay are extinct volcanos, even as their counterparts in nearby Auvergne.[11] It is unclear whether either Faujas or Desmarest drew upon the other's work, however. It is also unclear whether Faujas met any of the Montgolfier family in his tours of their province. "Who is this Faujas?" Joseph asked Etienne in one letter in the summer of 1783.[12] By then Etienne had come to know him, and to like him on the whole. Like many an enthusiast, Faujas was a highly affable person.[13]

He never imagined there was a show to steal, moreover, since he was not party to deliberations in the Academy and had no way of knowing that Etienne was on his way to Paris. In opening a subscription and engaging the services of Charles, he most probably thought only to do a service in the good cause of progress and utility.

Charles was equally an enthusiast, to which quality he owed much of the success of the public course he gave in experimental physics. Just as Faujas had attached himself to Buffon, Charles had come under the wing of Benjamin Franklin, who encouraged him to abandon bureaucracy for science. A note in Etienne's hand among the Montgolfier papers alludes to Charles in passing

as the son of the marquis de Castries, minister of marine affairs. If so, his illegitimacy and the eminence of his father's family would explain the ambiguities of his early life, as well as his access to Franklin. Most of what little we know about him comes from a younger friend, an infantry officer in the Napoleonic armies, Sainte-Fare Bontemps, who wrote a memorandum for Fourier on which the latter based the *éloge* delivered before the Institute of France after Charles's death in 1823. Charles had been well educated for life in polite society. Among other accomplishments in literature and fine arts, he was a gifted flutist. When he was old enough to need a position, a trivial post in the Ministry of Finance, treasurer of *haras* (horse-breeding), was found for him. He left that for scientific lecturing in 1781, outfitting a laboratory in the Place des Victoires at his father's expense. According to Bontemps, his object in science was to perfect the art of experimentation to such a degree that it would convey the truths of physics to the eye in as exact a manner as mathematics does to the mind. That endeavor involved him in a "constant battle against matter and all its imperfections," a hard struggle from which he often emerged the winner.[14]

Charles was, of course, conversant with the properties of hydrogen. In demonstrations of its extraction from acids reacting with metals, he sometimes applied a soapy film to the open end of the glass tube venting his apparatus so that it blew soap bubbles. They bobbed up to the ceiling, and he would hold a lighted taper to two or three and arrest the ascent in a puff of flame. The term "charlière" for hydrogen balloons never won quite the currency that "montgolfière" still has for the hot-air variety. Charles would not have wished it otherwise. He readily acknowledged that the idea of expanding his soap bubbles into full-scale flying machines occurred to him only when the news of Annonay reached Paris. Even then he did not imagine himself to be making an invention, but only to be repeating the feat of lofting a balloon. Etienne withheld all information on how he and Joseph had floated their machine until the day in September, Friday the 12th, when he was ready to demonstrate the thing himself. The *procès-verbal* from the *Etats particuliers* said of the gas only that its density was half that of ordinary air. Since the density of inflammable air in the laboratory was an eighth to a tenth that of air, something somehow different must have been employed by the Montgolfiers.

How in any case could they have procured the amount of hydrogen they would have needed in a remote town devoid of chemical resources? Paris was a different matter. Funds were plentiful, thanks to the subscription. Time was short, for the same reason. The public expected a show for its money, and soon. No one had yet tried extraction of hydrogen in greater than laboratory quantity, however, or contained it in vessels other than laboratory apparatus. Fortunately, a prominent artisan, one Bernard, had developed an impermeable fabric that would serve, a sturdy taffeta impregnated with a solution of rubber in turpentine, a "gomme élastique" or india rubber. The design called for a spherical bag, twelve feet in diameter. It would be tiny compared to the Montgolfier balloon, which was thirty-five feet in diameter, with a thirtieth of the capacity. Even so, Charles and his associates would have to produce 900 cubic feet of hydrogen, a gas previous volumes of which had been measured in cubic inches.[15]

The principal assistants were a pair of brothers, A.-J. and M.-N. Robert, well-known instrument-makers who supplied Charles with most of his apparatus. Faujas and his fellow promoters scheduled the launching for 27 August from an emplacement in the Champ de Mars. To have tried mounting and inflating the balloon there before the eyes of all Paris would have been foolhardy, and the decision was taken to ready it for launching in the seclusion of the laboratory courtyard. Materials were ready by the 23rd. The balloon was suspended in a scaffolding and filled with atmospheric air. The globe was then collapsed upon itself and a valve in the orifice closed in order that it might be reinflated with inflammable air. One of the Roberts had improvised a generator in the form of a chest of lead-lined drawers. They were to be charged with iron filings onto which oil of vitriol (sulfuric acid) would be poured. Each opened at the back into a con-

duit that led by way of a siphon for washing the gas through the valve into the balloon. The notion was of a multicell device for producing hydrogen continuously. When the metal in the top drawer was used up, the acid would be diverted to the second while the contents were replenished in the first, and so on. The arrangement was altogether too complicated and proved a disaster, wasting time, material, and gas.

After two hours of struggling with it, the Roberts despaired and substituted a simple oaken barrel filled with iron filings (Fig. 9). Into it they poured successive doses of sulfuric acid, stoppering the bunghole each time. Hydrogen came off spasmodically and belched in great puffs into the interior of the balloon. When further acid produced diminishing effervescence, they shut the valve, dumped the sludge, and put in a new batch of metal. The assemblage produced gas so rapidly that the Roberts could never have managed it without the extra hands provided by several volunteers, among them Faujas. For there were problems, not to say bugs, to be eliminated only by improvised methods requiring cool heads and steady nerves. The reaction in the barrel produced so intense a heat that the water diluting the acid vaporized in part and passed with the hydrogen into the balloon. There it condensed, producing droplets of concentrated sulfuric acid that formed near the bottom of the bag. The corrosive blisters had to be extracted in short order lest the liquid eat through the lining. They could be tapped only through the valve, which had to be disconnected at frequent intervals while these tiny puddles of vitriol were teased out by shaking and manipulating the fabric from the outside. Soon after the operation began, the copper tube connecting the barrel to the valve grew too hot to touch and had to be swaddled in wet cloths. At the same time the undersurface of the balloon got so warm that several workmen were told to spray it with small water pumps.

Otherwise, writes Faujas, it would have "risked the greatest danger." And just let the modern reader imagine for a moment what was going on here. In a small, enclosed courtyard in a densely populated section of the city, a handful of largely

EXPÉRIENCE AÉROSTATIQUE

9. Generating hydrogen in the Place des Victoires

inexperienced people were collecting an unprecedented quantity of the most inflammable gas known through a tube too hot to touch into the confinement of a rubberized bag that was close to catching fire if it was not first chewed through by sulfuric acid. Well might Faujas observe that this first attempt was hard.

After a long day's work, the balloon was one-third full. At nine o'clock in the evening the decision was taken to quit for the night. The bag was left hanging flabbily on its framework, and the elder Robert made sure the valve was shut. What then was the surprise on returning at dawn on the 24th to find the balloon fully inflated! It could scarcely have inhaled a full volume of air through its skin. Alas, in an excess of caution one of the workmen had also tried the valve before departing, and thinking to close it, he opened it instead. There was nothing for it but to collapse the bag and begin anew. A twelve-foot balloon might not seem like much, observed Faujas, but to fill it with inflammable air required 1,000 pounds of iron filings and 498 pounds of vitriolic acid, not to mention the enervating effect of breathing in whiffs of the gas over a period of many hours.

The second day went more smoothly. By six o'clock in the evening the balloon was half-full and beginning to stir a bit within its harness. An hour later it was exerting a strong upward thrust. The next morning, the 25th, all was well. Only a little gas had seeped out overnight. Since the trial was still two days off, it seemed better to rest the fabric than to fatigue it by further filling. On the 26th, preparations began for moving the machine to the Champ de Mars for launching on the 27th. Early in the morning the crew removed the harness and substituted a leash of strong cords, allowing a test flight on a short rein. To everyone's delight the balloon bobbed up handsomely to a height of 100 feet. The apparition behind the façade of a globe floating above the rooftops would scarcely pass unnoticed, and the sponsors had arranged for two municipal guards at the doorway, one afoot and one on horseback. The curious thronged from all over Paris, however, and so great was the crush that Charles and Faujas felt constrained to admit a few at a time, whether to disarm or to titillate so natural a curiosity.

Clearly, the only hope of transporting the device undamaged to the Champ de Mars lay in moving it under cover of night. But how to get it out of the courtyard? One alternative might have been to pass it over the roof, but the risk of fouling the ropes among chimney pots in the darkness was too great. It would have to go out through the porte-cochère, therefore, which was a good deal less than twelve feet wide. The transfer began at 2:00 a.m. Since the balloon was still only half-inflated, it could be squeezed in the middle enough to slip it top to bottom through the passage. Crew members on both sides eased the fabric past the doorjamb. Outside in the Place des Victoires, the contrivance was righted and attached to a handcart. Preceded by torches and escorted by a detachment of the night watch, the crew drew their bobbing globe along the rue des Petits-Champs, turned down the rue de Richelieu into the rue Saint-Nicaise, traversed the Car-rousel, crossed the Seine on the Pont Royal, and made their way the length of the rue de Bourbon (now the rue de Lille) in front of the Invalides to arrive at their destination by dawn. The procession dumbfounded the few night owls encountered in the silent streets. A cabby stopped his fiacre, dismounted, and bowed before the balloon, his cap sweeping the pavement.

At the launching pad prepared in the Champ de Mars, the retaining cords were fixed to iron stakes driven into the ground. Generation of the remaining complement of hydrogen began immediately, while troops cordoned off the entire park. With the practice gained already, the reaction went smoothly. By noon the balloon was well filled out. At 3:00 p.m. ticket-holders were admitted through the barriers. The best places were in the windows of the Ecole militaire and in the parterres of the Champ de Mars itself. Other spectators thronged the roofs all around as well as the bank of the Butte de Chaillot across the Seine, while carriages choked the road from Versailles along the quay. In such a crowd the borderline between festivity and menace is easily traversed. The weather began to turn ugly, as the mood might have done. Black clouds loomed in the west. Cries for action arose, scattered at first but soon general. By five o'clock the globe was fully inflated and straining at the retaining cords. At a signal from the site a cannon fired, and up leaped the first balloon in Paris to the cheers of the multitude (Fig. 10). Out of sight in two minutes at an altitude of 1,500 feet, it momentarily reappeared across the Seine through a break in the clouds concealing Montmartre, and was gone.

It was a pity that the public thus forced the pace, for the impetuosity largely spoiled a design for combining popular with scientific interest in the experiment. Faujas's book contains a long, highly technical report on the flight path, a memoir conceived in a spirit that bespeaks talents of a very different order from any yet encountered in this story. The contributor was an accomplished young engineering officer, Jean-Baptiste Meusnier, whose career engaged one of the finest mathematical minds of his generation with prob-

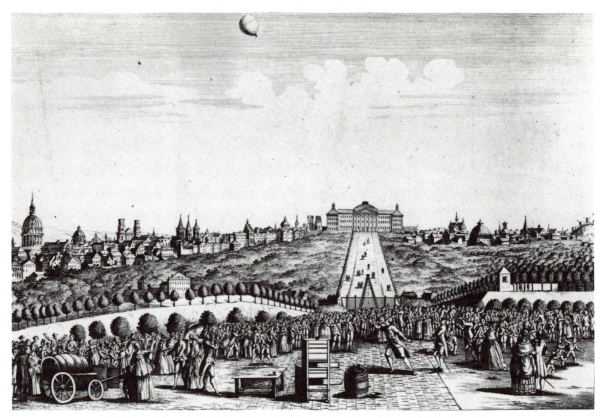

10. Launching the *charlière* from the Champ de Mars. Gimbel Collection 1160

lems of technology.[16] This preoccupation was characteristic of the entourage of Gaspard Monge, professor in the royal engineering school at Mezières, principal founder of differential geometry, and renovator of descriptive geometry. Meusnier was the best of Monge's former students. He had arranged with the military authorities to spend half the year in Paris working up for publication the records on mechanical inventions in the Academy of Science. The occupation placed him right where he wanted to be, in the midst of the scientific community. It was Meusnier's idea to make of the Champ de Mars demonstration an experimental verification of hypothetical laws of motion. Faujas could never have thought of that for himself. The problem is stated in the language of a builder of mathematical models: to consider "a voluminous moving body displaced in the air to a considerable altitude and subject in its motion to the action of two opposing forces, one of which varies as the density of successive layers of the atmosphere, while the other depends on the laws of air resistance."[17]

The former of those two laws, Meusnier observed, rested on largely abstract considerations uncontrolled by experience. He acknowledged right away that he was probably not the only one to conceive the notion that exact observation of the flight of a balloon would furnish the needed data. A little later he learned that he was indeed in good company. The news of Annonay reached Saint Petersburg sometime in August. There in the Russian capital, the aging embodiment of rational mechanics, Leonhard Euler, purblind in his last years, wrote out calculations on his slate deriving "the laws of vertical motion of a globe rising in calm air in consequence of the upward force owing to its lightness." On 7 September he

~ 32 ~

died of a stroke, and his son copied off the equations and sent them to the Academy of Science in Paris. Its *Mémoires* thus had the privilege of inaugurating mathematical analysis of the flight of aircraft with the publication of Euler's valedictory.[18]

Meusnier had the details of the proposal for comparative observations ready for Faujas and his associates on the 26th of August, the day before the flight. Three sets of readings taken simultaneously from different vantage spots would in principle permit triangulation of points along the path at successive intervals. In order to provide a margin for error, Meusnier decided to employ four observers, each furnished with a quadrant for taking azimuths and altitudes and a stopwatch with a secondhand. The astronomer Joseph Le Paute Dagelet, professor of mathematics at the Ecole Militaire, undertook to enlist his colleagues and to coordinate their services. He stationed Guillaume Le Gentil at the Observatory of Paris, E.-S. Jeaurat on the roof of the *garde-meuble* in Place Louis XV (now the Place de la Concorde), and a mathematics teacher called Prévost in one of the towers of Notre Dame. Dagelet took his own place in the cupola of the Ecole militaire, immediately overlooking the Champ de Mars. From there he would signal the others so that all sightings might be referrable to the same time scale. Notice was very short. Dagelet was able to reach Jeaurat and Le Gentil, both members of the Academy, only at eleven o'clock in the morning of the 27th, with the balloon already emplaced. They joined in the project enthusiastically, but there was no time to write down an agreed-upon procedure, let alone to rehearse the transmission of signals, on the success of which the whole thing would turn. Planning had to be by word of mouth.

The scheme was for Dagelet to keep the preparations for launching closely under scrutiny and to have a pennant hoisted when release of the balloon was imminent. At that moment all four observers would synchronize their watches and ready their telescopes for tracking. Alas, the impatience of the crowd created disarray around the launching site below. Rain obscured the view.

From the Ecole militaire it looked as if the crew was hastening the hour, as indeed they were. One of Dagelet's assistants fumbled in his pocket for the pennant, but the cannon sounded and the balloon was off before the other three observers could have spotted it. Anyway, the little flag was too small to see except through the telescopes, which were focused on the more interesting object of the balloon itself. Once released, the globe rose much faster than expected. What with the confusion and the overcast, all that Prévost and Le Gentil managed to observe was the apparent position of its disappearance into the clouds. Even if their watches had been coordinated, ruefully reflected Meusnier, there was no reason to suppose the visibility identical from Notre Dame and the Observatory.

Thus vanished into incoherence the project for triangulation, or rather quadrangulation. Fortunately Jeaurat in the Place Louis XV noted the time when he heard the cannon. That bit of good luck permitted collating his observations with those of Dagelet in the Ecole militaire right on top of the site. Meusnier retrieved what he could from the near-fiasco by elaborate calculations approximating the time and location of eight positions in the path from these two small sets of data (Fig. 11). Lost from view, both scientific and profane, the little *charlière* flew on through the rains at ever increasing altitude for three quarters of an hour. About twenty kilometers north of Paris it burst and plummeted to earth near Ecouen. The peasants among whom it fell attacked with pitchforks and dragged the remains into the village of Gonesse, near the present-day airport of Le Bourget. Their panicky defiance immediately became a favorite theme in the iconography (Plate IV). From the debris Charles and Meusnier were able to determine that the rupture was caused by growing imbalance between internal and external pressure at increasing altitude.[19] More important than the post-mortem, or than the partial results of a frustrated mathematical analysis, was Meusnier's continuing engagement in the development of aerostatics, which he went on to promote into aeronautics almost from the start.

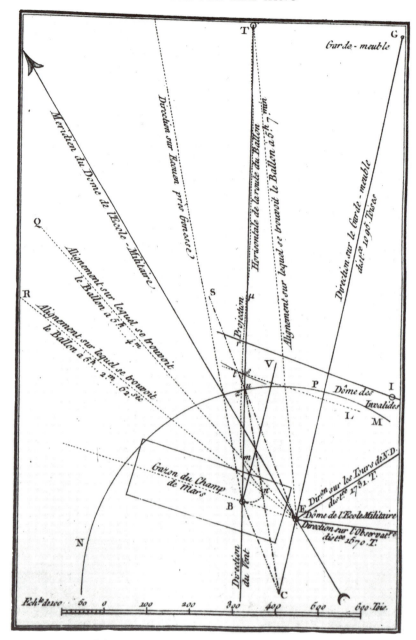

11. Meusnier's plot of the flight path of the *charlière*

3. To Set before the King

Journalism feeds on spectacles of dissension, creating quarrels where none exist and amplifying differences into disputes. The popular press, and Grimm in his *Correspondance*, ranged Faujas and his subscribers against Charles and the Roberts over alleged faults in design and inflation that supposedly led to rupture of the balloon, and simultaneously attributed pique over the whole enterprise to Etienne Mongolfier. It was put about that Etienne had been turned away from the Champ de Mars for want of a ticket.[20] Whether chagrined at word of this slight (real or invented), or more largely at the denigratory tone of the public prints, Faujas in his expansive way launched a second subscription, this one to underwrite the striking of a medal honoring the achievement of Etienne and Joseph Montgolfier in inaugurating flight.[21] Again the initiative was his. Nothing in Etienne's own hand gives any indication of his being out of countenance in the manner imputed to him. The one thing certain is that the entire experience gave him a rooted distaste for the method of funding through popular subscriptions. Later in the year, he vehemently warned Joseph against thus subjecting himself to the whim of the public in order to finance construction of the enormous balloon that his brother was cogitating for Lyons.[22]

Intermittent depression and irritation rather than jealousy seem to have afflicted Etienne, if we may judge from the responses to his infrequent letters home in August. His brothers chided him lightly on occasion but were generally warm and supportive, mingling encouragement for the balloon with news of business and the family and imparting commissions to be executed in the capital. One or another wrote by virtually every post throughout the summer, often adding to each other's letters. Thus on 31 July the abbé Alexandre, whose light touch made him the family favorite, replied that Etienne must have had indigestion when he wrote some sour complaint addressed to his wife. He, the abbé, has had a stomachache for a week but means to handle the discomfort better. Now then, what's it all about? So we haven't sent you Imbert's address. Surely you can get it in the controller general's office. You say nothing—thus the abbé—about our letters since asking for that.

It seems to me that you have become possessed by the spirit of an author and inventor. You're afraid that the Périers will get ahead of you. [The brothers Périer were the importers of Watt's steam engine.] That is, perhaps, a good deal less certain than you imagine. But in any case, your credit for the invention can't be disputed. You reproach yourself for having been obliging with the *Etats particuliers*. Come on now! What else

made you famous? What else brought you to the attention of the Minister? What else made the Academy take you up? What else, if it wasn't that public experiment? Is it not a bulwark raised against all the counterfeiters and other hornets that would like to devour your honey? Go to, my friend, a little more patience, and you'll feel better. I notice every day that it's a drug impossible to overstock.[23]

A few days later, on 4 August, the abbé wrote again, to the effect that Jean-Pierre, who had dined unwisely in town, was better (Jean-Pierre adding a grumpy postscript that the abbé always put things in the worst light and wanted him to eat as lightly as his wife, which was impossible). Etienne's wife (Adélaïde) was keeping up her spirits, but her condition made her sleepy in the morning. He, the abbé, had disturbed her before her hair was done, but she had forgiven him. They badly needed an experienced foreman to oversee the cylinders. Etienne was to see whether Desmarest couldn't find them someone. These and a hundred other details of family and factory streamed in on Etienne from Vidalon.[24]

Joseph's letters, mainly from Lyons, mingle the personal with the technical in a style that may best be called explosive. Most of his correspondence with outsiders is in his wife's hand, for he was incapable of spelling properly. Within the family circle he let himself go and usually wrote in his own deformed words. His letters look illiterate, therefore, but do not sound so when read aloud. For example, in his first reply (5 August) to Etienne, inspection yields the meaning of "Je matandais bien que la chose nestait pas mure." . . . "I was certainly prepared to find that the time was not ripe" (and that the balloon would be regarded merely as a curiosity). Only when spoken, however, does "Mais je suis bien comptant que nous ayons pris datte" give "But I'm very glad (content) that we have priority." Joseph hated writing. Still, once he started, thoughts tumbled from his mind, and his pen raced along following where they led as best it could. Here they led to the next machine he envisaged, which must be no paltry improvement but an affair that would take imagination by storm, a monster balloon 150 feet in lateral diameter and 100 feet high. Joseph calculated that it would cost 15,000 or 16,000 livres. But—as he has just written Argand—why settle for less? If the government lacked the will or vision, as he gathered from Etienne it very well might, then let his brother find a rich man, or else let him confront the authorities with the alternative of taking their invention to England. There were plenty of wealthy patrons in that country.[25]

The next day Joseph was in Vidalon, where he joined in the worry over the tone of Etienne's correspondence. Relax a little, he wrote. You will ruin your health. Etienne was not to fret over the anxiety lest Joseph be deprived of his share of fame by being absent from Paris. You know I don't think like that (if we may paraphrase), and there is no point whatever in sending a copy of my portrait. Joseph, for his part, was uneasy over a phrase in Etienne's letter implying that the latter was going up in the machine himself. Don't do it—at least not unless I come to Paris to dissuade or accompany you.[26] Back in Lyons four days later, Joseph let himself go on the preliminary specifications he had imagined for the mega-balloon in which he did there take to the air with passengers in January of the following year. Characteristically, he then veered off in mid-paragraph to improvements he was making in his printing scheme. Finally, he took up Etienne's news that the government was greatly interested in developing techniques for extraction of commercial soda from the salt in sea water. Joseph had no doubt that that could be done. He suggested two possible methods. His language in the second conveys his way of conceiving chemical phenomena: "The decomposition could also be tried with chalk, because of the double affinity involved, the base of marine salt feeling a strong affection (*estant tres amoureuse de*) for the fixed air contained in chalk."[27]

Even while rallying to support Etienne's morale, Joseph complained that he had not been told what his brother actually had in hand. As late as 4 September he wrote that Etienne appeared to have put aside their "machine diosta-

tique" in order to concentrate on business. Well, he, Joseph, recognized that that is where their future lay. He regretted the time he had taken from his heat pump. Perhaps some day they might come back to aircraft.[28] In fact, however, Etienne was working intensively all this while. His laments in private must have been the safety valve affording release from tension, or a potential cushion in case of disappointment. For he began consulting with the commission named by the Academy early in August, well before the flight of the *charlière*, and continued his preparations while the attention of Paris fastened on that experiment. He had no need of a subscription. The commission had immediately undertaken to defray his expenses, and the Ministry of Finance assumed the obligation when officials there realized that it would overburden the Academy. The controller general put Etienne in touch with high persons at court to arrange for a demonstration at Versailles before the royal family. Technical things interested Louis XVI, and the king assented to a public exhibition to be mounted in the great court in front of the château on 19 September. Etienne further agreed to stage a private trial a week earlier for the benefit of the academic commissioners, and of course for his own, in the courtyard of the Réveillon factory. There he had installed equipment and begun breaking in construction workers and a ground crew, sharing the direction with Ami Argand and Réveillon himself.[29]

Apparently Etienne's ideas had expanded as the summer lengthened and anxiety waned. Early references in the correspondence are to a globe forty feet in diameter, only slightly larger than the Annonay balloon, and we know that materials for such a sister-ship had been cut and sent along with him to Paris in July. Joseph kept urging Etienne to think in showier terms, pointing out that at this stage a crowd would be more impressed by the scale of a machine than by its capacity to lift a load, which would be invisible.[30] That could come later. Etienne did not answer to that point, and his brother learned about the design only after the demonstration was over, though it seems likely that his advice intensified

Etienne's own sense of the importance of rising to the opportunity and meeting the expectations of the public.

Etienne did communicate to Joseph doubts he had developed about the tensile strength of taffeta and paper. Réveillon and he had explored the feasibility of substituting cloth coated with varnish. Unfortunately, he did not then persist in that design, because of the expense. Faujas emphasizes how Etienne made economy a point of honor in view of the carte blanche accorded him by the commissioners.[31] The machine he had ready for them on 12 September modified the fabric of the Annonay envelope only to the extent of covering the taffeta with paper inside and outside instead of lining it with a double layer. If all went well, it would be transported to Versailles a week later to be flown before the king.

This second *montgolfière* was a splendid object, seventy feet tall and only forty feet in diameter. Inflation curved it out gracefully on a geometric profile consisting of three segments, the central section being a prism twenty-four feet high, the cap a twenty-seven-and-a-half-foot pyramid, and the base an eighteen-and-a-half-foot truncated cone. True to his education, Etienne thought like an architect about the design, and Réveillon like a decorator. For surely it was in consequence of the latter's association with the project that the iconography of balloons has evolved out of the patterning of 18th-century wallpaper. This was the first of them to be adorned like a pleasure dome turned inside out. The *charlière* fabricated by physicists and instrument-makers was merely a dumpy, round flying machine, unimaginatively striped in red and blue. Not so the Réveillon *montgolfière*, fit to float above a king, and still more so over the particular queen who was Marie Antoinette. The background shade was azure, and the effect that of a tent at some *fête-champêtre* with its *pavillon* and ornaments personifying the sun in color of gold. The weight was 1,000 pounds. When inflated, the gorgeous aerostat would displace 4,500 pounds of atmospheric air by a volume of gas weighing 2,500 pounds. Its lifting force would thus balance an additional weight of 1,000 pounds.

That made a bulky mass of intractable material to handle on the ground. In order to assemble the pieces, match the edges, and sew the seams, the crew had to lay the whole thing out in the garden of the factory. No interior space was big enough. When rain threatened, as it did intermittently in the equinoctial season, the enormous length of material had to be folded over loosely so that the layers of paper were neither creased nor broken and then brought under shelter. Twenty men were needed to move it, and they had to be gingerly. "No machine," wrote Faujas, who was there as he had also been in Charles's courtyard, "ever caused so much anxiety and trouble."[32] Réveillon was resourcefulness itself, throwing all his energy and virtuosity into the task of readying the great bag. For a time it seemed as if the weather would force postponement. Then the morning of Thursday 11 September dawned clear and still. Finishing touches were applied, and the working trio—Etienne, Réveillon, and Argand—decided on a trial among themselves that evening. It went perfectly. Nine minutes over the lighted brazier sufficed for filling the envelope (Fig. 12). The craft lifted eight men holding it captive off the ground and would have borne them aloft if others had not jumped for the ropes. Word was sent round forthwith to the commissioners of the Academy requesting their presence at 8:00 a.m. the next day, Friday the 12th, and the bag was left hanging in its scaffolding overnight.

By five o'clock in the morning the weather had changed. Rain began to fall, lightly at first. Etienne lit the burner and inflated the balloon enough to dry the fabric. It would in any case have been out of the question to dismount the thing and lay it out all wet on the ground. The commissioners failed to arrive before nine o'clock. By then a considerable company of distinguished people had assembled, all eagerness and enthusiasm despite the drizzle. There was no choice but to go ahead. Etienne had fifty pounds of straw briquettes fed into the fire, and he regulated the rate of burning by tossing in some ten pounds of woolen shreds from time to time. Within ten minutes, the quiet flame had produced a vapor so expansive—thus

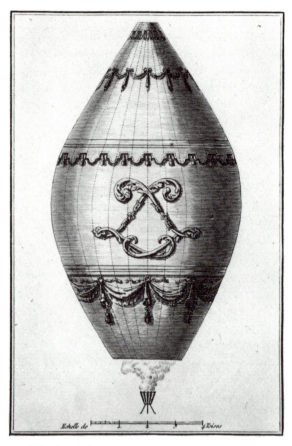

12. The first balloon constructed in the Réveillon factory

Faujas—and endowed with such force that the balloon began to ripple longitudinally and to shape up. In order to demonstrate its lifting power, Etienne added ten fifty-pound weights. Argand and he were hanging onto the cords, and as the bag filled it lifted them together with the leaden load a few feet into the air. If the crew had not grabbed for the retaining lines, it would have immediately leapt to a great height when they let go and dropped back onto their feet.

At this moment of imminent triumph, the splendid sack towering into the gray sky, the rain increased. Argand urged cutting the cords and staging a flight even if it meant losing the balloon. Etienne, the cautious one, vetoed that course since it would have meant breaking their commitment for Versailles. He sought instead to bring the craft down lest, bobbing in the wind, it brush

against the heater and take fire. In retrospect, Argand's would have been the better solution. The rainfall became a steady downpour. The decorated bands of paper peeled from their backing of fabric and trailed their gaiety in the courtyard. All spectators were full of sympathy and prodigal in their praise of what might have been. The academicians drew up a generous attestation on the spot, encouraging Etienne to persevere in his imaginative experiments.[33]

Etienne enclosed a copy of this *procès-verbal* in a letter to Joseph, observing in his frank way that it failed to convey the ultimate dejection of their attempt since the commissioners had departed before the rain was at its worst. What would have been a beautiful spectacle was then a heap of wet cloth amid piles of soggy wallpaper in a drowned garden of the faubourg Saint-Antoine. In the face of catastrophe, Etienne exhibited the coolness one might have expected of him in the early stages of his mission. "Too bad," he wrote, "the machine had a pretty appearance and would have made a good impression." After this, they have resolved to make another "which will not be vulnerable to fire, wind, or water, and which will be easy to service." They now intended to impregnate the fabric with an impermeable mixture, which might even prove no costlier. Joseph was not to allow their wives to repine over the disaster. Let them look on it as another experiment, like the one at Annonay.[34]

Etienne's mood had apparently hardened late in August, steeled by the competition of the *charlière* and by a healthy involvement in the labors of the Réveillon garden. Then and early in September he began to take the family into his confidence about the plans for Versailles. Not content merely to match the spectacle of the Charles balloon with a *montgolfière*, Etienne and his associates contemplated moving matters a stage further, into the transportation of living beings. The story that Louis XVI personally forbade a manned flight and insisted on experimenting first with creatures other than human is probably apocryphal. It is more likely that the idea of flying animals originated with Etienne, Argand, and Réveillon. But what beasts to choose? According to Jean-Pierre, Etienne's first thought was a sheep. The abbé counseled against it—altogether too placid an animal. "I should prefer a dog, or anything else that would make itself heard in the air." Why not a cow, or better yet a young bull of 300 or 400 pounds: "whatever its sex, it could be transformed into beef on the principle of *hic et haec homo*."[35] Joseph was also all enthusiasm, now that his brother had plucked up his spirits. "Bon jour, cher frère," begins one of his great long screeds of technical rumination. Try to take a cow. That will create an extraordinary effect, far more so than a panicky sheep that no one will be able to see.[36] Jean-Pierre, ever the man of business, urged his brother, first, to get some American orders out of Franklin and then to profit from the prospective publicity by securing a contract to supply paper for the India Company. To this letter Adélaïde (who wrote little) added a lazy and affectionate postscript:[37]

Do you feel the way I do, my love? I seem to be surrounded by a sense of illusion and of prestige. Your success astonishes me. I'm not yet used to your being a celebrity. I don't know whether I ought to laugh or to yield to hopes of a successful outcome. I guess I want that, moderately at least. But we'll have to watch out. It would be too painful to renounce these chimerical prospects if we once get used to them. I believe that you're more sensible than I am, and that you'll be as modest when you get back from Paris as when you left, and also satisfied with the outcome whatever it may be. I'll limit myself to urging you to look after your health. Follow your brother's example. All his fame hasn't cost him a mouthful (*un coup de dents*) nor an hour of sleep. It would be better to be away three weeks longer and to come home in good health. You'll appreciate that it takes a good deal of generosity for me to urge that. Your presence would be a joy to me on the eve of the baby's coming. But I do my part and accept what has to be. . . . I no longer indulge myself in the hope of seeing you here before the end of October. My time is near. I beg you only to keep on sending us your

news, even if it's only a word. I'm feeling well. We appreciate that it's hard for you to find the time to satisfy all our curiosity. Save your descriptions for a more leisurely moment.

She does just want him to ask their aunt what name the latter wants given to her goddaughter if it's another girl, and she has a few scattered commissions—don't take time to shop for me—and a word of news about persons in Annonay. "I'm very tired and going to bed. Give all our relatives a big hug. I've still got a thousand things to tell you but I'm dying for sleep."

The Réveillon demonstration had originally been intended for a week earlier, it would appear, for the abbé in a letter of 4 September thinks it to be occurring that very day: "There you are covered with glory, dear brother, but also (I imagine) exhausted. I suppose that your new machine took off today, and that in a week at most the mail will bring us your news. You must now get back to business and try to get hold of the various merchants who could give us some orders, for we are in great need of them."[38] When Etienne received that prodding, he had no time even to read letters, for he and his associates were striving to build a new balloon from scratch against the deadline of the demonstration promised for Versailles on the 19th. Abandoning paper, they reverted to the alternative of taffeta coated with varnish. The model they constructed in four frantic days and nights was fifty-seven feet in height and forty-one in diameter. A good deal smaller than the great craft destroyed in the rain, it had a capacity of 37,500 cubic feet and displaced 3,192 pounds of air. The "gas of M. Montgolfier"— i.e., hot air—that filled it weighed 1,596 pounds, to which the combined burden of fabric, cage, sheep, duck, and rooster (for those were the animals chosen) added 900 pounds. The initial lifting force was thus equivalent to 696 pounds, generated by consumption in the burner of fifty pounds of straw and five of shredded wool. In the evening of the 18th, a trial inflation succeeded admirably, except that again a gust of wind whip-sawed the balloon against one of the masts and ripped a seam near the summit. There was time only to baste before transporting equipment and people to Versailles early the next morning.[39]

The final arrangements for inflation were far more sophisticated than in the Réveillon attempt a week previously. Agents were sent ahead to Versailles to construct an octagonal stage high enough to walk under in the courtyard of the château. The working space below was concealed from public view by an apron running around the perimeter. In the middle of the platform was a circular opening fifteen feet in diameter and beneath it an iron stove four feet high and three feet in diameter with a direct draft. The material of the balloon was then so disposed on the scaffolding that the dome covered the opening while the remaining fabric was pleated under it. A skirt reached right down to the ground, enclosing the stove. The crowd, of course, was enormous. All the windows of the château and its dependencies, and even the roofs, were occupied with spectators who had been pouring in since early morning, from Paris and from the countryside. Instead of seeing a limp bag hanging loosely from two jury-rigged masts, they looked down upon a great spread of brightly colored cloth. On the firing of a signal, the fabric began to stir and rise, apparently on its own, assuming shape, and off it went, its bleating, quacking, crowing passengers in tow (Fig. 13). But let us allow the exultant Etienne to tell the story of the trial and of the flight, in the letter he wrote to Adélaïde, his wife, late in the very evening of his triumph.[40] (Etienne did not then know that their child, another daughter, had been born just a week previously, the day of the Réveillon fiasco.)

NEWS FROM THE AIR
19 September 1783
Aboard the Aerostat Réveillon
"We feel fine. We've landed safely despite the wind. It's given us an appetite." That is all we could gather from the talk of the three travelers, seeing that they don't know how to write and that we neglected to teach them French. The first could say only "Quack, Quack"; the second, "Cock-a-doodle-doo"; and the third, no doubt a member of the Lamb family, replied only "Baa" to all our questions.

I'll have to be the historian in their place, therefore. You already know how in last Friday's rain the paper stretched and the cloth shrank so that the materials stripped apart in the machine that had taken me two months to make: *the work of two months disappeared in a day*. You know, too, how the new one that we started at nine o'clock Saturday evening was finished Thursday morning. We thought we had won the day and wanted to try it out and make the last adjustments, but the skies ordained otherwise. A downpour threatened us with another day like Friday and forced us to get it all under cover hastily. Several of the members of the Academy arrived, and all downcast we went to dinner.

The weather began to mend. With trepidation we hoisted the top into place and began the operation. Suddenly there was a gust of wind. *Cric-crac* the top split open, torn in several places. We secured the craft, called for caulkers, and held a consultation on the repairs we would have to make. The one who talked the loudest got his way, as usual. I think it was Monsieur Argand. We gathered up the damaged part and reinforced it beneath the netting with a double layer. The tears being folded under, it no longer gave evidence of leaking air. The wind stilled momentarily, and we could try again. In six minutes the machine was inflated. It took off, and remained suspended twelve feet in the air secured by strong ropes.

Everybody clapped their hands. Someone led me down to the bottom of the garden so that I could get a better impression of the effect. Though I was scarcely combed and had a three-day beard, not having been near the hairdresser in that time, one lady embraced me, and then I had to make the rounds of all the others. What with the precaution of refusing entrance to anyone except the commission from the Academy, there were only two or three hundred people in the garden. There were compliments. There were

13. Liftoff at Versailles, by the chevalier de Lorimier

speeches. While this was going on, we brought the machine down to its emplacement, got it ready to transport, and waited for the wagon from the Menus [the recreation hall at Versailles]. Instead of arriving at six o'clock, it got there only at half past eight. Before we had finished packing and loading, it was almost eleven. Worn out, we went to bed, really exhausted for people who had to be up at four.

We got ourselves together in the morning, washed and shaved, and left at five o'clock, reaching Versailles at eight. People were beginning to get restive over not seeing us arrive. The Secretary of the Menus took me to Monsieur the marquis de Duras. I gave him a report on the probable success of the experiment. He asked me to write out a précis to show the king, for fear that there might be a mistaken idea of the altitude to be attained and the distance to be traveled. I was about to carry out his instructions, but after a moment he said to me that he thought it might be better for me to present this précis to his majesty myself. At 11:30 I was ushered in to the levee. I presented my précis. I then returned to the machine to unfold and arrange it, etc., etc.

A few moments later, the king and queen arrived with Monsieur and Madame, the comte d'Artois, Madame Elizabeth, etc., etc. [the brothers, sister-in-law, and sister of Louis XVI], all of whom one after the other passed beneath our scaffolding, got under the machine, had the workings explained to them, and saw that the machinery consisted only of a burner full of straw. Monsieur de Cubières, who came with the king, yelled to Monsieur Réveillon to call me, since I couldn't see them all, being on the other side of the scaffolding. The king, who had my précis in his hand, took Monsieur de Cubières by the arm, and said, "Never mind. Don't worry. Here is good old Montgolfier [Voici le petit Montgolfier] who will explain it all to me anyway."

At one o'clock, we set off a round of ammunition and lighted the fire. Two or three puffs of wind raised doubts about the feasibility of the experiment. However, by dint of muscle and gas, we overcame all obstacles. The machine filled in seven minutes. It was held in place only by ropes and the combined efforts of fifteen or sixteen men. A second round went off. We redoubled the gas, and at the third round, which I may have had fired too soon for fear that the wind might come up and interfere, everyone let go at once. The machine rose majestically, drawing after it a cage containing a *sheep*, a *rooster*, and a *duck*. A few moments after takeoff a sudden gust of wind tilted it over on its side. Since there was insufficient ballast to keep it vertical, the top afforded the wind a much larger surface than the part where the animals were. At that instant I was afraid it was done for [Plate V]. It got away with losing about a fifth of its gas, however, and continued on its way as majestically as ever for a distance of 1,800 fathoms [just over two miles] where the wind tipped it over again so that it settled gently down to earth.

I went right up to the royal apartments and found the king still engaged in observing the machine with his field glasses. He showed me the locality where it had fallen, expressed his satisfaction, and at my request gave orders that people go to the place where it lay stranded in order to verify the condition of the animals. The controller general was there, who indicated his satisfaction and invited me to dinner with the members of the Academy. I went to beg off from Monsieur de Cubières, with whom I had agreed to dine; I saw Pache, who beckoned me into the rooms of Monsieur de Castries. He also invited me to dine, but I could not accept. At the controller general's, the talk was all about the machine. During dinner, I was told about its condition when it landed, that it had traversed 1,800 fathoms from its point of departure, it was torn in the upper part, the animals were in fine shape, and the sheep had pissed in the cage.

I went along to report to Monsieur le marquis de Duras, who was at Madame d'Ossun's. I was taken into a pretty apartment under the eaves. In the inner room, bathed agreeably in the half-light of dusk, an attractive gathering of twenty or thirty ladies held court. They could have served as models for painters called on to represent assemblies on Olympus. A new opera by Sacciny [Sacchini] was being performed. Madame d'Ossun had the most flattering things to say to me. She made me sit next to her to listen to the music. After having stayed for half an hour, I took my leave. They wished to keep me, but I pleaded that Monsieur de Duras had asked me to prepare a précis describing the condition of the machine so that he might show it to the king, and that I must tend to it. They made me promise to return and gave instructions that the door be opened for me.

I had to see Monsieur de Cubières, and went to his quarters. There I found more company. "Here," he said, "is a gentleman who has written a book, a poem, about the machine, composed of a song, of a leaflet, of a verse, which runs: 'The creator of this globe is still merely a mortal man.' "

After departing in order to rejoin my people at the Menus, I lost my way and walked for three quarters of an hour. Finally I arrived, overcome with fatigue, and right away had to return to the château. "Quick, the queen is asking for you!" I took Monsieur Argand by the arm. We hurried off. I arrived again at Madame d'Ossun's apartment. "Where have you come from?" cried the Maréchal. "I've had people looking for you everywhere. You've kept the queen waiting. She has already come out two or three times to talk with you." I went into the outer room, where Madame d'Ossun also chided me agreeably over not acceding to her invitation to return. The queen came out. I gave her

a detailed account of the machine, read her the précis drawn up for the king, and told her of our further projects, for that machine as well as for others. She listened to me kindly. On the way out from seeing the queen, Monsieur the Marquis asked me if I was happy with my reception. You can judge how I replied. We rejoined Argand, and I went back to our group, none of us feeling the least bit tired. For I am willing to admit that, in spite of a philosophy that appreciates things at their true value, I have not been insensible to the pleasures of this day, and I have forgotten the work, the trouble, and the worry that it cost me. At last we all went to bed very happy but very tired.

Well before the launching, two of the astronomers who had tracked the Charles balloon stationed themselves in the Observatory of Paris, Le Gentil with a three-foot quadrant and Jeaurat with an instrument he did not specify. The balloon rose above their horizon near Mount Valérien, and they estimated its maximum altitude above ground level at 240 and 253 fathoms (1,440 and 1,518 feet) respectively. That was only a quarter of the height attained by the Annonay prototype, one reason being the loss of hot air on near-capsizing. The strain of that narrow escape had further torn the seam damaged the previous evening, and the combined effect of these accidents limited the flight-time to eight minutes instead of the twenty predicted by Etienne. None of that spoiled the success, however. Hastening to the woods of Vaucresson, where the *montgolfière* alighted at a crossroads, called Carréfour-maréchal, were the eager Faujas, the abbé d'Espagnac, the chevalier de Lorimier, and Alexandre Brongniart. They found the deflated craft lying flat across the lawn, one side caught up in the branches of a small oak. Already on the scene was François Pilatre de Rozier, a young man who, a few weeks before, had put in his bid to fly the first balloon to be entrusted with a human being.[41] Two months later he did pilot the next of Etienne's creations, the *montgolfière* that sailed across the capital from a launching in the château de la Muette on 21 November.

4. MANNED FLIGHT

Pilatre de Rozier had a gift for offering himself up to scientific causes in a way that disarmed the skepticism with which scientists normally greet the enthusiasms of the public. He was well placed to make known his willingness to become a winged guinea pig. Twenty-six years of age, Pilatre was the impresario of a popular science establishment under the patronage of the comte and comtesse de Provence, the king's brother and sister-in-law, Monsieur and Madame in the usage of the court. This Musée, which he liked to call the first approved by the government, was situated in the rue de Valois, a few steps from the café du Caveau in the Palais Royal, where Faujas opened his subscription.[42]

There the scientific demimonde forgathered under the aegis of the duc d'Orléans, the king's cousin. Pilatre gave talks in his Musée on topics of physics and chemistry. According to an intimate, he sometimes had trouble in finding the right words, and qualities other than eloquence accounted for his success. He was unfailingly agreeable to an audience consisting for the most part of ladies of fashion. He never put them at a disadvantage. His purpose was to entertain, instructing no further than might be welcome. He perfectly understood that his hearers preferred the éclat to the reality of science. Interspersing demonstrations of electrical and chemical effects with jokes and gallantries, he sustained a mood of gaiety in the lecture hall (Fig. 14).[43]

What with charm, pluck, and enterprise, Pilatre had made good his escape from a very petty bourgeois background in Metz. There his father put him out to pharmacy after he faltered, first in schooling and then in a brush with surgery. He began his chemistry and natural history in the shop of an accomplished apothecary, one Thirion, whose company was sought out by the duc de la Rochefoucauld, an amateur of science then in Lorraine with his regiment. The connection

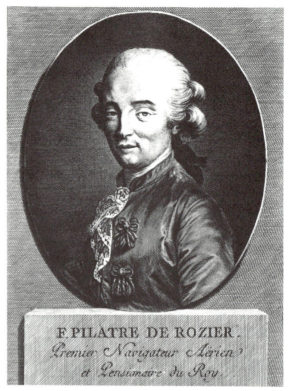

14. Pilatre de Rozier, portrait by Pujos

15. Pilatre de Rozier breathing fire

stood Pilatre in good stead when he ran away to Paris, where a doctor with whom he lodged befriended him. Upon the death of this benefactor, his widow having (it is reasonable to infer) made a man of the lad, refused his juvenile offer of marriage. By dint of frequenting public courses in the capital, Pilatre acquired more than a smattering and less than a serious competence in chemistry and physics. Like many another young hopeful, he composed memoirs and submitted them to the Academy of Science, aspiring to notice and—who knows?—to election by that increasingly august body. These investigations include analyses and preparations of several dyestuffs, an experiment describing the shattering of a sheet of glass by the spark from a Leyden jar, fabrication from white phosphorus of a spontaneously combustible candle, and studies of properties of noxious gases. He used his own lungs in estimating the tolerance of the human body for breathing hydrogen. In his public demonstrations he would light the gas he exhaled with a candle (Fig. 15).[44]

Mephitic gas was a more serious concern. Sanitary workers would sometimes be overcome and suffocate while cleaning out the trenches of public conveniences. Pilatre demonstrated, again on himself, that breathing the fumes causes spasms in the epiglottis, an effect to be aborted only by swallowing the gas. He imagined and constructed a respirator equipped like a skin diver's snorkel with a tube attached to an air tank. The lieutenant-general of police of Paris, the chevalier Pierre Le Noir, had his underlings locate a trench noxious enough to test the efficacy of Pilatre's device with a view to its adoption by the municipality. Pilatre donned rubberized coveralls and descended to the bottom of this foulest of cloaca. There he lay upon the excrement under a three-foot layer of mephitic gas for a period of thirty-four minutes before exhausting his air supply. His invention was duly approved by the Academy of Science and the Royal Society of Medicine.[45]

Of such mettle was the first airman. But was he the first? The distinction is always accorded him, not so much for his public demonstration of free flight on 21 November since the marquis

d'Arlandes shared that voyage, but rather for his feat of soloing a month earlier in the same balloon held captive in tests run on 15, 17, and 19 October. Before that, however, Etienne himself flew the new balloon in experiments that were not then, and have never since, been reported (unless one cryptic sentence in the account of the academic commission may be called a report: "We shall say nothing of several preliminary experiments, but will turn at once to that which was performed in our presence on 15 October"). Etienne may simply have preceded Pilatre on the 15th, but it seems more likely that he tried the machine out several days before that. He later mentioned to Joseph having lightened the gallery though he did not then tell his brother he had been up himself, perhaps because Joseph had expressly urged against any such venture.[46] Neither do we have the letter in which Etienne did recount the escapade to Adélaïde. Her reply, however, leaves no doubt about the fact: "I have just received your letter, my dear one, where you tell us about your embarking. Although it did not give me much pleasure, I congratulate you on your success and specially on your safe return. I don't much like these aerial voyages. Don't imagine, my dear, that I disapprove of what you are doing. Everything you do is right in my eyes, but I'm an echo in these complaints. Maybe I make a mistake sending along all this chatter."[47]

Discussing the background experiments for the November flight, Faujas later observed that the promoters had learned the importance of conducting tests as privately as possible.[48] In this instance, they succeeded in keeping the word from everyone except Etienne's family including, as bad luck would have it, his father. Amid all the pressures, Etienne overlooked accompanying the news for Adélaïde with an innocuous letter that Pierre might read. The publicity attending the Versailles flight had only heightened the old man's uneasiness, and some piece of persiflage in the *Courrier d'Avignon* convinced him that Etienne was dead. His gathering anxiety made life miserable for everyone at Vidalon. If they did not get a letter the next day, wrote the abbé desperately on the 22nd, "*Ma foi*, I'm leaving home."

They dared not reassure their father by reading him the letter to Adélaïde because it told of his traveling in the balloon. "But that word is terrible."[49] Still no letter came, until the brothers and sister in Vidalon had no choice but to show their father this last. At least it would convince him that Etienne was alive. Its further effect was an assertion of paternal authority. Pierre summoned his eldest, Jean-Pierre, Montgolfier l'aîné, and dictated a command to his youngest son: "He requires you to give him no further cause for distress and . . . not to get in the machine. You've already got out of it what you wanted to know." Those lines are countersigned in an old man's spidery hand, "Ton père, Montgolfier."[50]

That call to order did bring Pierre a letter from Etienne. He is mortified to have caused anguish by his silence. He has been terribly busy. The time got away from him. He had thought that his uncle's letter would have been reassuring. He has never taken the slightest risk. When he went aloft, the balloon was fully retained with ropes on all sides, and he was exposed to no possible danger. He did not wish to trust anyone else to verify the handling of the ropes. More recent experiments show that there was nothing to fear. He means to write them up for the Academy of Science and then desist and spend his time on their business interests. He is going to Orléans tomorrow to see about the warehouse and to settle accounts.[51]

The further experiments that Etienne mentioned to his father were those of 15, 17, and 19 October. He had in the meantime modified the balloon, apparently on the basis of the captive flight he had been obliged to confess. In its completed form, the height was seventy feet, the lateral diameter forty-six feet, and the capacity 60,000 cubic feet. Its volume was over 50 percent greater than that of the Versailles globe. The decoration again showed Réveillon's hand. Signs of the zodiac in gold were interspersed with fleur-de-lis around the dome; a belt of ceremonial royal initials alternating with flaring suns girdled the waist; a flight of eagles ringed the base amid festoons and garlands, their open wings bearing the great sphere aloft, azure against the background of the sky. The circular understructure consisted of a wicker gallery with a curtain of cloth painted to resemble formal drapery. The orifice it surrounded measured fifteen feet in diameter. The weight of the whole contrivance, including passengers, was calculated to be 1,600 pounds. The most delicate aspect of the design consisted in the suspension beneath the aperture of a burner that could be tended by means of a pitchfork from the gallery without setting fire to the fabric—a possible eventuality, observed Faujas, that would have "forever discouraged the continuation of such fearful experiments."[52]

Etienne and his associates were less successful in keeping privy this further and critical round of experiments in manned flight. They took the precaution of warning the public by a notice in the *Journal de Paris* for 11 October that the tests soon to be conducted concerned only scientists, and that the more significant they might prove for the physics of flight, the less entertaining they would be to persons who were merely curious.[53] Despite this announcement, or more likely because of it, people flocked to the faubourg Saint-Antoine once the word was out, and as always many of them were too eminent for their eagerness to be denied. Once again, therefore, Etienne and the others in charge were exposed to the gasps, groans, and finally applause of a throng of spectators, whose enthusiasm ever threatened to sour into scorn during intervals of tedium.

Since dates were not announced, the experiments on 15 October were still relatively unencumbered by an audience. Then it was that Pilatre was granted his wish to be the pilot. He hopped aboard, counterbalanced by a one-hundred-pound weight at the opposite point in the gallery. The purpose of his first ascension was to perfect techniques of landing. Etienne limited the altitude to eighty feet, and there Pilatre floated comfortably for four minutes and twenty-five seconds before settling to a soft touchdown. Evidently, Pilatre did not share the desire for privacy of the responsible parties. Printed copies survive of a "faire-part" like a wedding announcement which he distributed to acquaintances informing all and sundry of the time and place of the next flight on which he would be embarking at the invitation of Monsieur Montgolfier.[54]

Whether on that account, or through word of mouth, an immense crowd assembled for the next experiment two days later, on Friday the 17th (Fig. 16). "It would be difficult," wrote Faujas, "to bring together a more brilliant gathering." Unfortunately, a wind sprang up, and Pilatre could rise no higher than on the Wednesday. The effect, moreover, was less impressive since the balloon was obviously in trouble, laboring at an angle of 45° with the ropes chafing. Then it was, added Faujas ruefully, that we could have wished we had resisted the importunities of the public.[55]

By the 19th the weather had settled and remained clear and relatively still for the entire day, a Sunday. More than 2,000 people crowded into the Réveillon premises in time for a series of flights beginning at 4:30 in the afternoon. Pilatre again flew alone with the heater unlighted in the first attempt. The second time he had a live fire so that he might control his altitude. With the ground crew carefully paying out the cords, he floated up some 250 feet above the craning heads and remained stably aloft for over eight minutes, occasionally replenishing his blaze. Thereupon, a slight east wind deflected the machine over the neighboring garden, where it threatened to sink into the branches of a great tree. Cool and ready, the intrepid Pilatre fed straw and wool into his burner and rose smoothly above the danger, thus— in Faujas's account—refuting skeptics who held that balloon travel must forever be inhibited by the likelihood of landing in the woods.

In his remaining two flights on that great day, Pilatre had company. One Giroud de Villette, an employee of the Réveillon firm, replaced Pilatre's counterpoise in a nine-minute ascension that extended the retaining cords to their limit of 324 feet. The effect was splendid, visible from all over Paris. Afterward Giroud wrote an open letter to the press, extolling the dexterity with which Pilatre, "this intelligent physicist whom I had the honor to accompany," manipulated the burner. Giroud could observe the operations from the point opposite through a four-inch peephole. It occurred to him that a simple and inexpensive machine like this could prove invaluable in military operations, allowing a commander to be informed through signals of the positions and movements of an enemy. Giroud regretted only that he had neglected to take his field glasses.[56] In some way he soon afterwards gave offense, however, to Réveillon as well as to Etienne. The latter wrote Joseph before the Lyons flight in January 1784 warning against his machinations.[57] With that Giroud disappeared from the annals of aviation.

Daylight and fuel remained for a fourth, equally felicitous demonstration. This time the passenger was the marquis d'Arlandes, a major of infantry who also accompanied Pilatre in the November flight for which these tests were the preparation. All the prospects were encouraging. "It's a much shorter distance," predicted Faujas, "from the aerostatic machine of today, which is even now carrying men, to a machine that will hold a large number than it was from some savage's primitive canoe to a 100-gun ship of the line making light of the action of the waves and sailing the seas with impunity from pole to pole."[58] Etienne had yet to endure the reproaches from Annonay about having flown himself, and his immediate reaction was equally enthusiastic. A brief and airy account for Joseph in Lyons sustains the cheery conceit that opened his narrative of the Versailles extravaganza addressed to Adélaïde:

Aboard the Aërostat Réveillon
at 300 feet above the earth,
8 8ᵇʳᵉ 1783

Dear brother,

I continued my experiments on Friday and on Sunday [17 and 19 October]. I was impeded on the former day by the wind, which caused several little accidents that slightly tarnished the brilliance of the experiment, which did however fully establish the possibility of lifting men. I wanted to increase the force of imbalance a little [me procurer un peu plus de rupture d'équilibre] and I lightened the gallery by 200 pounds. Then I had two people get in the machine, which was held by four ropes 300 feet long. The machine rose their full length, and held steady for a quarter of an hour. The people in the gallery let it descend and raised it again several times in succession, and even succeeded twice in adroitly manipulating it so that it nearly grazed the ground and then rose again without touching down at a moment when the wind had carried them out of plumb with the garden. They came down in a neighboring garden above a tree which brushed against the machine, but that accident only served to show that exposure to such risk was not very dangerous and that the machine could be lifted without returning to earth. Thus, we have perfected the machine as far as we could have hoped with the means at our disposal.[59]

Evidently this exultant report to Joseph crossed in the mail with the strictures addressed to Etienne from Vidalon about his having flown himself. However dashed he may have been, that contretemps was not the origin of his divided feelings about the entire enterprise. Etienne's ambivalence, as we have seen, went back at least to the time of his arrival in Paris. Following the fine results of 19 October, both Pilatre and d'Arlandes urged speed in readying the craft for its free flight. Along with everyone else, they knew that an improved hydrogen balloon was being developed for the same purpose by the Robert brothers, and naturally they wanted to be the first to fly unleashed. Pilot and copilot had to contain their impatience for over a month, however, while Etienne dealt with problems of design, of family, and perhaps of self.

Far from resolving his difficulties, the success at Versailles and the subsequent notoriety had compounded them. "People talk only the machine to me"; he wrote irritably, "I get to talk only of the machine; I do nothing but the machine. . . . If I go to a commercial office, I'm forced to talk about the machines we've made and the machines we mean to make."[60] This in late September or early October, when (Etienne went

on) he saw no chance of tending to business for at least another two weeks. The immediate reaction of his brothers to his triumph before royalty and court had, naturally enough, been enthusiasm tempered by relief. "What a happy day for all of us . . . ," began Joseph, who, in response to word of the fiasco of the first Réveillon tests on 12 September, had reproached Etienne mildly for sacrificing solidity to gracefulness in the design. Only now he could not understand why the balloon had risen a mere 1,500 feet. The *Journal de Paris* must have made a mistake.[61] As for the abbé, he had been all for rushing to Etienne's side on receiving the news of the 12 September tests. Their friends in Annonay could not understand how he could bear to stay home. "My dear abbé," exclaimed the marquis de Girodon on encountering him in the street, "Who would ever imagine finding you here! What! You're not in Paris? But that's absolutely absurd!" After Versailles, he wrote again proposing that Joseph should come to take on part of the technical load inside the Réveillon walls, where his awkwardness in company would pass unnoticed, while he, the abbé, could help with public relations.[62]

"Bravo," wrote Jean-Pierre apropos of Versailles, "No one could do better. We all say Bravo!" Now, as to practical advantages that may accrue, he approved the idea of securing a particle of nobility. Etienne could make clear that he could accept no distinction that did not apply equally to Joseph, and could point out that they had an aged father who had been a businessman "with the most brilliant distinction" for seventy years, on whom it would be fitting to bestow honors redounding to the credit of the family. On the other hand, Jean-Pierre disapproved the notion of seeking the designation of *Manufacture royale* for Vidalon. Such privilege was an empty thing and would only intensify jealousy among their fellow papermakers who were already denigrating Etienne's trip to Paris as a maneuver really intended to discomfit the Johannots. The only distinction needed for the business was the reputation Etienne had already won for it with his introduction of hollanders and discovery of the

Vue du Jardin de la Manufacture Royale de Papiers peints de M. R. veillon.

16. Testing in the Réveillon courtyard, October 1783. Pilatre is at the left

best method for sizing vellum. No, no—the important thing was to get some money, "a good sum."[63]

This letter, along with many others on the crying need for orders, makes it clear that at times the flow of cash at Vidalon dwindled to a trickle, as it had done now. Let Etienne (urged his brother) strive to obtain a reward big enough to pay off Joseph's debts and to meet a partial lien on the factory held by their nephew Marc-François Seguin. The latter had married Augustine, the oldest daughter of Raymond, the deceased heir apparent, and (as will be explained later) had a claim either to a one-third interest in the factory or to a cash settlement. He was to make his choice by 30 November 1783. Happily, he opted for the money, but this anxiety too hung over Etienne as he struggled with perfecting the passenger balloon in Paris.[64]

The matter of Joseph's chronic insolvency was more straightforward. Since the invention of the balloon, he had been neglecting his business more and more. "I really can't blame him," wrote Jean-Pierre, "other than that physics is much more to his taste. The success of all his experiments raises his imagination to a height from which he cannot easily lower himself to attend to the base question of providing payment." It would be fine to get him out of hock ("sortir Joseph de son maudit tripot de lettres de change"). But a more comprehensive solution might be conceivable. Etienne's comrade from school days, Jean-Nicolas Pache, had become chief secretary of the naval ministry and then comptroller of the royal household. He enjoyed the confidence of his patron, the maréchal de Castries. Might not Etienne bespeak Pache's good offices to become supplier of paper to the government? They could then merge the Vidalon and Voiron plants into a single enterprise. "Don Joseph" could ostensibly head the latter, since his wife was perfectly capable of running it, while in reality devoting himself to physics. Etienne would remain in Paris as director (régisseur) of the whole business with immediate oversight of the outlet in the capital. Jean-Pierre could promise his own backing from Vidalon and that of his sons, who would soon be ready to

assume responsibility (Etienne's children were all girls and younger). The abbé looked twenty years younger at the thought of his brothers' forming "a single heart, soul, and household." He would cheerfully take on all and any tasks. And speaking of the abbé, could not Etienne now get the king to grant him an abbey? He would make worthwhile use of the income; he did, after all, have his doctorate from the university; and his impartiality in discharging judicial duties was much appreciated in the region.[65]

The abbé himself, light though his epistolary style, was the one brother most given to harping on the worldly wisdom of getting something tangible. He and Etienne knew only too well how apathetic Joseph was in these matters.[66] "Modesty is a becoming virtue. A middling status [la médiocrité] has its charm. But modesty pushed too far becomes pusillanimity and laziness, and the middle range can easily degenerate into poverty, and that is frightful."[67] A few days later the abbé was at Etienne again, and now it was not only Joseph—the "petit comité" at Vidalon has begun to worry about Etienne's apparent lethargy.[68] So far he had nothing to show for his success except the reimbursement of their expenses by the crown. That was one thing about which Etienne could write their father.[69] Whether irritated by these further exhortations, or merely to stave them off, Etienne let the family understand that he had decided to sit on his hands until he got definite assurances. He would be home before the end of October if, as he was coming to think, continuing the work in Paris would do nothing to advance their fortunes.[70]

These many disenchantments afflicted Etienne throughout the time in which he was preparing and executing the manned-flight tests of mid-October and for several weeks thereafter. Is that the reason that over a month elapsed before the la Muette flight? His correspondence in that interval concerns business rather than balloons. Considering how expeditiously he had moved when he wanted to, in September and early in October, it seems probable that he really was deliberately holding back, even as he said. If so, he was running a risk. Meusnier was collaborating with Charles and the Robert brothers, and appears to have taken relatively little interest in the hot-air craft. Contriving, filling, and launching miniature hydrogen balloons of goldbeater's skin became a fad from early in September. Anyone with a cabinet of apparatus for natural philosophy could make these scientific toys. Among those who did was the duc de la Rochefoucauld, the sort of patron who liked to do the science that was within his grasp.[71] Etienne was clearly no longer indispensable to the development of the Montgolfier invention. Whether reflections of that sort, or promises of acceptable reward, or both caused him to relent, we do not know. At all events, he overcame his hesitations in time to beat out the competition, but only just. On 15 November he appeared before the Academy of Science, at the invitation of its commission on balloons, to read a memoir drafted by Joseph (who delivered it himself ten days later at a meeting of the Academy of Lyons) on the principles that had guided the brothers in arriving at their invention.[72] On 21 November, just under a week after Etienne's presentation, Pilatre and d'Arlandes took off in his balloon from the garden of the château de la Muette. On 1 December Charles and the younger Robert staged the second airborne journey, departing from the courtyard of the Tuileries palace.

The château de la Muette, in the western outskirts of the capital, was the seat of the court of the two-year old dauphin, a puny child who died in 1789. There he and his five-year old sister, the "enfants de France," were confided to the care of the duchesse de Polignac. Their governess was one of the favorites who brought the queen, their mother, into discredit through extravagance and indiscretion. A distinguished neighbor was Benjamin Franklin in his house on the bluff of Passy overlooking the Seine. That Madame de Polignac should have offered the gardens of the princely nursery for the departure of the first passenger flight is evidence enough that stock in the Montgolfiers was still high at court. Unlike the Réveillon yard, the grounds were spacious enough to allow an ascending balloon to clear surrounding structures handily. In what remained of his

innocence, Etienne hoped that the date and place of the launching might be kept confidential until the deed was done, and no announcements were made.[73]

Even if all concerned had respected his wishes, however, and of course they did not, the construction of a platform in the royal park could hardly have been kept secret. We do not know what if any modifications he made in the aircraft between the complete success of the 19 October experiment and Thursday 20 November, when he was ready for this next attempt. Only the day before, the 19th, the Robert brothers put a notice in the *Journal de Paris*, advertising arrangements for the flight they projected, originally for 29 November, and opening a subscription at six livres for two tickets.[74] That can only have spiced the rumors about the *montgolfière* (which was underwritten by the government). Inevitably, a considerable crowd had already gathered at la Muette as Etienne and his crew set about their tasks. Once again the weather—which had been entirely favorable on only one day, 19 October, among the six occasions when he had flown balloons in public—betrayed his hopes. Wind and rain suddenly bore down upon the scene, and he had to adjourn the demonstration. He hoped it would be until the morrow, but who could know whether conditions would then permit giving the public the sensation it craved? In the mass psychology of these gatherings a feature may be recognized that characterizes thrill-seekers in any arena, whether Roman circus, Spanish bullring, or modern prizefight. Only perfection reconciles spectators to the survival of the performer.

The prospects looked fairly promising on the morning of Friday 21 November, and a larger crowd than on the Thursday had assembled by eleven o'clock. Great white cumulus clouds advanced from the horizon, preceded by fitful gusts. Under pressure of all the expectations, Etienne pushed his preparations and in an interval of calm succeeded in inflating the balloon, whereupon d'Arlandes and Pilatre climbed into harness in the great breadbaskets which were their stations aboard. Before sending them off to float away, Etienne planned one more tethered test of lifting force. So soon as the would-be voyagers had ascended a little way, his enemy the wind struck another blow, tilting the balloon at such an angle that the retaining cords chafed against the fabric. In a moment, the whole magnificent contrivance was borne ignominiously to ground, where it would have caught fire except for the rapidity of volunteers who sprang into action and saved the day. Elements in the crowd at once turned mocking and menacing. People of another sort, however—in Faujas's words "all those distinguished by rank or knowledge in that assembly"—reacted in a spirit of sympathy and encouragement. Certain persons came forward to help, among them several great ladies who contributed their art as needlewomen.[75]

Repairs were completed in an hour and a half. By then the breeze had died sufficiently so that a worrisome alley of poplars downwind presented no danger. In eight minutes the balloon was reinflated. It is interesting for the conceptual development that Faujas now spoke of "the gas, or rather the rarefied air that it contained." At 1:54 p.m. d'Arlandes and Pilatre were off, over the eyes of the multitude and of the official team of observers who on completion of the voyage signed the *procès-verbal*.[76] Among the latter group was Franklin. This was the occasion of the often-told story of his being asked what use the thing was, and replying "What use is a newborn baby?" The terrace of his house in Passy also offered a vantage point from which artists sketched, or in some cases imagined, their impressions of the balloon along its flight path (Plate VI). Neither the official summary, nor in this instance Etienne's own account, fully succeeds in recreating the event, however. Instead, we shall follow the log written out for publication immediately afterward by François Laurent, marquis d'Arlandes.[77]

There may be some injustice in his being the less remembered of the two airmen, for if he is to be believed—and the account is consistent with the record of Etienne's procrastination in the preceding weeks—d'Arlandes had been charged by "persons of the greatest eminence" to approach Etienne and bring home to him how a final experiment launching a man in free flight would

put the seal on the glory of his invention. Etienne took the point, "like a man with good sense who knows what he's doing." D'Arlandes then reminded him of a promise Etienne had made that he, d'Arlandes, should be the one to make the experiment. Etienne agreed, and d'Arlandes went off at once to la Muette, where he fixed on a location for the launching, hired laborers, and set them to work. Only on the day before the flight did Etienne, on prudent second thought, suggest that d'Arlandes take a companion, and proposed Pilatre. D'Arlandes accepted readily, having been well impressed with Pilatre during the Réveillon experiments. All this he afterward felt bound to impart in order to explain why, given a "professor of physics" as companion, he hadn't left it to the latter to describe the voyage. "For I was the one chosen by M. Montgolfier to run this experiment. It's permissible to be proud of being selected, and unnatural to imagine that I could yield to anyone else the right to publish its success." Now then, except that Etienne may all along have ambivalently let them both expect to fly, this claim is plausible, the more so in that d'Arlandes, of a noble family in Dauphiny, was a familiar of the court as Pilatre could never conceivably have been. Also, he does not come across as vain. On the contrary, he wrote cordially and enthusiastically of Pilatre's manipulations when they were aloft, and rather self-critically of his own (Fig. 17).

At all events, the two of them were the first ever to experience the curious stillness of ascent in a free balloon. Their sensation was of an undefined release and separation, not at all to be defined by the adjective "majestic" pompously and tritely applied to their departure by observers left below. The wind out of the northwest was light. As they rose above the treetops, it spun their craft through an angle of 180° so that Pilatre was fore and d'Arlandes aft. They retained those relative positions throughout the flight, able to see each other through matching peepholes at either end of the lateral diameter (Plate VII). Looking back and down in the early moments, d'Arlandes was struck by the apparent silence and immobility of the spectators. Astonished and perhaps frightened by the spectacle (he thought),

17.

M.^r LE MAR.^s D'ARLANDE,

they were the ones who needed reassuring. He waved and, when that produced no effect, flourished his handkerchief. That gesture did produce a kind of surge arrested by the garden wall. It was as if no other obstacle divided crowd from travelers. Thereupon—or so it is fair to assume in the perspective of latter-day ballooning—the city wore the static and literal appearance of a canvas by some naïf painter or of the model landscapes surrounding a peasant crèche or a child's toy train at Christmastime.

However that may have been, Pilatre in a few moments aroused d'Arlandes from contemplation by calling out sharply, "You're not doing a thing, and we're not climbing at all." "Sorry," apologized d'Arlandes, and forked a bundle of straw onto the burner, poking the fire a bit with the tines. Turning and gazing back along the Seine, he could make out the conjunction with the Oise and identify the towns of Poissy, Saint-Germain,

Saint-Denis, and Sèvres. Next he glanced straight down through the central aperture and saw that they were right over Chaillot, whereupon Pilatre recalled him to the unreality of their situation. "There's the river, and we're dropping. Come on, my good friend, *the fire!*" The wind now shifted slightly, and instead of taking them over the Invalides, bore them the length of the Ile des Cygnes along the course of the Seine (Fig. 18). "It's damned hard to make it across that river," observed d'Arlandes. "You said it," called back Pilatre, "You're not doing a thing." "I'm not as strong as you are," said d'Arlandes, "and anyway we're doing all right."

But he turned to and poked the fire again, pitching in another bundle of straw. Too closely packed, it did not catch at first, and d'Arlandes had to lift with his fork and shake the stalks loose. They flared into flame, and suddenly he felt himself hauled up as if by the armpits. "Now we're really climbing," he called out, and immediately afterward heard a popping noise high in the dome. He could see nothing amiss, but suddenly felt the whole machine give a sharp shudder. "What are you doing?" he cried to Pilatre, "Are you dancing, or what?" "I didn't budge," called back the latter, and d'Arlandes bethought him that perhaps the shock was a change of wind that might at last carry them beyond the river. He looked down, and sure enough they were coasting along between the Ecole militaire and the Invalides. Again they set to work stoking the heater when d'Arlandes heard a second sharp report way up in the rigging. Thinking it might be a broken cord, he scrutinized the inside of the bag, and saw that a sector to his right was perforated with round holes, several of them fairly large with smoldering edges eating back into the fabric. "We've got to put down," he yelled. "Why?" asked Pilatre. "Look," said d'Arlandes, managing at the same time to extinguish the sparks he could reach with a sponge fixed on his fork. He then felt the tissue underneath the damaged portion to see whether the seam was holding along the bottom rim. It was not. The threads had loosened. "We've got to put down," he cried again. "We're right over Paris," objected Pilatre. "No matter," in-

18. The first aerial voyage, a view from Franklin's terrace

sisted the marquis, "But look—isn't there any danger on your side? Is it holding together?" "Yes," Pilatre reassured him, and when d'Arlandes examined the damage near him more closely, he recognized that it was arrested, and they could, after all, cross the city and make for the country.

This moment of near-panic now past, he looked down again to find that they were sailing over the seminary for overseas missions—"Missions étrangères"—near the site of the present-day Bon Marché department store. On peering forward through the apertures, d'Arlandes had the round towers of Saint-Sulpice directly in his line of vision. Moments later they were over the Luxembourg and crossing the ramparts at Port-Royal into broken country. "Feet on the ground," he cried to his partner, and let the fire dwindle. The "intrepid" Pilatre, however, who—d'Arlandes acknowledged—"never lost his head" judged that they were headed straight for the windmills on the Butte-aux-Cailles between there and Gentilly, their great sails turning broadside to the wind (Fig. 19). D'Arlandes tossed in a final bale of straw. Up they lifted, with a slight swerve to the left. "Beware the mills," shouted Pilatre, but sighting through the peepholes from the rear, d'Arlandes could see that their craft was headed right between them. "Ready for landing—*Arrivons*," he called. The aircraft just cleared a pond alimenting mill wheels that powered the machinery of one of Réveillon's competitors, Brenier and

19. The "Croulebarbe" windmills on the Butte-aux-Cailles

Company, and bumped to a halt with the ominous windmills distant a hundred yards on either side. The point of landing on the Butte-aux-Cailles is nowadays in the heart of the 13th arrondissement and was then just off the highroad to Fontainebleau. The two passengers had been in the air for twenty to twenty-five minutes, and had burned only a fraction of their fuel. Etienne later observed privately that the machine would have been capable of flying four or five times as far if only the pilots had kept their nerve.[78]

Immediately before touchdown d'Arlandes took hold of the railing and lifted his weight onto his arms. The wind carried the fabric forward so that it merely brushed against his head as he leaped to earth. Spinning around, he was astonished that, instead of towering over him, the great globe had collapsed forward into a huge swatch of fabric strewn along the ground. Pilatre was nowhere to be seen. As d'Arlandes rushed around to disentangle him, Pilatre crawled from under the mass in his shirt sleeves, having stripped off his redingote just before landing in order to be unhampered. Their first care had to be preventing the whole thing from catching fire. The gallery was too heavy for them to move, however, and there was nothing for it but to tear away the fabric, under which the fire was still smoldering. Once the heater was exposed to the air, the remaining straw blazed up. The two managed to fork the glowing embers into one of the baskets in which they had ridden and shove it aside.

Just as that danger was averted, peasants and workingpeople rushed up, grabbed Pilatre's redingote, and began fighting over it. Happily the police now arrived upon the scene, none too soon, and, with their authority, the machine was secured and saved. Its remains were loaded on a wagon and transported within the hour back to the Réveillon factory. D'Arlandes feared lest Pilatre take a chill, since their excitement and exertion had left them overheated, and urged him to take shelter in the nearest house. As the sergeant of the guard made a way for him through the mob, Pilatre encountered the duc de Chartres, son of the duc d'Orléans and the future Philippe Egalité, who with other notables had galloped across Paris in their wake. Finally carriages arrived, but the garments that someone had lent Pilatre were so seedy that he was ashamed to return to la Muette. So d'Arlandes went off to receive congratulations alone, "although with the greatest regret over parting from my brave companion."

In comparing their relative importance in the history of aviation, it is to be noted that d'Arlandes, whatever his claims to have been the first choice for pilot, had apparently now had enough. At least, he does not reappear. Pilatre, by contrast, was soon off to Lyons, there to board the monstrous craft that Joseph was even then designing for the next generation of *montgolfières*.

5. THE MOMENT OF HILARITY

The approach of the Robert brothers to realizing a return on their investment by the sale of tickets was more straightforward than Etienne's instinct for shrinking from publicity and badgering the Treasury for favors. The subscription was in their name; Charles had evidently come to prefer the role of scientist. The prospectus announced their intention to fabricate a globe of taffeta twenty-six feet in diameter to be impregnated with india rubber and filled with inflammable air "in accordance with the theories of M. Charles."[79] The Roberts estimated their costs at 10,000 livres, and stipulated that subscribers would acquire no claim to a share of property in the machine. Initially, the plan called for a set of preliminary experiments to be performed, if weather permitted, in a balloon held captive at an altitude high enough to permit interesting observations of phenomena of electricity, atmospheric density, heat, and gravity. The prospective physicist was unnamed, but would, of course, have been Charles, who wished to make his mark scientifically and to establish the utility of flight for serious research. Having accomplished as much, he would descend, making way for the two Roberts. The brothers would then embark in free flight ("en ballon perdu").

In order to advertise the demonstration further, the balloon and its accessory equipment went on display several days ahead of time in one of the public rooms of the Tuileries palace. On 26 November it was moved out and suspended at the entrance to the central promenade running the length of the garden. Soldiers of the Swiss Guard provided security, and even lent a hand with the operation of filling. The Roberts had put to good use the three months since they had painfully inflated the first *charlière* in the courtyard of the laboratory in the Place des Victoires, and had devised a more sophisticated generator in the interval (Fig. 20). The arrangement of

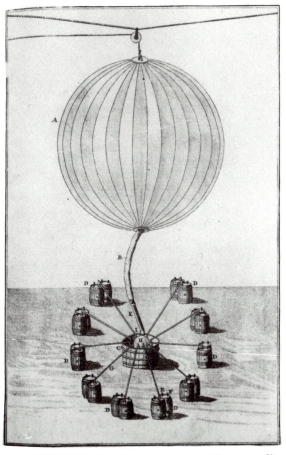

20. The improved hydrogen generator. Faujas credits this device to the first Blanchard flight (below chapter IV, section 1), but the Meusnier account, and iconographic sources, make it appear that Blanchard's suppliers adapted the arrangement from Charles and Robert

barrels in a ring, each communicating with a central conduit, became standard in the mass production of hydrogen for lighter-than-air craft.[80] When the iron filings (or scraps of zinc or of other metal) in one were used up, the flow of acid would be diverted to the next. There would thus be time for cooling and recharging before the circuit was completed. Pipes of tinned iron (soon replaced by lead) carried the vapor from each reactor into a trough fitted with a hood so that bubbling through water would wash it. Meusnier credited this precaution with the greatly increased levity of the hydrogen employed in this second Charles-Robert balloon.[81] A less concentrated sulfuric acid also obviated the alarming spasms and excessive heat of the earlier battle with the gas from a single, overworked barrel.[82]

The Roberts were unable to predict how long it might take to extract the 9,200 cubic feet of hydrogen they would need. The original *charlière*, twelve feet in diameter, had contained only one-tenth that quantity. With no other experience behind them, the entrepreneurs badly underestimated the time required to fill the larger model. Much grumbling by subscribers had to be weathered when the demonstration originally scheduled for Saturday the 29th had to be put off until Monday, 1 December.[83] Over that weekend a balloon crew once again found itself working night and day to meet the expectations of the public, for even the fine new apparatus at first proved balky. Hearing of the trouble, a skilled chemist who (says Faujas) remained incognito out of modesty, but who may most probably have been Lavoisier, came by to consult on the right proportions of iron, acid, and water. Thereafter everything went smoothly. The globe swelled handsomely. There was no doubt it would now be ready. Chemistry had rescued physics.

Monday 1 December began with fog. By noon the last wisps had dissipated leaving the weather calm with a barely detectable east wind and a temperature the equivalent of 40° Fahrenheit. What with all the publicity, the gathering crowd soon dwarfed all the others. Half the population of Paris was on hand, according to Faujas. Other chroniclers agree. A central enclosure around the basin of the Tuileries garden was reserved for members of the academic bodies and for the wealthy and fashionable, who had paid the premium price of four louis (ninety-six livres) a place. The rest of the great park overflowed with subscribers at the regular three livres an entry. Gatecrashers looked for chances to scramble over the fence or to swarm up the rampart along the bank of the Seine (Plate VIII). The quay opposite, balconies and rooftops of all the houses within sight, the bridges and the Place Louis XV (now Place de la Concorde)—all were jammed. Security guards lined paths within the Tuileries garden and surrounded the emplacement for the balloon at the center of the high-priced enclosure.

Artillery pieces on the terrace of the palace heralded the transfer of the balloon from its filling station to this launching site. In one respect the flight plan had been changed. The notion of sending Charles aloft initially to make experiments in tethered tranquillity had quietly been dropped, no doubt in anticipation of what would certainly have been the impatience of the multitude confronted with so static a spectacle. Instead, Charles replaced the older Robert in the gondola to make the flight itself. A curtain raiser of an experiment preceded the main event. Announced by the renewed firing of cannon, a green trial balloon, five-and-a-half feet in diameter, was sent aloft to mark the direction of the winds and blaze the trail. It rose almost vertically to a great height and was visible for about a quarter of an hour, a diminishing dot of color disappearing into the northwest. We know that this time Etienne Montgolfier was on hand, for the promoters had invited him to honor the day by himself releasing the tiny globe. In this detail, as in all respects, they had spared no effort to learn from their oversights as well as their experience on the Champ de Mars in August.[84]

Technically, the lessons that Charles had the Roberts incorporate in the new balloon derived from the bursting of its predecessor in consequence of uncontrolled ascension into a thinning atmosphere. They now reinforced the bag itself by encasing the upper hemisphere in a strong netting, from which the gondola was suspended

by an arrangement of a dozen or more ropes. Equally important, the pilot might relieve the internal pressure by means of a system of two orifices. A cord leading through the interior controlled a one-way valve at the top through which Charles could spill hydrogen without admitting air. A second opening near the bottom led into a kind of sleeve, or "appendix," the cuff of which he could hold in his hand and manipulate with greater sensitivity to the internal pressure. Provided he had adequate ballast aboard, he could thus trade off release of gas against lightening of load in an effort to maintain constant pressure in the bag at uniform altitude for a flight of considerable duration. The decoration of the new balloon, though not a patch on the splendor of the Réveillon-inspired *montgolfières*, consisted of vertical bands of yellow and ocher and made a brighter show than had the first *charlière*. Only the rococo dreamboat of a gondola fully expressed the taste of the reign, however. Its stern was prettied with fleur-de-lis surmounted by a crown, and its sides adorned with golden pinions, rather stubby ones actually. Friends had taken care to provide the conveyance with bottles of champagne and furs and blankets against the chill of distant climates, as if it were a chariot headed on a long journey. Charles had equipped himself more practically, with a barometer and thermometer, both of mercury, a telescope, maps, and pencil and paper.

From far back in the crowd nothing seemed to be happening after the departure of the trial balloon. Rumors of malfunction ran to and fro, and the mood turned restive. Finally at 1:30 Charles and the younger Robert took their places facing each other at either end of their gondola. Sensing that the moment needed lightening, Charles opened a bottle and the two lifted glasses to the multitude, or to as many of them as could see the gesture. Attendants had already eased loose the cords. At a signal from Charles, the ground crew let go. Like a champagne cork in the sky, off went the bark to the popping of artillery, one passenger waving a white pennant and the other a red one (Figs. 21, 22, 23). A kind of universal amazement and silence fell upon

A L'HONNEUR DE M^{RS} CHARLES ET ROBERT

21. The Charles-Robert ascent, looking toward the château des Tuileries

La plaiſanterie confondüe ou les Intrépides Voyageurs.

22. The Charles-Robert ascent, looking toward the garden of the Tuileries

the crowd. Nothing, wrote Charles a few days later, would ever equal that "moment of hilarity" he felt on leaving the earth. The sensation was more pervasive than pleasure. It was happiness. At no point did he or Robert feel the slightest anxiety.

Their ascent, like that of the pilot balloon, was nearly vertical (Plate IX) to an altitude of something over 1,800 feet, as measured by the simultaneous fall of the barometer from 28⁴/₁₂ to 26²/₁₂ inches. That was the height at which Charles intended to level off. They were then over the village of Monceau, where a wind current began carrying them northwest, across repeated bends in the Seine toward the valley of the Oise. The rays of a bright sun beat upon the surface of the balloon causing the hydrogen to dilate. Opening his fist, Charles let the excess gas escape through the appendix. Throughout the flight the temperature was in the range of 10° to 12° Réaumur (in the 50s Fahrenheit). When they began descending, he would toss out small amounts of ballast to maintain altitude. Fifty-six minutes after departure, they heard cannonfire, the signal from the Tuileries that now they were lost to view. In another hour enough hydrogen had been released so that the bounce on dropping ballast grew sluggish. They were then approaching the plain of

23. The Charles-Robert flight: successive positions as viewed from the left bank of the Seine, just below Pont Royal

LE MOMENT D'HILARITÉ UNIVERSELLE

ou le Triomphe de MM.⁵ Charles et Robert   au Jardin des Thuileries le 1.ᵉʳ Xᵇʳᵉ 1783.

Présenté à mon Pere   pour son 89.ᵐᵉ Anniversaire.

Se vend chez M. le Noir au Louvre   Voyés le Journal de Paris du 2 Xᵇʳᵉ

Nesle, and it seemed wise to put down on an inviting stretch of fields. Lower and lower they sloped, as if on a long inclined plane. Ahead loomed a row of trees that the gondola might fail to clear. Charles tossed out another two pounds of ballast. The craft bounded over the obstacle, like a hunter's mount clearing a hedge, he wrote, and coasted along for another hundred feet or more at one or two feet above the ground, the peasants running after it like children pursuing a butterfly. Charles and Robert came to rest near a hunting lodge owned by an Englishman called Farrer, who hastened to the site (Plate X). Soon two more exalted witnesses arrived. The duc de Chartres, having tracked Pilatre and d'Arlandes across Paris, had provided himself with splendid horses and a companion, the duc de Fitz-James (grandson of the Old Pretender). Together they had galloped after the aircraft, the distance from Paris being about forty kilometers (Fig. 24).

Charles had not forgotten his scientific purposes, and now decided to take advantage of the relative isolation to perform the observations originally planned for a preliminary captive ascent. By leaving Robert behind, he could lighten the load by 130 pounds, and reduce the remaining weight (including his own) to 438 pounds. Robert dismounted accordingly, to be engulfed by the knot of thirty or forty peasants. Charles had only three or four pounds of ballast left, and asked those nearest to dig him some earth. Someone went off to find a spade, which never materialized. Stones would do, he said. There were none in the field. The day was waning, and he dared not wait. "My friends," he said to the peasants holding on to the rim of the gondola, "Let go all at once . . . when I give the signal, and I'll fly off." ("Mes amis. Retirez-vous en même temps . . . au premier signal que je vais faire, & je vais m'envoler.") They did as he asked, and off he darted "like a bird" rising to an altitude of 9,000 feet (1,500 *toises*) in ten minutes. In order not to upset the balance, he made his observations and recorded his data on his knees in the center of the gondola. The barometer had fallen over nine inches to a level of $18^{10}/_{12}$, and the thermometer from 7° above freezing to 5° below (approximately from 50° to 20° F). The balloon,

which had been slack at takeoff, swelled visibly, and he was obliged to vent hydrogen both from the appendix and the upper valve. Its escape was attended by condensation. From that effect, he concluded that equilibrium of pressure in a gas is restored much faster than equilibrium of heat. He was above the clouds, which appeared to be rising from the earth in a form like that of their normal appearance, but grey and monotonous in color. To his great surprise air currents at that altitude were far more variable than much lower down. But for us, and perhaps for him, Charles's perception of the quality of his experience, alone two miles above the surface of the earth, is more interesting than these first meteorological observations of the upper atmosphere:

> The cold was sharp and dry, but not at all unbearable. I could then examine all my sensations in complete tranquillity. I listened to myself living, so to say, and I may report that in the first moments I experienced no discomfort in this sudden change of pressure and of temperature. . . . I stood up in the middle of the gondola, and lost myself in the spectacle offered by the immensity of the horizon. When I took off from the fields, the sun had set for the inhabitants of the valleys. Soon it rose for me alone, and again appeared to gild the balloon and gondola with its rays. I was the only illuminated body within the whole horizon, and I saw all the rest of nature plunged in shadow. Amid this inexpressible delight, this ecstasy of contemplation, I was recalled to myself by an altogether extraordinary stab of pain that I felt in my inner right ear and maxillary glands. I put it down as much to the dilation of the air contained in the cellular tissue of the organism as to the coldness of the external air. . . .[85]

Whatever the explanation, it was time to go down. He had promised the duc de Chartres not to stay more than half an hour, and he had been aloft for thirty-five minutes. Opening the upper valve from time to time, as well as the appendix, he descended fairly rapidly, releasing gas until the bottom of the balloon had flattened to the point that

Mᵍ. le Duc de Chartres et Mˡ. le Duc de Fitz Jame
signent le Procès Verbal qui constate l'arrivée de MM. Charles et Robert
dans la Prairie de Nesle près d'Hedouville.

24.

an observer might have taken the whole thing for a parachute had one yet been invented. At sixty or a hundred feet above the ground, he braked by throwing over the few pounds of ballast he had left and settled gently to a landing in open country near La Tour de Laye, about a league or three miles from his point of departure, even while reflecting that had he wished to do so, he could have remained aloft at least another twenty-four hours.

So ended the first six months of artificial flight (Fig. 25).

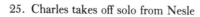

25. Charles takes off solo from Nesle

GLOBE AEROSTATIQUE

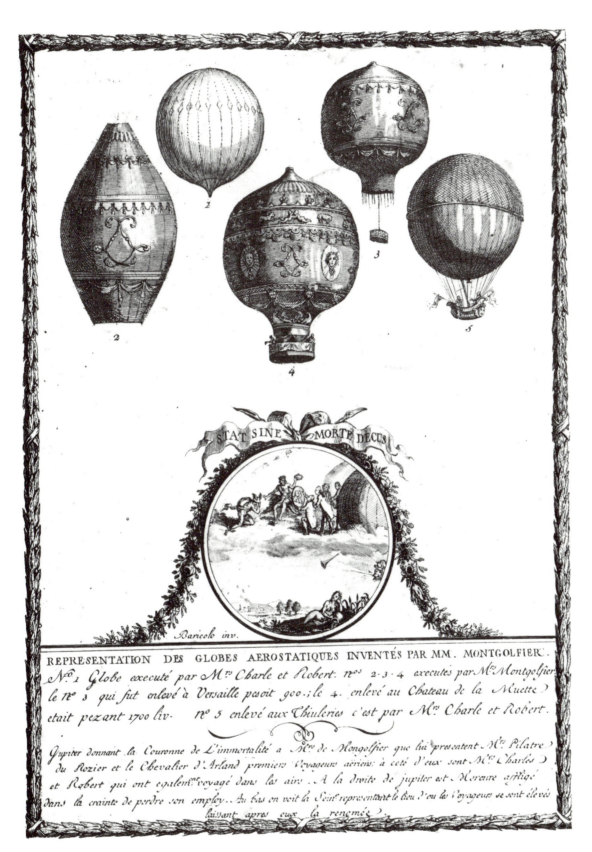

REPRESENTATION DES GLOBES AEROSTATIQUES INVENTÉS PAR MM. MONTGOLFIER.
Nᵒ 1 Globe exécuté par Mᵣ Charle et Robert. nᵒˢ 2.3.4 exécutés par Mᵣ Montgolfier.
le nᵒ 3 qui fut enlevé à Versaille pesoit 900.; le 4. enlevé au Château de la Muette
etait pezant 1700 liv. Nᵒ 5 enlevé aux Thuileries c'est par Mᵣ Charle et Robert.

Jupiter donnant la Couronne de L'immortalité a Mᵣˢ de Mongolfier que lui présentent Mᵣ Pilatre
du Rozier et le Chevalier d'Arland premiers Voyageurs aériens: à coté d'eux sont Mᵣˢ Charles
et Robert qui ont egalemᵗ voyagé dans les airs. A la droite de jupiter est Mercure affligé
dans la crainte de perdre son employ. Au bas on voit la Seine représentant le lieu d'ou les Voyageurs se sont élevés
laissant après eux la renomée

26. Aircraft constructed in 1783. The representations are not according to scale

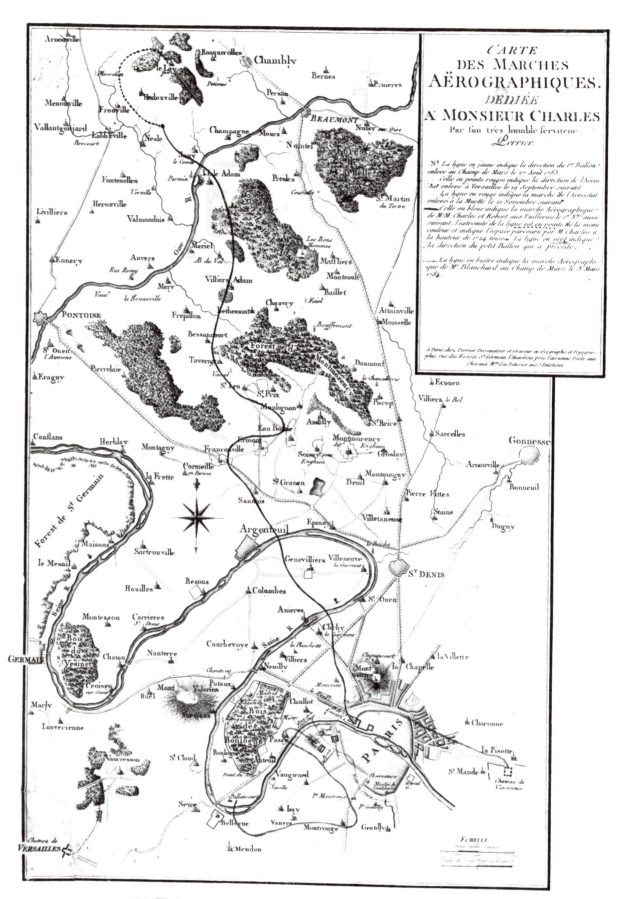

27. Flight paths over Paris, including Blanchard's of 2 March 1784

1. Honors

Throughout December 1783 the Academy of Science occupied itself with reaching provisional judgments upon the accomplishments of the past half-year in aviation and with planning for its development in the future. The commission named in July, though appointed to consider the Montgolfier invention, had naturally included the Charles balloons within its purview. Its members had attended all the experiments and demonstrations except the test in early October when Etienne privately tried the balloon himself. Among the eight commissioners, the two who counted for most were Lavoisier and Desmarest, Lavoisier because of his preeminence in science and his influence with government, Desmarest because of his knowledge of the background. All except the latter had been ignorant of the Montgolfier technique until Etienne exhibited it in the disastrous demonstration of 12 September in the Réveillon factory. By the time of their report in December, they made no doubt that hot air balloons drew lifting force from the expansive effect of heat whereas the Charles variety depended on the production of a gas different from the atmosphere.[1]

In the eyes of the commissioners, the contrast had thus become one between physical and chemical methods, though they did not put it that way. Etienne may have helped to sharpen the distinction, albeit unwittingly. The commissioners referred in their report to the memoir that he had read before the Academy on 15 November. They stated that he and his brother had systematically investigated the lifting potentiality of every vapor lighter than air, and had considered steam, hydrogen, and various products of combustion before settling on the dilation of ordinary air by heat as the simplest and cheapest technique. In fact the 15 November memoir—the same that Joseph, who wrote it, presented before the Academy of Lyons on 25 November—was nothing like so categorical. The brothers dismissed the possibility of inflammable air with little more than a mention. The expense would have been prohibitive. In the latter part of the memoir, Joseph developed the opinion that the effects of electricity augment the buoyancy due to heat.[2] It would appear, therefore, that the commission attributed its own view of the alternatives to the inventors. In any case, they acknowledged the justice of the Montgolfier choice. After all, combustion of eighty pounds of straw and seven or eight of wool at Versailles had sufficed to lift a load of almost a thousand pounds in less than ten minutes.

The Charles alternative, the commission allowed, was far costlier in the current state of the art. At the same time it was natural that chemists and physicists in the capital, many of them preoccupied with newly discovered gases in their own research, should have looked to hydrogen. The success of the Charles-Robert flights was undeniable, and who knew whether a gas lighter than hydrogen might turn up? The science of gases, even like the age of flight, was in its infancy. The Montgolfiers for their part had already proposed several improvements in their technique. Clearly, it was much too soon to make a choice. All that could be said provisionally was that the facility and economy of the Montgolfier method bade fair to make it preferable for civil uses, whereas the hydrogen alternative, lifting the same weight with a much smaller balloon and requiring no replenishment of fuel in flight, might well offer advantages for scientific uses. The meteorological observations Charles had made at a great altitude showed how much was to be learned.[3]

The tilt toward hydrogen is unmistakable, and the tip of Lavoisier's finger may be felt upon the balance. After hearing this report on 23 December, the Academy adjourned. Thereupon Lavoisier immediately convoked a further meeting of the same group, a most unusual step since such a commission would normally disband when its work was done. In his view questions of great urgency for the future of aviation remained to be resolved, and Meusnier must be the one to explore them. Clearly—though this is not the reason Lavoisier then advanced—the coincidence with his own investigations into the composition of water had already attracted his interest to the problem of collecting hydrogen in large quantity.[4] At an earlier meeting of the Academy, on 6 December, Lavoisier intervened in a discussion of the hot air and hydrogen alternatives with a suggestion on methods by which the latter gas might be generated more cheaply. In that same session Meusnier completed the reading of a magnificent memoir on the engineering of the hydrogen balloon he imagined for the future, a craft designed to reach a stable altitude in perfect equilibrium with the medium in which it floated. He must have begun working on that memoir soon after completing the analysis Faujas had commissioned of the flight of the first *charlière* from the Champ de Mars. It is a splendid piece, at once highly technical and highly visionary.[5]

It is also lengthy, and Meusnier began the reading on 3 December. The Academy invited Charles to attend that same meeting in order to present his account of the flight with Robert from the Tuileries just two days previously. Charles and Meusnier thus appeared before the scientists together, the one the pilot and experimentalist, the other the designer and engineer. At the end of the month the *Journal de Paris* published a three-page note in which Meusnier recalculated, on the basis of the data Charles had recorded, the exact altitude the latter must have reached on the two legs of his journey through the air. He refined the rougher estimates Charles had made in the hurry of his own narrative, correcting for fine points of instrumental error and of varying atmospheric density.[6] It was clearly the combination of just such precision with imagination that

appealed to Lavoisier and led him to select Meusnier to act for the revived commission in exploring the unsolved questions of aviation. What they were, and how Meusnier proceeded to seek answers, are topics to which we shall return.

Whatever Lavoisier's inner thoughts about the comparative merits of hot air and hydrogen, the outward actions of the Academy gave Etienne no reason to feel slighted. On 10 December it accepted Desmarest's motion that he and Joseph be elected to corresponding membership. It equally adopted the proposal with which the commission concluded the 23 December report, to the effect that the brothers jointly be awarded the prize of 600 livres founded by an anonymous donor for discoveries in the arts. The phrasing qualifies them as "savants" who had created an entirely new art "marking a new era in the history of human invention."[7] The baron de Breteuil, minister of the royal household, had quietly conveyed to the permanent secretary of the Academy the king's express desire that appropriate recognition be accorded to the Montgolfiers no less than to Charles.[8] In the nature of the procedures, Louis XVI had personally to approve the solution to the problem of rewarding Etienne and Joseph equally, accomplished by the issue of letters patent conferring the particle on their father. Thus was the family style elevated to "de Montgolfier." The citation dwells on the distinction of Pierre's career in industry, and the exploits of his sons are merely mentioned.[9] Nothing indicates that the old man was ever reconciled to flight. Indeed, Jean-Pierre again warned Etienne to be more discreet in letters home. A reference to injuries that Réveillon suffered in falling backward off the launching platform at la Muette had caused another crisis of patriarchal anxiety.[10]

Etienne was scarcely more capable of keeping an easy mind than his father. His initial disquiet amid all this success does him credit, however. He alone, being in the capital, was decorated with the Order of Saint-Michel, and evidently wrote home in dismay that he had been unable to refuse despite the unfairness to Joseph. At once his brothers rallied, as the family always did when trouble deeper than irritation threatened. He had already reported being menaced by this honor, to which the abbé replied lightly, saying it would be an empty thing compared to tangible reward, and that anyway Etienne was not rich enough to be a nobleman.[11] Now that the invidious disaster had struck, the abbé's mode of assuaging his brother's guilt and chagrin (and perhaps his secret pride) is a masterpiece of healing wit. The letter opens (so as not to touch the nerve) on the line that the real problem was the one he had been harping on all along:

> I thought you more of a philosopher, my dear friend and brother. And now, say what you please, I find that, though I get more carried away than any of you, I'm better at resigning myself to the things that happen in life. Remember, I beg you, what we've been telling each other in our letters. If nothing comes of it, we'll just have to console ourselves. Well, something has come of it. To be sure, it's less than you expected, and you take on like a child. You write us in a tone to infect us with your worries. If J.-P. and I, well-fortified by philosophy, had not resisted the emotional plague that you tried to transmit to the family, we'd have had a hard time protecting your wife from catching it. As it is, I regard her as barely convalescent. We've had to employ gentle and harmless remedies. As for Marianne, whose temperament is more robust, we have brought her around to agreeing that it's all for the best. So she is completely cured, except that sometimes she says, "But no money at all, when we've spent so much." Still, I can reassure you that these exclamations are infrequent, and always in a low voice.
>
> Let's be serious. What ails you is having got nothing for Joseph. You know him well enough to be sure that he won't doubt for a moment but that you did everything in your power. You didn't succeed. That's not your fault. "Yes," you'll tell me, "that's how you see it, but what about the public!"[12]

The public be damned, rounds off the abbé, turning to the idea of forming a commercial partnership between Joseph and Etienne to deal in paper and to develop aviation.

Best of all, Joseph chimed in with a letter scrawled from Lyons the same day. He has been working so hard on his own balloon that he has not found a moment to write, but if the king had only one ribbon, he is delighted that Etienne should have it. "Just between us," he goes on, "you will put it to better use." For himself, he finds the preference for solitude growing on him in proportion to his exposure to the life of society, and it would have been of little value. Anyway, he is thrilled with the particle of nobility for their father. Thereupon Joseph turns to details of the design of his enormous balloon, wondering at the end whether their uncle could help with another letter of credit? He just happens to need 12,000 livres to get on with the construction.[13] Relieved (one may imagine) at this shift of focus, Etienne gave every appearance of enjoying the reversal of roles whereby in the remaining weeks of December and early in January he seconded his brother with technical advice. He even managed to write cheerfully about canvassing the capital for money.[14]

For Etienne shared in the sense of the family that the time had come for channeling its flow of aid and comfort toward Joseph. His qualities of innocence were felt to require the protection, not just of their moral support, but of their presence.[15] Augustin came on from Rives together with his wife, arriving in Lyons on 17 December. Joseph's wife, Thérèse, let her father look after himself in Annonay for a time. The abbé came up from Vidalon with Adélaïde, Etienne's wife, who left her child of three months and escaped the confinement of the factory.[16] Brothers, wife, and sisters-in-law formed a phalanx around Joseph as he struggled to adapt his designs to the demands imposed by subscribers and would-be passengers, Pilatre de Rozier leading the pack. Etienne warmly commended his recent pilot's qualities of skill and personality to his brothers. "Embrace him for me," he wrote, and Pilatre arrived in Lyons on Saturday 27 December.[17]

2. THE *Flesselles*

Joseph had been meditating his own balloon since mid-summer at a time when Etienne was visiting an earlier phase of discouragement upon the family. From the beginning, Joseph's mind ran on increasing the size, and on the nature of the lifting force. A letter to Etienne of 18 August tells of experiments looking to improve the adhesion between cloth and paper, and also of the thought that a rectangular balloon 200 feet high on a square base 100 feet on the side might make a more impressive sight than would another globe.[18] The intendant of Lyons, the chief officer of government in the region, was a magistrate called Jacques de Flesselles. Like everyone else, he had been excited by the news of the Annonay exploit, and he invited Joseph to the residence from time to time to talk of that and of other technical matters.

In the last days of August, Flesselles prevailed on him to make a small flying machine to demonstrate at his country house. Joseph used the same paper and cloth that he and Etienne had employed at Annonay, but now he varied the form, constructing a truncated pyramid, eight feet high on an eight-foot square tapering to a four-foot top, rather like a symbol of Freemasonry. Underneath the mouth he suspended a cylindrical frame of iron wire in which he inserted the fuel, a roll of thirty-two sheets of printers' paper soaked in olive oil. Rising rapidly, his polyhedral bubble was carried first toward Lyons, then toward the north, and finally west where it disappeared behind the hills after a flight of more than twenty minutes. Enchanted, others of the company begged him to repeat the experiment in their properties. Its success provoked the floating of a subscription on the part of leading citizens.[19] That got under way after news of the Champ de Mars *charlière* had reached Lyons but before Joseph received Etienne's account of the fiasco of the Réveillon experiment on 12 September.[20] Even without that chastening word, Joseph at first gave his backers modest undertakings. The sale was limited to 360 tickets at twelve livres each, his initial engagement having been to construct an inexpensive machine capable of lifting a considerable load, 8,000 pounds including its own weight and, possibly, a horse.[21]

As always Joseph harbored more extravagant

inner thoughts. On receiving the great news of Versailles, he wrote Etienne a letter of congratulations bursting with the enthusiasm that was natural to him, now that he no longer had to affect to share his brother's posture of reluctant sacrifice of business interests to the calvary of invention. He concluded with a confession of what he really had in mind: a cylindrical flying machine 100 fathoms in height and 150 in diameter—i.e., 600 feet and 900 feet—which would weigh 42,000 hundredweight (over 200 tons). He would float it by burning about 200 pounds of wood a minute in order to maintain a temperature of 70° (about 190° F) inside. It would cost 4,000,000 livres to construct. Oh, he knew there was no chance of getting the government to take on anything of that magnificence. But he could not stop thinking about it and working out the dimensions:

> . . . so keen is my desire to see the building of a vessel big enough to be without an equal since the world has existed. If I'm crazy, I'm incurable. For I can't get the image of that construction out of my imagination. I correct and perfect it every day. It's an occupation that serves me as an antidote to vexation. Still, if ever it is to be developed, I guess it would be better to begin with a small-scale model.[22]

Joseph's notion of small was not that of other men, and it was a further feature of his inventor's temperament that he should have combined cost-consciousness in his actual engineering with indifference to paying the expenses incurred. Following this vision of a mega-balloon, a monstrous letter of 10 October gives detailed calculations on relations between capacity, weight, fuel requirements, quality of materials, and costs.[23] The analysis is an example of Joseph's do-it-yourself manhandling of the calculus and deals with factors that Etienne, for all his greater elegance, seems not to have taken into account. Partly they arise from the scale of the model Joseph actually meant to construct and partly from the modesty of the subscription. He observed that the lifting force of the contained gas bears more intensively on the upper reaches of a balloon, and that important economies could be effected by employing cheaper fabrics in the lower hemisphere. Since his obligation in this instance was to lift 8,000 pounds, he thought to stay within his budget by resorting throughout to fabric coarser and heavier than expensive grades. It made no difference whether the weight was in the body or the ballast. His design also respected the consideration that he had reproached Etienne with overlooking. The elongation and tapering of the Réveillon balloon had subjected it to excessive torque from the lateral pressure of the wind.[24] Joseph's model was spherical, and he proposed reinforcing the upper hemisphere with a ribbing of strong cords from which would be suspended an airborne box stall.

Calculation and experimentation occupied Joseph throughout October and November. Panels of fabric were all cut out and ready to assemble in early December, at the time when the excitement of manned flights in Paris reached Lyons. Thereafter, he turned to the problem of accommodating his design to the irresistible pressure to substitute passengers for the horse. The adaptation Joseph imagined is described in the letter of 18 December to Etienne, the same in which he disclaimed pique about the Order of Saint-Michel. For the wicker gallery he thought to substitute a platform of horsehair mats spread on a radial arrangement of fir boards with the heater at the center. The drawing is his own (Fig. 28). The balloon was to be a perfect sphere one hundred feet in diameter topped by a sugar-loaf dome twenty feet high and forty in diameter to lend a touch of grace to the profile. The volume of this, the fifth *montgolfière* intended for the public, was thus to be approximately 525,000 cubic feet, a figure to be compared to the 60,000 cubic feet of the machine in which Pilatre and d'Arlandes had flown over Paris and to the 37,500-cubic-foot model at Versailles. To generate the lifting force, Joseph planned to abandon straw and use a wood-burner, a Liège stove as the model was called. The weights would be as follows, within an allowable error of 3 percent:

Lumber for the platform	1,000	pounds
Water	1,000	"
Stove, mats, pails, sponges, etc.	1,500	"
Fuel	1,200	"
Men	1,500	"
Balloon	8,000	"

He had thus almost doubled the original scale in order to allow for ten or twelve passengers. A further novelty was his hope of making a long flight. The launching was to be at noon so that a midday wind might carry them thirty or forty leagues (say 125 miles) before nightfall and touchdown. Joseph then intended to depart directly for Paris to join Etienne in promoting further development.

Like the cost-accounting, the work-plan for assembling the aircraft combined practicality in principle with impracticality in practice. The spherical body consisted of 16 doubly tapered segments, each composed of 7 pre-cut panels, which together with the dome made 113 pieces of fabric (Fig. 29). They were to be joined by 14,944 frogs. Each piece was identified with two numbers stenciled on all four corners, so that "14 6," for example, designated the sixth panel of the fourteenth segment. Joseph calculated that a man working alone would need thirty-two hours to hitch the parts together. He wanted the thing done in public, however, and fast, so that the fabrication would enhance the spectacle. To that end, he recruited sixteen teams of workers, one for every segment, each consisting of a foreman, an assistant, three volunteers, and an "homme de paine."[25] In addition to these ninety-six men on the assembly line, he would hire a work-gang of fifty-four auxiliary laborers. If everyone observed good discipline, and Joseph was training them to that end, the whole operation would take less than two hours. With all these preparations to concert, he did not expect to try the first experiments before 29 December.[26]

In fact, assisted by Augustin and the abbé, Joseph tried a preliminary inflation of the dome alone on 26 December. To their dismay, the coarse sackcloth proved full of holes when stretched.[27] The very next day Pilatre blew in accompanied by the marquis de Dampierre, another nobleman drawn like d'Arlandes to the derring-do of flight. In cloak and dagger fashion the two of them affected incognito, Pilatre as Monsieur Roland and Dampierre as Monsieur Henri.[28] Preceded by Etienne's warm recommendation, Pilatre now set up as an expert in design. Augustin and the abbé both wrote Etienne of the modifications he presumed to impose, it may be rightly. (It may also be that Pilatre was acting on reservations about the specifications imparted by Etienne himself.)[29] The leaky dome was to be eliminated and replaced with a cap fitted conformably to the sphere and made of two layers of taffeta with a sheet of paper between them. The number of passengers was to be reduced to six. The wooden platform and iron stove were to give way to a wicker gallery and a brazier burning straw and wool again, the latter to be soaked in olive oil. The fabric in the part around the mouth was to be taffeta fireproofed with alum (clearly Pilatre had learned a few things flying over Paris with sparks eating

out the bag). Finally, Joseph's netting was to be replaced with one of finer mesh covering only the upper hemisphere.

All this took time. The date of an experimental inflation had to be put off, from December 29th to January 4th or 6th, and then to the 9th or 10th. Repeated delays produced the inevitable skepticism in public opinion, mockery by pamphleteers, irritation among officials and subscribers, and disenchantment on the part of thrillseekers from afar, some of whom grumbled off in dudgeon. All these modifications were accepted after long discussions among Joseph, his brothers, and his backers. Pilatre had come into their midst like a *deus ex machina* dispelling discouragement about the sieve of a dome, and their first reaction was warm. They found him charming, wrote the abbé, and Joseph dashed off a note to Etienne to say they were enchanted.[30]

Soon they were disenchanted. As the preparations continued to drag despite frantic activity, Pilatre's untrue colors began to show up under pressure. The abbé confessed to reservations on 9 January. It was a day when all had gone well, he wrote Etienne, and they hoped to manage the launching on the morrow. True, Monsieur Pilatre could not flatter himself with having made many friends in Lyons, but at least he was getting on well with Joseph, the only person he dared not push around. Joseph, on the other hand, had won the hearts of all.[31] In the course of a further week of wrestling with design and apparatus, even Joseph had had enough of Pilatre's officiousness. Writing to Etienne on the 16th, he said that Pilatre always contradicted everyone else, that he took advantage of Joseph's forbearance to suppose that he could always get his way, that he upset everything, that it would have been far better if he had never set foot among them, having cost the venture at least 200 louis of unnecessary expense and always stirring up a row. In experiments with the tethered balloon, Joseph could never feel sure but that Pilatre might order the crew to cut the cords and soar off alone, stealing the whole show.[32]

Probably it was part of Joseph's charm that he never could refuse people. Besides Pilatre and

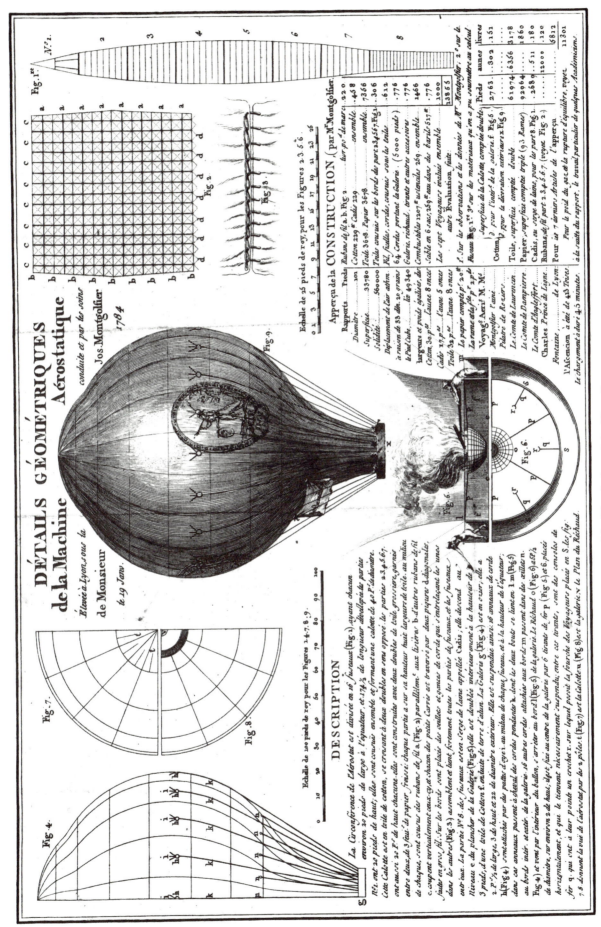

29. The design of the *Flesselles*

Dampierre, he had vaguely promised places to two local noblemen, the comte de Laurencin and the chevalier de Laporte d'Anglefort, and more seriously to a royal shaveling, Charles, son and heir of the prince de Ligne. The latter, a magnate of the Austrian Netherlands (as Belgium then was) had taken 100 subscriptions. The young prince was a comrade and competitor of the duc de Chartres, the same who had pounded across Paris after Pilatre and d'Arlandes, and then galloped through the northern suburbs after Charles and Robert. His seat, the château of Saint-Cloud on the western outskirts of the capital, was even then accommodating construction of the next Robert balloon. All these blooded and incompetent people, together with the immediate entourage of the intendant, Flesselles, and the notables of the Academy of Science of Lyons, formed an inner circle of would-be collaborators, ever at the elbows of Joseph and his brothers.

Joseph, of course, enormously complicated the task of perfecting the aircraft by his undertaking to carry it out in public. The sections of fabric were cut and then modified in a shop and yard assigned to him in central Lyons. A rather mean workplace it was, in Augustin's view.[33] The pieces were to be assembled and the launching staged in the area called Les Brotteaux, outside the city on the left bank of the Rhône. There a platform was constructed and equipment installed on Wednesday 7 January. Fitting the pieces together took two days of pesky labor instead of the two hours of Joseph's master plan. At half-past five in the dark of the morning of Saturday the 10th the first inflation succeeded in twenty minutes. The object was to raise the balloon enough to attach the gallery, but the whole forenoon got used up in untangling ropes and adjusting the netting. A new fire was lighted at twelve o'clock, and this time it took twenty-seven minutes before the bag grew taut. By then the emplacement was aswarm with spectators. Such was the noise that the work force fell into confusion, and the day ended in chaos. Amid the divided counsels of the evening, Pilatre proposed to leave forthwith for Paris to fetch Etienne's balloon and bring it back in substitution for Jo-

seph's, which he considered beyond redemption. Joseph's reaction to this threat was that Pilatre need not fret over the danger, but he did agree that hope for a long flight would have to be abandoned.[34]

Monday the 12th brought a little encouragement. The crew managed to get a few ropes properly attached to the gallery—four out of the eighty required! Joseph had been fueling the operation with bundles of fagots, but on this day someone threw in a bale of straw soaked in alcohol. So sudden was the heat that the balloon surged up three or four feet and dragged fifty or sixty workmen kicking and scuffing some fifteen feet along the ground. The strain of all this told on the mediocre fabric. Seams split. Holes opened. Two more days went into patching. On the 15th, it looked for a few hours as if patience and doggedness would have their reward. Inflation began at 2:45 and required only seventeen minutes. The work force, better-instructed, got the remaining ropes for the gallery fastened in an hour. Five pounds of fagots an hour sufficed to keep the pressure constant. At four o'clock, six would-be passengers climbed aboard for a tethered test. Along with thirty-two hundredweight of ballast, the balloon lifted them a foot off the ground. Jubilant, they urged cutting the ropes and converting experiment into flight. What with the lateness of the hour, they were overruled, and takeoff was put over until the next day.

Who overruled them it is impossible to say, since by now authority was diffused among the Montgolfier family, leading subscribers, and local officials. When anyone had the last word, it was usually the intendant himself, Flesselles. If so in this instance, he had reason to regret his caution. Rain came on in the night, changing to sleet by morning, and on Friday dejection was the order of the day. Exposed to the elements, the fabric sagged under a weight of slush. Unwilling to leave bad enough alone, Joseph and his cohorts tried to inflate and dry it. They heated the stove too intensely, and the cap of the balloon caught fire. Fortunately, someone had thought to mount pumps on the edge of the platform, and the blaze was extinguished before the whole machine was lost. Now snow threatened. Refusing to admit defeat, the Montgolfier brothers and their crew cut away the charred ruins of the cap, a segment fifty feet in diameter, and replaced it with sound fabric, newly lined with paper. The external net had also been damaged in the fire, and they substituted an arrangement of sixteen ropes placed meridionally to lend tensile strength.

Those repairs took all day Saturday and Sunday. On Sunday night a heavy snow fell. Monday dawned clear and so cold that the sodden fabric was frozen stiff as a board. This time a gentler thawing was achieved by means of charcoal burners placed under the platform. As the glaze loosened, Dampierre, d'Anglefort, Laurencin, and several of the greatest merchants of Lyons, people who had never laid hand to a domestic instrument, grabbed brooms and began sweeping. By noon the fabric was pliable, and the crew proceeded to a gingerly inflation, taking two hours to the task. On peering up into the enormous sack, the permanent secretary of the Academy of Lyons was appalled to see daylight through a raft of holes.[35] With all that it had been through, the fabric was clearly on the verge of disintegration. It was equally apparent that the sixteen reinforcing ropes had been spaced irregularly and that strain would be greater in the wider intervals.

Friends and well-wishers who for several days had been urging the prospective passengers to desist, now redoubled their efforts on the brink of what looked like disaster. Unheeding, Prince Charles, Dampierre, Laurencin, and d'Anglefort leaped aboard. Pilatre hung back. He had been insisting for some time that three people would be as many as the weakened aircraft could safely carry. One can sympathize with him. After all, he alone had been up in a balloon, a much better one. He again proposed, what his companions had so far rejected, that the four of them draw lots to see which two should accompany him. In vain. All were noblemen. All were armed. All drew their pistols. Dampierre, d'Anglefort, and the prince threatened to blow out the brains of anyone who tried to dislodge them. Laurencin threatened only to blow out his own brains.

Thinking they might listen to a lady, Adélaïde, Etienne's wife, tried pleading with the titled hijackers. Never. The intendant, Flesselles, urged them to be reasonable and to dismount. Instead, they yelled at the crew to cut the cords. Thereupon, Pilatre jumped into the gallery, acting on the impulse that things had gone too far to let them fly without him. Joseph, quite forgotten in the imbroglio, followed on his heels. Thus there were six, one passenger for each of the stations provided with a harness like a seat belt, that being the number intended after converting the original project of ballast plus a horse into one for manned flight. Now the crew loosed the cords. As the craft shuddered off its platform, in jumped a seventh aeronaut, a local worthy called Fontaine, who had been fidelity itself among the inner circle of Joseph's collaborators (Fig. 30).[36]

Compared to the Réveillon decorated globes in Paris, the Lyons *montgolfière* made but a dull appearance. The cap was white and the body grayish with four large medallions, one pair representing History and the other Fame. A gesture toward *trompe d'oeil* gave the impression that the sphere reposed on a truncated and inverted cone of varicolored stripes flaring up and out from the gallery that rimmed the heater. The one touch of panache was a banner blazoning the name *Le Flesselles*, with which the intendant's wife had christened the vessel amid the confusion of its launching. Pilatre had managed to throw out all the ballast and three-quarters of the fuel after failing to get rid of passengers. Even so, the overburdened craft, instead of taking off, dragged itself under a light wind across the platform, bumped off the edge onto the ground, and got caught for a moment on a post in the fence surrounding the enclosure. A couple of crew members shouldered it free, and it then became evident that another of them had lost his head and held on to his rope. He stood there stupidly with everyone yelling at him to let go, and only when someone cut the cord with a hatchet did the *Flesselles* at last gather the force to rise slowly above the throng of 100,000 spectators. Men clapped their hands, cheered, and threw their hats after the aircraft (Fig. 31). Ladies wept and fainted.

The seven passengers saluted the multitude from on high, ascending to an altitude of 2,400 or 2,600 feet in twelve or fourteen minutes. At one point a breeze carried them toward the Rhône, and shifting, brought them back almost overhead (Fig. 32).

Suddenly a segment ripped open in a four-foot tear near the cap, where the already shoddy and fatigued fabric had been further weakened by fire the previous Friday. The descent, by all accounts, was rather that of a parachute than of a balloon, though no one could make the comparison at the time. Only later in the year did Joseph participate in invention of the parachute. Reacting quickly, Pilatre pushed the fire to its utmost to slow the fall. Even so, the speed accelerated, and *Le Flesselles* hit the ground in three minutes. In the

words of an eyewitness, the shock proved "supportable" to the voyagers. The place of landing, or impact, was in a field behind a house belonging to an architect called Merand, only a short distance from the launching platform. Out sprang the passengers in less than thirty seconds and scrambled clear of the balloon collapsing over them. The spectators came floundering through the mud left by melting snow, the first of them arriving on the scene in time to put out the fire which had spread from the heater to the fabric.

Among them was the abbé, who could spy Joseph from afar. The mounted police assured him that everyone was safe and sound. He could see that Pilatre had got himself onto a horse. Apparently old Pierre had after all come on from Vidalon, for the abbé rushed into the intendant's

30. Launching the *Flesselles*

Première Expérience de la Machine Aérostatique, nommée Le Flesselle, construite à Lyon, sous la direction de M. Joseph Montgolfier, dessinée dans ses proportions à ⅓ Ligne par pied

Départ de la Machine Aérostatique, le 19 Janvier 784 montée par l'Auteur, et par M. le Prince Charles de Ligne, le C. de Laurencin, le C. Dampiere, le C. d'Anglefort, Pilatre de Rozier, et Fontaine.

Dédiée, à Madame De Flesselle, Intendante De Lyon

Par ses très humbles, très obéissants Serviteurs, Cogell, & St Aubin.

EXPÉRIENCE AEROSTATIQUE
Faite à Lyon en Janvier 1784, avec un Ballon de cent pieds de diamètre.
Vuë prise du Pavillon méridional de Sᵗ. Antonio Spréasico, aux Brotteaux.

Voyageurs Aëriens:
M. Montgolfier L'Ainé; M. Pilatre de Roziers.
Le Prince Charles, fils ainé du Prince de Ligne
Mᵗ. Le Comte de Laurencin Ch. de Sᵗ. Louis, de Lyon
Mᵗ. le Comte de la Porte d'Anglefort Lieut. Col. d'Inf.ᵗᵉ Ch. de t. L.
Mᵗ. Le Comte de Dampierre Off.ᵗᵉ aux Gardes francoise
Mᵗ. Fontaine .... de Lyon

un espace infini nous séparoit des cieux;
mais, grace aux MONTGOLFIER que le génie inspire,
l'aigle de Jupiter à perdu son Empire.
et le faible mortel peut s'approcher des dieux ....
Nota L'on prépare une Seconde Planche, qui donnera bientôt et très exactement les Plans, coupe, profils, détails, calculs,
résultats et autres objets rélatifs à cette Machine.

* Le 19 a Midi 48 Minutes. La Machine s'est élevée
à plus de 3000 Toises portant 7. Personnes
dans la Galerie.

.... VASSELIER de l'Acad.ᵉ de Lyon

A Lyon chés Joubert fils Mᵈ. Estampes 4.ᵉ rue Mercière

31. The *Flesselles* airborne

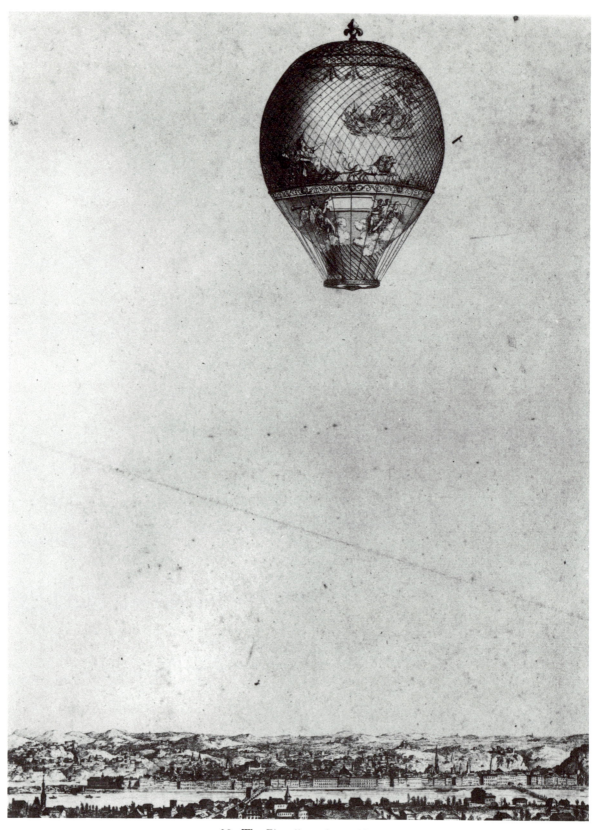

32. The *Flesselles* at its zenith

headquarters to tell their father all was well. No one was there, however, except the young Prince Charles, who in transports of joy nearly strangled him with a great bear hug. Laboring back to the launching site in mud up to his knees, the abbé next found Fontaine, the seventh passenger, who said Joseph had been haled off in triumph to Lyons.

The first arrivals among the crowd made as if to carry Joseph on their shoulders. When he resisted, they commandeered a carriage, proposing to eject the ladies within. Joseph would have none of that and instead got in among them. The officer, their escort, climbed up on the box beside the coachman. Dampierre and d'Anglefort hung onto the step at either door, and four or five others of the immediate circle rode behind like lackeys. Led by a brigade of mounted police, and followed by an ecstatic retinue of four or five thousand celebrants, the carriage bore Joseph and his companions into Lyons and across town to the Hôtel Blanc, where Dampierre and Pilatre were lodging. There the hall porter, befuddled with drink, tried to bar their entrance, beating at the carriage with his staff. Indignant, the crowd would have lynched the drunken concierge had Dampierre not risen to the occasion with a speech begging their indulgence and a respite for changing clothes.

Thereupon Prince Charles invited the entire party to dinner, after which Flesselles came round to take them to the opera. *Iphigénie in Aulis* was on the boards that evening. The performance had already begun when the intendant and Madame appeared in their box with Joseph, his wife, the abbé, and Pilatre, followed by all the voyagers except Fontaine, who had not dined. Applause and bravos broke out, and the action on stage was interrupted. The actor singing Agamemnon came forward bearing garlands with which Madame de Flesselles crowned each aeronaut. Pilatre doubled Joseph's crown by adding his own, and Prince Charles placed his on the head of Joseph's wife, Thérèse. Meanwhile Fontaine was discovered in the parterre, and the intendant descended with his award and brought him forward together with Augustin. The latter had concealed himself behind a pillar, being still in rough clothes

from overseeing the dismantling of the aircraft out in Les Brotteaux. Agamemnon then returned to his tent, reemerging in order to sing an appropriate (and the abbé thought a bad) couplet. Once again the opera was stopped by overwhelming applause when Clytemnestra sang the piece, "Que j'aime à voir ces hommages flatteurs."

Supper at the residence of the military commandant followed the performance. He and his wife had three daughters—the "three Graces" in the spirit of the evening. Their gallant father had them embrace the heroes of the occasion, and the meal ended with music performed by a young merchants' chamber group conducted by Fontaine. Madame de Flesselles and he then opened the ball with a minuet. Figure dancing followed. Joseph and the abbé stole off to bed, leaving Augustin to see the ladies home.

"Have you had enough of that?" the abbé asked Etienne, winding up the letter that contains much of this detail. "For the rest," he concluded in an unvarnished sentence, "the *procès-verbal*, if it is accurately done, may, it seems to me, make up for the small measure of success of this experiment."[37]

3. What Next?

The abbé Alexandre's account crossed an angry letter from Etienne written the very day of the flight of the *Flesselles*. Forgotten for the moment was the encouragement Etienne had joined in giving Joseph. The violence of the tone is more pronounced than in other expressions of fraternal irritation that escaped his self-control, not so much betraying as proclaiming the intensity of conflicting pressures. They bore on Etienne from father and factory at Vidalon, from courtiers at Versailles, from ministers of state in Paris, from scientists in the new commission of the Academy, from camp followers of flight all over, and now from brothers, sisters, cousin, and wife making fools of themselves in Lyons.

In this instance the immediate provocation was a letter from his Adélaïde in which she must have all innocently imparted the notion of her joining Joseph and rushing to Etienne's side on the momentum of a successful flight in Lyons. "I'm distressed to see," wrote Etienne, scolding his kindly and enthusiastic abbé of a brother, "that busying yourselves with the machine has turned your head and more so my wife's." He cannot imagine how she got the idea of coming to Paris, which she says the abbé approves, unless the purpose would be to make him, Etienne, feel that he had stayed too long himself. Well, if that was the object, the maneuver would succeed. Just let Joseph and Adélaïde set foot in the capital. He would depart the next day. As for the talk of a subscription to underwrite further development on a heroic scale, he would not presume to say how such a thing might go in Lyons, but in Paris it would dissipate in a quarter of an hour all the esteem he had been at pains to nurture. Persons of means in the capital might give lip service to worthy causes, but had no idea of contributing to constructive purposes the money they spent on women and horses. Even were a subscription to succeed, the price would be delivering Joseph and himself hostage into the hands of the public. For his part, he had been bending every effort to persuade the government that only an outright grant of 50,000 to 100,000 livres would suffice to construct a machine capable of realizing the possibilities for aviation. But if the abbé, along with Joseph and his own wife, were determined to continue meddling instead of tending to business, why he, Etienne, would take the opposite course, abandon flight, and get back to paper where he belonged. In all that he had been doing, Etienne added, he had followed the advice of the worldly-wise, and foremost among them, their uncle.

To this blast the same good Uncle Jacques added a postscript, one of the few words we have from him: "People here say your machine has burned up. It's downright astonishing that we know nothing from you about the essentials. Better if it had never existed, but perhaps the only course is not to speak of it. . . . May you forget all about your balloons, and we'll forget all your preposterous notions. Let's make up for all the time wasted."[38]

The abbé had more trouble absorbing these reproaches than he did with anything ever ad-

dressed to him by members of the family whose balance wheel he was. The rebuke had, he replied, surprised him not a little. Clearly Etienne had been in a fury when he wrote, and could rest assured that the effect of his letter had been electric, "and the shock violent." The abbé would be grateful to know what their uncle meant by his "preposterous notions." His part in Adélaïde's plan had been merely to advise her to let her husband know in advance. But Etienne need not worry. Crestfallen, his wife had crept back to Vidalon. He, the abbé, having thus been ordered out of aviation, would follow within the day. To the charge of failure to communicate, he pleaded the nights spent on the emplacement struggling with the problems of the Flesselles, not to mention the treachery of Pilatre (about whose true character Etienne might have warned them). But enough of mutual reproaches. Before assuring Etienne of his determined affection, proof against all trials, the abbé felt bound to convey the opinion, in which he had company, that it was high time for Etienne and Joseph to be reunited in their efforts.[39]

This, the abbé's hurt rejoinder, crossed another letter from Etienne, written on 26 January when the news of the Flesselles had reached Paris. Now he sought to soften the impact of the dressing-down he surely wished he had not sent. He opened handsomely enough with congratulations and passed on, not precisely by way of apology, into a rumination on the ways of the world. May the glory his brothers have won not issue in chagrin, but by now they should have had enough rest to reckon with the realities. The more enthusiastic public opinion seems to be, the more fickle it is. Admiration inevitably greens into jealousy, and fame entails demands that it costs popularity to refuse. Reflect above all, he charged his brothers, on what the spectacle had cost, now that they were paying the piper. Joseph's fantasies of setting up in England or other foreign parts might be all very well if they were twenty years old and without responsibilities. Even then, wealthy people would not throw their treasure out the window any more readily abroad than in Paris. As for money dangled by the prince de

Ligne, that might be acceptable provided he would agree to construction of a machine at Annonay and pay up before work started. In practice, however, allusions to approaches by foreigners will only redound to our disadvantage unless word of them comes from someone other than ourselves. Even then, to be seen rejecting some outside offer would win greater favor than to use it as a bargaining counter. On balance, we, the Montgolfiers, have more to gain from business than from all these adventures. "All things considered, we'd do better to put up with the churlishness of our workers than with the fatuity of our patrons." For the delays imposed by ministers of state drove him nearly wild. To be honest, however, he had to admit that in their place, he would do the same. He would temporize. At all events, he meant to be home by the good weather, even if he had to leave the execution of his projects in the hands of Réveillon.[40]

Actually, Etienne remained in Paris until June 1784, dividing his energies between balloons and paper. His strategy deliberately exploited the official interest in each of these objects for the leverage it afforded in prising concessions from the government that would advance his ventures in the other. In regard to aviation, he was ever the businessman of modest means who had sacrificed the material interests of family and firm in order to carry forward development of a device of inestimable value to the public, though of none to himself, and who could no longer do so without commensurate financial backing. In regard to business, he traded on the prospects for flight in seeking further privileges that would enable the Montgolfiers to consummate their rationalization of papermaking. Let us consider this latter, the commercial, aspect of his activities briefly before recapturing the vision he had simultaneously formed of the future for aircraft.

Pierre's leadership in the industry had been a principal factor mentioned in the letters patent ennobling the old man, and in January Etienne set about securing the designation of "Royal Manufactory" for Vidalon itself. The project became the more urgent when Matthieu Johannot and one of his sons turned up in Paris letting it

be understood that the Montgolfiers had abandoned paper for flight and notoriety, that their factory was in difficulties financially and technically, that anyway, it had been Matthieu and not Etienne who had introduced the fabrication of vellum in France, and that the main Johannot plant of Faya should be the one entitled royal.[41] Etienne might, indeed, have cited the souring of relations with the Johannots as an instance of the penalties attaching to fame. Until the installation of hollanders in 1780, Pierre Montgolfier and Matthieu Johannot had made common cause in production of their papers while competing in the marketing. They had the same interest in factory discipline and in diminishing the power of the workers to resist technical innovations. Both Montgolfier and Johannot had abstained from hiring away skilled people trained by the other, and neither would employ a man who had quit the rival plant without his former boss's consent.[42]

The favor shown the Montgolfiers by Desmarest in the late 1770s, and through him by the authorities, put a strain on this relative solidarity. Discord broke into the open in 1780, when Matthieu Johannot and his son Jean-Baptiste joined Pierre's own nephew, Antoine Montgolfier, at Vidalon-le-bas in protesting the subsidy of 18,000 livres by which the Estates of Languedoc enabled the senior Montgolfiers to convert several vats in Vidalon-le-haut to the service of hollanders.[43] Desmarest then described the Johannot factory (it may be quite unjustly) as capable of emulation but not of innovation.[44] Joseph's debts compounded these antipathies. Sums owed the Johannots were among them, and lawsuits further envenomed feelings.[45] In 1783 relations degenerated so far that the Montgolfiers suspected the Johannots of hiring the scribblers whose poison pens lampooned and vilified their invention of aircraft in the pamphlets of the gutter.[46]

The Johannot design of stealing a march on the aspirations Etienne had conceived for Vidalon could be thwarted, of course, but only by frequenting the corridors of power and accosting the very patrons whose delays over the balloon exasperated him almost beyond bearing. Etienne had access to the maréchal de Castries, minister of the navy, through his friend from student days, Jean-Nicolas Pache, long a familiar of the Castries household and now a bureaucrat. Through another intimate and contemporary, Antoine Boissy d'Anglas, of the landed gentry in Vivarais, he could also get the ear of Lamoignon de Malesherbes, formerly keeper of the seals, charged with responsibility for censoring publication, and much respected among philosopher-statesmen for the liberalism and equanimity with which he discharged what might have been a painful duty.[47] At the Ministry of Finance, Lefevre d'Ormesson, the controller general who had imparted the news of Annonay to the Academy and brought Etienne to Paris, had been replaced in November 1783 by the much more notable Calonne. Among the permanent staff Etienne had long known a senior official, one Blondel, inspector general at the Bureau of Commerce, who had the paper industry in his detail.

The busiest body in spinning and pulling strands throughout this web of influence was another young blade of the Vivarais, the comte d'Antraigues. More officious than Boissy d'Anglas, d'Antraigues was newly arrived in Paris and took up Etienne's cause as a means of cutting a social swath. His uncle, the comte de Saint-Priest, ambassador successively to the Sublime Porte and to the States-General of Holland, and now intendant of Languedoc, was an intimate of Etienne's Uncle Jacques Montgolfier at the archbishopric of Paris. D'Antraigues was also a cousin of Blondel, and that relationship provided an auxiliary link to Malesherbes through the person of Blondel's sister-in-law, Madame Douet de Laboulaye, wife of a tax farmer. She had the confidence of the official who handled sovereign functions, such as tax-collecting, farmed out to private financiers. It was not enough to know these people, however. Etienne must dance attendance on them. He must accompany Madame Blondel to a concert where they might encounter the soprano Mlle. de Saint-Huberty, who was anxious to meet him and who could be useful. He must join an expedition to bend over the tomb of Rousseau at Ermenonville. He must be at the beck and call

of this climber of a d'Antraigues and accede gracefully to summonses like the following, one among dozens that assailed him:

> It is absolutely necessary that I see you tomorrow morning, my dear Montgolfier. Arrange to be at my house tomorrow morning at nine or ten o'clock. That's not all. You will not be able to return that evening to sleep at Monsieur Réveillon's, for at 8:30 I'll take you to a locale where you'll be very pleased to be. Blondel should be able to fix up your business on Tuesday. Under those circumstances, Madame Blondel and I think you'd better not be absent from Paris. Our friend Réveillon will surely think the same, and will not expect you to accompany him at a moment when your interests require your presence in Paris. . . . Adieu, my dear friend. Do not fail me tomorrow morning. It is altogether essential.[48]

Etienne had also to bespeak Desmarest's recollection of the latter's first visit to Annonay, when Etienne had displayed sheets of vellum, the surfaces as smooth as parchment, that he had recently perfected. Did Desmarest recall how they had been discussing the design of molds there before the fireplace, how both old Pierre and Matthieu Johannot were present, and how Etienne had replaced the wire sieve of conventional molds with mesh woven out of threaded brass? If so, would Desmarest kindly attest anew to his having initiated the product in France?[49] All these démarches succeeded in the end, and on 19 March Calonne notified Etienne of the award he coveted for Vidalon, being persuaded (according to the covering letter) that this added mark of favor would redouble his activity and zeal.[50] At the same time, the Johannots were let down with the striking of a bronze medal signifying commercial distinction. It was ever the wisdom of the old monarchy that worthy petitioners should be consoled with something.

The lilies of France might now be embossed above the doorway at Vidalon, and the porter might wear the royal livery. No member of the Montgolfier family other than Etienne took much interest in this particular honor, however. In vain Jean-Pierre had advised against what he thought an empty name that would only intensify jealousy. The designation had no pecuniary value, and had come to signify something similar to the appointment nowadays of certain products to the British monarch. Like a life peerage, it pertained to Etienne personally and was not transmissible to partners or heirs. That he set such store upon it gives a glimpse into the inwardness of his motivation, which was more complex than the simple service of vanity. Whatever he might tell himself and friends, the leadership he exerted among family and associates was somehow more intrinsic than the mere influence of a hardheaded businessman temporarily bent on public service.

No—what set Etienne apart was a kind of platonic aspiration for higher things, a drive for perfection that would not be denied. Felt by others, this was the quality that had led his father to single him out over his older brothers. That same power made them put up with the affronts he visited on those close to him when frustrated or thwarted. In this instance, nominal affecting of Vidalon to the crown accorded with his sense of the fitness of things. A spirit of didacticism pervaded the enlightenment of the 18th century, moral fervor masking itself as education. In keeping with this instinct, Etienne wished to make of Vidalon, not a spearhead of some unimagined industrialism, but a school, an institute of papermaking wherein competitors would become pupils graduating into colleagues, once they had learned the lessons of rationalization that no other establishment could impart so well.[51] Even the churlishness of his workers might—who could tell?—be abated in the light of reasoned practice. Already in effect was the stipulation that the Vidalon entrusted with introducing hollanders should be conducted as an open, model factory (though there is no evidence that it ever was).

Thus, it will seem less surprising than might otherwise appear that Etienne the promoter, rather than Joseph the inventor, turned out to be the zealot for whom aviation became a cause, dissimulate though he might and did. In the weeks after the flawed flight of the *Flesselles*, Joseph got a few grandiose remarks off his chest about taking service with Catherine the Great in Russia, and read a memoir about dirigibles before the Academy of Lyons.[52] Thereupon, he turned attention (in part by way of ideas for locomotion in balloons) back to his interests in heat and power, in typography, in chemistry, in machines in general. His remaining contribution to aviation, the impetus he gave to the parachute, derived from the rate of descent of the *Flesselles*, bordering on catastrophic, and from his collaboration with the marquis de Brantes on the one additional balloon that Joseph designed.

De Brantes was another of the noble butterflies taking wing in the wake of the *montgolfières*. He hailed from Avignon, where he had long known and admired Joseph's virtuosity. Excluded from the company aboard the Flesselles, he resolved to build and fly his own balloon, incorporating in the construction various improvements that Joseph imagined in the light of the experience at Lyons. The globe was much smaller, only forty-two feet in diameter, and Joseph recommended that de Brantes alone should take it aloft. Features of the design exhibited a greater sophistication than anything yet seen in hot-air balloons (Fig. 33). An improved suspension for the gondola increased stability. Instead of a great mouth gaping open at the bottom and spilling hot air at every tilt, the aperture consisted of a valve to be opened only when lifting force was called for. Its adjustability eased the strain on the fabric by making possible a gentler takeoff and a moderated acceleration upward. The heater, finally, was an adaptation of the chimney lamp invented by the Montgolfiers' great friend, Ami Argand, and perfected by Joseph.[53] Its fuel was a three-to-one mixture of olive oil and grain alcohol impregnating a circular wick of spun cotton. The principle was that of a convection draft, air for combustion being carried up through the center of the wick by means of an iron tube that acted as a blower. The opportunity to apply that device had been decisive in disposing Joseph to respond to de Brantes's initiative. He did not attend the flight itself.

No flight ever came off quite as planned. De

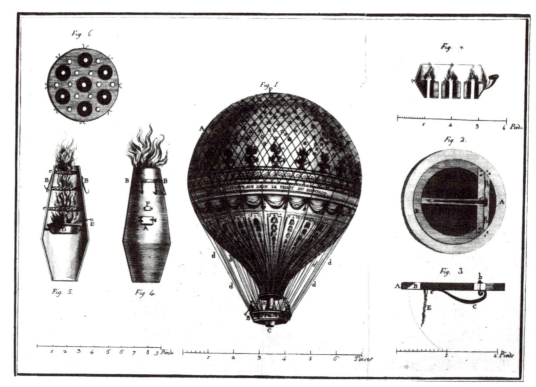

AÉROSTAT

Conſtruit par les ſoins du Marquis DE BRANTES, d'Avignon.

DEVISE PLACÉE SUR L'ÉQUATEUR.

LE génie eſt du Ciel le don le plus parfait ,
MONTGOLFIER qui l'obtint , maître de l'Empirée ,
M'entraîne ſur ſes pas à la voûte Ethérée ;
Et je rapporte aux Dieux le tribut du bienfait.

Par M. ARTAUD, ancien Rédacteur du Courier d'Avignon.

CET Aéroſtat, conſtruit en papier gros raiſin, ſoutenu par un reſeau de ruban de fil & doublé de papier brouillard , a été lancé de la maiſon de MM. les Céleſtins de Gentilly , près le Village de Sorgues , dans le Comtat, le 4 Avril 1784. Il s'eſt élevé dans l'eſpace de 7 minutes ¼ à la hauteur de 1000 toiſes, ſans autre feu que celui reſté dans le fourneau, lorſque les amis particuliers des Voyageurs ont témoigné leur crainte à ceux-ci, & les ont forcés de deſcendre de la galerie. Le Marquis DE BRANTES s'étoit propoſé de monter ſeul avec une galerie plus petite & la lampe, figure 6 & 7 , mais on l'obligea de donner parole qu'il ſe choiſiroit un Compagnon dans la perſonne de M. SCANEGATY , Phyſicien. Il fut dès-lors obligé de ſe ſervir d'une plus grande galerie & du fourneau, figure 4 & 5. Ce moyen néceſſita un plus grand poids, qui nuiſit enquelque ſorte à l'aſcenſion de l'Aéroſtat & au ſuccès de l'expérience. Le Ballon partit donc ſeul avec la galerie vuide & le fourneau, à la demande de tout le public, & au grand regret de M. DE BRANTES, que ſes amis s'efforcerent de retenir. La rapidité avec laquelle il s'éleva dans ce moment, ne laiſſa point de doute ſur la poſſibilité où il étoit d'enlever un plus grand poids. Faute de Pilote le Vaiſſeau Aérien eſt deſcendu, après la conſommation des combuſtibles, ſur un grand arbre, dont les branches l'ont entiérement détruit. Un léger vent de Nord-Oueſt ne lui avoit permis de s'éloigner du lieu de ſon départ que d'environ une demi lieue. (*)

EXPLICATION DES FIGURES

FIGURE I.

A Le Globe enflé dans tous ſes points , compoſé de 22 fuſeaux.
B La galerie en oſier de 2 pieds de largeur ſur 4 de hauteur , recouverte d'une toile peinte.
C Le fourneau ſuſpendu par 8 gros fils de fer au cercle du Globe , il traverſe la galerie dans ſon centre
DD Cordes au nombre de 22. Elles partent de la naiſſance du filet à l'équateur du Globe , & viennent s'attacher à des ganſes fixées autour de la galerie , pour la ſoutenir extérieurement.
EE Cordes ſervant à ſoutenir la galerie intérieurement ; elles partent du ſommet du Globe où elles ſont arrêtées , ſur le cercle extérieur de la ſoupape , & deſcendent le long des bords de chaque fuſeau juſqu'à l'ouverture. C'eſt ſur ces mêmes cordes que les fuſeaux ſont réunis entr'eux par une couture.
F Point où la ſoupape eſt fixée au Globe.

FIGURE II.

La ſoupape vue en deſſous.

FIGURE III.

Coupe de la ſoupape.
A Cercle extérieur ſur lequel viennent ſe réunir les pointes de chaque fuſeau , & les cordes qui le ſoutiennent.
B Cercle mouvant ſur les charnières bb , & repouſſé par le reſſort C. Le fond D eſt de papier collé ſur toile.
E Chaîne qui aboutit à la galerie par l'intérieur du Globe ; elle ſert à ouvrir la ſoupape au beſoin pour retarder une aſcenſion trop prompte , ou pour deſcendre ſubitement, &c.

FIGURE IV & V.

Coupe & élévation du fourneau en fer blanc battu, dont toutes les feuilles qui le compoſent ſont ſoudées, clouées & agraffées.
A Porte pour jetter les combuſtibles de pailles ou autres.
B Crochets qui ſervent à ſuſpendre le fourneau à l'ouverture du Globe.
C Cordes s'oppoſant au paſſage des flammeches qui pourroient être portées dans l'intérieur du Globe.
D Rechaud en fil de fer à claire voie , entouré d'une plaque de tôle ; le fond eſt en baſcule , agiſſant au moyen d'une chaîne E , qui répond à la porte du fourneau. Cette baſcule peut ſervir pour ſe dégager dans l'inſtant de tout ſon feu.
La petite porte F, figure 5 , ſert à jetter par intervalle quelques papiers huilés ſur la première grille afin d'entretenir dans le Globe une flamme toujours égale ſuſqu'à ce qu'il parvienne à la hauteur où l'on veut ſe ſoutenir.

FIGURE VI & VII.

Plan & coupe de la lampe en fer blanc, compoſée de 7 mèches de 6 pouces de diametre , perfectionnée d'après les conſeils de M. ARGANT. Les mèches ſont traverſées par un tube , où l'air venant en deſſous fait effet de ſoufflet dans le centre de la flamme , & donne à celle-ci une forte activité. Chaque mèche a

ſon porte-mèche & ſon éteignoir à charnière , pour n'en laiſſer allumées que la quantité néceſſaire à l'entretien du Globe , ſelon qu'on veut s'élever ou s'abaiſſer à volonté , & les éteindre toutes en cas de beſoin. La lampe eſt armée de huit doubles crochets en fil de fer , qui ſervent à la ſuſpendre au centre de l'ouverture du Globe. De la bonne huile d'olive , mêlangée avec un quart d'eſprit de vin , forme le combuſtible dont la lampe eſt remplie : les mèches ſont de cotonn filé.
La figure 6 repréſente le plan de la lampe , avec tous ſes ſoupiraux.
La figure 7 donne la coupe de la même lampe avec l'entonnoir latéral , ſervant à alimenter le combuſtible. On voit les ſoupiraux traverſant la flamme.
Cette lampe , ſoumiſe au jugement de M. JOSEPH DE MONTGOLFIER lors de ſon paſſage à Avignon, fut approuvée par ce célèbre Phyſicien , qui augura très-bien de ſon effet , & encouragea l'expérience de M. DE BRANTES , après avoir eu pluſieurs converſations avec lui , & l'avoir exhorté à ſe ſervir de cette lampe , & à monter ſeul dans la galerie. Cet avis , qu'il n'a pu ſuivre , a été un des principaux obſtacles à ſon voyage aérien.

PROPORTIONS DU GLOBE.

Diametre. . . . . 42 pieds.
Surface . . . . 5540 pieds.
Capacité. . . . . 38775 pieds.

POIDS QUE LE GLOBE AUROIT EU A PORTER

POUR L'ENLEVEMENT.

De deux perſonnes.		D'une ſeule perſonne.	
Globe	170 llv.	Globe . . . . : .	170 llv.
Cordes & filet	90	Filet & cordes	90
Soupape & cercle	50	Soupape & cercle	50
Uſtenſile , Baromètre , &c.	50	Uſtenſile , barometre, &c.	50
Fourneau	50	Lampe toute garnie	120
Grande galerie	00	Huile & eſprit de vin pour alimenter . .	25
Combuſtible en papier huilé	00	Petite galerie	60
Les deux Voyageurs environ	00	Un Voyageur ſeul	150
	1.40		895

33. The de Brantes balloon with Argand burner

Brantes scheduled his ascension for Monday 29 March 1784 in the park belonging to a Celestine convent near the village of Sorgues in the Comtat Venaissin. Torrential rain forced postponement, at first until the Thursday. The delay allowed meddlers to interfere. The Comtat was an enclave surrounding Avignon and also under papal sovereignty. On the Wednesday a nuncio arrived bearing an order from the vice-legate forbidding the flight. Someone had warned the authorities that the paint decorating the globe was inflammable. Just as de Brantes straightened that out, he was served with a second injunction prohibiting him on grounds of safety from flying alone. Compliance required substituting a heater of greater capacity for the Argand lamp. Reluctantly, de Brantes chose a companion, one Scanegaty, a local physics teacher.

The weather was ideal on Sunday 4 April— Palm Sunday. An immense crowd gathered. For some reason its psychology amplified the official anxieties, and the mood settled into one of concern for the safety of the aeronauts rather than the more normal impatience over delay that often sharpened into thirst for blood. De Brantes began inflating his globe at noon. He soon realized that the substitute heater was failing to generate enough force to lift two men. Accordingly, he reverted to the original plan and asked Scanegaty to dismount. With that, the public became his collective protector. Nearby spectators began to weep and to beseech him to relent. The chief dissuaders brought forward his wife and children, whose tears and pre-orphaned sobs added pathos to the general lamentation. De Brantes had no choice but to desist, lest he appear an unnatural monster. Neither could he let Scanegaty risk what was forbidden to him. There was nothing for it but to launch the aircraft on an unmanned flight. It performed as well as might be, rising to an altitude of 2,000 fathoms and coming to grief half a league distant in the branches of a great tree. The servants and farmers on de Brantes's estate nearby bewailed its passage, thinking their master lost to his dependents. But however heartwarming, the experiment was far from answering to the expectations that de Brantes and Joseph had formed.[54]

Among their intentions was development of parachutes. The letter in which de Brantes reported to Joseph on the near-fiasco of his beautifully engineered aircraft concludes with a drawing and a discussion of a parachute (Fig. 34). He asked Joseph's opinion of the proportions, since the two of them had collaborated on experiments with similar devices several weeks previously in Avignon. The sketch shows the profile of an open parachute twenty-two feet in diameter together with the detail of one of the twelve panels comprising the surface.

Joseph himself described those experiments in a letter to Etienne of 24 March. Evidently, their model was a smaller one, seven to eight feet in diameter across the open bottom. A dozen seven-foot cords attached a sturdy wicker basket to the hemisphere of fabric. Four inflatable pig's bladders were fastened underneath the carrier to cushion the shock of impact. Leading a sheep, he and de Brantes climbed with this contraption to the top of the highest of the towers surmounting the papal palace. There they were a hundred feet above the level of the pavement. With the animal in the basket, the whole affair weighed fifty pounds. Joseph balled the bundle into a compact mass and hurled it from the parapet with all his strength. It fell like a plummet for about fifty feet. The chute then opened and its passenger drifted gently down into the street, where it scrambled free and ran off, baa, baa, into the crowd. Spectators caught the creature, caressing it and making much of it, and brought it along with the parachute back to the palace.

Joseph and de Brantes repeated the experiment five or six times, always with equal success. The sheep showed no ill effects, and de Brantes, writing about the disappointment of his own flight, assured Joseph that it was still in fine fettle two weeks later. Joseph meanwhile had written Etienne urging his brother to have several parachutes made for the new balloon the latter was building. A spread twenty feet in diameter, he calculated, would let a man down gently from any height. Twenty-five ells of silk would suffice for each, and the cost would be about ten louis the parachute. The cords should be attached one or two feet above the lower rim at the seams that

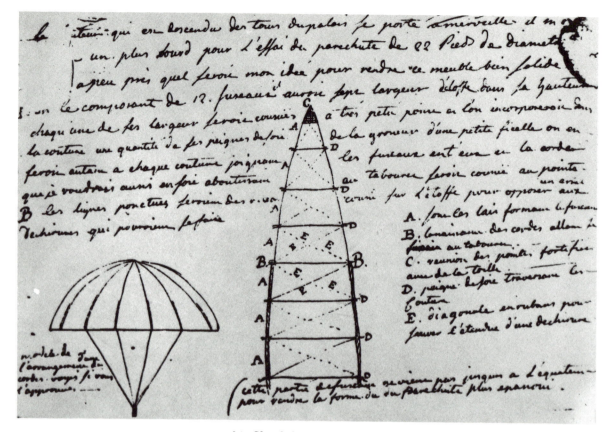

34. Sketch for the parachute

joined the panels. The specifications, even to that for an auxiliary cord to assure opening, are essentially those of the de Brantes sketch. With such instruments, observed Joseph to Etienne, you could "rain a whole army into a city, just as we've been raining sheep."[55]

Writing to his brother, Joseph affected to have derived the idea of the parachute from abstract aerostatical considerations of conservation of momentum. In fact, priority in the invention belongs rather to an obscure mechanic and clockmaker of Montpellier, Louis-Sebastien Le Normand. Le Normand had read a fanciful travel book which told of an Oriental potentate whose slaves entertained him by leaping from a considerable height while slowing their fall by parasols. Why not? he evidently thought, for on 26 November 1783 Le Normand took two thirty-inch parasols, rein-

forced the stays, and jumped off a height of one story. He landed with only a jar, and tried further experiments with weights, cats, and dogs in the presence of numerous spectators.[56]

Among those present was a physicist, the abbé Bertholon, known for writings on medical electricity, lightning rods, and other topics of natural philosophy. Bertholon was the type who took things up. He made much of the parachute in a book on ballooning and aerostatics in general that came out later in 1784.[57] A reader might take away the impression that the idea had been his. Joseph for his part certainly knew of Le Normand's experiments. He was in Montpellier in early March 1784, and Le Normand later said that Joseph approved of the word "parachute." Joseph has consequently been reproached for not recognizing the true author.[58] Probably he never thought of it, however. He was nearing the end of his own involvement with aviation. He published very little on any of his own inventions, and that little many years later.

At any rate, he never claimed credit himself for discovering the parachute, unless his letters to Etienne are to be read that way. The idea became known through the writings of Bertholon, and the actuality through demonstrations at the hands of the epigones of flight. On 4 June 1785 Jean-Pierre Blanchard let a dog float down from a balloon flying over Paris. The first human jump, also into Paris, came long after. On 22 October 1797 Andre-Jacques Garnerin leapt from his balloon at an altitude of 700 meters and alighted in what is now the Parc Monceau (Fig. 35).[59]

By then the Montgolfiers had put flight far behind, and let us return to Etienne and what he had imagined at the outset. For his vision of the future of aviation was very different from the extravaganza that ensued throughout 1785. Two conditions had to be met before flight could satisfy more than curiosity and thrill-seeking. First, balloons must become navigable like boats, or "dirigeable" to use the contemporary adjective since Anglicized into the noun for blimps and zeppelins. Second, if airships were to have a claim on the resources needed for their development, they must be proved capable of serving the ends of commerce. Etienne thought both these objects within reach. But the government—and here the voice might equally be Joseph's—must enlarge its thinking.[60]

Etienne gave the Ministry of Finance one of two choices, corresponding to the estimates he had mentioned in scolding the abbé. The first, which he described as economical, would cost 50,000 livres. Its success, though sure, would be slow. With such a subsidy, he would construct an aerostat to carry seven or eight people with sufficient food and fuel to remain aloft for long periods. Their mission would be to station themselves at various altitudes and locations in order to determine wind patterns. From adequate data a structure of meteorological theory could be deduced that would permit mastery of the elements instead of subjection to their caprices. The crews,

moreover, would gain experience. For, true to his temperament, Etienne also imagined founding a school for aeronauts.[61]

In Etienne's view, however, only his alternative proposal firmly grasped fortune by the forelock. The expense would be 100,000 livres, but success would be rapid and would take the form of returning a profit on the operation. Given a subsidy on that scale, he would build a flying machine big enough and sturdy enough to transport merchandise from one end of France to the other.[62]

At no time did Etienne, the businessman supposedly ruled by balance sheets, show the slightest sympathy for the plight of ministers responsible for a government in deepening financial trouble—unless his admission that in their place he too would temporize is to be so construed. That was probably an expression of his own ambivalence, however, which was such that he never dared commit himself fully to his beliefs and hopes. "The fruit would be beautiful," he wrote the abbé in mid-February, "but it's not for us, and we'll be dead before the sun of practice and experiment will have ripened it. It's a tree planted for our nephews." Yet he would spare no effort: "I'll neglect nothing that lies within my power."[63]

Instead of accepting one of these bold initiatives, or refusing both, Calonne accorded the balloon project a kind of holding grant, a mere 8,000 livres.[64] The amount was scarcely more than Etienne had expended on the three machines he had built during the previous autumn. The Réveillon fiasco, the Versailles spectacular, and the passenger balloon of la Muette had cost 6,579 livres, 13 sous, and 5 deniers.[65] Of that sum only 6,000 livres had been reimbursed by the royal grant of December 1783. Even so, Etienne did not spurn the 8,000 livres (as Joseph in disgust urged him to do).[66] Lowering his sights, he resolved to do what he could with those funds, convinced that the only way to get the government to cover the existing deficit was to accept its terms.

These constraints threw Etienne back on achieving a measure of direction by mechanical means. He did not despair of thus supplementing

EXPÉRIENCE DU PARACHÛTE.

Le 1.er Brumaire an 6. (22. Octobre 1797. v.S.) à 5.h 28.m du soir, le citoyen Garnerin, s'éleva à ballon perdu au parc de Monceau, un morne silence regnoit dans l'assemblée, l'intérêt et l'inquiétude étoient peints sur les visages. Lorsqu'il eut dépassé la hauteur de 330 Toises, il coupa la corde qui joignoit son parachûte et son char avec l'aérostat, ce dernier fit une explosion et le parachûte sous lequel le C. Garnerin étoit placé descendit très rapidement, il prit un mouvement d'oscillation si effrayant qu'un cri d'épouvante échappa aux spectateurs, et des femmes sensibles se trouvèrent mal. Cependant le C. Garnerin descendit dans la plaine de Monceau, il monta à cheval sur le champ, et revint au parc de Monceau au milieu d'une foule immense qui marquoit son admiration pour le premier qui ait osé entreprendre cette expérience hazardeuse, il en avoit Talent, et le courage de ce jeune Aéronaute. En effet le C. Garnerin est le conçu le projet dans les prisons de Bude, en Hongrie, où il fut longtems prisonnier d'Etat à la suite du sanglant combat de Marchienne, en 1793. j'Allai annoncer ce succès à l'Institut National qui étoit assemblé, et l'on m'entendit avec un extrème intérêt. Lalande .

à Paris, chez l'Auteur rue Nicaise au coin de celle Honoré N.o 497.

35.

the major hope, which was improved weather prediction. On the contrary, he first mentioned a propeller in a letter to Joseph late in December 1783. Might a little windmill—a "moulinette"— be mounted in the gondola and be turned by a crank, giving the aircraft the same force that a wind would have generated in revolving the sails at equal speed in the opposite direction?[67] Joseph was then amid the stress of mounting the Flesselles, but he found time to return a careful answer. Its tenor is another instance of the reversal of roles through which he became the realist relative to the future of aviation and Etienne the visionary. Meanwhile, Etienne had also mentioned the idea of oars. Don't think of it, wrote Joseph. He had carefully considered the question, and was persuaded that no such contrivance could win a mechanical advantage that would compensate for its own weight together with the load imposed by men and provisions.[68]

Never one to be merely negative, Joseph had at the same time imagined an alternative method. Pilots might deform a slack balloon in one sector by manipulating a harness of ropes, and then achieve a reactive impulse by reinflating and letting the dent spring back into form. The paper he read before the Academy of Lyons in November had developed a reaction scheme of a different sort.[69] A balloon might be provided with lateral vents through which a pilot could release bursts of hot air, achieving a jet effect. In general, however, Joseph was more firmly persuaded than his brother that only a reliable knowledge of wind patterns would ever permit balloonists to choose directions. He was dismayed, he wrote, at the talk of cross-Channel flights and trusted that Etienne would warn anyone contemplating such folly of the dangers. In less dire vein, he also hoped that Etienne would not make them look foolish by persisting with these chimerical designs.[70]

Etienne took encouragement from a more analytical quarter. Locomotion was the first problem to which Meusnier addressed himself on being named staff member of the renewed commission on aeronautics. On 14 January he read a memoir before the Academy comparing the effects of oars pulled against the resistance of water and of air.

He found that surfaces of equal area should have triple the relative effect in balloons that they do in boats, since the ratio of the weight of the vessel to that of the oars was much less in aircraft.[71] On the strength of that, and ignoring his brother's more intuitive advice, Etienne abandoned the part of balloon-builder for a time and came forward like Meusnier in the guise of engineer. Throughout the last two weeks of January and all of February, he devoted the time he could salvage from lobbying to working out a mathematical analysis of the problem of rowing a balloon (Fig. 36).

On 6 March Etienne appeared before the Academy to read his memoir "Sur la théorie des rames appliquées aux machines aérostatiques."[72] To follow his reasoning will be worthwhile light exercise in 18th-century engineering mechanics and will exhibit the extent of his competence and ingenuity. The model analyzed is a balloon moving at uniform velocity relative to the surrounding medium under the impulsion of a pair of oars (sometimes he says wings) beating at a steady pace. From hydraulic engineering Etienne adopted the convention that resistance to the passage of such a vessel is the same as it would be to a plane surface two-thirds the area of the largest cross section perpendicular to the direction of motion. He then designated by

a this surface of resistance,
b the total effective area of the oar-blades,
V the velocity of the balloon,
u the velocity of the center of impulse of the blades.

Resistances are as the squares of velocities, and since at uniform velocity, resistance to passage of the balloon equals that to the stroke of the blades,

$$(a\,V^2) = b\,(u - V^2),$$

and

$$V = u\,(\sqrt{b}\,/\,\sqrt{a} + \sqrt{b}) \qquad (1)$$

This velocity is sustained by the force (f) that the oarsmen expend at rate or speed γ, and the product γf is the quantity of action.

The modern reader may pause to notice that this quantity has the dimensions of kinetic energy—mass times velocity squared. Etienne ex-

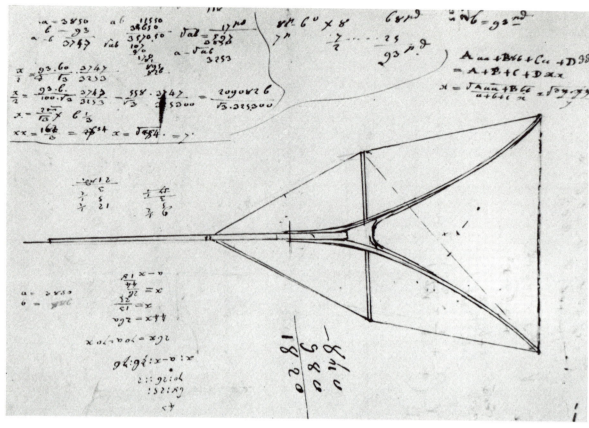

36. Etienne's sketch of an oar, or sweep, to propel a balloon

plicitly recognized that no arrangement of machinery could increase the yield from a given quantity of action. What in later times would be called work, he expressed in terms of the height to which the quantity of action measured by the velocity of the blades is capable of raising unit mass. That is given by the formula $(u - V)^2/2\,g$, where g is the velocity acquired by freely falling bodies at the end of the first second. In order to evaluate air resistance, Etienne adopted another widely observed convention, which equated it to the weight of a column of air with its base equal to the resisted surface and its height the same as that to which the velocity of the moving surfaces would raise unit mass. If Φ is the weight of a cubic foot of air, the resistance will then be given by the formula $(u - v^2)\,\Phi\,b/2\,g$, which yields the equation

$$\gamma f = (u - V)^2\,\Phi\,b\,u/2\,g \qquad (2)$$

By substituting for u the value obtained from equation (1), this becomes

$$\gamma f = a\,\Phi\,V^3\,(\sqrt{a} + \sqrt{b})/2\,g\,\sqrt{b} \qquad (3)$$

from which follows

$$V = \sqrt[3]{\frac{2\,\gamma f g\,\sqrt{b}}{a\,\Phi\,(\sqrt{a} + \sqrt{b})}} \qquad (4)$$

Equation (4) gives the velocity of the balloon in terms of quantity of action, surface of resistance, and surface of the oar-blades. It was particularly gratifying that this value varied only as the sixth root of the combined surface of the blades. What would otherwise have been unwieldy sweeps could thus in principle be limited to a workable size without much reducing the speed of the aircraft.

In order to apply his theory to numerical examples, Etienne drew on a famous memoir of 1753 by Daniel Bernoulli analyzing the effects on ships of agents auxiliary to the wind. Bernoulli varied the factors of force, rate, and fatigue to arrive at formulas for estimating the maximum work that oarsmen could perform over given periods of time.[73] Etienne for his part took it as experimentally established that a rower moving the handle of an oar at two-and-a-half feet per second makes an effort equivalent to lifting twenty pounds. That he is in fact working only half the time, or during the power stroke, allows a 50 percent margin for absorbing losses to friction and other imponderables. If each stroke is three feet long, the beat will be twenty-five per minute. Substituting these values into his equations, Etienne calculated the expected speed of a balloon seventy feet in diameter propelled by a pair of oars each with a blade of one hundred square feet and a shaft twenty-two feet long pivoted four feet from the handle. It would make 994 fathoms, or about 2,000 yards an hour.

A second example solves the expressions for a balloon twenty-six feet in diameter moved by oars forty-nine square feet in surface. This smaller craft would travel at 2,249 fathoms or about 4,500 yards per hour.

Etienne's memoir was one of dozens on the problem of dirigibles submitted to the Academy amid the general enthusiasm for flight in the first six months of 1784. The permanent secretary, Condorcet, named a serious trio of commissioners, Coulomb, Bossut, and Leroi. They gave Etienne good marks, bringing in their report within the week and recommending that his piece be published in the collection called *Savants étrangers*.[74] It never was, perhaps because Faujas printed it forthwith in the sequel to his *Description* of the early ventures in aviation.

All the while Etienne was making calculations for the design of his fourth balloon.[75] A sketch for what he dreamed of building survives (Fig. 37). It would have been a splendid aircraft, 108 feet in lateral diameter, furnished with a roomy gondola, and capable of crossing the English Channel. Alas, construction was out of the ques-

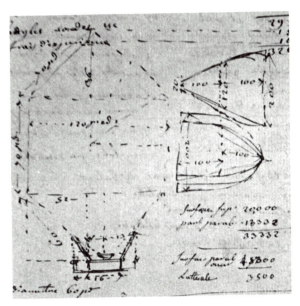

37. Sketch for a cargo balloon by Etienne de Montgolfier

tion on a meager subsidy. Early on, Réveillon wanted Etienne to compromise and make two smaller balloons to provide a backup in case of accident. That, too, would have overtaxed the grant, and Etienne had vowed to risk no more family money in aerostatics.[76] The machine he did build in the weeks following his appearance before the Academy was still a considerable affair. Eventually it made a fine appearance, thanks largely to the decoration by Réveillon. The latter continued the hospitality of his factory and also participated in the design.[77] His was the proposal that the dome be flattened and the top segments made of leather instead of cloth, the better to withstand the upward thrust of the lifting force inside. Etienne adopted that idea, which accorded with his own preference for an elongated shape. Completed in early May, the new balloon measured seventy-four feet in diameter at its greatest width and eighty-six feet in height. The profile tapering down from an umbrellalike upper surface was suggestive of a medusa or jellyfish floating quietly. The effect was somehow more sedate than the globular assertiveness of its predecessors had been. Named for the queen, it was launched on Wednesday 23 June in front of the chateau at Versailles (Plate XI).

"Marie-Antoinette" was floated, however, without Etienne, who had returned to Vidalon earlier in the month. Amid the gathering frustration of the winter and spring of 1784, his correspondence often recurs from time to time to the prospect of leaving Réveillon to oversee fabrication, of returning home, and of picking up the threads of business. In finally acting on this impulse, he never acknowledged that he half-thought thereby to convince the government of his indispensability and to loosen its purse strings as the price of getting him back. He merely sent Réveillon instructions to disassemble the new machine and to crate the parts for shipment pending word.[78] Nevertheless, the most plausible construction that can be placed on the letters with which he afterward—in July and August—bombarded Laboulaye, Malesherbes, Castries, and Calonne is that he much wanted to be recalled.[79] He wanted to be persuaded that the public interest required sacrificing his preference for family, privacy, and paper, and to be told that the funds were his if he would undertake the grand-scale mission he had defined. Equally clearly, his real friends—Réveillon, d'Antraigues, Argand—thought him unwise thus to leave the scene of action.[80]

Events soon proved them right. Pilatre was availability itself and the first name on the lips of all Paris when flying was the topic. On Monday 14 June a marshal from the controller general appeared at the Réveillon factory with an order informing all concerned that the king intended the balloon to be demonstrated the following week, on the 21st. Pilatre de Rozier was to be the pilot and would take delivery forthwith. Réveillon was in the country when this summons was served. That same evening Pilatre did come round and had the three bales containing the balloon moved to a warehouse in the Place de la Porte Saint-Antoine.[81]

Clearly, members of the royal family had remained unmoved by Etienne's elaborate views on the long-run prospects for aviation. Their own thoughts scarcely went beyond the entertainment they wished to stage in order to dazzle a notable visitor. Under the name comte de Haga, King Gustav III of Sweden was then making one of the ostentatiously incognito tours affected by 18th-century royalty. Nephew of Frederick the Great, Francophile, idol of enlightened society, he wanted to see a balloon, and Marie-Antoinette wanted to show him one. It went down badly at Versailles that he should have passed first by Lyons, where local enthusiasts mounted a flight in his honor on 4 June. Joseph de Montgolfier had nothing to do with the "Gustav," as the craft had to be called. His erstwhile passenger, the comte de Laurencin, was a principal source of funds, and the impresario was a painter called Fleurant. The ascension went off much better than the demonstration of the Flesselles had done, and was chiefly remarkable for the presence aboard of a female aeronaut, a noted Lyonnais beauty called Madame Trible. This time Laurencin gallantly ceded the place he had thought to occupy.[82]

When Etienne left Paris, he knew of the royal desire to entertain Gustav III. His absence, observed Réveillon later, made a bad impression at Versailles.[83] The king's order commandeering the balloon permitted no evasion, but Réveillon did all he could to defend the integrity of his friend's creation. He required Pilatre to return the machine to his own work yard as a condition of overseeing the reassembling and decorating. The outcome, he feared, was bound to be damaging for Etienne in one way or another. If the flight succeeded, Pilatre would reap the credit. If it failed, the design would get the blame.

The flight went very well. Pilatre refused the services of the marquis de Dampierre, the "Monsieur Henri" of the Flesselles, and chose a scientist for companion.[84] A chemist, Joseph Proust gave courses in his Musée in the rue de Valois. He is known to the history of chemistry for the Law of Definite Proportions, stated in 1794 when he was in service in Segovia, where he made most of his career. After two days of waiting for good weather, Pilatre and Proust took off before the court and assembled royalty at 4:45 in the afternoon of 23 June. Present were Etienne's uncle and aunt, the Jacques Montgolfiers, in the company of Réveillon, his wife, and their daughter Céleste.

Réveillon wrote Etienne an account of the departure early the next morning, before he knew whether there had been a safe landing.[85] To all appearances, Pilatre had handled the aircraft skillfully. Striving for altitude, he disappeared through the clouds, high though the cover was, and remained hidden from view for seven or eight minutes. If so much fuel had not gone into that, Pilatre later said, he could have traveled a long distance.[86] As it was, after forty-five minutes he came down twelve leagues to the northwest in a glade in the forest of Chantilly. Nearby is the château that was the seat of the king's cousin, the prince de Condé. Having watched the approach, their serene highnesses hurried thither through the woods in the company of several retainers. All joined in witnessing the *procès-verbal*. The forest is now parkland, and the site is still called the carréfour Pilatre de Rozier.

The same accident occurred there as had marred the landing of the la Muette machine and the Flesselles. Embers in the heater set the gondola on fire. When the blaze was extinguished, the travelers were hurried back to the château for refreshments and sent off in a carriage to Versailles. In the excitement the deflated fabric of "Marie-Antoinette" lay unguarded for a time. Villagers were free to vandalize before anyone thought to gather up the remains.[87]

Réveillon again moved rapidly to protect what was left of his friend's interests. He foresaw that Pilatre, not content with identifying the exploit wholly with himself, would also move to recover the wreckage for repair and future exhibitions. Accordingly, Réveillon immediately set about securing authority from the controller general to repossess all that had been salvaged.[88] Only about half the original yardage remained undamaged. Réveillon then further got permission to pack and send it off to Etienne at Vidalon, an operation he completed in mid-August.[89]

A letter Pilatre wrote Etienne purporting to acquiesce in these arrangements goes far to justify the suspicions about his good faith that grew in all who had to do with him. Echoing the abbé and Joseph in Lyons, Réveillon and d'Antraigues now joined in warning Etienne of machinations

tending toward a takeover. And indeed, when Pilatre's letters are read in sequence, the evolution of the tone and terms recalls to mind the character of Uriah Heep. In early October 1783, Etienne is "My dear Master." Following the tethered tests in that month, a jocular familiarity still knows how to keep its place, and throughout November and December, he is alternately "My dear Captain" and "My dear Admiral." After the Flesselles flight in January, notoriety advanced Pilatre's standing in just those fashionable circles where Etienne was perforce paying court, and Pilatre addressed him an invitation as "My dear Brother." Now, writing of the "Marie-Antoinette" on 30 July—over a month after the event!—Pilatre began abruptly and got around to a salutation only in mid-sentence: "I follow your orders, my dear Master, and am sending the details you request. . . ."

Thereupon, the manner partakes of intimacy, flattery, and insolence. Pilatre affects to take pleasure in the laurels he has won solely for the adornment they bring to Etienne's image. He would have been infinitely complimented by the success of the experiment if only Etienne had presided in person over its execution. The brothers Robert, by contrast, had just run a flight at Saint-Cloud (of which more in a moment) "with all the ignorance of a pupil in physics." They had also (Etienne should know) permitted themselves, and specially the elder, conceited and injurious remarks about "my best friend." Initially, the controller general had decided that "Marie-Antoinette" would be returned to him, Pilatre. But after Réveillon's representations, and Etienne's own letter to the minister, "I decided"—thus Pilatre—"to send it back to you."[90]

In fact, of course, the controller general had already decided that, but little else went Etienne's way in Paris. His papers contain several drafts of a letter to Calonne regretting his absence from the demonstration for King Gustav and excusing himself on the grounds of urgent business and straitened circumstances. By now Etienne's regrets were real enough.[91] The dilapidation of his machine had reduced him to begging the Ministry of Finance for funds to restore it to a serviceable condition there in his own establishment at Annonay. That would require 12,000 livres, he estimated. Should a grant be forthcoming, he and his brother would eagerly concentrate their energies on the further development of aerostatics with a view to realizing its utility.[92]

It may be surmised that all the scheming and importunity would have wearied the responsible officials, even if Etienne had not offended the court by playing Achilles in his tent, and even if financial stringency had not placed the government in a worse situation, relatively speaking, than the Montgolfier family. As it was, there was clearly no chance of a favorable response. Early in October, an inspector of finance, one De la Roche, replied to Etienne's renewed request, and rather curtly. The controller general had read his last letter and had determined to appropriate no further money for aerostatical experiments.[93]

A less tenacious man than Etienne would have taken that as final. For a time he did perforce subside there in Vidalon, meditating and calculating before resuming the offensive for commercial aviation some two years later, in 1786. In the interval he participated only vicariously in the experiments and stunts conducted in quite a different spirit in Paris and throughout Europe. Already on 25 February 1784, the young nobleman Paolo Andreani had piloted the first flight outside of France, taking off from his property of Moncuco near Milan. Our history concerns the Montgolfier connection, however, and not all aviation or its popularization. We shall limit ourselves to a summary account of the flights involving the main actors in their story, therefore, drawing in large part on what Etienne knew of the episodes as it is reflected in his correspondence.

1. THE BARNSTORMERS

At noontime on 2 March 1784 Etienne was once again in the Champ de Mars amid a throng gathered to observe the experiment of a competitor, Jean-Pierre Blanchard, who once again was employing the competing system of inflammable air.[1] The spirit of the occasion, however, was very different from anything that had gone before. In Blanchard we meet with the first of the barnstormers. He put on numerous ascensions—it is disputed whether the eventual number was fifty-nine or sixty—before his death of natural causes in 1809. Is he to be called a professional aviator? At all events, he flew, he flew for a living, and he had no other means of support. His widow, the first woman to solo, assumed the mantle for another ten years and made sixty-seven flights before falling into Paris amid flames, victim of her practice of varying the spectacle by setting off fireworks from the gondola (Fig. 38).

An inventor born in Les Andelys on the border of Normandy in 1759, Blanchard dreamed of making flying machines all the while that as a young mechanic he had to work on hydraulic devices. In 1781, two years before the Annonay experiment, he constructed a mechanical would-be bird with four lifting wings fore and aft and four propellent wings amidships, all spring-driven. He later acknowledged that the success of the Montgolfiers convinced him of the futility of this approach. He followed Charles and the Roberts, however, in preferring hydrogen to hot air.

On 5 February 1784 Blanchard announced his intention of launching a flight on the 28th of the month and offered tickets for sale.[2] A more efficient gas generator than Charles and Robert had employed for their ascension from the Tuileries was the signal contribution of Blanchard's initial

venture. He enlisted the services of a firm of industrial chemists, Messrs. Vallet and Alban, manufacturers of acids and alkalis at Javelle. Vallet built him an apparatus in the form of a ring of ten pairs of barrels. Substitutions of pieces of sheet iron for filings smoothed out the action of sulfuric acid. The globe was twenty-six feet in diameter, and Vallet filled it in twenty-seven hours, a contrast to the three-day battle waged by Charles and Robert to inflate their balloon using a similar apparatus in the Tuileries. Later modifications reduced the time to two hours.[3]

The Blanchard airship included an ever-open parachute attached to the suspension cords, a rudder, and a motor in the form of double-bladed paddles swiveled to rotate vertically on either side of the gondola and worked by a treadle (Fig. 39). Launching had to be put over to 2 March. As subscribers gathered, Blanchard completed his preparations with the help of the intended co-pilot, a Benedictine physicist called Dom Pech. They were ready shortly before the appointed hour of noon. Just then a teen-age cadet, Dupont de Chambon, burst out of the Ecole Militaire demanding to be taken aloft. Rebuffed, he drew his sword and wounded Blanchard in the hand. In the scuffle, barometers, thermometers, and telescopes were broken, together with the mechanism for revolving the propellers.

Bleeding but undaunted, Blanchard resolved to salvage what he could and took off with his companion for a flight at the mercy of the elements. Alas, the buffeting had also taken its toll of hydrogen. The balloon labored under the weight of two people. Blanchard was obliged to put down almost immediately and Dom Pech to disembark. Thereupon, the remaining buoyancy sufficed to carry Blanchard to an altitude estimated at 12,500 feet. He felt dazed by the cold and by the rare-

*M.S. Blanchard Célèbre Aéronaute
au moment de son ascension aérienne suivie à Turin
Le Soir du 26. avril 1812*

38. Madame Blanchard rising above Turin in 1812

39. Blanchard's first balloon, launched from the Champ de Mars, 2 March 1784

faction of the air. He also felt hungry and ate a slice of pâté.

Later, Blanchard pretended to have jury-rigged a sail with the slack fabric in the lower reaches of his balloon and to have tacked against the wind with the auxiliary device of waggling his rudder. Faujas and others were coolly unconvinced by this claim. In fact, Blanchard was carried hither and thither by contrary air currents at different altitudes. Ultimately, he described a rough spiral and landed after an hour and a quarter in the plain of Billancourt, the equivalent of two kilometers from the Champ de Mars.[4] Etienne wrote home about the near-fiasco.[5] He also exchanged correspondence with the famous lawyer and chemist, Guyton de Morveau, about the elaborate aircraft that the latter constructed and tried on 25 April in Dijon under the auspices of the Academy of that city, whose most prominent member Guyton was.[6]

Etienne took some interest, finally, in preparations for the one experiment in Paris that proved a total fiasco and turned aerostatics into a subject of ridicule for a time. The promoters were a professor of physics in the capital, the abbé Miollan, and an associate called Janinet. As bad luck would have it, their choice fell upon hot air rather than hydrogen. They proposed to construct a very large montgolfière, 112 feet high by 84 feet in diameter, to demonstrate both capacity for loads and dirigibility. Locomotion was to be achieved by jets of hot air released by the pilot through portholes incorporated in the globe at angles of 90° to each other. Experiments with the balloon tethered in the gardens of the Observatory on 17 and 30 June 1784 succeeded admirably. In the second round, the airship carried nine people weighing in all 1,300 pounds, together with ballast of sacks of stones adding another 669 pounds. Twenty laborers were needed to hold her captive.[7]

All optimism, Miollan and Janinet enlarged the globe by another 40,000 cubic feet and scheduled the public demonstration for ticket-holders on 11 July in the garden of the Luxembourg at high noon. Both Réveillon and Meusnier were present and wrote Etienne accounts of the humiliation. It was a broiling day, and humid, with the thermometer at 28° R (87° Fahrenheit). The balloon simply would not inflate. For three hours the unfortunate impresarios struggled with heater and huge, shapeless bag. In vain. The throng, reported Réveillon, was the largest ever.[8] Impatient murmuring turned to anger in the heat of a stifling afternoon, and finally spectators who had paid for a show fell upon the hapless machine, dismantling it in a trice and forcing promoters and crew to take to their heels. Miollan and Janinet escaped with their lives, but not with their dignity, which was the butt of innumerable lampoons transforming them into a cat (miaou, miaou) and an ass (âne) (Fig. 40).

Meusnier attributed the disaster to their having followed Etienne's example in eliminating the clumsy masts between which the empty bags were at first suspended, but failing to replace them with a leather cap or superstructure to give the limp fabric some initial spread.[9] Two years later

Miollan was still appealing to Etienne to come to the defense of his battered reputation with testimonials that the design had been sound and the excessive heat the culprit.[10] The successful experiments at the Observatory had both occurred at five o'clock in the morning with the thermometer at 9° R (about 51° Fahrenheit). Etienne answered kindly from Vidalon agreeing and observing that combustion was less efficient the higher the temperature, that the differential between internal and external density would have been much reduced, and that the proportion of fixed air (carbon dioxide) in the products of combustion would have been higher and a further drag.[11]

However that may have been, the disaster may be taken as a convincing early instance of the merit of staging ascensions in the cool of the early dawn.

2. AERONAUTICAL ENGINEERING

In point of theory and design the most meticulous of the accompanying developments was the series of investigations that Meusnier put in hand under the aegis of the Academy of Science. Meusnier—it will be recalled—was the lieutenant of engineers whom Faujas had engaged to coordinate the tracking of the first *charlière* on 27 August

40.

LA MONTAGNE ACCOUCHANT D'UNE SOURIS
ou la Prophetie accomplie dans le Luxembourg

L'An mil sept cent quatre vingt quatre
Un Chat miaulant, faisant le Diable à quatre
    Mettra l'allerte dans Paris.
On verra l'animal tellement se debattre
Qu'une Montagne en toille et Papier gris
    Accouchera d'une Souris.
Se vend A Paris chez Bligni cour des Thuillerie.

Ce qui devra bien plus surprendre,
C'est qu'aulieu de monter, quoique fait à ce prix
On verra la Montagne honteusement descendre
Et malgré vingt essais, sermens et beaux écrits
Se trouver par le Peuple à l'instant mise en cendre :
Voila ce qu'a grands frais et surtout en payant
    Vous fera voir ce Chat miaulant.

1783. He was the brightest and best of the pupils schooled mathematically by Monge.[12] Already a correspondent and technological consultant of the Academy, Meusnier had been drawn into collaboration with Lavoisier before the end of 1783 and had designed a pair of gasometers for use in the latter's experiments on the composition of water. We have already noticed how the central line of Lavoisier's research into the nature of combustion intersected with the beginnings of aviation. On 24 June 1783, a few days before word of the Annonay balloon reached Paris, Lavoisier (in cooperation with Laplace) had succeeded in synthesizing several droplets of water by sparking a jet of hydrogen mixed with air in a closed flask.

Over the next several months, Lavoisier perfected the demonstration for the ceremonial public meeting of the Academy on 12 November. Since Monge had made the same discovery independently (and Cavendish before either of them), Lavoisier's special touch is more evident in its exploitation.[13] As always, his strategy called for confirmation of synthesis by quantitative analysis, and he needed a method for decomposing water in order to show that its elements were those from which he had compounded it. At the same time prospects for aviation had greatly increased interest in the properties and production of hydrogen for its own sake. Might not water be more economical and tractable a source from which to extract the light gas on a large scale than was sulfuric acid? These were the reasons that led Lavoisier to have the Academy prolong the life of its commission on the Montgolfier invention after the report of 23 December and to retain the services of Monge's protégé. An engineer, Meusnier had experience in the design and construction of apparatus that would approach machinery in scale. A mathematician, he was accomplished in the abstract analysis of quantity.

The first meeting of the renewed commission occurred on 27 December 1783 in the Hôtel de la Rochefoucauld with the duke in the chair. Lavoisier led the discussion. It culminated in the consensus that research and development of aircraft should proceed along four lines: first, lessening the weight and permeability of the fabric; second, choosing and generating the gas; third, stabilizing altitude while conserving both ballast and buoyancy; and fourth, securing a measure of control over locomotion and direction. A further reason for employing Meusnier was that, as we shall see, he had already solved the third problem in principle.[14] In order that he might be a member as well as agent of the commission, the Academy elected him to a vacancy on 28 January 1784, preferring him to several senior candidates. Thereupon, Lavoisier and La Rochefoucauld interceded with the high command of the army in order to secure Meusnier an extension of his normal six-month leave so that he might have a full year free for aeronautical investigation.[15]

Extraction of hydrogen from water occupied Meusnier from the start of this program of research; and largely in service to Lavoisier, he proceeded to design the experiment that is famous from the history of the chemical revolution. A gun barrel slightly inclined to the horizontal was heated incandescent in a bed of coals. Water dripping into the upper end was decomposed by contact with the inner surface, where the red-hot iron combined with oxygen and liberated hydrogen to be collected from the lower end in a pneumatic trough. Lavoisier and Meusnier perfected this operation during the month of March 1784, on one occasion producing 125 pints of hydrogen pure enough to be nine-and-a-half times lighter than air. On the 29th Lavoisier invited their colleagues of the academic commission to his laboratory in the Arsenal to observe a demonstration. Three weeks later, on 21 April, he put Meusnier forward as principal author to read a memoir describing the experiments before the Easter meeting of the Academy, the second public session in a row to be occupied with Lavoisier's research on the composition of water.[16]

It remained to enlarge the scale to the dimensions of a practical exploitation both for analysis and synthesis. Meusnier modified the two gasometers that the instrument-maker Mégnié had finished in December 1783 and ordered other large vessels for collecting gas. The summer and autumn months of 1784 were occupied with trying out and improving the procedures and apparatus. No amateur, Lavoisier observed later, could imagine the pains and the time required to develop and perfect a course of precise experiments. Only in February 1785 were Meusnier and he satisfied with their results. On the 27th and 28th they scheduled demonstrations to which they invited members of the Academy and other notables. In the most considerable of these exercises, they packed a gun barrel with iron rings and decomposed 335 pounds—about 45 gallons—of water. The hydrogen occupied eleven bell jars, from which it passed into one of the redesigned gasometers. The second stood ready, filled with oxygen by the pyrolysis of mercuric oxide. A jet of hydrogen was then admitted into a portion of the oxygen in a sealed flask and ignited by an electrostatic spark. The weight of water produced equalled the combined quantities of the two gases. The scale and precision convinced the most skeptical observers, and such was the demonstration that carried the day in Lavoisier's campaign to supplant the phlogiston with the oxygen theory of combustion.[17]

What with the importance of that research, and of Lavoisier's position in the Academy, Meusnier may well have put more energy into chemistry than into aeronautical engineering in the year of leave that the corps of engineers had granted him for the latter purpose. Of course, decomposition of water could have been justified by the second of his instructions, which called for study of the relative merits of hydrogen and of hot air. As to the third line of research, stabilization of altitude, he had already arrived at a solution. The doom of the first *charlière*, which rose until it burst, had suggested the problem in August, 1783, before ever a balloonist faced the problem Meusnier analyzed. An eventual pilot could arrest his ascent prior to such a catastrophe only by venting irreplaceable hydrogen. He would then begin losing altitude. To reverse his descent, he would have to toss out ballast, bobbing up a bit, only to resume his slow fall from a lower height than before. His flight would consist, therefore, of a decaying series of bounds of increasing amplitude.

In addressing the problem of steadying the state of equilibrium at constant altitude, Meusnier observed that two alternative strategies were conceivable. Either the volume or the weight of the aircraft might be varied in order to bring it into balance with the weight of air displaced. In practice, however, he could think of no way of altering the volume of a globe in precisely inverse proportion to atmospheric density. How, then, might the weight be modified, and the volume held constant, otherwise than by a destabilizing discharge of gas or ballast? But that is just what a fish does, Meusnier evidently thought, admitting or expelling from its bladder enough water to stay in balance. What, Meusnier asked rhetorically, "could be added to an isolated body, if not the very air in which it swims? That is what no one has thought of, and yet all the difficulties would immediately disappear."[18]

The principle, of course, is that which still serves to regulate the depth at which a submarine floats and the height at which a blimp levels off. The printed record creates some confusion about its initial application, however. Meusnier published it in July 1784 in *Observations sur la physique*, the monthly founded by the abbé Rozier (no relation to Pilatre). The full title (Fig. 41) is germane to unraveling the circumstances:

MÉMOIRE

Sur l'équilibre des Machines aéroftatiques , fur les différens moyens de les faire monter & defcendre , & fpécialement fur celui d'exécuter ces manœuvres , fans jeter de left , & fans perdre d'air inflammable , en ménageant dans le ballon une capacité particulière , deftinée à renfermer de l'air atmofphérique.

Préfenté à l'Académie , le 3 Décembre 1783 (1).

Avec une Addition contenant une application de cette théorie au cas particulier du Ballon que MM. Robert conftruifent à Saint-Cloud , & dans lequel ce moyen doit être employé pour la première fois.

41.

MEMOIR

On the equilibrium of aerostatic machines, on various ways for causing them to climb & descend, & specifically on a technique for carrying out these maneuvers, without jettisoning ballast or losing inflammable air.

Presented to the Academy
3 December 1783[1].

With an addition containing an application of this theory to the special case of the Balloon that Messrs. Robert are constructing at Saint-Cloud, in which this method is to be employed for the first time.

Conformably with that legend, the Robert brothers did in fact launch a balloon from the park of the château of the duc de Chartres. Theirs was the first aircraft shaped like a cigar, albeit a thick one. It was supposed to consist of a cylindrical central section twenty feet long and thirty feet in diameter sandwiched between two hemispheric segments. (If the artist is to be trusted [Fig. 51 below], the actual appearance was egg-shaped.) On 15 July, the date of their experiment, the issue of the journal containing Meusnier's memoir could scarcely have reached subscribers. It is natural to suppose that things were as they seemed, that Charles had abandoned aviation following his solo communion with the universe on 1 December 1783, and that thereafter the Roberts worked instead with Meusnier in developing a machine to test-fly the stabilizer he had described to the Academy during the same session wherein Charles recounted his unique adventure.

Nothing of the sort, however. The archives of the Academy contain a sealed note deposited by the mineralogist, Balthazar Sage, on behalf of the two Roberts on 9 June 1784. In it they pointed out that an elongated balloon would become unbalanced if it should lose inflammable air from either end. The need to obviate that danger had led them, so they said, to the invention for which Sage was now claiming their priority:

... these physicists have had the idea of putting a balloon a quarter of the size of the aerostat in the middle part. This will be filled with atmospheric air intended to escape when the inflammable gas expands. ... There will be no loss of inflammable air and no emission of fumes that might create the risk of setting fire to the aerostat through an electric spark.[19]

When Meusnier objected that the principle of this device was identical with that which he had proposed to the Academy on 3 December 1783, six months previously, Robert—according to the minutes of the Academy—recognized straight off that such was indeed the case.[20] The contretemps makes sense of a footnote appended to the title (above) of Meusnier's memoir, where the date is mentioned. It reminds readers that priorities are of great moment in science, and that the Academy records dates with much care. The method in question, the note goes on, had been imagined in the time when Charles and the Roberts were preparing the Tuileries flight of 1 December.[21]

It would appear, therefore, that the Roberts had been out of touch with Meusnier in the interval, and that they never meant to steal his idea. The probable explanation is that they subconsciously remembered their earlier exchanges with him so that the notion of a bladder came to mind as a solution to the problem of keeping an even keel and lessening the risk of fire. For those are the advantages they claimed. A pair of practical artisans, they say nothing about generalized conditions of equilibrium.

Soon after the 15 July flight, Meusnier on his side wrote to Etienne—and it is interesting that throughout this period he was communicating rather with Etienne than with these tradesmen—that their reticence with respect to the actual invention was what led him now to go ahead and publish his conception.[22] Thus, the full explanation may further be that Meusnier saved appearances, together with his intellectual property, by adopting the Robert balloon as the application of his principle even though he had had nothing to do with its actual construction.

To that end, the Roberts evidently supplied him with the data on its characteristics.

The "addition" to Meusnier's memoir has two main aspects: first, analysis of those characteristics, and second, development of a general strategy for navigation.[23] The order of composition was probably the opposite, however. Numerical application of his theory to the case of the Robert balloon must have occupied him intensively between 9 June 1784, the date of the sealed note, and the experimental flight at Saint-Cloud on 15 July. The overall capacity of that aircraft was 28,274 cubic feet. Fully inflated, it would displace 2,457 pounds of air at ground level. The internal balloon or bladder was nineteen feet in diameter, with a capacity of 3,591 cubic feet or 312 pounds of air.

The initial object of the calculation was to obtain figures for load and gas pressure that would define the optimal trade-off between strain on the fabric and speed of ascent. Meusnier's method of estimating the strain seems curious at first reading, almost as if it were a throwback to the model of the globe by which Otto von Guericke of Magdeburg had demonstrated the reality of atmospheric pressure in 1657. The latter's famous experiment pitted two teams of horses tugging against each other to separate a pair of tightly fitting hemispheres after the space inside was evacuated. Similarly, or rather inversely, in the case of the Champ de Mars *charlière*, Meusnier calculated the force that tended to split the little balloon into hemispheres. He estimated it to be equivalent to the weight of a column (or disk) of mercury of which the height measured the excess of internal over external pressure and the circumference equaled that of the great circle of the balloon. He then divided that figure by the length of the circumference in order to get the tensile strength required of the fabric in pounds per linear foot.

The rational deduction from an arbitrary, not to say a willful, assumption is the hallmark of the forward-looking engineer. By that same method Meusnier calculated that an excess of internal gas pressure equivalent to one inch of mercury would make the Robert balloon eighty-eight pounds

lighter than the air it displaced. In the hemispheric end sections, that pressure would impose a tension of 594 pounds per linear foot of fabric. In the cylindrical center portions, the force tending to separate its halves longitudinally would be twice as great, or 1,188 pounds. The Roberts had already realized that they must reinforce the barrel section with belting. Even so, no fabric could withstand such pressures, and Meusnier advised limiting the levity to fifteen or twenty pounds. An excess of internal pressure of only two or three *lignes* (about five millimeters) of mercury would effect that. Extrapolating from the observations of the Champ de Mars and the Tuileries balloons, Meusnier predicted that such an imbalance would produce an initial vertical velocity of three feet per second. Whether that was sufficient to rise above surrounding hazards would depend upon terrain and weather.

Meusnier also drew on the characteristics of the Robert balloon to illustrate the general strategy he had already imagined for the navigation of aircraft at the pilot's choice of altitude.[24] He could see, again a priori, that equipping a balloon with his stabilizer would give it a vertical range for ascending and descending at will without loss of ballast or hydrogen. In order to rise, a pilot would allow air to escape the bladder under pressure from the surrounding hydrogen. In order to descend he would reinflate the bladder by use of a simple bellows. The lower limit of equilibrium was the level at which the bladder was full of air. To descend further, a pilot would have to release hydrogen. The upper limit was the level at which the bladder was empty and collapsed within the body of the balloon. To rise further, he would need to jettison ballast.

For any given aircraft, the distance between these limits was a constant determined by the dimensions of balloon and bladder. In the case of the Robert balloon, the band was 566 *toises* (3,396 feet) in depth. Absolute altitudes varied inversely with load, however, and Meusnier constructed what he called a nautical table. From its columns an eventual pilot might read off the limits of stable flight for a series of initial weights ranging from 2,048 down to 848 pounds. In every instance he was also given the barometric pressure corresponding to each of the two critical values. A barometer would thus serve the pilot as altimeter, and he could estimate both his altitude and his place within the zone of maneuverability, ascending or descending reversibly in search of favorable winds.[25]

In the preliminary, theoretical part of the memoir Meusnier stipulated that the separate air compartment might consist either of an internal bladder, or of a shell surrounding the great bag of hydrogen. He preferred the latter alternative, since the arrangement would partially insulate the gas from sudden changes of temperature, would constitute a buffer to lessen loss from leaking, and would be simpler mechanically to vent and refill. Later on, in the "addition" prepared in July 1784, he urged the further precaution of an automatic valve set at a safe threshold to release hydrogen into the atmosphere in case heat from the sun or other causes produced sudden surges in internal pressure. With its stabilizer inside, the Saint-Cloud balloon embodied neither of these suggestions. The omission may be further evidence that the Meusnier calculations applied to it after it was under construction. Near-catastrophe and much embarrassment would have been averted if the Roberts had modified their machine in accordance with these ideas—though, to be sure, they may not have known of them in time to do so.

The duc de Chartres (it will be recalled) had tracked both the Pilatre-d'Arlandes and the Charles-Robert flights on horseback. Now he decided to go up himself in the balloon he was subsidizing. The project annoyed his cousin, Louis XVI, and even more so the queen. She detested him for his common touch and resented him for the popularity that eluded her. Saint-Cloud is on the western outskirts of Paris, less than halfway to Versailles, and a considerable crowd had gathered by the early morning of 15 July. Visible novelties were the elongated gondola, a large rudder, and an arrangement of paddles to be worked from a central shaft (Fig. 42). Besides the duke and the two Roberts, there was a fourth passenger whose identity we do not know. He may well have been the Roberts' brother-in-law, Collin-

Hulin, who accompanied them on their next and final venture.

At 7:52 of a still, overcast morning, they were airborne. Disappearing through the ceiling within three minutes, they remarked the feather-bed effect of a blanket of cloud below: "Never was a spectacle inspiring horror so interesting."[26] Turbulence ruled the air, and they heard a snap. The silk cords that suspended the stabilizing bladder in the middle of the envelope had parted. Bright sunlight beat upon the upper surface and heated the hydrogen inside. The barometer fell rapidly, and they judged themselves to be rising at a comparable rate. One of the Roberts set about releasing gas. In vain. The displaced bladder had stopped the vent. Attempts to free it with a long stick failed. Up, up they sped, accelerating toward the bursting point, when suddenly the duke had the presence of mind to grab the flagstaff and punch a couple of holes in the belly of the balloon. A tear of seven to eight feet opened between the punctures. They descended "very rapidly" (say the Roberts in their report), down through the cloud cover straight toward a pond called the Garenne. Throwing out a sixty-pound sack of sand, they slowed enough to gain the bank, from where a peasant woman watching her cows took flight. One of the six bottles of wine aboard was broken by the shock, but no one was hurt.

The young duke never flew again.

Undaunted, the Roberts repaired their balloon for a second attempt at locomotion, reverting to subscription for the financing. On 19 September 1784, the anniversary of the Versailles demonstration, they took off together with Collin-Hulin from the Tuileries for what proved the most trouble-free flight so far. Departing at high noon, they were lost to view at 1:50 p.m., riding a southeast wind at varying altitudes. Witnesses reported their passage above the plains of Picardy all that afternoon. A cavalry officer wrote in to the *Journal de Paris* from Ravenel, as did a landowner from Montdidier. As dusk gathered the aviators put down after a flight of six hours and forty minutes in the park of the prince de Ghistelles on the edge of the village of Beuvry near Béthune and not far from the northern frontier (Fig. 43). Com-

Gouvernail

Rames ou Ailes

Bout de la Galerie

les Armes de Chartre

Bout de la Galerie

les oiseaux

Echelle de 48 pieds.

12   24   48

EXPÉRIENCE DE LA MACHINE AËROSTATIQUE DE M. ROBERT,
faite à St Cloud le 15 Juillet 1784;

Ce Balon qui a 52 pieds de longueur sur 32 de diametre et dont la construction a pour objet l'application des
moyens d'ascension et de descente a volonté, fut enlevé en presence de la Famille Royale et fut applaudi universelement.
Sa hauteur ne peut être estimée des spectateurs aux yeux des quels il fût invisible en 3 minutes; Il a tenu l'air environ ¾ d'heur.
Sa descente se fit très rapidement près l'Etang de la Garenne, dans le Parc de Meudon.

42.

DESSENTE DES IMMORTELS ROBERTS

Le Prince de Ghistelles sortant de faire enlever un Ballon devant son Château apperçu les Srs Roberts, on leurs crûd de dessendre ce qu'ils firent a l'instant en se detournant d'un Moulin, par le moy= en de leurs rames. Un cri général fut Vive Roberts.

A midi le 19.7^bre 1784 les Srs Roberts et Colin Hullin leurs beau-frere entrerent dans le Char, qui étoit sur le Bassin des Thuilleries; d'où ils s'enlevèrent aux ac- clamations de la plus brillante assemblée; peu après ils s'abaisserent et s'éleverent successivement et prirent route par la Pi- cardie et l'Artois, où ils dessendirent le même jour à 6 h. 40.' chez M. le Prince De Ghistelles à Beuvri, près Bethune distante d'environ 53 lieues de Paris.
Après que le Procès Verbal fut fait par les Notaires Royaux et signé des Princes; il furent Couronnés dans le Château, ainsi que dans la Ville de Bethune par le Marquis De Gori qui leur donna une superbe fête.

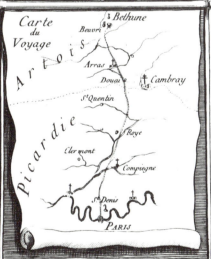

Carte
du
Voyage

Artois

Bethune
Beuvri
Arras
Douai
Cambray
St Quentin
Roye
Clermont
Compiegne
St Denis
PARIS

Picardie

A LA GLOIRE DES Srs ROBERTS.
Air, du Vaudeville de Figaro.

En s'élevant sur nos têtes,
Ils reçurent nos adieux;
Pour eux quels beaux jours de fêtes
Lors qu'ils plannent dans les cieux;
Par la foudre et les tempêtes,
Jupin instruit l'univers,
Du voyage des Roberts......(bis)

Talens, Prudence, Courage,
Vous élèvent jusqu'aux cieux;
Par ce céleste voyage,
Vous régnez avec les Dieux;
Partout sur votre passage,
L'on vous dresse des autels,
Et vos noms sont immortels......(bis)

a Paris chez Berthet rue des Noyers au coin de celle St Jacques maison du M^d de Vin.

43.

bining the effects of rudder and sweeps, they had managed to sail at an angle of 22° at most to the wind direction and not (as Blanchard and others pretended to do) to tack against it. They had eliminated the stabilizer after the near-disaster at Saint-Cloud, and the Meusnier device was never used again until the age of dirigibles late in the 19th century.[27]

On 13 November 1784, Meusnier presented the Academy with a précis of all the work he had accomplished on behalf of its commission for aviation.[28] He, too, had addressed himself to the problem of locomotion, the fourth and last of its charges, immediately upon his appointment. We have already noticed how, on 14 January 1784, he read a memoir (which has not survived) "on the proportion between oars in air and in water," and how Etienne in his own paper on aerial oars adopted Meusnier's conclusion.[29] It was that blades of equivalent surface would have a relative effect three times as great in the atmosphere as in the sea. On the strength of this comparison, Meusnier conceived of a giant double-bladed affair that was far more interesting in design than Etienne's imaginary sweeps, for its principle was that of the helical propeller. A system of cranks turned by many hands would rotate paired helicoidal surfaces like sails of a windmill in a plane perpendicular to the direction of flight. Meusnier agreed with Etienne, and had perhaps coached him, in the belief that the most efficient "rames"— that was still his word—would prove capable of producing a maximum velocity of one league (about four kilometers) an hour, and that knowledge of wind patterns was the prerequisite to navigation. Nevertheless, that small maneuverability would make all the difference in landing at the precise place of choice, and also in positioning the aircraft relative to the flow of air currents during flight.

It followed that Meusnier's ideal airship should have been greatly elongated, its proportions those of a modern zeppelin. His preference for that shape derived both from the obvious dynamical desirability of favoring headway by reducing air resistance and also from analysis of the relation of the strength of fabrics to the form of the surface.

The very first of his instructions had been to study ways to improve the impermeability and lessen the weight of the envelope. The instrument-maker Fortin, often employed by Lavoisier, produced an admirable varnish that answered to the former of these purposes. For the latter, Meusnier followed the model of the great and patient work on ship-rigging prepared by Duhamel du Monceau in 1747, extending the method from the one-dimensionality of ropes to the two dimensions of textiles. Over a period of many months, he hung weights on swatches of cloth, testing the tensile strength of twenty-one qualities and weaves of silk, taffeta, canvas, linen, duck, twill, and various mixtures. He recorded the closeness of weave—threads per square inch— both in warp and weft, and determined a "quotient of resistance" or ratio of supportable load to weight of fabric in both directions. Since tensile strength was greater lengthwise than crosswise, the more elongated the balloon, the less the weight of fabric that would be required to withstand the pressure of the gas inside the envelope.[30]

Stability was here the limiting factor, since the longer the aircraft, the more subject it would be to pitching and even to upending should hydrogen stream to the higher extremity. Differential geometry was Meusnier's mathematical forte, but his analysis of the motions and forces that affect aircraft shows what it was—and for that matter is—to be an engineer. Rather than thinking of a balloon as a simple body occupying a certain space and weighing so much, Meusnier divided the weight into two parts (Fig. 44, 1) corresponding to the gondola and the balloon itself. The part P is the weight of the former with its contents, which may be supposed to act as if concentrated at the center of gravity G. The part of the weight represented by E derives from the balloon, its rigging, and its content of air and hydrogen. The air in a stabilizing bladder is supposed to occupy the lower layer. O is the center of the balloon and C the center of gravity of the hydrogen. When the balloon is in equilibrium, the lifting force equals (P + E) and acts along the vertical axis.

Suppose now that the balloon pitches longitudinally like a ship in the turbulence of atmospheric waves (Fig. 44, 2). The air content of the stabilizer flows like bilge in the hold of a ship to the lowest portion of the envelope. The center of gravity of the gas is thus displaced to C'. For small displacements, the lifting force $(P + E)$ acts in a line that intersects OG at M. (Geometrically, M is the cusp of the curve that forms the envelope of the line of lifting force.) If we compound the lifting force $(P + E)$ with the force E acting at O in an opposite and parallel direction, the resultant P will meet the line of centers OG at N.

Meusnier's analysis of the conditions of stability turns on determination of the location of this point, which he calls a *metacenter*. The force P acting at the metacenter N, and the weight P acting at the center of gravity G of the gondola, create a torque, of which the tendency is to restore the balloon to the position of horizontal equilibrium. Meusnier gives the following formula for determining its location,

$$n = \left(\frac{P + E}{P}\right) \cdot 3/2 \left(\frac{l^2 - h^2}{h^2}\right) \left[\frac{(h - x)^2}{3h - 2x}\right]$$

where n is the distance from the center of the balloon O to the metacenter N, h is the minor axis, l the major axis, and x the mean height of the center of gravity of the hydrogen when the balloon is on the ground. Meusnier then defines the moment of stability as the product of the weight P into the distance from center of gravity of the gondola to the metacenter—that is, P × NG. Since the torque is proportional to NG, the greater that distance, the better the aircraft will withstand the disturbance of pitching fore and aft. Meusnier concludes that for optimal stability the major axis must be not more than double or at most triple the minor axis.[31]

The November 1784 report to the Academy consists of a verbal and qualitative statement of these, the characteristics of the aircraft of the future, including the principle of the air bladder. Meusnier concluded this précis with an estimate of the costs and followed Etienne's example in proposing two models, a cheaper and a more expensive, to the patronage of government. A combination of vision and detail, his engineer's notion of what might be expected was at once more fanciful and more precise than the businessman's. The estimates were respectively eight and over thirty times anything ever mentioned by Etienne, whose figures of 50,000 and 100,000 livres were already unrealistic from the point of view of a Treasury sliding into the bankruptcy that undid the old regime in 1789. The smaller of Meusnier's aircraft would cost 400,000 livres and carry six men on experimental cruises within the European continent. They would gain practice with aerial navigation and obtain data on the constitution of the upper atmosphere.

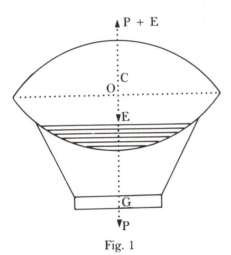

Fig. 1

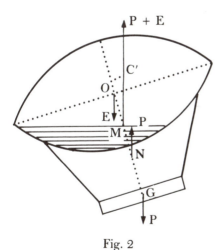

Fig. 2

44.

The larger model, a hand-powered zeppelin, would carry a crew of thirty men with provisions for sixty days. They would venture overseas and into distant latitudes. They might well circumnavigate the globe. As Meusnier worked out the details in the specification or "devis" that he developed in the next few years, his first rough estimate of 3,000,000 livres grew to 2,564,333/10/0 livres for aircraft and provisions together with 742,990/1/8 for the hangar and supporting equipment on the ground: a grand total of 3,307,323/11/8. The scale of the proposal was thus on an order of magnitude proportional to the space program in our own day. That this enormous figure should be completed to the refinement of 11 sous, 8 deniers is altogether characteristic of the author.

The form of the airship was an ellipsoid with major axis of 260 feet and minor axis of 130. Its surface would contain 90,752 square feet; its capacity would be 2,300,688 cubic feet and its total weight 133,663 pounds. With a keel fifty-nine feet, ten inches long, the gondola was to be constructed of oak with fir fittings and designed in the form of a ship in case it should be necessary or desirable to put down at sea. The hangar would have been 336 feet long, 228 feet wide, and 180 feet high—the size of a cathedral.

But enough of the figures. The quality of Meusnier's imagination comes through in his drawings better than in his numbers, impressive though they may be. After his return to active duty at the port of Cherbourg in 1785, he occupied the hours of idleness that fill (or empty) military life at his drawing board. There he readied the drafts for a publication that his death in the siege of Mainz in 1793 left unachieved. The originals are lost, but an atlas of copies found its way after vicissitudes into the military archives of Vincennes. We print a selection that will exhibit the salient features, in their precise attention to the detail of all the parts no less than in the sweep and range of the whole conception. The specifications of weight, moment of inertia, and cost for every set of structures occupy three separate tabulations. We have thought it might exemplify Meusnier's capacity for detailed planning

to abstract just one of them—the table of weights for the anchoring mechanism.[32]

45-54. THE MEUSNIER ATLAS

A selection of ten of the sixteen plates, together with a table of weights pertaining to the landing gear. Omitted are Plates 1, 2, 3, 12, 15, and 16, which have less interest graphically than those reproduced here.

45. 4th Plate. Fig. 10, Side view of the gondola with iron hasps for the suspension hawsers; Fig. 11, Front view of the gondola, showing the forward pair of bellows; Fig. 12, Rear view of the gondola; Fig. 13, Detail of iron hasp

46. 5th Plate. Figs. 14, 15, and 16, Detail of attachment of suspension hawsers; Figs. 17 and 18, Front and side views of propeller hub; Fig. 19, Crosswise view of the propeller axle, to illustrate its suspension; Figs. 20 and 21, Blade of a propeller; Figs. 22 and 23, Gears for revolving the propeller

47. 6th Plate. Fig. 24, Side view of gondola, propellers, and rudder. The tubes V are for filling the hydrogen compartment with lifting gas, and the tubes U are for pumping air into the stabilizing bladder by means of the two pairs of bellows fore and aft

48. 7th Plate. Fig. 25, Front view of the gondola and fore propeller

49. 8th Plate. Fig. 26, Interior of the dirigible, showing the two hydrogen compartments, expandable to the limit A. Below A is the stabilizing air bladder, filled through U and vented through X

50. 9th Plate. Fig. 27, Lengthwise view of the dirigible, to show the suspension system

51. 10th Plate. Fig. 28, Frontal view, to show suspension. 11th Plate. Fig. 29, Anchor in the form of a dart, weighted to penetrate a depth of four feet in medium soil when dropped from an altitude of fifty fathoms (300 feet); Fig. 30, Pulley block with ratchet to prevent reversal of wheel; Fig. 31, Block and tackle, one of twenty-four serving to moor the dirigible

52. 13th Plate. Figs. 33 and 34, Front and side views of the moored dirigible sheltered under its tent

53. 14th Plate. Fig. 35, Ready to drop anchor; Fig. 36, The dirigible aground, downwind from the point of anchoring; Fig. 37, The dirigible secured by twelve cables; Fig. 38, The dirigible under shelter of its tent

DÉTAILS D'UN PROJET DE MACHINE AÉROSTATIQUE.

Fig.^{re} 10. Vue en long de la Gondole avec les Armures
de Fer qui servent a la Suspendre

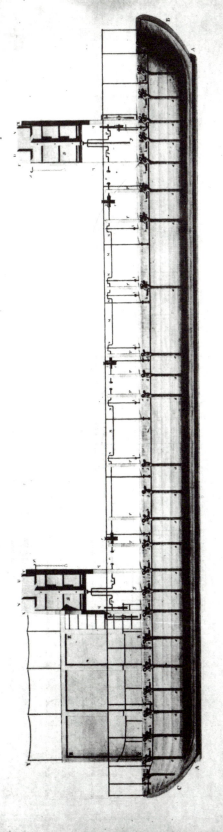

Fig.^{re} 11. Vue de l'Avant de la Gondole.

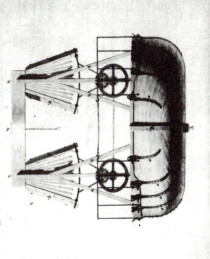

Fig.^{re} 13. Détail plus en grand d'une
des Armures de Suspension.

Échelle de

Fig.^{re} 12. Vue de l'Arrière de la Gondole.

Échelle de

45.

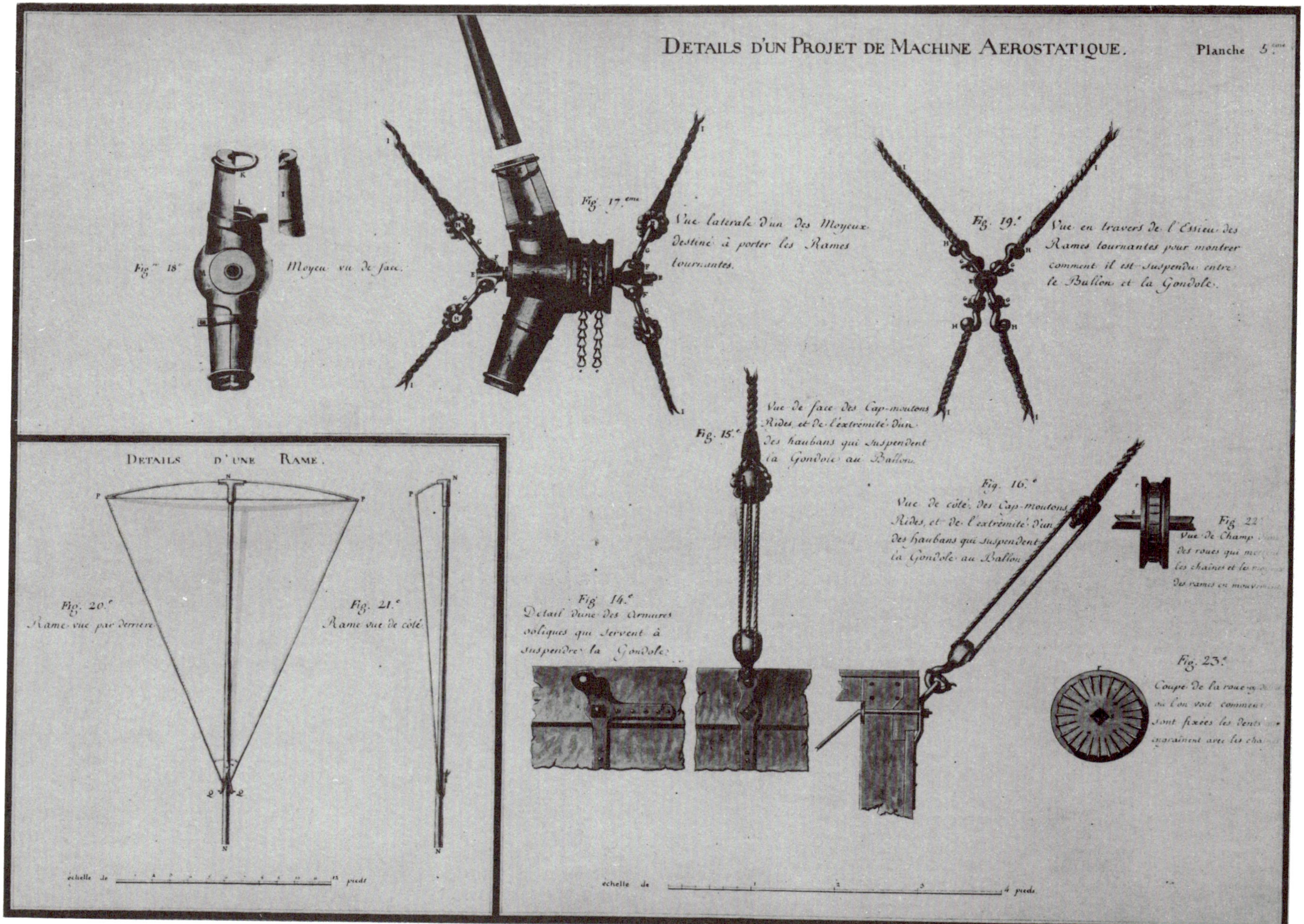

DETAILS D'UN PROJET DE MACHINE AEROSTATIQUE.

Fig. 19.e Vue en travers de l'Essieu des
Rames tournantes pour montrer
comment il est suspendu entre
le Ballon et la Gondole.

Fig. 17.^{em}

Vue Laterale d'un des Moyeux
destiné à porter les Rames
tournantes.

Fig. 15.^e

Vue de face des Cap-moutons
Rides et de l'extremité d'un
des haubans qui suspendent
la Gondole au Ballon.

Fig. 16.^e

Vue de côté, des Cap-moutons
Rides, et de l'extremité d'un
des haubans qui suspendent
la Gondole au Ballon.

Fig. 18.^e

Moyeu vu de face.

Fig. 22.^e
Vue de Champ.

Fig. 23.^e

Coupe de la roue
du l'on voit comment
les roues qui m...
les Rains et le cr...
de rames en mouve...

Fig. 14.^e

Detail d'une des Vernures
obliques qui servent à
suspendre la Gondole.

DÉTAILS D'UNE RAME.

Fig. 21.^e
Rame vue de côté.

Fig. 20.^e
Rame vue par derriere.

echelle de .... 4 pieds

echelle de .... 6 pieds

46.

DÉTAILS D'UN PROJET DE MACHINE AÉROSTATIQUE

Fig.re 24.me VUE EN LONG DE LA GONDOLE ET D'UNE PARTIE

DU BALLON POUR MONTRER COMMENT LES MOYENS DE DIRECTION

OU RAMES TOURNANTES SONT DISPOSÉES

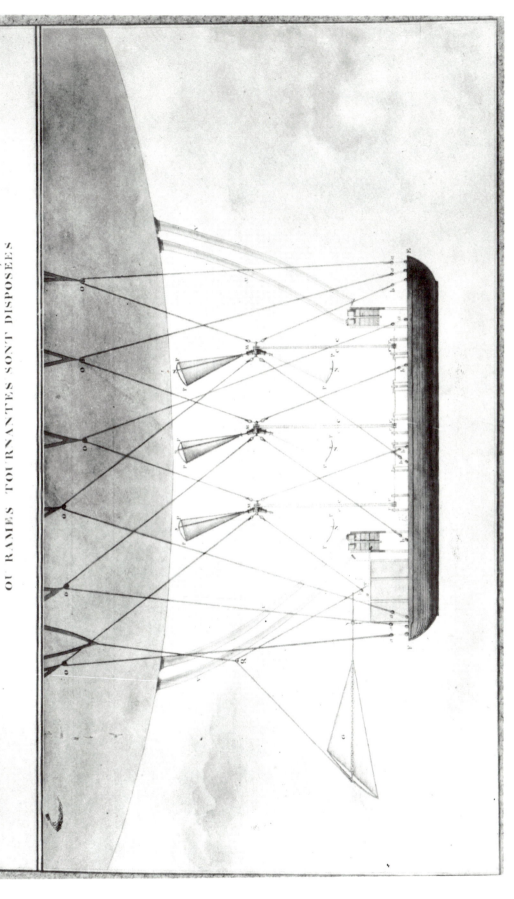

47.

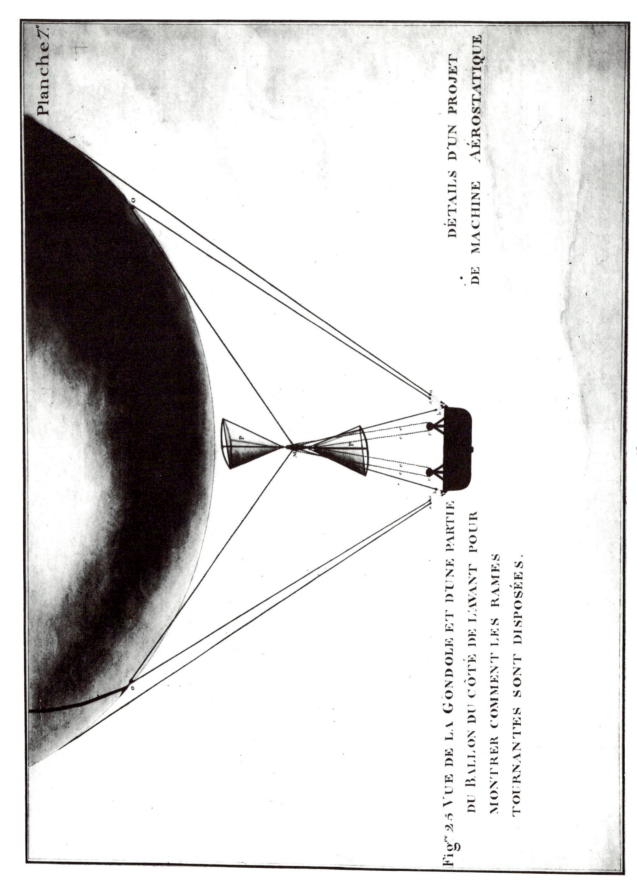

Planche 7.

Fig.re 2.5 VUE DE LA GONDOLE ET D'UNE PARTIE
DU BALLON DU CÔTÉ DE L'AVANT POUR
MONTRER COMMENT LES RAMES
TOURNANTES SONT DISPOSÉES.

DÉTAILS D'UN PROJET
DE MACHINE AÉROSTATIQUE

48.

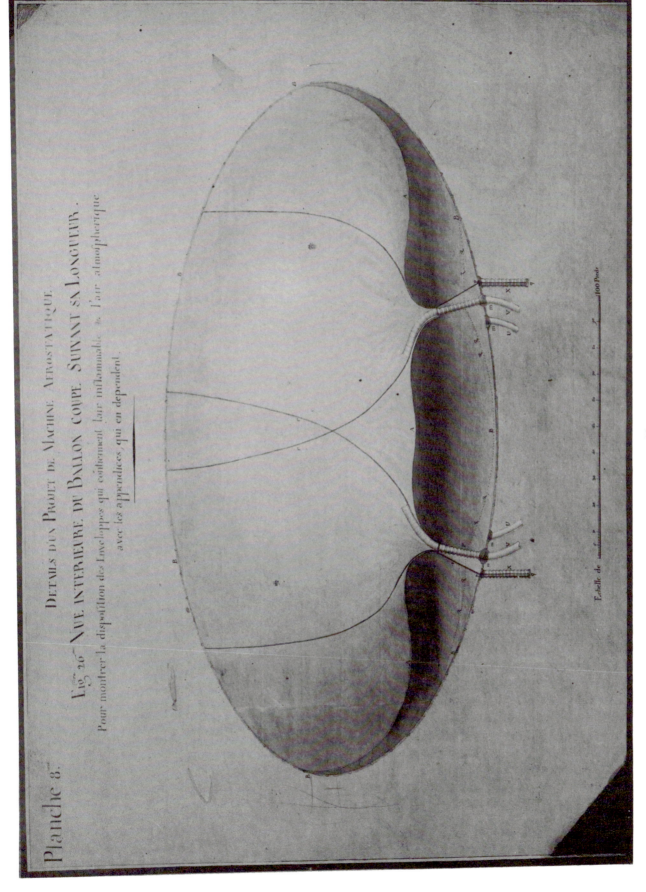

Planche 8.

DÉTAILS D'UN PROJET DE MACHINE AÉROSTATIQUE.

Fig. 26. VUE INTÉRIEURE DU BALLON COUPÉ SUIVANT SA LONGUEUR.

Pour montrer la disposition des Enveloppes qui contiennent l'air inflammable & l'air atmosphérique
avec les appendices qui en dépendent

Échelle de   100 Pieds

49.

DÉTAILS D'UN PROJET DE MACHINE AÉROSTATIQUE.

FIG.ⁿ 27.ᵐᵉ VÛE EN LONG DU BALLON ET DE LA GONDOLE, POUR MONTRER
les haubans de Suspenſion, l'aſſemblage de Sangles qui ſert de filet, les échelles de cordes, marche-pieds et filets de ſureté.

Échelle de.   60 Pieds.

50.

DÉTAILS D'UN PROJET DE MACHINE AÉROSTATIQUE

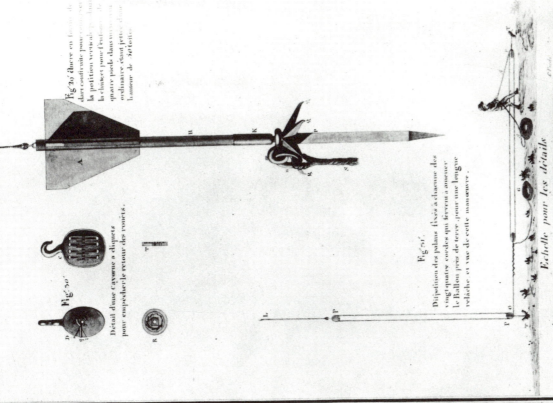

Fig. 26. Barre en forme de dard conduite pour comprimer la position verticale : placer la cliquet pour l'entonnoir, de quatre pieds dans l'entonnoir ordinaire étant jettée dans la mineur de 50 toises

Détail d'une cazorne à clapets pour empêcher le retour des rouëts.

Fig. 30.

Fig. 31.

Disposition des palans fixés à chacune des vingt-quatre cordes qui serviront à amener le Ballon près de terre , pour une longue relâche, et vue de cette manœuvre .

Echelle pour les détails

Fig. 28. VUE DE FACE DU BALLON ET DE LA GONDOLE POUR montrer les haubans de suspension l'assemblage de sangles qui sert de filet.

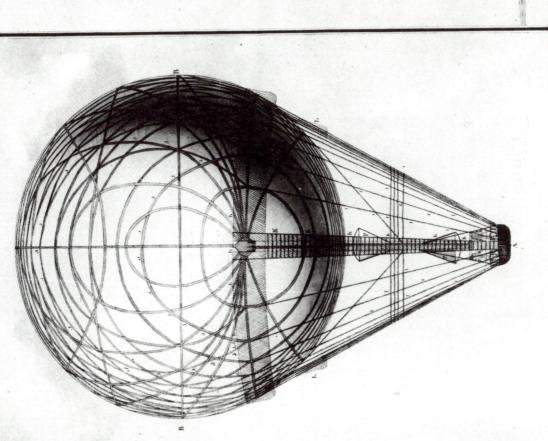

51.

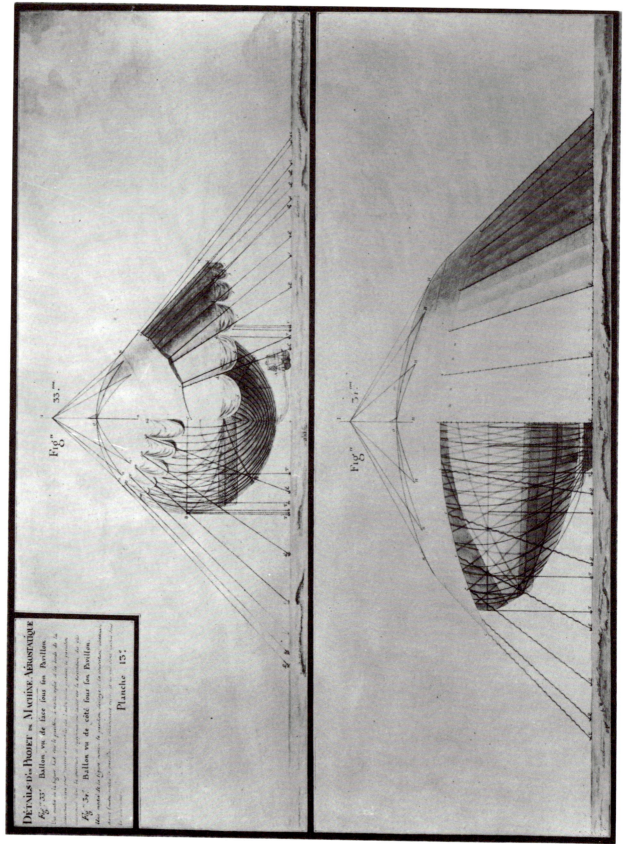

DÉTAILS D'UN PROJET DE MACHINE AÉROSTATIQUE

Fig. 33.ᵐᵉ   Ballon vu de face sous son Pavillon.

Fig. 34.ᵐᵉ   Ballon vu de côté sous son Pavillon.

Planche 15.ᵉ

Fig.ʳᵉ 33.ᵐᵉ

Fig.ʳᵉ 34.ᵐᵉ

52.

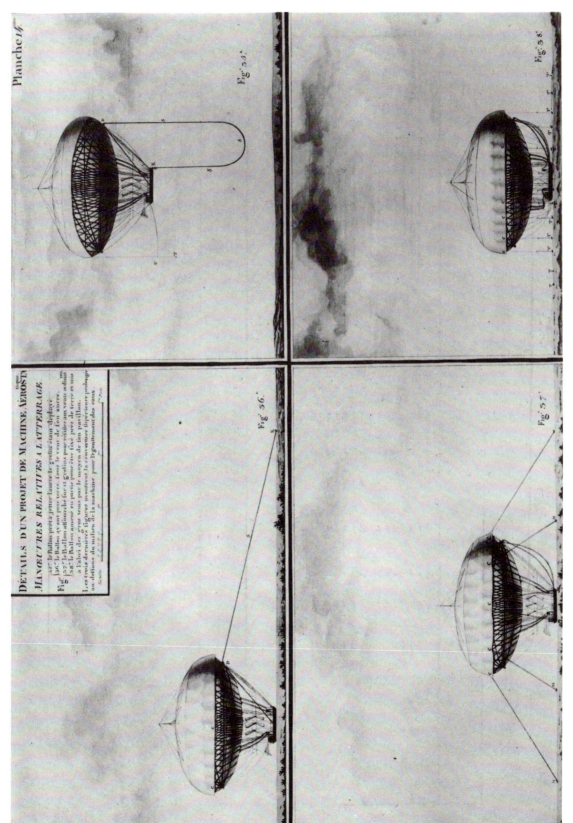

Planche 14

Fig. 55.

Fig. 58.

DÉTAILS D'UN PROJET DE MACHINE AÉROSTA.
tique

MANŒUVRES RELATIVES A L'ATTERRAGE.

55. le Ballon prêt à jetter l'ancre faire le grapin s'ouvrant déployé.
Fig. 56. le Ballon ayant pris terre, sous le vent de son ancre, ...
57. le Ballon attaché, far 12 grelins pour résister aux vents soutenu ...
58. le Ballon amené en partie près de terre ou mis
à l'abri des gros tems par le moyen de son pavillon.
Les trois dernières figures montrent la couverture supérieure prolongée
au dessous du milieu de la machine pour l'égouttement des eaux.

Échelle

Fig. 56.

Fig. 57.

53.

MÉMOIRE ET DEVIS DU PROJET D'UNE
MACHINE AÉROSTATIQUE.

Poids des agrès.

	Poids. livres
La grosse ancre	280
La seconde ancre	200
Le grapin	100
Grelin de la grosse ancre de 600 pieds de long et de 7 pouces 6 lignes de grosseur	813

Nota.—En prenant 20,000 pour le quotient de résistance du chanvre en cordage, ce grelin est susceptible de porter 27,080 livres, tandis que l'action d'un vent de 10 lieues à l'heure contre le ballon en repos ne serait que de 25,000 livres.

Grelin de la seconde ancre de 400 pieds de longueur et de 5 pouces 6 lignes de grosseur	291

Nota.—Ce grelin est susceptible de résister à l'action qu'un vent de 8 lieues à l'heure exercerait contre le ballon.

Grelin pareil pour grapin	291
Les deux cayornes de chacun des palans verticaux qui servent à amener le ballon à terre, pesant ensemble	30
Le garant de chacun de ces palans a 13 lignes de grosseur et 480 pieds de longueur, pèse	14

Nota.—La force ascensionnelle du ballon qu'il faut vaincre pour l'amener à terre est de 57,000 livres, ce qui donne pour chacun des 8 cordons ou brins de garant qui composent le palan une tension d'environ 300 livres; d'après cela on a calculé la grosseur du garant pour un effort de 1,200 livres; suivant ce calcul chaque palan et son garant pèse ..

	44
Chaque palan horizontal et son garant de 360 pieds de longueur et de 3 lignes de grosseur, pesant ensemble 25 livres, 30 palans pareils pèseront	750
Les 24 palans nécessaires pour la manœuvre et 6 de rechange pèseront	1,320
30 paires de piquets auxquels se fixent les palans verticaux susdits	720
Chaque piquet a 30 pieds de longueur et pèse 12 livres.	
30 piquets simples de même force que les précédents et auxquels se fixent les palans horizontaux	360
90 piquets simples pour les cordes du pavillon dont 30 pesant 20 livres chacun, ensemble	600
60 piquets de 12 livres l'un	720
120 piquets pour fixer à terre les bords de la toile du pavillon, à 6 livres l'un	720
24 petits piquets pour fixer les cordes de la couverture de l'hémisphère supérieur	72
15 masses de fer pour chasser les piquets, à 15 livres chacune	225
Poids total des agrès	7,462

54. Table of Weights, landing gear of the Meusnier dirigible

3. THE FIRST AIR CRASH

Flush with a pension of 2,000 livres a year from the king, Pilatre continued a correspondence unwelcome at best to Etienne after the success of the *Marie-Antoinette* on 27 June. Affecting to be his former master's intelligencer, he wrote on 6 October with an account of the marathon flight of the two Roberts and Hulin to Béthune.[33] They had won such acclaim for the exploit that Etienne (Pilatre calls him "my good friend") could well imagine that "Pilatre must have his revenge." He continued with the further news, bound to be bitter to Etienne, whom the controller general

turned down in a letter dated the very same day,[34] that Calonne had given him a new commission, which was to cross the English Channel.

Here was how Pilatre proposed to outdo his rivals. "Inflammable gas" (it would clarify and falsify his ideas to call it hydrogen here) is advantageous for its lifting force, and "igneous gas" (hot air) for facility of descending and ascending at will. Therefore he has conceived the notion of combining the two in his next "*montgolfière*." He was even then constructing a globe thirty-five feet in diameter to be inflated with inflammable gas. Beneath it he would attach a second balloon on the model of the *Marie-Antoinette*, though much smaller. Its capacity would be 300 cubic feet. If all went well, he would ride this tandem rig across the sea to England between 10 and 20 November. As an afterthought, and further enticement, he added that he intended to cut costs by extracting his inflammable gas from fecal matter.

Pilatre had already returned to this, his first line of research so to say, while bidding for scientific attention earlier in the year. In April 1784 he had submitted a reworking of his memoirs on mephitic gases to the Academy of Science in hopes of election to membership. The commission to which they were referred praised his courage but concluded that he would do better to support his claims with new experiments.[35] Nothing dashed, Pilatre returned to the offensive on 12 June. In the following week he would put on an aerostatical experiment for which he would extract the inflammable air from excrement, "which contains a large quantity of it."[36] He never kept that promise, of course. Pilatre was, however, in good company, that of the large majority of persons knowledgeable about chemistry, in lumping together as a single species all gases that would burn—whether methane, hydrogen sulfide, hydrogen, or any other.

There is also a question whether the idea of a tandem balloon was original with Pilatre. Among the numerous writings on aviation that appeared in 1784 is an anonymous *L'Art de voyager dans les airs*. For the most part, this little book excerpts, pirates, paraphrases, and digests the articles published by Faujas in the two volumes of *Description des expériences de la machine aérostatique*.[37] One passage, however, is not drawn from Faujas. After comparing the two main types of aircraft, the author observes,

> What is more, physicists would do well to exploit both these methods, and I think that by combining in a single aerostatical machine the effects of inflammable gas and those of air dilated by fire that MM de Montgolfier employ, it should be possible to achieve long-distance voyages with no risk to the travelers.[38]

It is unlikely that Pilatre wrote this work. Anonymity was not his way. It seems possible, however, and even probable, that he knew it. Not much got past him, except good sense. At all events, his letter telling Etienne of this scheme concluded with a request for advice, both from Etienne and Joseph, "your dear brother." He means his enterprise to "keep the flag of the Montgolfiers waving."[39] A note in Etienne's hand says that he replied on the 14th. We do not have the letter, but in later years he said that he warned Pilatre of the danger he would be incurring and advised against it. Others did likewise if we may believe a chorus of "I told him so" expressions of regret.[40]

Pilatre was deaf to the counsels he had invited. He enlisted the services of a skilled artisan, one Romains, and fashioned his double-decker pretty much according to the specifications he had outlined to Etienne. To all remonstrances, he replied that if by chance any inflammable air escaped through the impermeability of the varnished fabric, the gas was so light that it would rise faster than sparks from the heater underneath the lower module.

Construction proved costlier than he had anticipated. According to Réveillon, the Treasury sank 40,000 livres in the venture, five times anything Etienne had yet been granted. Early in the new year, on 4 January 1785 to be precise, Pilatre and Romains established their base on the bluffs overlooking the channel at Wimereux, near Boulogne-sur-Mer. There he learned that another of his rivals had not been idle and that Blanchard was even then poised in Dover Castle with a companion to attempt the Channel from the English coast.

Blanchard had fallen back on Rouen after the parlous start of his career in the Champ de Mars on 2 March 1784. There in the capital of his native Normandy he perfected his art in public demonstrations that realized his hopes, one on 23 May, another on 18 July. Thence he passed to England, departing Dieppe on 14 August without his balloon, over which the customs made difficulties. He arrived in London in time for the first proper ascension in the British Isles, executed not by an Englishman, but by a daredevil attaché of the Neapolitan embassy. Vincent Lunardi flew a hydrogen balloon that he had made himself from the Artillery Ground on 15 September 1784. One of its two oars fell off almost immediately, narrowly missing a spectator.

Meanwhile, Blanchard associated himself successively with two physicians who professed scientific interests, John Sheldon, an Englishman, and John Jeffries (Fig. 55), an American loyal to Britain and a graduate of Harvard College. Blanchard made two ascensions in October, the second with Sheldon, but neither of them was satisfactory. On 30 November he tried again, this time with Jeffries. They took off from the Rhedarium in central London and traveled down into Kent while Jeffries recorded elaborate meteorological data. By year's end they were ready for the Channel and arrived in Dover on 17 December. Jeffries published the narrative of their exploit a little later, and paid the bills at the time.

After three weeks of waiting, the wind stood fair for France on 7 January 1785, and they were off. About halfway across, their balloon began to lose altitude. First they threw out ballast, and then provisions, anchors, grappling hooks, cordage, water, ornamentation, and even lining stripped from the gondola. Finally even the coats on their backs went over the rail, followed by Blanchard's trousers. All to little avail, for with four or five miles still to go they were below the level of the cliffs of Calais, the waves licking at their underparts. Bracing for an icy bath, they donned cork jackets, when suddenly and inexplicably their balloon took a new lease on flight, rose above the danger, and carried them in their undergarments across the shoreline and inland for an additional forty-eight minutes after their two-hour crossing. They came down in the branches of a tree in the forest of Guînes, hard by the spot where Henry VIII had met François Ier on the Field of the Cloth of Gold.[41]

Pilatre bit the bullet, played the good sport, and participated in the official welcome offered by dignitaries in Calais. Afterward he traveled with Blanchard and Jeffries to Paris. Thereupon, he perched atop his cliff, his equipment sheltered in a tent, awaiting conditions that would allow his making good his own commitment, however dulled its edge. Unfortunately, the prevailing wind was the northwester that Blanchard had ridden.

Months went by. Pilatre visited Paris from time to time, and even England.[42] Finally the wind pattern changed in June, and takeoff was announced for the 15th of the month.

Spectators gathered from all over the Pas-de-Calais. The day promised to be very hot. First Pilatre and Romains filled the upper-stage globe with hydrogen generated in the conventional manner by sulfuric acid acting on iron filings. When the lower-stage *montgolfière* had been inflated in its turn, the hydrogen component was floated over it. An arrangement of cords linked the two nettings. Pilatre and Romains took their places at seven o'clock in the morning and ordered the retaining cords cast off. Eyewitnesses agreed that they rose to an altitude of perhaps 6,000 feet in a matter of twelve minutes. Thereupon, the two parts of the bi-balloon appeared to separate more widely. Instants later a flame shot from the very top. For a few moments they hung motionless as the upper module became a globe of fire.

Opinions differ whether a spark from the *montgolfière* burner below caused ignition or one produced electrostatically by friction between a copper ring and a steel sleeve in the safety valve for hydrogen above.[43] Searchers found the fabric of the hot-air balloon nearly intact among the boulders of the shore and near it the shattered bodies of the aeronauts.

Thus perished the first airman in the first air crash (Fig. 56).

Three days later, on 18 June, Meusnier read the Academy of Science an account of the accident sent him from Boulogne.[44] In October 1785 Joseph de Montgolfier and Ami Argand visited Pilatre's grave. They were on their way to England, for Joseph had rallied to Argand's side there in the latter's battle to defend the patent on his lamp.[45] Through the good offices of Réveillon, Etienne contributed to a subscription for erecting a mausoleum to house Pilatre's remains.[46]

4. COMMERCIAL AVIATION

At home meanwhile in Vidalon, all passion far from spent, Etienne peopled the skies of his imag-

J. Russell pinx.ᵗ
Crayon Painter to his
Royal Highness the
Prince of Wales.

Caroline Watson sculp.ᵗ
Engraver to her Majesty.

JOHN JEFFRIES M.D.

*We appear'd at this time to be about three quarters of the distance towards the French shore; and we had fallen so low as to be beneath the plane of the French Cliffs. ——— We were then preparing to get up into our Slings, when I found the Mercury in the Barometer again falling, & looking around, soon observ'd that we were rising, & that the pleasing view of France was enlarging & opening to us every moment, as we ascended so as to overlook the high grounds.

* Dʳ JEFFRIES NARRATIVE, ——— SECOND VOYAGE.

Publish'd according to Act of Parliament, April 3.ᵈ 1786, by James Robson, Bond Street.

55. John Jeffries, M.D.

ination with argosies of airborne merchandise. Though bound to deplore Pilatre's death in public, and to swell the decent chorus of tributes to the victim's courage and regrets over the excess of his zeal, Etienne privately considered that the shock might well be beneficial. Aviation needed to be turned from mounting spectacular stunts to proving its utility. The public must be brought to think of airships, not as motifs prompting the latest frippery in couture, coiffure, or porcelains (and the disaster at Boulogne did indeed deflate the fashion), but as instruments of commerce.

To that end Etienne composed a memoir "Sur l'utilité des aérostats." Drafted late in 1785 or early in 1786, it reviews the history of the discovery Joseph and he had made and considers the prospects. The tone is reflective, or was meant to be. Etienne failed, however, to resist throwing up his hands in an aside about the official mentality that would lavish thousands in public funds on a junket of seven leagues across the glamor of the seas while refusing the least sou to development of inland transport over comparable or greater distances.[47] He had to admit the justice of the criticism that so far aerostats had served only to excite the curiosity of the public. A contrary complaint, namely that aviation ministered only to the vanity of scientists, he found quite unacceptable. True, lacking a great fortune, his esteemed friend Meusnier had perforce limited his analysis to the theory of flight. But to dismiss the work accomplished as an empty exercise would be philistine.

Such a judgment would be as absurd as it once would have been to disdain the science of celestial navigation and abandon seafaring just because, despite the perfection of mathematical theory, a vessel might still be incapable of sailing a straight line in the teeth of contrary winds to a given destination. Aviation was at the stage where shipping had been right after the first voyagers hollowed out and launched a canoe onto unknown waters. Was it to be denied a comparable chance to prove its value? The skies were now as open to exploitation as the seas. Etienne was confident that men would one day—albeit not in his time—travel their whole extent as readily and fearlessly

as, after much individual sacrifice and daring, they had come to do the oceans of the world. What alone would bring that to pass would be the uses of trade and commerce.

For commerce, Etienne continues in a philosophical vein, is "the lifeblood of an ordered world."[48] Considered in its essentials, it consists of providing countries with goods they lack in exchange for the superfluous portion of those that abound, whether through industry or nature. It is through trade that the nations of the world communicate. In the eyes of the merchant the boundaries that separate peoples disappear. Commerce breaks through even the barriers raised by geography. Northern countries obtain the productions that nature denies to industry and that require sun. Reciprocally, countries of the southern regions have access to commodities peculiar to northern climes and unobtainable from their own baked and arid soil. Thus are formed lines that link all peoples pole to pole.

Prosperity does not depend on trading in particular localities. The essential relations are not among the famous cities where exchange happens to occur, but among manufacturer, consumer, and agriculturalist. Demand is always there, and the market for commodities from afar is assured provided only that the cost of transport be kept as low as possible. And precisely there lay the opportunity for aviation. Seizing it was beyond the modest means of a family of middling manufacturers. Oh, he would have readily invested all that was needed had theirs been a great fortune. Failing that, he still hoped for vision on the part of government, the object of his peroration:

Thereupon, we shall see aeronauts departing on a north wind with confidence that in the tropics they will meet with the trade winds that will carry them to America, laden with the productions of European civilization. The shift in direction that this steady wind makes when it reaches the northern continent will facilitate their return by carrying them toward that favored country [whose inhabitants] at the price of their blood have just acquired the liberty of which their efforts

56. A German illustrator's impression of the crash of Pilatre's Channel Balloon. The object on the left may be an imaginary observation balloon or the other half of Pilatre's ill-fated aircraft. Or perhaps it is meant to represent Blanchard and Jeffries earlier on.

prove them worthy. West winds are almost constant over the ocean that separates us from that happy continent, and will return these new argonauts to their fatherland.

Thereupon, too, our new Columbuses, after having collected all the observations recorded for us on the winds of Africa, will venture out over that unknown continent, the interior of which we may well have no other way of penetrating. Thereupon, finally, the inhabitants of our colonies will no longer feel penalized by the lack of roads for sending the products of their industry to the ports, but readily taking advantage of alternating landward and seaward breezes, will easily transport the fruits of their peaceful occupations to the nearest seaside. . . . Then and only then will mankind have acquired a new domain. The hand of time, the work of ingenuity, and experience for which there is no substitute will assure him domination over it.

Etienne's fancy was nothing if not concrete. Surviving among his papers are many sheets (for example, Figs. 57 and 58) on which he compiled potential itineraries and timetables for his cargo aircraft. One memorandum, perhaps intended to accompany the essay just discussed, takes the reader on an airborne peddler's journey worthy of Jules Verne, except that the object is not fictional.[49] It was written to convince the authorities of the feasibility in principle of an experimental trading voyage. For the sake of argument, Etienne stipulated only that it be supposed that the winds recorded in Paris in January and February 1785 had blown uniformly throughout the country. If such an assumption was favorable to his venture in certain localities, it was unfavorable in others, and the differences would even out.

Paris was the starting point and 10 January the day of departure. The cargo was to consist of mirrors, a vulnerable item on the roads, together with rolls of wallpaper and other luxuries. Weighing anchor and taking off at 1:00 p.m., our aeronauts rode a six-league-per-hour wind to reach Sully-sur-Loire at 3:30. On the 11th a shift into

the northwest carried them forty-eight leagues beyond Cluny. On the 12th the wind backed into the north, and the party sailed over Montbrison, Saint-Flour and Pierrefort to descend at Rouergue. The next day, their fourth, they made good their arrival by way of Albi at a destination near Toulouse. There they could choose between the highway for Montpellier or the banks of the Languedoc Canal. Either location would allow them to vend their merchandise to retailers in Toulouse, and any surplus would be snapped up by traders supplying the neighboring towns by road or water.

For the return trip the hold would be charged with products of Languedoc—cloth, vegetable oils, and *eau de vie*, together with poultry, for which the region around Toulouse was famous. On the 15th, 16th, and 17th, the expedition was becalmed, a circumstance that gave time for bargaining. Then on the 18th, a southeast breeze took them thirty-eight leagues to Libourne for a few profitable exchanges. On the 19th, the weather was from the south. Taking on several crates of seafood to be sold the next day at Saumur, they proceeded on the 20th over Chateau Gontier and Laval to Avranches. The travelers thought better of continuing on to Cherbourg, lest they be swept out to sea, and paused for a few days, selling and buying all they could. On the 29th a southwester took them to Bayeux. They might have flown on to England and begun anew in London, but elected to await a shift for central France. En route to Rheims, Etienne had his crew anchor at Ermenonville that he might figuratively cast his laurels on the grave of Rousseau, and we will not follow further.

Etienne was altogether serious about these proposals, and for a time it seemed he might yet prevail. There in the privacy of Vidalon, he began repairing the wreck Pilatre had made of the *Marie-Antoinette*. One of his intimates, Pache (who had retired to his native Neuchâtel from the service of the maréchal de Castries) advised him to return to Paris and see to his own interest.[50] Etienne preferred to enlist the good offices of another friend and a compatriot, Antoine Boissy d'Anglas. The entry Etienne gave him to the salons of Madame

Blondel, of Madame Douet de Laboulaye, and to the acquaintance of the comte d'Antraigues, were the future statesman's introduction to Paris society.[51] He capitalized upon it and prevailed on Malesherbes to take up Etienne's cause in the inner circles of court and government.

Through these channels Etienne submitted a new proposal to the administration early in March 1786. He would undertake to construct an aerostat capable of carrying a burden of 40,000 pounds, of remaining aloft for five days, and of flying nonstop from Annonay to Paris. Evidently he had lowered his sights, for he now estimated the cost at 60,000 livres. Of that, he would be willing to risk 20,000 himself. Malesherbes was among the most respected of courtiers, and Calonne reversed his cutoff of October 1784, agreeing to these terms on 25 March 1786. In April the Treasury duly paid over its share of 40,000 livres to Etienne. At the same time, the king intervened personally to improve upon the conditions. The moment that Etienne himself arrived by air at the helm direct from Avignon, he would be reimbursed the remaining 20,000 livres.[52]

We do not know how far Etienne went in fulfilling his engagements. Certainly progress was slower than he had expected. Almost a year later, in February 1787, a brief memorandum records that winter weather had interrupted the experiments he was making in order to determine the most advantageous proportions. The machine was over half finished, however, and he had spent the winter evenings calculating navigational tables for speedy conversion of observational data into information on position, altitude, and winds. He hoped to begin experiments in the spring preparatory to making the long trips for which the machine was being designed.[53]

Those journeys never came about. Fragmentary correspondence through the summer of 1787 suggests that expenses were running over Etienne's estimates and that he was seeking further subsidy. Apparently he was loath to furnish his intermediaries with precise information on the state of construction. Calonne fell from office in the spring of that year, to be replaced by Laurent de Villedeuil. One of the less effective of the ministers of finance in the fiscal extremity of the monarchy, he was more sympathetic than Calonne to Etienne and to the claims of aeronautics. When he in turn resigned late in August 1787, hope went with him. Grasping at straws, Boissy d'Anglas tried to buck up Etienne and urged him to furnish specifications and an accounting to be referred to a carefully chosen member of the Academy of Science. Should it be Lavoisier? Desmarest?[54] Etienne did reply, but the setbacks were too much for him, and he now joined Joseph in abandoning the invention that had made their name famous.[55]

Had management of the family business suffered from Etienne's absorption in aviation? Such was the burden of his father's constant complaint, of course. The old man may well have been right. Etienne said so himself often enough in his pleas to the authorities, and there are confirming indications. Sales of Montgolfier paper plunged in 1783-1784 whereas demand for the Johannot product held steady.[56] It seems probable, however, that the decline, though intensified by effects of Etienne's absence, resulted from a problem that had contributed to his going to Paris in the first place. The difficulties originated with the adaptation of production to the use of hollanders and with the consequent renovation of the labor force. From a memoir on regulation of the paper industry that Etienne addressed in August 1786 to Blondel, who was still intendant of commerce, it appears that trouble with discipline was continuing at Vidalon. The number of inside workers was down to 150, though the factory was designed to employ 225 people. He hoped soon to be back to that.[57]

Etienne never did realize his dream of converting Vidalon into a school or institute of papermaking. Immediately after his return from Paris in June 1784, he addressed himself to the provincial authorities, appealing directly to the archbishop of Narbonne, presiding dignitary of the Estates of Languedoc. Clearly his importunities over subsidy for the hollanders had worn out his welcome in Montpellier, for the syndic observed to the intendant of commerce (Blondel again, probably) that "Monsieur de Montgolfier, capi-

57-58. Itineraries for a cargo balloon, in the hand of Etienne de Montgolfier

talizing on the good luck that has brought him his so-called (and so far, at least, altogether useless) discovery, wanted to try to augment the marks of favor that he has already received, whether with respect to that or to the paper mill at Annonay. I could not, however, refrain from observing to him that, as to the latter object, the Estates had already carried the views of the minister into effect."[58]

The long and technically fruitful association with Desmarest may have left Etienne even more prone than other manufacturers in France to look to agencies of government for protection of enlightened enterprise from the slings and arrows of outrageous competition. In addition to enlisting Malesherbes in the cause of the cargo balloon,

Boissy d'Anglas had a further commission from the Montgolfiers in 1786 and 1787. Through the good offices of the same statesman, he set about securing for Vidalon a monopoly of the supply of paper for a new stamp that would be required to validate sales subject to an excise tax that the government was meditating. The controller general must be given to understand that Etienne had no wish to be granted an unfair advantage. But if he could be assured of an outlet for that one product, his mind could rise above the daily battle for markets and his attention be freed for matters of public utility.[59]

There was trouble of a more embarrassing sort. In June 1785, Réveillon had to write his old friend a regretful letter. He had hesitated to do so, but to fail in frankness would be wounding to their confidence in each other. He had to say, then, that the last shipment of paper from Vidalon was of an inferior quality that should never have come out of the Montgolfier vats. Of sixty-seven reams, only twelve were passable, and only four were close to what they should have been, though even so not quite up to standard. He was astonished, so much so that he had shown samples to Etienne's Uncle Jacques, who confirmed his judgment.[60]

Two visitors to Annonay, one in 1786 and the other in 1787, have left records of the impression made on them by the principal manufacturers. In both instances, the comparison is to the advantage of the Montgolfiers in point of urbanity and of the Johannots in point of enterprise. Victor Dupont de Nemours, a nineteen-year-old son of Pierre-Samuel, the physiocrat who made the name of that family famous, spent a week in Annonay in July 1786. His father, then an administrator in the ministry of finance, sent his son on several tours of industrial inspection in those years, partly by way of educating him and partly to gather personal information that would supplement the dry statistics that crossed his desk in official reports. Victor and his two companions thought Annonay an ugly city and badly laid out, though surrounded by charming country. They had letters introducing them to the Montgolfiers. Soon after their arrival, Etienne called to escort them to Vidalon, where he and others of the family reproached them hospitably for lodging in the town. The visitors found the house and garden truly picturesque, there in the cleft of the ravine. The factory, however, suffered from a faulty installation, the several workshops having been added on at different times. A fine new building was said to be in the planning stage.

As to the Johannots, the Dupont party spent

only one day at Faya, strictly on business, and Victor says little about personalities. There the owners were about to complete a new factory, which they had begun building three years previously. It was splendid. An expanse of fifty windows ventilated the drying racks and admitted light to the workshops. Already the Johannots had six hollanders in place and intended to install two more. In general, Victor noted, these people supervised their operation with more care and attention to every detail than did their counterparts. They did a larger business in France and abroad, notably in England.[61]

In 1787 a second visitor, better qualified to judge, left a still more damaging comparison. Emric David, a printer and publisher in Marseilles, made a tour of paper mills throughout Dauphiny and Languedoc in October of that year. Several customers, he reported, considered both the Johannot and the Montgolfier paper to be very expensive and thought that the latter had gone off in quality. David found Jean Johannot, old Matthieu's son, to be a straightforward, uncultivated person, polite but unceremonious, inventive and alert to possible improvements. Among the Montfgolfier brothers, Joseph (at home for once) struck him as large of stature, simple in bearing, and to all appearances stronger physically than intellectually. Etienne was a short man, slight of build, bald, and a little affected. The impression was that of an academic, "guiding himself in the conduct of his art by mathematical rules and calculations involving *force* and *resistance*. He seems to prefer tightly articulated processes to experimentation by trial and error." So far as David could tell, "there was nothing in that household that people had less wanted to be involved in than balloons." His contrast in summary is worth giving verbatim:

At Johannot's I think one sees greater cleanliness and a calmer order—at Montgolfier's, more ostentation. At Johannot's, machinery of better quality and greater precision—at Montgolfier's, more expenditure for labor. Johannot seeks improvement by trying lots of experiments. Montgolfier wants to achieve

it by sure-fire methods. Johannot, used to the ways of business since his young days, brings to manufacturing the active and speculative spirit of a merchant. Montgolfier wants to be a scientist and to take the academic route.

A further line is crossed out in the manuscript: "All in all, I believe Johannot's is the more perfected." At Johannot's, finally, the superfine grade was certainly far superior. Montgolfier used more pulp in his product. In the last analysis, both factories might be useful suppliers: the Johannots for the finest paper and the Montgolfiers for inferior grades.[62]

In sum, the spirit of modernization that Etienne brought to Vidalon had a more positive effect on principles than on profits. Fiscally, the business labored under difficulties compounded by legal clouds obscuring the ownership of the property. For neither Etienne nor Pierre, his father, had a clear title. On the marriage of the oldest son, Raymond, in 1761, Pierre had settled one of the two factories on him, retaining the business and the profits. The expectation was that the arrangement would be *pro forma* and that the father would gradually yield management to the son and remain the honored head of firm and family in the custom of the country. In 1767, Vidalon-le-bas went to a nephew. In 1771, Raymond died, leaving his four daughters legally the owners of Vidalon-le-haut. Their mother soon quarreled with the patriarch and departed, and their guardians refused to accede to an agreement retroceding the factory to old Pierre.

Accordingly, when Etienne took control of the business, as distinct from the factory, the legal basis was a lease of the property from his nieces and an agreement on sharing profits in the family. His father now arbitrarily valued the factory at 36,000 livres and stipulated that Etienne should inherit either that sum or the property if his nieces should agree to sell their shares. One of the four died. As we have seen, Marc-François Seguin, who married the oldest of the three remaining in 1782, amicably accepted payment of 12,000 livres for his wife's interest. The second married Gilbert de Colonjon in March 1784, at a moment when Etienne was developing his scheme of locomotion for the Academy in Paris. Lawyers, his mother-in-law, and greed possessed the bridegroom soon after, and he refused in his wife's name to accept settlement. A few years later the third daughter married Matthieu Duret, a nephew, physician, and Joseph's sometime protégé, well disposed to the family. Among them all, they brought the Colonjons around, but not before the good faith of Pierre and Etienne had been traduced and the family name vilified and trailed through many a courtroom.[63]

5. REVOLUTIONARY INTERMEZZO

With all that, the Revolution came to Etienne as something of a welcome break in 1789, a chance for a new beginning and a new ordering of affairs. So also it did, for a mixture of private and public reasons, in the lives of the great majority of French manufacturers and businessmen. Etienne was anything but a politician by temperament. Instead, he had the capacity to inspire confidence in others like himself. He might have been a statesman if he had been born to power. As it was, his fellow citizens elected him mayor of Davézieux in March 1789. On the eve of revolution, that tiny commune just north of Annonay thus affirmed the standing of its leading citizen. Boissy d'Anglas wrote to congratulate his erstwhile mentor.[64] For Etienne's old friend was indeed a politician at heart. He had bought an honorific post as *maître d'hôtel* of the comte de Provence and had been admitted to the bar. Enthusiasm for the corridors of power was already evident in his lobbying on behalf of the Montgolfier interests in balloons and paper throughout the years just past. In the elections for the Estates-General, which convened on 5 May 1789, Boissy was chosen to represent the third estate, the commoners, of Annonay in the body soon to declare itself the National Constituent Assembly. His correspondence gave Etienne a sense of vicarious participation in the great events swirling across Paris, and Etienne went to the capital to see for himself

late in June. He was there, lodging as always with his uncle, in the headquarters of the archdiocese, when the Bastille fell on 14 July, and he remained throughout the tense days culminating in the renunciation of feudal rights in the Constituent Assembly on 4 August, departing for Annonay soon afterward.[65]

Etienne's participation in the ensuing events of the Revolution was largely administrative and commercial, as befitted his temperament. In January 1790, the Constituent Assembly decreed conversion of the ancient patchwork of provinces, overlapping crazily with the *généralités* and lesser fiscal and juridical units of local government, into the modern structure of departments. At the instance of Boissy d'Anglas, Etienne was named to the board of administrators of the Ardèche, the new designation for much the same territory as that of the Vivarais of yore.[66] Only under Napoleon in 1800 did concentration of departmental authority in the hands of a prefect replace regional government by commission. The original "directories" consisted of some ten persons who chose from among their number a president and a secretary general to exercise responsibilities day to day. Etienne remained behind the scenes. His name appears only a few times in the minutes of its meetings.[67]

In March 1790 his colleagues put him on the committee of three charged with organizing subdivision of the Ardèche into districts and cantons. The task was touchy politically, since the boundaries would determine the constituencies that would name electors for the National Legislative Assembly to be chosen by indirect vote in September 1791. A letter Etienne wrote the abbé from a remote corner of the department deplores the thanklessness of public service. He was finding the various communities he visited to be as fully under the sway of self-interest as were individual persons.[68] The abbé, suffering from laryngitis, had just written of their sister, the Reverend Mother Thérèse, who had been "prophesying at his bedside" and mistaking her dreams for inspiration. She was also worrying about the future of her convent at Boulieu. The abbé described the local radicals as "Franciscan zealots," and closed his letter—which he had dictated to Jean-Pierre—with "Farewell, my friend" in English. The latter was more outspoken about the self-importance of the hometown worthies in the two Masonic lodges, now become political forums: "Annonay has meetings every evening at six o'clock. What fine things two assemblies composed of the elite of the learned and the lawyers, etc., should accomplish! For the sake of future generations, and lest the fruits of their labors be lost, they will no doubt favor us with their publication."[69]

Commerce rather than politics always brought out the visionary in Etienne. What fired his spirits in the Revolution was the abolition of internal tolls and tariffs, which made possible communications uninterrupted by artificial barriers. To exploit the opportunity, he teamed himself with Joseph once again, their notion being to create by water and by land the national system of transportation that Etienne had imagined for the air, and that forty-odd years later their great-nephew Marc Seguin began realizing in the form of bridges, steam navigation, and railways. To that end, Etienne went to the National Assembly through the good offices of Boissy d'Anglas, still his man in Paris, with a proposal for a venture that in economic principle would have looked very like a modern railroad or airline. The existing service of *diligences*, or stagecoaches, provided by a quasi-governmental administration, was inadequate for passengers, mail, and freight. Its responsibilities, for the Paris-Marseilles route as a starter, would be turned over to the partnership formed by the Montgolfier brothers. Their principal innovation would be to take full advantage of transport by water along the Seine and Yonne in the upper sector and along the Saône and Rhône from the Burgundian heartland to the Mediterranean. They had designed appropriate boats, docking facilities, and carriages for the purpose, and would undertake to construct and maintain their floating and rolling stock and also to keep up and, where necessary, to build roads and bridges. In return they would be granted an exclusive charter, for a term of fifteen years, to carry mail, freight, and passengers. They might

also charge private conveyances tolls for using their facilities.[70]

It required justification, not to say special pleading, to come forward with such a petition at a time when monopoly, privilege, and special favor were being everywhere struck down in the name of liberalism. In a covering memorandum addressed to Boissy d'Anglas, Etienne invoked the right of inventors to protection of their property in their ideas, at least for a time, if society was to have the benefit of their exploitation. The arguments were the same as those being employed to justify the provisions of the first comprehensive patent law in France, adopted by the National Assembly on 7 January 1791.[71] They read a little lamely here, however, since it was a question of a new enterprise rather than some specific device. The Assembly failed to act on the proposal. As we have seen, Etienne was never one to abandon ideas easily. He renewed this one in a memorandum that is undated but that he must have drafted in 1793 or 1794. It alludes to interruption of communication by the Prussian armies and by the British Navy along the coasts, a situation that would have been much eased had his scheme been adopted, as he hoped it still might be.[72]

In the spring and summer of 1791 Etienne took some little part in local discussions of national politics. Like his brother, the abbé, and indeed like many public-spirited people of their class, he was a Freemason. In March 1791 the central lodge, the Grand Orient in Paris, quite politicized in the Revolution, resolved to transform its affiliates throughout the country into open societies in correspondence with the Jacobin Club in the capital. That these bodies would evolve into the radical organization of 1793, and become the political basis of government under the Terror of 1793 and 1794, was not to be predicted at the outset. Boissy d'Anglas was one of the founders of the Jacobins, and anything but a democrat. The final letter in the political series he wrote Etienne, which ends in 1791, contemptuously dismissed the notion of including "plebes" in the political process.[73] Moreover, in the Ardèche, a relatively backward region, peasant resistance to Paris and all its works was a more natural feature of the Revolution than political radicalism.[74]

Even so, Etienne appears to have been distinctly on the cautious side of the political center in Annonay. At first he attended meetings of the new Society of Friends of the Constitution, as the Jacobins called themselves. Combining the two lodges "Vraie Vertu" and "Vraie Amitié," it was inaugurated there on 24 March 1791. He accepted its commission to encourage enlistment of volunteers in the militia. In July he was among all the king's horses and all the king's men trying to piece the Humpty Dumpty of constitutional monarchy together again after Louis XVI and his family fled from the hands of its friends in Paris, only to be captured at Varennes before reaching the shelter of its enemies, the emigré noblemen with the Austrian armies on the frontier. On 2 July Etienne moved a resolution affirming the confidence of the Annonay society in the subsequent measures taken by the National Assembly and deploring the position adopted by sister societies in favor of a republic. He put his weight behind two other motions of a moderating nature. By a proposal of 21 July the society would urge the National Assembly to move the seat of government away from Paris, ever the source of violence and disorder. By another of 31 July it would reunite itself with the once liberal and now backpedaling Feuillant Society. None of these three measures carried, and Etienne thereafter quietly withdrew from participation in the society and, so far as might be, from partisan activities generally.[75] He was the recipient of many views on politics in his further correspondence, and he emitted few.

He returned his attention to local affairs and to the business. Jean-Pierre and increasingly his son, Jean-Baptiste, had resumed responsibility for the daily operation of Vidalon (if, indeed, Etienne had ever fully taken it back on returning home in 1784), and they needed his help from on high. Effects of the Revolution had damaged the paper industry before the military and economic crisis of the summer of 1793.[76] The supply of rags had dwindled. Younger workers went

into the army. Even if more than a skeleton work force had remained, it would have been impossible to find enough food for them. Clients were unsure of their needs, and orders fell off along with the capacity to fill them. Supplying the government with paper on which to print *assignats*, the currency backed by land confiscated from Church and aristocracy, failed to redeem the uncertainty over terms of trade caused by its rapid depreciation. The problem was compounded by the Jacobin policy of controlling prices.

Amid these instabilities Etienne could draw on his experience and influence to secure orders on the best possible terms from local authorities, agencies of state, and other customers. From April until November 1792 he spent most of his time in Privas, the administrative center of the Ardèche. How he divided his energy between the business of the family and of the department is unclear. The only record is an exchange of letters with Jean-Pierre and Jean-Baptiste.[77] Nothing is said of the declaration of war that France was to wage against most of Europe for the next quarter-century. After the overthrow of the monarchy by the uprising in Paris on 15 August, Jean-Pierre angrily supposed that some malign configuration of comets and planets must account for follies and irrationality unparalleled in history. He also imagined that anarchists at home might be in the pay of emigrés abroad, extremists from left and right leagued to destroy order.[78] Jean-Baptiste clung unrealistically to the imperative of preserving the constitution.[79] Apart from that, the letters concern the affairs of Annonay and Vidalon. Workers and townspeople were proving more skeptical of payment in *assignats* than were country folk. Jean-Baptiste was disbursing none of their own reserve of specie. Deliveries were impossible to assure.[80] Jean-Pierre suspected that their correspondence was being opened and read by unknown agents. Lest that be the case, Etienne began enclosing his replies under cover of envelopes addressed to his wife.[81] Jean-Pierre also regretted that the only horse he could send his brother was a sorry nag.[82] Late in August he wrote of closing the chapel in Vidalon for fear of anti-clerical political sentiment in Annonay.[83] Old

Pierre had the oratory moved to the secrecy of a nearby farm he owned, and there Father Clozel continued to say clandestine masses.

Early in December 1792 Etienne departed for Paris. The reason may have been that Johannot was also there, busy gleaning orders. Apart from one reference to the instability of politics and the unreliability of people in general, the reader of Etienne's correspondence would never know that the two competitors were in the capital at a time when they might have witnessed the trial and execution of Louis XVI and observed the struggle between Girondists and Jacobins in the Convention, where deputies of the Plain (among them Boissy d'Anglas, again representing Annonay) were eventually overwhelmed or reduced to silence by the radicals of the Mountain.

Etienne occupied himself primarily with obtaining commissions from the government. The Montgolfiers had developed a counterfeit-proof paper for *assignats*. Beyond that he warned his brother that the currency might depreciate even faster in the future. They must on no account enter into contracts calling for deliveries at a price fixed in advance. On the contrary, they would do well to give estimates on the high side and where possible delay shipment of current production until the picture clarified. Etienne urged his brother and his nephew to stock rags for pulping against the certainty of higher costs and also to lay in a supply of grain.[84] Detail about the treatment of four or five employees makes clear that he was still the active head of the company, as does a letter of late January 1793, one of those written when Etienne was out of sorts, scolding Jean-Baptiste for having failed to send certain accounts, bills, and samples of playing cards: "That is not the way to do business."[85]

We know little of life in Vidalon during the Terror of 1793-1794. The reader may, however, wish to learn what became of others who figured in the birth of aviation. Among those associated with the Montgolfiers ten years earlier, the two who became politicians, Boissy d'Anglas and Pache, enhanced their influence in the Revolution and outlived it. Throughout the Terror, Boissy d'Anglas concealed his reservations suf-

ficiently to survive as a deputy. He helped end it by joining with Tallien and Barrère in the opposition that rallied the Convention to overthrow Robespierre on 9 Thermidor. In the ensuing months of August and September 1794, Boissy d'Anglas organized the supply of provisions to Paris. His sang-froid as president (or Speaker) of the Convention in the face of the events of 1 Prairial Year III (20 May 1795) won him national reputation. On that day a mob of Jacobin extremists burst into the hall demanding bread and liberty. Féraud, deputy for the Hautes-Pyrénées, tried to block the door. A rioter shot him dead, whereupon the others fell upon the corpse, cut off the head, and paraded it on a pike before the chair. Boissy d'Anglas gravely saluted the bloody object. In the hush the National Guard arrived and arrested those of the band who failed to make good their escape back to the faubourg Saint-Antoine.[86]

Pache, Etienne's comrade from school days in Paris, became a partisan of the Terror. From lackey and tutor to the son of the maréchal de Castries, he evolved into a democrat of extreme Rousseauist persuasion, and was all the deadlier for a glacial, desiccated manner. Returning to Paris from his retirement—and possibly a breakdown—in his native Switzerland, he drew upon his experience of the Marine Ministry under Castries to serve Roland as adviser—more accurately, as informer—in the Ministry of the Interior before August 1792. On the declaration of a republic, he took the War Ministry, where he set about purging the officer corps and the bureaucracy of holdovers from the old regime. Through his influence, the important mathematician, Gaspard Monge, like himself a former protégé of Castries, became minister of marine affairs. Scientists and technicians of Monge's entourage, Jacobin to a man, served under Pache, heading up the chief agencies of the War Department throughout the autumn and winter of 1792-1793. The Girondist faction retained enough power to force Pache from office on 2 February 1793, whereupon he drew upon his strength in the Paris sections, which elected him mayor on 17 February. In that office he served, exerting leftward pressure upon Robespierre, for whom it became too much. Pache was removed shortly before the debacle of 9 Thermidor. Unlike many former Jacobins, he escaped reprisals and lived out his days in silence in the country.[87]

Among the followers of Monge on whose expertise Pache drew was Meusnier. After his year of aeronautics mingled with chemistry, Meusnier had returned to military duty and risen to the rank of colonel. He was the highest serving officer who had Pache's full confidence politically. The radical faction preferred attack across the Rhine and into Germany over the thrust into Belgium, suspecting (quite rightly) that Dumouriez, the commander in Belgium, was disloyal to the Revolution. Thus Meusnier found himself in the field, posted to the forces occupying the city of Mainz in the Rhineland. Placed in command of the outlying fortress of Kastel on the right bank, he was wounded in the counterattack by which the Prussians recaptured the entire stronghold. He died on 13 June 1793.[88]

The deaths by guillotine of Lavoisier and Malesherbes need no comment here.

Two aristocrats who figured in our story were no more fortunate. The comte d'Antraigues was elected to the Estates-General in 1789 to represent the nobility of Villeneuve-de-Berg in the Vivarais. He conducted himself with an inconsistency that bespeaks flippancy, not to say instability, and emigrated to Geneva late in the year or early in 1790. After publishing a tract on divorce, he secretly married the mistress to whom he had introduced Etienne, the opera singer "la St.-Huberty." D'Antraigues plotted successively in Spain, where he raised a legion to invade Languedoc; in Russia, where he acted for the future Louis XVIII; in Italy, where Napoleon had him arrested in Trieste in 1797, whence he escaped to Austria; and in England, where George Canning took him on as an intelligence agent in the Foreign Office. As he and his wife got into their carriage on the outskirts of London one evening in 1812, they were assassinated by an Italian servant whom they had dismissed the previous day.[89]

Jacques de Flesselles, the genial and urbane magistrate for whom Joseph named the balloon in Lyons, moved from the intendancy there to become *prévôt des marchands* in Paris shortly before the Revolution. The responsibilities were essentially those of mayor of the city. Disorders that culminated in the capture of the Bastille on 14 July 1789 started several days beforehand. Two deliberative bodies were by then sitting as parallel municipal councils in the city hall, the newly formed assembly of electors who had chosen the deputies representing Paris in the Estates-General, and the long-standing board of aldermen at whose meetings the *prévôt des marchands* presided. A joint committee bickered suspiciously over its inability to reconcile their purviews. In duty bound, Flesselles had continued reporting to the court and the commander of the garrison in Paris. On 12 July a hostile elector questioned Flesselles on these messages before a meeting of the joint committee open to the public. Unused to justifying himself before a crowd, he stammered in reply. Murmurs swelled to a demand that he be haled before the tribunal sitting at the Palais Royal. Very well, "Let's go to the Palais Royal," he agreed, starting down the great staircase. Before he reached the bottom, a young man drew a pistol and shot him through the ear. His head was among the first in the Revolution to end upon a pike. It led the parade to the Palais Royal. His body was trailed alongside through the mud of the gutter.[90]

Réveillon had come close to encountering a similar fate. What with his wealth, his philanthropy, and his prestige among manufacturers, Réveillon was a member of that same Assembly of Electors. He was one among thirty-six commissioners selected by the larger body on 27 April to draw up the list of grievances that the city wished to see redressed by the Estates-General. Representatives of the higher bourgeoisie were generally perceived as oppressors by the still obscure and mostly nameless leaders among sectors of the working class. Réveillon was here singled out as the main target, perhaps because his factory was in the midst of the seething faubourg Saint-Antoine. After the names of the commissioners were announced, he was hanged in effigy in the Place de Grève before the city hall. The next day, the 28th, the garden where Etienne had constructed his aircraft was invaded, and the factory pillaged. Several vandals died of their own folly, mistaking for potables the contents of flasks containing sulfuric and nitric acid in the dye shop. Two were apprehended, and later hanged: Jean-Claude Gilbert, a blanket-maker (*couverturier*) and Antoine Pourat, a day laborer (*gagne-denier*). Réveillon fled to the shelter of the Bastille nearby. It was put about, though never proved, that the authorities there had deliberately delayed aid from the garrison in order that the excesses might have time to cast a shadow on the forthcoming meeting of the Estates-General. Réveillon was granted in-

demnification, but never recovered heart to resume the business.[91]

As for the balloon itself in the Revolution, it is not recorded that either Etienne or Joseph took any notice of its employment for military observation in the victory that Jourdan won over the Austrians and Dutch at Fleurus near the Belgian border on 26 June 1794 (Fig. 59). Nor was there any Montgolfier participation in an effort to develop its wartime capabilities and to train aeronauts, which was among the projects assigned to a proving ground at Meudon as a feature of the mobilization of science and technology under the Terror.[92]

After the fall of Robespierre on 9 Thermidor

59. Balloon observation at the Battle of Fleurus, an Austrian view

Ger. v. Auerbach Défontaines.   Gest. v. Ant. Klauber 1816.

Sieg bei Fleurus den 26ten Iuny 1794.

in the revolutionary calendar (27 July 1794) and the end of dictatorial rule by the Committee of Public Safety, Etienne emerged from the seclusion he had apparently imposed on himself and others of the family. The only letter we have from him during the Terror was addressed to Desmarest on 8 February 1794. The two had been out of touch for years, and Desmarest had evidently asked Etienne's opinion of a proposal for reform of nomenclature and rationalization of units of weight and measurement in the paper industry. A fine idea, Etienne replied, apologizing for tardiness in his response, and regretting that he had not been able to think about it properly, what with the pressures resulting from "the active part that every good citizen is obliged to take in public affairs."[93] With the return to what he trusted would be order and stability in mid-summer, Etienne himself drew up for the guidance of the new authorities yet another, and the last, of his memoirs on the importance of the paper industry, its disordered state, and its present needs. The tax on exportation of finished goods levied under the Terror must be repealed, though it was equally important to prohibit exportation of rags and raw materials for sizing. The precondition of all healthy commerce was a return to monetary discipline and stable prices. (In the event, inflation worsened drastically in the next few years of free enterprise.) The problem that he addressed at greatest length and with strongest feeling was the one that had bedeviled his entire career at Vidalon, labor discipline. The state must uphold the authority of masters and enforce the terms on which workers hired themselves out.[94]

Old Pierre, who had been born with the century, died on 1 June 1793. Among his sons, only Etienne and Joseph outlived their father for some years. Augustin, whose plant at Rives in Dauphiny had been closely linked with Joseph's at Voiron, had died on 27 September 1788. In order to have tax-free access to the market for paper in and around Lyons, Augustin moved his operation to Beaujeu in Beaujolais in 1785. There he enlarged and modernized a small mill in Les Ardillats, very near the birthplace of his grandfather Raymond, the one who had married into Vidalon. Ever highhanded with his work force,

Augustin was burned out within a few months of going into production. He died of pleurisy contracted amid the effort at reconstruction, leaving (for he was twice a widower) eight orphans, the oldest a girl of thirteen. Pierre sent a governess for them and a manager for the plant from Vidalon.[95]

That did not work well, and in 1791 the abbé Alexandre together with his sister, Mother Thérèse, came on from Annonay to take over the factory and bring up their nephews and nieces. Thérèse's convent at Boulieu had gone the way of religious foundations in the Revolution, into dissolution, and anti-clericalism in Annonay had increasingly distressed the spirits even of the goodnatured abbé. From time to time he spoke of emigrating to America with his sister and their charges. There they might start a new life with the help of Benjamin Franklin, whom Etienne had known in Paris. In Les Ardillats, the abbé was compromised by sheltering a friend and fellow clergyman, the canon Pressavins, who had been denounced in the local Jacobin society. Failing to find Pressavins in the factory, a band of vigilantes arrested the abbé instead. After two or three weeks of prison, in Beaujeu and in Lyons, he contracted a respiratory infection, probably pneumonia, and died in Vidalon on 19 July 1794, soon after his release.[96]

In accordance with Augustin's will, Jean-Pierre succeeded the abbé as guardian, and he in his turn now moved to Les Ardillats for the better part of a year, leaving the management of Vidalon entirely to his son, Jean-Baptiste. Among the business affairs of the family in 1794 and 1795 was liquidation of Joseph's factory at Voiron. A third of the capital value was due to Jean-Pierre, who journeyed on foot to Voiron for the closing. He took his share in *assignats*, which made a bulky set of packages that he concealed in the lining of his breeches. After a few days at home in Vidalon, he set out for his country house in Saint-Marcel, a little way up the Deûme. A gale was blowing, and an attack of asthma forced him to take shelter behind a wall in Boulieu. He died there on 26 November 1795. Jean-Baptiste found his father's body after some hours, but only a month later did the family learn from Joseph that his clothes had been full of money. By then they had been through the laundry, and the certificates were reduced to pulp, fit only for recycling in the paper mill.[97]

Under the Directory, which ruled France from 1795 until 1799, Etienne took a civilian post in the administration of the War Department, that of paymaster for the artillery in the Army of the Alps, with his office in Lyons. He used his influence to secure release of his future son-in-law from the army on the grounds that papermakers were exempt from conscription. Barthélemy Barou de la Lombardière de Canson had been in the service since the *levée-en-masse* of 1793. He was of an aristocratic family in Annonay, his father having been a Musketeer. After Jean-Pierre's death, Etienne reorganized the Montgolfier company to include Barou de Canson in the partnership with himself and his nephew, Jean-Baptiste. Two years later, in October 1798, Barou de Canson married Etienne's second daughter, Alexandrine.[98]

At the age of fifty-four, Etienne began to fail in health. He was much in Lyons in 1799. Feeling unwell there on 31 July, he left his apartment for Vidalon in the company of his nephew. At Serrières he was too ill to complete the thirteen kilometers remaining of the journey and stopped to rest in a property adjoining the Montgolfier warehouse on the outskirts. He died the next day, there where the road leaves the Rhône to climb the bluffs toward Annonay. Jean-Baptiste continued in association with Barou de Canson for another four years—wherefore the paper produced at Vidalon bears the trademark Canson-Montgolfier to this very day—and then departed amid hard feeling to start his own factories at Grosberty and Saint-Marcel, a little higher along the Deûme.[99] Adélaïde, Etienne's widow, moved to Paris, making her home for a time with Joseph in a house he had taken in the rue des Juifs, now the rue Ferdinand-Duval. She died in 1845 at the age of ninety-seven.[100]

Joseph, finally, entered into a second burst of inventive activity during the Revolution and became a person of note in the technical community of the capital in the last fifteen years of his life.

With his factory at Voiron off his hands in 1795, he moved to Paris two years later, largely at the instance of Ami Argand, fellow inventor and long an intimate of the family. The latter's discussions with Joseph in 1781 and 1782 on the nature of heat and burning had certainly contributed to the design of the Argand lamp. In that device a glass chimney accelerates the draft that supports combustion of oil impregnating a tubular wick.[101] As we have seen, Joseph adapted the design to the plans for the marquis de Brantes's balloon in Avignon in March 1784.[102] Argand had helped Etienne and Réveillon construct the Versailles balloon in the previous September and had then departed almost immediately for London. His object was to make arrangements for producing his lamp in Birmingham under the protection of a British patent.

His patent was infringed almost as soon as it was granted. In the midst of the ensuing lawsuit, Argand repeatedly begged Etienne to rally to his side and testify to his originality, else "I shall be ruined forever."[103] His letters were extremely emotional, even by the standards of a sentimental time. On arriving in London, he was astounded by the coldness of the English temperament.[104] Etienne, just home from his own partial defeat in Paris, was in no mood to fight Argand's legal battles in London and Birmingham. Argand bore no grudge, however. His letters continue to be effusively affectionate, one of them ending in an acrostic, "Amore, more, ore, re."[105] Joseph did join him in 1785-1786 in the aftermath of the balloon and could thus visit the Soho Works of Watt and Boulton. Like most episodes in the jungle of patent litigation, the story of the Argand lamp is a tangled one, but need not detain us other than to note that Argand lost his suit.

Late in 1786 Argand turned to an additional interest, a method for distilling *eau-de-vie*, in the development of which Joseph again collaborated. As early as 1792 he and Joseph had talked of liquidating their local enterprises and moving to Paris as a team. In 1797 when they did take the plunge, amid the fever of speculation that set in with the Directory, their object was to float a company that would exploit four processes, all involving in one way or another Joseph's ideas on heat and motion. The other partners were to be Joseph's son, Pierre-François (known always as Joseph *fils*); his son-in-law, Philippe Arribert; and a third party called Jean Béranger associated with the latter. Argand and Joseph corresponded at length and in detail with Etienne about problems of design, organization, capitalization, and subsidy from government.[106]

The first of the four lines had developed out of Argand's long-standing involvement in *eau-de-vie*. Joseph had designed an improved still that recirculated heat from the condensing coil to the fractionating column, and yielded a byproduct of vinegar. The second item of their would-be stock in trade was a process for evaporating wine into a concentrate for economy of shipping. The basis was a technique that Joseph had invented for desiccating fruit and fruit juices. As their third service, he now proposed to prepare dried herring by the same method. Fourth and most important was a pump, the hydraulic ram. It appeared to fly in the face of the conventional wisdom that water could never be raised above its own level by harnessing its own motions, and its development will occupy us in the final chapter.[107]

1. An Internal Combustion Engine

In 1839 Marc Seguin published a large book on the importance and construction of railroads, *De l'influence des chemins de fer et de l'art de les tracer et de les construire*. He had recently built the first to be completed in France. It led sixty kilometers from Lyons to Saint-Etienne, across the divide between the valleys of the Rhône and of the Loire, and opened for business in 1833, carrying coal and in the next year passengers. Among other surprises, for the book is not a work of physics, is the tabulation of data that yield a very good value for the quantity later called the mechanical equivalent of heat.[1] Marc Seguin had had the idea, he said in the preface, forty years before, from "the illustrious Montgolfier, whose nephew and disciple I am happy to be." Monsieur Montgolfier—his Uncle Joseph—"thought that caloric [heat] and motion are only different manifestations of one and the same phenomenon, the primary cause of which remains entirely hidden from our eyes."[2] Marc Seguin for his own part, he continued, had further been led to consider whether some other vehicle might prove more efficient than steam for transmitting the motive power of heat. What he had in mind was air, and though he did not mention his uncle in this connection, we shall see that the internal combustion engine may also be traced directly back to Joseph and the heat pump (*pompe-à-feu*) that figures in the latter's correspondence with Etienne in the year of the balloon, 1783-1784.

Not that Joseph thought in any such categorical terms about these matters. His word for the mental processes that produced his ideas was meditation. The notion of analysis would have been quite foreign to him, and it would be impossible to specify the moment at which he invented, let alone perfected, an idea or concept. They grew on him. His letters, rambling, warm, ill-spelled, lengthy screeds that they are, hold many kinds of interest. Among them is the access they give to a wide and usually inaccessible substratum of information that becomes science and technology only when it is formulated as knowledge. Before that it is a gathering awareness of how nature runs growing out of the experience of people with a feel and instinct for the machinery in operation in the workshop of the world. Many things have to be known in that milieu before they can become science, and science is less the discovery than the statement of them. One would not wish to argue that this is all there is to science, but it is an aspect.

At all events, the reaction of Joseph to word of the Lavoisier-Laplace demonstration that water is a compound will illustrate the point. He had known that all along, he replied to Etienne, who reported the news from Paris soon after arriving to develop aerostatics in the summer of 1783. Not that Joseph had learned it from either of Lavoisier's rival claimants to priority, whether Monge or Cavendish. Of Joseph's command of chemistry, Matthieu Duret observed that he had the science in his bones and not from books.[3] His response to Etienne comes in the middle of a sixteen-page letter about balloon design and the nature of heat, and is worth detailing. "It really piques me that your Parisians have beaten me out by their analysis of water. I felt great over having suspected that the base of dephlogisticated air could produce water by combining with inflammable gas. I rather think I mentioned my suspicion to Mr Argand (please tell me how he's getting along)."[4]

The idea had come to him through noticing that flatirons used by laundresses, like cast-iron cooking pots and heavy castings of all kinds, are covered with moisture soon after they are placed over a bed of coals, even though they were perfectly dry beforehand. They continue to show water until they grow hot enough to evaporate it. It could not have come from the charcoal, which was incandescent, nor from the metal, since droplets would then have appeared rather on the upper surfaces and entailed a loss of weight. So water must have derived (Joseph implied) from the burning of inflammable air produced in the decomposition of charcoal, which process he intended to investigate further. He suspected, in fact, that he had already produced it by the detonation of inflammable air in an iron retort. He had touched off five *gros* (about fourteen grams) of gunpowder and three hours later found half that weight of water in the vessel.

From this effect he concluded that the explosive force of gunpowder does not result from the separation and sudden expansion of dephlogisticated air contained in saltpeter (it would be anachronistic to say the oxygen provided by potassium nitrate). Nor does it come from dilation of inflammable gas (to say hydrogen would be an oversimplification). Nor, finally, is it the effect of the subtle elasticity of heat itself, or not entirely—as he had thought until then. No, the force of the explosion comes from the prodigious dilation of water produced by combination of the base of dephlogisticated air with inflammable gas. That reflection had led him suddenly to modify his ideas on "our" heat pump, and he had done many more experiments that he could not describe right then. They would talk about them when Etienne came home.

As for the "elements of water," he had had the same idea as your "Parisian wizards," by which Joseph meant that he too had confirmed the evidence for its composition by decomposing it. To that end, he melted twenty pounds of old type metal in a cast-iron cauldron. When the molten lead was almost red-hot, he plunged a piece of potter's clay into it with a pair of tongs. Having been dried in ordinary air, the clay retained much moisture. He let the metal simmer for an hour. A scum formed on the surface. He skimmed it

off, and it proved a brittle substance, partially alkalized. The bath, on the other hand, had become acidic ("*aigre*"). When he placed scraps of cold iron on the cauldron above the molten metal, no humidity formed. Joseph concluded, therefore, that the water retained in the clay had been decomposed, and that the part retained in the type-metal was the base of dephlogisticated air or perhaps dephlogisticated air itself. The contrary possibility was inflammable gas. On the former hypothesis, what had volatilized was inflammable air or maybe heat. On the latter, it was the base of dephlogisticated air. In either event, he had clearly separated the water in the clay into its constituents, even if he could not tell which of the two had remained in solution in the leaden bath and which had evaporated. He intended to find out by making further experiments. That would have to wait, however. Too many people kept calling on him and asking for things.

Now then, it would be quite beside the point to say that Joseph was wholly mistaken about the significance of the sweat on heated irons, or that in relation to gunpowder he was right about the provision of dephlogisticated air (oxygen) from saltpeter (potassium nitrate) and wrong about the secretion of inflammable air (hydrogen) by charcoal (carbon). A point could be the obvious one that he meant different and vaguer things by those terms than Lavoisier was coming to mean, though it would also have to be that Lavoisier, albeit in less measure, meant different things from what a chemist of 1883 or 1983 would have meant.

It is more pertinent to observe that, relatively informal though Joseph's views were on the identity and nature of individual chemical substances, and also on the distinction (if he even saw one) between chemistry and physics, he nevertheless knew the properties of things as well as if he had been Lavoisier. He knew how to obtain them, and he knew the effects of mixing, melting, heating, and igniting them. Just because he did not see the difference between his own reasonings and those of the Parisian wizards, he is not on that account to be compared in the quality of his comprehension with a Pilatre de Rozier. Joseph was no less appalled at the notion of combining the two types of balloon than if he had been able to call the gas that filled the upper module hydrogen and to distinguish it from its hot-air rival down below chemically instead of physically. By the 1790s, moreover, Joseph had come to think of chemical substances in a more specific manner. He also, like Marc Seguin after him, adopted Lavoisier's term "caloric" for the material basis of heat (not that this usage would have made him at home in the company of modern physicists, however acceptable his idea that heat is convertible to motion).

As to heat, we cannot find an explicit statement of its underlying identity with motion further back than the 1790s, but the running series of observations to Etienne in 1783-1784 are instructive about how Joseph came to think that. Apropos of gunpowder again, he imagined that it ought to be possible to fabricate an equivalent explosive without using the conventional saltpeter, charcoal, and sulfur. For the sudden expansion on ignition must be due only to the decomposition of the combination that air makes with the base of heat, "the most expansive and the most elastic fluid known." Only think of water again, and of how rapidly heat dilates it at the moment when the constituent gases combine, before ever the forces of aggregation have had time to resist expansion.

Think, too, how water dilated into vapor draws out heat from bodies with which it is in contact. That is why fog feels frosty, why regions dotted with lakes and traversed by rivers are temperate, why we wet down the roof in the heat of summer, and why a thermometer with a moist bulb registers a lower temperature than that of the surrounding air. That, further, is why a man who emerges from a swim shivers more than when he was in the water. Maybe, Joseph runs on, that same chill factor is what makes a baby cry when it comes into the world, and it may also be what depresses a woman when a man unskilled in his marital duties deposits his semen elsewhere than in the place intended by nature—though the sensation of excessive coldness that results locally deserves special study. It might well yield insights into the relation between heat and life.

"But I'm going too far. That's not my line. Back to business (Revenons à nos moutons)."

In part that business was balloons, and Joseph turns from the dilation of water vapor by heat to its role in creating lifting force, wherein it was the principal factor. Accordingly, every care must be taken to obtain heat economically and to conserve it once produced by use of insulated conduits, reservoirs, etc. The only known method for procuring it was decomposition of dephlogisticated air (that is, combustion), and Joseph thought it urgent to put in hand research on alternative methods for "fixing" dephlogisticated air in an appropriate base, thus releasing the heat with which it is combined in nature. Pending that, however, the most efficient approach appeared to be combustion in a column of air of which the velocity could be regulated at will. The method produced a controlled quantity of heat capable of yielding enormous power by expansion. Joseph was not more explicit, but he must have been referring to the Argand burner, on which he was collaborating, with its manageable draft through a tubular wick. He applied an adaptation of that device (it will be recalled) to the second balloon he designed, the aircraft commissioned by the marquis de Brantes and launched in March 1784.[5]

Not by heat alone, however, was the air in a balloon dilated. All the foregoing (and much more) is in his 10 October letter. Joseph was explicit about other factors contributing to lifting force in an earlier letter to Etienne, written on 18 August when he still had no precise information on the dimensions of the machine his brother proposed to build in Paris. Etienne was to bear in mind that, mixed with air rarefied by heat, the bag would in the second place contain other "aqueous and oily vapors" exhaled by combustion and dilated by heat. Third, would be a certain quantity of "inflammable air" also deriving from the combustible. (Like Pilatre—and many another—in this, Joseph had in mind here that organic matter gives off gases that burn, for example methane, not yet differentiated from hydrogen.) Finally, there would be electricity, like heat a fluid in its material basis. The balloon would pick up charge in its passage through the atmosphere, and electricity would combine with all these vapors to increase their elasticity. (Joseph writes *"logmintation"* for *"l'augmentation."*)

The last effect would vary according to climatic conditions, and Joseph reminded Etienne that, in one of their private tests before the Annonay demonstration, they had flown a trial balloon in a fog and observed how the warm vapor inside the bag de-electrified the cold mist. The balloon rose higher than it had done when heated still more strongly on a very dry day. Thinking on the forthcoming experiment in Paris, Joseph advised his brother to launch the machine in the early morning when the air was coolest and most humid and before the rays of the sun had time to beat upon it. (The advice remains good regardless of the premises.) Joseph suggested further that the retaining cords be of silk so that the machine might be insulated from the ground during inflation and build up charge from the action of the heater and the friction of its own unfoldings. It might even be a good idea to give it a shot from an electrostatic generator.[6]

Joseph enlarged upon the buoying effect of electricity in the memoir he read before the Lyons Academy on 25 November.[7] He there supposed that the electrical fluid spreads on the surfaces of bodies and lightens them. In principle, they could be raised by electricity alone if they could be subdivided far enough to present adequate surface in proportion to their mass. The flotation of clouds may be an instance. When they discharge their electricity in bolts of lightning, the droplets of water coagulate and rain upon us. Electricity took on increasing importance in Joseph's mind throughout the ensuing winter and spring, no doubt because he was all along accompanying his aerostatical constructions and his advice to his brother with developing what interested him more fundamentally, his heat pump. In that device, as we shall see, he produced expansive force through ignition of combustibles in a closed vessel by means of an electric spark.

Recurrent allusions to the heat pump in Joseph's correspondence are tantalizing on first reading his letters. He rejoiced in the success of his experiments, but was cryptic on the design, which, of course, was known to Etienne. Joseph always speaks of "our" heat pump. The references begin immediately after Joseph wrote Etienne of his disappointment in the performance of a steam engine he went to see in Nîmes. It is important to note the date, 16 May 1783. Evidently Joseph made that visit just when they were laboring to perfect the balloon in the privacy of Vidalon, and not quite three weeks before they staged the Annonay demonstration of 4 June. The steam engine in Nîmes had been built for a flour mill. It provided power to run a pump that recycled water to a reservoir supplying the millwheel. The cylinder had an inside diameter of twenty-three inches and the piston a stroke of seven feet two inches. Too small, Joseph thought immediately: the thing was only a ninth the size of English engines he had heard about and capable of only a fifteenth the power. The inspection convinced Joseph that miniature steam engines, boys doing a man's job, could never be made profitable, and that in any case the best use of steam was to produce motion by linking appropriate machinery to the direct drive of the piston, and not through the intermediary of a suction pump lifting water.[8]

It seems reasonable to conjecture that the origin of the heat pump lay in Joseph's determination to imagine something better. The next allusion is a petition in Etienne's hand, undated but clearly drafted within a few weeks of the Annonay balloon demonstration before he left for Paris. It is addressed to "Monseigneur" (who would probably have been either the intendant Saint-Priest or the archbishop of Narbonne), and it bespeaks governmental support for the further development of aircraft since they may prove valuable for commercial transportation and equally for their military potential. The balloon is said to depend on a new principle of mechanics, which the inventors have also applied to the construction of a pump that is very effective, easy to build, and economical to operate.[9]

With Etienne off in the capital, Joseph must have worked primarily on the development of this, their heat pump, throughout July and into

August, when Flesselles and the Lyonnais notables in part diverted him to the construction of the enormous balloon that flew to near-disaster in the following January. Joseph's letter of 18 August, already cited for his views on lifting force, is explicit. The relevant passage is significant enough in the development of power machinery to quote:

> . . . I have come back again to my first idea of employing compression of air as the principal agent in preference to compression of steam. To convey my idea in two words: an ounce of oil of vitriol [sulfuric acid] mixed in a closed vessel with two ounces of chalk [calcium carbonate] furnishes enough air to raise easily a hundredweight of water to a height of 50 feet, and by elaborating the machine, we could get more than ten times the effect. I can't get over wondering at the way in which . . . various aerial elastic fluids have the property of becoming weighty solids and losing their elasticity by combining with other solid bodies, from which they can be separated under certain known circumstances and resume their former properties. No one has exploited the thing for the prodigious power that results from the expansion of these fluids in closed vessels—an expansion to which in certain cases the union of heat and electrical fluid gives prodigious energy.[10]

That the "air" to which Joseph refers would have been carbon dioxide in no way lessens the interest of this passage. The importance is the proposal of a physical alternative to steam. The few experiments he had made, Joseph continued, were very encouraging. He would not pursue them, however, until Etienne returned, and would get back to perfecting their procedures in the paper mill.

Joseph did not stick to that resolve. Two months later, in the long letter of 10 October, he tells of further experiments, prompted in part by the abbé's suggestion that small-scale models of their heat pump might be feasible. Thinking small never appealed to Joseph. At first reaction, he con-

fessed, he found the idea "revolting." (And certainly he was right about the relation of efficiency to scale in steam engines.) Nevertheless, he agreed to try. It was already clear, he thought, that combustion of vegetable matter in small closed vessels was impossible except in the presence of saltpeter or some other source of dephlogisticated air (that is, an oxidizing agent). So he took another tack.

The notion came to him in the course of continuing reflections on the tendency of water vapor to soak up heat. The phenomenon might be related at least in part to its decomposition, which Joseph now imagined as a physical process. Like a mass of salt pulverized in a mortar, some of the corpuscles of water in a state of dispersion would be much larger than others, perhaps 10,000 times as large, and the smallest would approach the dimensions of the primordial parts of matter. These tiniest bits must each have a surface that would be immense relative to their mass, and would, therefore, adsorb heat so potently that they would disintegrate into "pure air" and inflammable gas. The latter in its lightness would rise above the upper reaches of the atmosphere, while the former mingled with ordinary air at all levels. That would explain why the air is purer after heavy rains.

If a way could be found to disintegrate water at will ("*sur le chant*"—Joseph means "*champ*"), the effect would cool the workshop (he does not use the word "laboratory"). Were that to prove possible, he and Etienne might substitute exploitation of the power furnished by the two airs (ordinary air and hydrogen here) for expansion of heat in the process they had developed for their heat pump. And Joseph tried it. He had the shop make him a cylinder of tin plate fourteen inches long and two inches in diameter reinforced by five iron bands. He filled it with a mixture of air and inflammable gas (hydrogen). At the bottom, a tube a foot long and a third of an inch in diameter communicated with the outside. Through it he introduced a glass of water into the lower half of the cylinder. He gave no drawing, but the arrangement must have looked like Fig. 60. He then passed a spark from a Leyden jar or electrostatic machine through the gases. The water shot out of the tube too fast for the eye to follow and jetted to the height of a second story. "That experiment," he told his brother, "gave me the idea that you could employ the method in a pump for fighting fires, and even in certain cases for a lift pump, but we'll examine that object more closely in our moments of leisure on your return."[11]

Throughout the ensuing winter, allusions by the abbé and Jean-Pierre in their correspondence, and indeed by Joseph in his, make it clear that experiments and further tests were proceed-

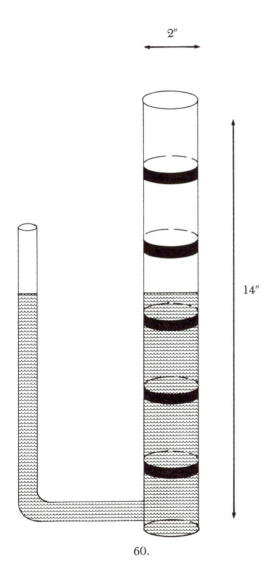

2"

14"

60.

ing in consultation among the brothers.[12] Apparently, it was the practical Jean-Pierre's idea to apply for an exclusive privilege from the government to manufacture the device once perfected.[13] In the absence of provision for patent rights in French law before the Revolution, such requests were normally referred to the Academy of Science for an expert opinion of their feasibility and value. Inventors, even like scientists, would sometimes seek to protect their priority and property in ideas that they were not ready to exploit by registering them under sealed cover, also in the Academy of Science. Thanks to that practice, we are not left dangling, as often happens in the annals of invention.

On 12 May 1784 Joseph wrote to say he understood from the abbé that Etienne was on the point of leaving Paris.[14] With his letter, he was enclosing a sealed envelope. It contained the description of their heat pump. The thing was so simple that he was afraid of being forestalled. Will Etienne deliver it into the safekeeping of the permanent secretary of the Academy? Etienne did so, on 29 May. Condorcet formally acknowledged receipt on 9 June, by which date Etienne had probably departed, leaving the field of aviation to Pilatre in effect, if not in intent.[15] One hundred and fifty-two years later, in March 1936, another permanent secretary authorized the opening of that envelope, and the Academy published the memoir it contained in its *Comptes-rendus*.[16]

The initial paragraph represents the invention as a device for domesticating the "prodigious exertion" with which gunpowder propels a bullet from a gun barrel. Joseph attributes the force developed to the confinement of the heat of sudden combustion. Perhaps it is increased by a quantity of electricity that may be supposed fixed in carbon, as one of its elements. Several experiments had persuaded him that the materials responsible for the force of gunpowder were inflammable air and dephlogisticated air, and that their "conflagration" alone constituted the explosion. Accordingly, he had sought to reproduce that effect and had imagined the experiment we have just described in which the gases were detonated in an iron vessel above a seal of water that was ejected to a great height.

"From that experiment," Joseph continued, "we concluded that it would be possible in accordance with the same theory to raise great masses of water up a hillside by procedures as simple as they would be economical relative to their effect." He does not give a sketch, but his description is so explicit that there can be no doubt about the details (Fig. 61).[17]

The machine consisted of a well dug into the bank of a pond or a river from which water is to be pumped. The bottom was several feet lower than the surface of the water, and the top of the well was vaulted with masonry to make an enclosed receptacle. One conduit (A) admitted water from the source and there were two air vents, one lateral (B) and one vertical (C), all with valves or stoppers as shown. A standpipe communicated with the reservoir (R), equipped with a retaining valve. The operator charged the chamber with a bundle of fagots introduced through the lateral shaft (B). The twigs, as dry and small as possible, were to be loosely bound. They were to be ignited "by means of electricity or in any other way." As they burned the air in the well expanded. The pressure closed the valves (B) and (C), forcing water up into the reservoir. When combustion was completed, the pressure equalized itself, and water flowed in through (A) reestablishing the level. After each firing, the operator removed the stopper (C) so that the exhaust could escape to be replaced by fresh air through (B). He then inserted a new charge of fuel, also through (B).

In a concluding paragraph, Joseph said that tests allowed the authors "to hope" they would be able to raise 12,000 cubic feet of water a day to a height of fifty feet with a consumption of 100 hundredweight of wood. They had been overseen while making these trials and feared lest their invention be appropriated by spies. Thus, they prayed the Academy to safeguard their priority. Joseph reported the numerical results, not to the Academy, but to Etienne in his covering letter. The hopes realistically permitted by

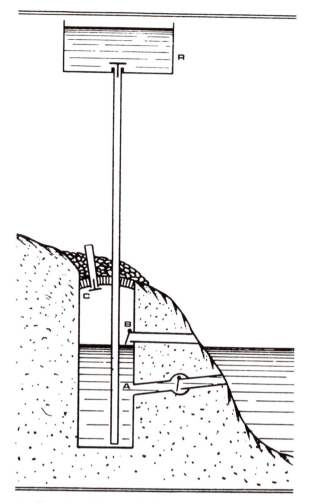

61. Drawing of Joseph de Montgolfier's Heat Pump, as described in the *pli cacheté* deposited in the Academy of Science

these tests would have been a good deal more modest. The data refer to models tried out in a workshop and not to the chamber sunk into a hillside, which may never have been constructed. Combustion of 12 *grains* (about 0.5 milligrams) of paper in an earthenware vessel with a capacity of 200 cubic inches raised a pound of water better than two feet. Burning one *gros* (2.82 grams) of paper in a tin plate receptacle of about 1,200 cubic inches pushed twelve pounds of water to a height better than six feet. Finally, two ounces (61.12 grams) of paper developed enough power in a tin plate container of four cubic feet to lift

120 pounds of water a distance of eight feet, though in this case the effect was less than it might have been because the chamber lost compression.[18]

2. THE HYDRAULIC RAM

Several years after registration of the heat pump by the Academy, Joseph sent Etienne another, very interesting letter. It is undated, but there is good reason to place it in 1786 or 1787. Joseph was in Voiron and, he wrote, concentrating largely on the technology of paper except for one device that he expected soon to perfect. Etienne was making one of his visits in Paris, and Joseph urged him to take the occasion to impress the government with the importance of this new invention. When completed it would enable one man to destroy a great city in a quarter of an hour, leaving only a heap of arms, legs, wood, and stones inhabited by ghosts. The object was to spare humanity the ravages of war by con-

vincing rulers that a weapon could be constructed of so deadly a nature that military operations against centers of civilization must become unthinkable.[19] There are no specifications, but probably the idea involved some sort of variant on the heat pump experiments, which themselves derived in part from Joseph's meditations on the operation of firearms. He did not forget his heat pump, although he turned in the 1790s to what did prove practical, a hydraulic variant, and never recurred to the weapon to end all wars.

In the matter of the hydraulic ram, it will be convenient to begin with a developed form of the design, illustrating the principle with a schematic drawing that Joseph printed in 1805 (Fig. 62).[20] The rampart (A) on the left is a dam. A conduit (BCD), the ram's body, taps a flow of water from the base through a screened conical opening (QT) and channels it into the assemblage at the right, which Joseph called the ram's head. Its function is to butt charges of water up to a cistern, not shown, at the top of the pipe (U), which is higher

62. The hydraulic ram, 1805 model

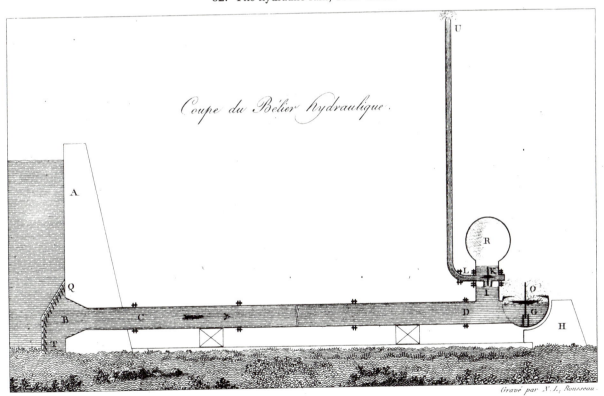

Coupe du Bélier hydraulique.

Gravé par N. L. Rousseau.

than the level behind the dam. As flow begins, water is free to escape through the outlet (O). When the current reaches a certain swiftness, it raises the stop valve (G), which is slightly flanged and weighted. The shut-off gives a "*coup de bélier*" and forces water up the alternate outlet (I) into the compression chamber (R). There the enclosed air cushion springs back in a reaction that closes the lift valve (K) and sends a surge of water up the supply pipe (U). Arresting the current in the conduit has meanwhile allowed the stop valve (G) to reopen of its own weight. Flow resumes until the critical velocity is again reached, and the cycle is repeated. In normal operation a ram was capable of 20 to 120 cycles per minute, depending on its dimensions. In a machine installed in a commercial laundry near Senlis, the principal conduit had a diameter of 7½ inches, and Joseph calculated its effect as follows:

> The head of water, or vertical distance, between the level behind the dam and that of the stop valve (G) was 3 feet, 2 inches.
>
> The vertical distance that water was raised from (G) to the cistern atop (U) was 14 feet, 2 inches.
>
> In 100 cycles, requiring 3 minutes, the water that ran through the ram amounted to . . . . 1,987 litres
>
> The water raised to the cistern amounted to . . . . 269 litres
>
> The force "expended" was 1,987 × 3⅙ = 6,293
>
> The force "obtained" was 269 × 14⅙ = 3,811
>
> Since 6,293 is to 3,811 as 100 is to 60, the "force received" was six-tenths of that employed, or as would later be said its efficiency was 60 percent.

Now, there are a number of interesting things about this passage, among others the mixture of metric and avoirdupois units in this early stage of adoption of the metric system. The formal science of machines had not yet evolved to the point that agreed upon units could be assigned to the quantities later called energy and work, or that Joseph could differentiate in name between them.

Nevertheless, the actual operations had become perfectly clear to him by 1805, the date of this explanation. That was not the case, as we shall see, when he made his first hydraulic ram. What is equally clear to us, moreover, if this machine be compared to the heat pump, is that Joseph had achieved the same effect by substituting the kinetic energy of running water for that obtainable (but only in a model) from the expansive force of heat acting on enclosed gases. No better example is available, or needed, of what was in his mind in his frequent references throughout these, his last years, to the identity of heat and motion as manifestations of the same cause.

Is it permissible to say he had come to know the cause even if he could not name it? True, his calculation of the efficiency of the ram is hydrostatical here, but his explanation of its working is as dynamical as his thinking. The reason that water is forced up through the passage (I) when the velocity of flow suffices to close the stop valve (G) is that "the live force with which it is animated cannot be annihilated."[21] A footnote gives his readers, whom he addresses as prospective purchasers, an engineer's rule-of-thumb for estimating the volume of flow through a pipe. It will be approximately two-thirds of the product of the area of the cross-section multiplied by the velocity a body acquires in falling a distance equal to the head of pressure. You could apply a similar approximation to a stream by holding a properly graduated ruler broadside to the current, reading off the velocity from the height that the water laps up the scale on impact, and multiplying the value by two-thirds of the area of a cross-section of the stream-bed. You could also throw in sticks and time them.[22] As will appear, Joseph designed the earliest models of the ram for use in streams and rivers, utilizing the velocity of the current passed directly through the ram's body instead of that obtained from a stand of water at rest.

Aided by his immediate entourage—his intimate collaborator, Ami Argand; his son-in-law, Philippe Arribert; and the latter's associate, Jean Béranger—Joseph installed a demonstration model in the courtyard of his house, 18 rue des Juifs, in Paris early in the summer of 1797. On

14 July he read a memoir on it before the scientific division of the Institute of France, the body that replaced the Academy of Science in the Revolution. The idea had come to him, he said, almost a year previously in the course of reflecting on certain natural phenomena that seemed as yet inadequately explained. He had in mind that tides rise higher on some coasts than on others, that a flow of water gushing upward from an orifice spouts higher at first than in its steady state, that waves in the sea dash up the tilted surfaces along a rocky shore. "We recognized"—he used the first person plural in these documents—that the true cause lies in the motion under way, and in the hammer-blow that results when it is interrupted.[23]

In their experiments they equipped the ram with two outlets, fitted with valves and a lift pipe as shown in Fig. 63 (Joseph's Figure 1), and laid it in a small, swift river. Those are the essential parts. The machine is simplicity itself, Joseph insisted, since there are no pumps, wheels, or gears, and the motor is simply the current of the river. Only at a later stage did he add the compression chamber (Fig. 64, Joseph's Fig. 2), and then as an auxiliary, of which the purpose was to smooth the flow of water up the lift pipe. The applications he imagined in this first presentation, and in the application for a patent, would furnish water for irrigation systems, canals, and cities. His ram would be far more economical and efficient than the urban pumping stations it could replace. As a leading instance, he mentioned the famous "Machine de Marly" that had been supplying water from the Seine to aliment the fountains of Versailles at enormous cost since the reign of Louis XIV.[24]

Prior to his appearance before the Institute, Joseph and his associates had apparently enlisted the interest of Jean-Charles de Borda, senior member of the Mathematics Section, and himself an ingenious and inventive engineer and former naval officer. For Argand soon complained that he could not understand how Borda could have got them so obdurate a commission to report on their invention.[25] The experts the Institute named were the abbé Charles Bossut and Antoine Cou-

sin. Cousin was a professor at the Collège de France, a mathematician and physicist who had largely abandoned science for municipal administration. Bossut was an elderly mathematician of didactic temperament, who had made a career of writing textbooks and setting the entrance examinations for the Royal Engineering School. Since he had published a treatise on hydrodynamics,[26] his was the major responsibility. He looked at the plans, and at the model (which drew its water from a raised tank), and declared it impossible in principle for water to ascend in the lift pipe above its original level. According to Argand, he waxed passionate in this prohibition. He may well have done. Nothing more righteously excited the indignation of mathematical specialists in mechanics than pretensions on the part of practitioners to build perpetual-motion machines, and that is precisely what Bossut took the ram to be.

Bossut could not (Argand again, writing to Etienne), "stomach the principle of the thing."[27] And, on first reading this correspondence, the historian is likely to take Bossut for an example of the inventor's occasional obstacle, a scientist who declares a priori that claims contravene some fundamental law of nature. There was that about it, of course. It could be said that Bossut evaluated the potential energy of the ram as was conventional for any hydraulic machine, in terms of the height of the column of water creating the pressure under which it operated, and that he failed to understand that Joseph was exploiting the kinetic energy of water in motion. When the initial application for a patent is consulted, however, it has to be admitted that Joseph himself either failed to understand the difference fully at this juncture, or else that he failed to make it clear.

The calculation with which he purported to illustrate the principle of the machine by way of a numerical example made no sense to anyone other than Argand and himself. He supposed the ram to be 100 feet long, the velocity of the current 7½ feet per second, and the height to which the water was to be raised 20 feet above the lift valve. The power ("puissance") of the ram is then 750,

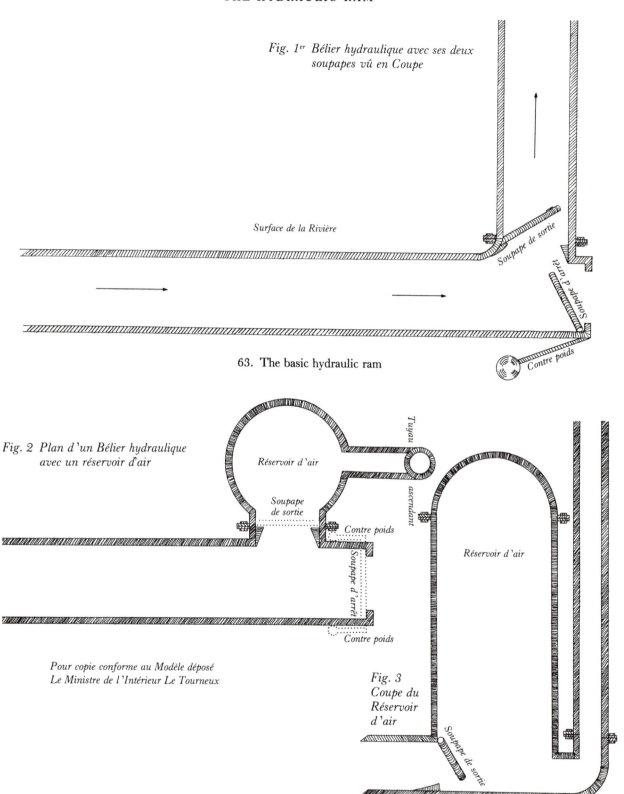

Fig. 1ᵉʳ *Bélier hydraulique avec ses deux soupapes vû en Coupe*

Surface de la Rivière

Soupape de sortie

Soupape d'arrêt

Contre poids

63. The basic hydraulic ram

Fig. 2 *Plan d'un Bélier hydraulique avec un réservoir d'air*

Réservoir d'air

Tuyau ascendant

Soupape de sortie

Contre poids

Soupape d'arrêt

Contre poids

Réservoir d'air

Pour copie conforme au Modèle déposé Le Ministre de l'Intérieur Le Tourneux

Fig. 3 *Coupe du Réservoir d'air*

Soupape de sortie

64. The hydraulic ram with air reservoir

the length multiplied by the velocity. Joseph assigns no units to this number, but divides it by 20. The quotient, 37½, is again velocity, the velocity that a body will acquire falling from rest for 1¼ seconds. (The value of gravitational acceleration was approximately 30 feet per second per second in the old French units.) That interval thus represents the "time of ascension" of the water, by which Joseph means (but does not say) the time in which the lift valve is open during each cycle. During 1¼ seconds, water in the body of the ram will flow a distance of 111½ inches. But since its velocity varies from 7½ feet per second to zero, only half of the last quantity should be taken as the effect. In other words, each stroke of the ram will push a column of water 56¼ inches up the lift pipe. Joseph justified omitting consideration of the actual quantities of water, since they depend on the diameters of the ram and lift pipe. The dimensions that matter are the longitudinal proportions.

Evidently Argand felt the obscurity of this, for he attached a supplement to their application for a patent in order to explain what they had in mind and to give other examples with numbers that made the arithmetic tidier, followed by an algebraic formulation. The principle is that the product of the "sum of the forces" of the water in the main tube, multiplied by the velocity, measures the effect. At the moment that the stop valve arrests the flow, it will release ("*lâchera*") this quantity of force, which is equal to $L \times V$, to use his symbols. Since force must equal effect, the product $L \times V$ will counterbalance a column of water of height E in the lift pipe during the time that the lift valve remains open. That time is given by the formula

$$\frac{L \times V}{30\, E}$$

If the time is known, the formula then serves to calculate the value for E, the height to which the ram will raise water.

Now then, even after clarification, what are we to say of this? Certainly, it illustrates how wide the gap could be between the capacity to imagine an ingenious piece of machinery and the ability to explain it in terms of the most elementary science. Obviously, Joseph took his quantities from hydrostatics, where pressure is indeed determined by the height and not the diameter of a standpipe, and he tried to apply it to a dynamical analysis. He thinks of the ram as a kind of standpipe laid on its side, in which velocity does the work of gravity, and arresting the flow produces an impact equivalent to pressure. What he needed to do was to equate the kinetic energy (live force) of the ram ($½\,M\,V^2$) with the potential energy of the lift pipe ($M\,G\,H$) (to use symbols more conventional than Argand's even then); and for that, of course, he needed to take account of the amounts of water involved.[28]

If, as seems virtually certain, Joseph presented that same reasoning in the memoir he read before the Institute, Bossut's resistance becomes less surprising. Fortunately, other and more noteworthy scientists were able to see through the argument to the reality behind it. Laplace, Lagrange, Prony, and Monge were impressed and encouraging. Even more fortunately, an unofficial demonstration was a great success. It came off on 30 August 1797. Besides the two commissioners, members of the Institute and certain notables were present. Among them were Lazare Carnot and François Barthélemy, two of the five persons constituting the Executive Directory, which ruled the country from 1795 through 1799.[29] Besides being the foremost military statesman of the Revolution, Carnot was himself an engineer and author of important writings that contributed to the foundations of engineering mechanics.[30] In after years Marc Seguin told the story, saying he had it from his uncle, that Bossut with a long-suffering air took a place right under the outlet of the roof gutter to which the ram would raise its charge, that he merely shrugged when Joseph urged him to move some paces aside, and that the rigid geometer got well and duly drenched.[31] However that may have been, the date was fortunate for Joseph and his hydraulic ram. In the next week, Carnot and Barthélemy were displaced from office and driven into exile by the neo-Jacobin *coup d'état* of 18 Fructidor.

Joseph's application for a patent was accepted

two months later, on 3 November 1797, under the designation "Hydraulic ram whose effect is to raise water from rivers by means of their natural slope, without pumps or wheels or other mechanisms of the usual sort."[32] The papers are signed by himself and Argand, with the notation that they are acting also in the name of Etienne. Those concerned in forming a family company—Joseph, Argand, Arribert, Béranger—kept appealing to Etienne, then in Lyons, to take an active part. Arribert and Béranger counted on him to compensate for their youth and inexperience in business.[33] Even the young Joseph, supposed to be one of the partners, looked mainly to his Uncle Etienne for the solution of his problems, the chief of which was himself.

Joseph *fils* inherited both his father's mechanical ingenuity and fiscal irresponsibility, although in inverse proportion. The product may have remained constant, but the result was a series of disasters in private life and business. His mother and his brother-in-law (Arribert) bore the brunt, and it was to Etienne, not to Joseph, that the latter turned when it became urgent to get the young man out of Voiron. The trouble was that he had become infatuated (*amouraché*) with the illiterate fifteen-year-old daughter of a bankrupt barkeeper. To remonstrances, he would only hold haughtily that "all our customs, all our social institutions, are based on nothing but vain prejudice."[34] Apart from that, Arribert was mainly responsible for the projects involving distillation of *eau-de-vie*, vinegar, evaporated wine, and dried herring, though he was also on hand for the tests of the hydraulic ram in Paris.

Argand, for his part, begged Etienne again and again to come to Paris to put in hand the financing, establish relations with government agencies, and turn the prospective business into a going concern. Everything is at a standstill, he wrote on 26 November, a scant three weeks after they had their patent. He himself was prostrated with migraine. He could not persuade "our apathetic and excellent Joseph" to do anything practical like calling on ministers and officials to advance their interests. Competitors, the Périer brothers with their steam engines, the Bralles with another kind of pump, were intriguing to get contracts for public waterworks at Sèvres and Marly. The minister of finance had been heard to say that their hydraulic ram was nothing but a lever to prise money out of the government. Arribert and Béranger were pressing him, but he was unwilling to go ahead unless Etienne was present. "I swear, my dear friend, if you don't come to back me up, I shall be forced to drop the whole thing, and we shall lose out on the best of business opportunities, both as to fame and wealth, all at once." And Argand added a desperate postscript to say that Joseph, instead of writing Etienne as he had promised to do, had gone off to look for another house. He would certainly make a bad decision, taking something altogether unsuitable and inconvenient out of false economy, and all "because you're not here."[35]

In fact, Joseph had already joined in the appeals to his brother, needing both advice and money. To his first intimations, Etienne had evidently replied with a stream of letters in July and August urging caution and inquiring about details.[36] Once the demonstration had come off, Joseph could take time to answer. "I very much hope," he wrote on 14 September 1797, "that this invention will work out better for us than the aerostats."[37] He must, he recognized, prepare a prospectus explaining the principle of the machine in a manner that will convince technicians, officials, and the qualified public. As Argand pointed out, Etienne himself had not grasped it at first,[38] and Joseph launched into another computation of the input and output of his ram, going into much greater detail than he provided in the patent application. He set the thing up symbolically, assigning letters to the dimensions of the pipes, the velocity of flow, the head of pressure, and the frequencies of the valves, and wrote equations relating all these variables. Five pages of cumbersome and unconvincing calculation conclude this attempt to explain himself to his brother,[39] who evidently—we do not have the letter—replied that no one could be expected to follow such a presentation.

On reflection, Joseph could only agree. Please, he said in effect, you do it:

... it needs to be put into a different form and style, and you have to be the one to do that. Not that our excellent Ami Argand isn't equal to it, but he is overburdened with work. Moreover, you are much more familiar with algebraic analysis. It's also true that he is more familiar with my way of counting, to the point that we understand each other immediately and that he uses my method readily. Still, since we're about to prepare a memoir for the public, we must certainly employ terms that are in common use. To that end, we have got to be sure that we understand each other and you have also got to familiarize yourself with our method of representing the thing.

And with that Joseph unleashed another ten pages of calculations.[40]

Evidently Etienne set to work and obliged, for the family papers contain the draft of a memoir in his hand giving exactly what Joseph needed but could not define. It represents an application to the hydrodynamics of his ram of the principle of conservation of live force (energy, to be anachronistic) in hydraulic systems. The introductory remarks rephrase the background considerations with which Joseph had opened his presentation before the Institute—the action of water in tides, waves, and jets contrasted to the inefficiency of water wheels, and the consequent desirability of building a machine in which it would use up its motion. "At the same time, we have considered that the live force of water with any given velocity cannot be destroyed except by a cause similar to that which produced it." When a certain mass of water takes on that velocity in falling from the required height, it acquires a live force sufficient to return it to the same height, or to send a lesser quantity to a greater height, provided the product remains constant. "Any other use of force is nothing but communication of motion"—that is, it is merely inertial.

The symbolic expression of the equality is
$$mv^2 = MV^2$$
where the lower- and upper-case letters represent the quantities mass and velocity respectively in the lift pipe and the conduit. It was then a matter of elementary algebra for Etienne to give the formula for the height to which water will be raised, $h = MV^2/4am$, and for the time in which the lift valve is open, $t = (V/2a)\sqrt{M/m}$. (In his expressions, a represents the gravitational acceleration, which Etienne defines in terms of the distance a body descends in the first second of free fall, although he wrote "first minute" in an instance of the carelessness in detail that on other occasions accompanied his clarity in principle.)

This idealized formulation presupposed that the velocity of water moving through the ram is either zero or V. In fact it is variable, and Etienne went on to simulate the real situation by forming differential expressions employing a "virtual velocity" that obtains at the moment the stop valve is opened. These equations express the relations between the time the valve remains open, the quantity of water that then escapes, and the mean velocity at which it flows. They thus permit a calculation of how much water remains within the ram to be lifted to a given height, or vice versa. Etienne recognized that the expressions involved approximations. Nevertheless, when the data from the demonstration before the Institute were tried, they proved to be good approximations.[41]

Let us pause for a moment to underline the personal circumstances. In general it is no doubt true that youth is better served than age in point of the capacity to innovate and learn. Yet here was Etienne, within two years of his death, educating his older brother, then in his fifty-eighth year, in the theory of the latter's most practical invention. From the account of the commercial model that opened this section, it is evident that Joseph learned the lesson, and it will be further evident that he drew upon it in developing his heat pump into a true internal-combustion engine, the last of his machines.

Meanwhile, over the course of the winter of

1797-1798, Joseph imagined two modifications in the design of the hydraulic ram. The first of them, which he called "Bélier en veine contractée," economized live force by introducing an auxiliary ram of reduced dimensions in series between the lift valve and the compression chamber. In effect, it reduced the loss due to shock by smoothing out the action. The second variation adapted the ram to installation on shipboard. The notion was to pump the bilge out of a hull by taking advantage of the rolling of the ship. The ram needed two intakes, therefore, which would suck up water alternately from starboard and from port and lift a fraction of it overboard. The machine took its power from the accelerated swish, swish, that the motion of the ship imparted to the swill.[42] Perhaps the reader will be interested in the specifications for the latter, along with a preliminary sketch (Fig. 65).[43]

On 26 May 1798, the patent was amended to cover these and other improvements. Etienne had rallied, contributing his presence along with his rationale. The new application is in the name of Montgolfier Frères and Argand and signed in his hand.[44] As for the Institute, Bossut remained grudging if not quite unyielding. For the August 1797 demonstration had been unofficial, however spectacular. Evidently the Montgolfiers were in a position to go over Bossut's head to the minister of the interior. On 11 December 1797, the president of the Institute received a letter from that high officer of state saying that the government was much interested in the prospects for the hydraulic ram, and requesting the commission to speed its evaluation.[45] Not until 20 May 1798 did it do so, and then there is evidence of further intervention. The Institute deferred consideration of the report until the commissioners should have had an opportunity to confer with Borda, Coulomb, and Prony.[46] When finally Bossut and Cousin did bring it in, on 29 June, their enthusiasm was notable by its absence. They no longer could deny that the machine worked, but only for small quantities of water over medium ranges did they find it preferable to a good pump driven by a water wheel.[47]

Although a draft of articles of association sur-

vives, the company that was to exploit the hydraulic ram along with other things never got under way.[48] Argand fell ill, became involved again in lawsuits over other patents, and late in May 1798 retreated to his home in Versoix, near Geneva.[49] Béranger went into politics and won election to the Council of Five Hundred, the lower house of the legislature. Arribert continued on his own with the lines involving distillation of *eau-de-vie* and vinegar and dehydration of food products.[50] As always the ideas of Joseph proved practical technically and grandiose commercially. "Our friends," he wrote to Etienne, "are agreed that I absolutely must be left to my meditations, and in fact I fully realize that I'm not much good at other things."[51]

It is agreeable to record, therefore, that in the years that remained to him, Joseph occupied a position in the Conservatoire National des Arts et Métiers, where he had no other responsibility. That institution, which is both a technological museum and a technical school, was founded in the general reorganization of scientific facilities that followed the end of the Terror in 1794. Its first collections consisted of machines and tools from the laboratory of the inventor, Jacques Vaucanson, who had willed his equipment to the Crown in 1782; of many models of inventions submitted over the years to the judgment of the Academy of Science; and of apparatus confiscated from aristocrats and others during the revolutionary years, both in France and in conquered regions in Belgium and the Netherlands. The Thermidorean Convention adopted the measure providing for the new establishment on 10 October 1794. Only in 1800, however, was the Conservatoire des Arts et Métiers fully installed in the former Priory of Saint-Martin-des-Champs.[52] Nowadays, the one-time refectory houses the library, and in the chapel is an exhibit displaying the evolution of the automobile.

From the outset the mission combined education of artisans in a trade school with provision of technological information for manufacturers. The initial staff consisted of a director, Claude-Pierre Molard, and four demonstrators. Molard was an expert on machinery, an encyclopedist in

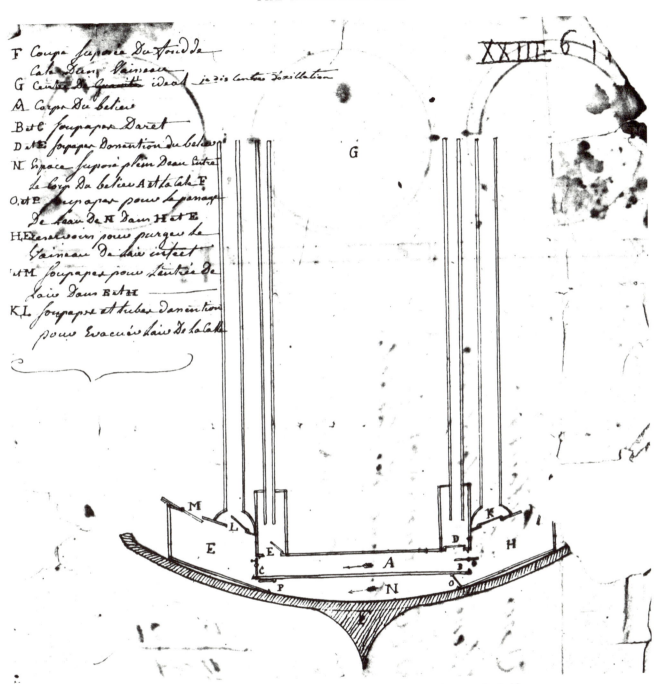

65. A hydraulic ram to be installed on shipboard for pumping out the hold

spirit surviving from the old regime. On 22 January 1800 Joseph was named to one of the posts of demonstrator. His duties were what he made them. Among other enterprises, he worked on improving the design and enlarging the capacity of the hydraulic ram. Protected by the patent, he licensed construction of several models by various entrepreneurs.

The dream of replacing the Machine de Marly remained Joseph's personal mill-o'-the-wisp. In 1807 he made a final effort to persuade the government to substitute a system of four rams working in parallel for its fourteen water wheels, each thirty feet in diameter, driving a battery of huge leaky pumps under the burden of enormous counterpoises. The whole monstrosity operated (so Joseph calculated) at an efficiency of 2.8 percent, a performance improved but little by recent modifications. Among the rams currently in service, one that MM "Wat et Bouleton" had installed in their Soho Works raised 224 cubic meters of water a distance of 28 feet every 24 hours with an effective yield of 64 percent of the power consumed. Another, belonging to an immediate client, Mayor Fay-Sathonay of Lyons, lifted 18 pints of water per minute to a height of 108 feet with comparable economy of means.

Force is money, Joseph pointed out, and now he clearly meant the same thing as either energy or work. Its unit is the quantity required to raise 1,000 kilograms of water a distance of one meter. Calculating its cost on the basis of the cheapest use of water power for milling grain gave a value of 0.2 francs per thousand such units, later called dynames.[53] The relative sophistication of this estimation, compared to the naïveté of the patent application ten years before, is itself a measure of Joseph's continuing capacity to learn. No doubt he had help with the composition, but what taught him was the intensive discussion of power engineering going on all around him in the early years of the new century. The reader may be interested to compare the development Joseph had given the machine by 1807 (Fig. 66) to the design he published in 1805 (above, Fig. 62). The minister of the interior was impressed and allocated 17,000 francs to the project of testing

the ram at Marly. Although the tests went well, the government never produced the funds to permit its adoption.[54] Nonetheless, the machine made steady progress in finding other applications. In a prospectus printed not long after Joseph's death, his son could say to customers that 700 hydraulic rams were in service throughout France, and the firm of Seguin Frères went on supplying them well into the 19th century.[55]

There at the Conservatoire in the apartment that went with his position, Joseph welcomed Marc Seguin late in 1800, a fifteen-year-old great-nephew who had been sent by his father to Paris for the education that Annonay could not afford. For, although the great scientific institutions of the capital, the Institut de France and the Ecole Polytechnique, prospered in the immediate aftermath of the Revolution, secondary education throughout the country suffered from abolition of the fine religious schools of the old regime. Recovery required many decades. Joseph put young Marc Seguin into a private boarding school during the week and shared his life and thoughts with the boy over weekends. Those were the thoughts of which Marc Seguin made a family cult. They reached back to the heat pump, and now Joseph was meditating on the deep unity beneath heat and motion, a fund of power to be drawn from nature.

He talked with many besides his young nephew in these years. In technical circles he attained, indeed, the standing of an oracle whose utterances were much respected. The head of the Gunpowder and Saltpeter Service recorded how "Montgolfier, all of whose ideas bear the stamp of ingenuity and simplicity," advised the Arsenal on adaptation of his techniques for evaporating fruit juices to drying out munitions with reduced risk of fire.[56] A French physician in Turin, Joseph-Marie Socquet, published a book on heat in 1801. The differences between "caloric" combined chemically and held in bodies physically was still unclear to science, as was that between both these forms and the modification of temperatures by radiant heat. He expected enlightenment on these and other matters when "citizen Montgolfier publishes the reflections and impor-

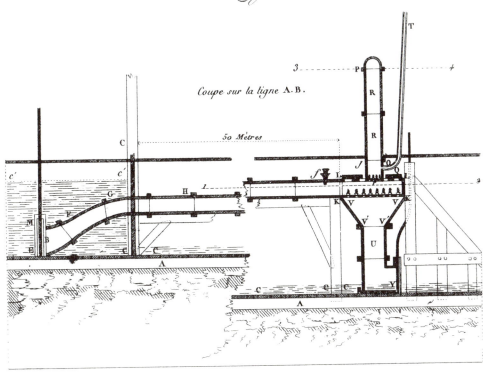

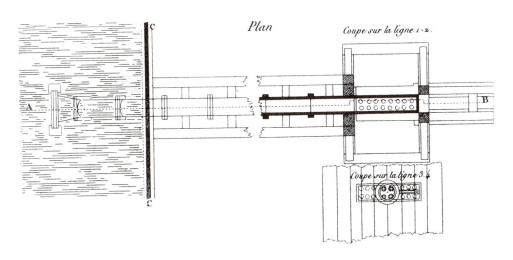

66. The hydraulic ram, 1807 model, intended to replace the Machine de Marly

tant results of his experiments," marked by "variety, precision, and simplicity." Meanwhile, Socquet was honored to acknowledge the gratitude he felt for the enlargement of his own understanding in the course of highly instructive conversations.[57] An even more significant recognition came from the two most enterprising industrial chemists in Paris, Nicolas Clément and Charles-Bernard Desormes. In 1804 they took Joseph into a consulting partnership in their firms, which produced soda, alum, and copperas in a new factory at Verberie on the Oise.[58]

Joseph also gained in the esteem of the scientific community proper throughout these years. Early in his tenure at the Conservatoire, in February 1801, he declared himself a candidate for membership in the Institut de France in the vacancy created by the death of Cousin (Bossut's associate on the ram commission in 1797). Joseph placed near the bottom, fifth out of six, in the election that followed. In 1807, when Coulomb died, he tried again, and this time swept all before him, taking thirty votes to fifteen for his nearest competitor.[59] Clearly, his reputation and personal standing had come to count, and not his writings, the normal criterion, for they were few and fragmentary. Thereupon, the duties of his post occupied him along with his life in the Conservatoire, and he served regularly on commissions that scrutinized proposals of others in the area of mechanical inventions (Fig. 67).

There is a poignancy in the identity of the last of them. On 13 March 1809 a prolific inventor called Cagniard de Latour brought in a proposal for a "Heat engine for raising water."[60] It was one among several machines imagined in those years of which the principle, even like that of Joseph's heat pump, was to draw power from the expansive force exerted by heat upon air instead of upon steam. An Archimedean screw captured air at the surface of a tank of water and swiveled it down to an orifice at the bottom of an adjoining tub of hot water, where it escaped. The inverted cups of a millwheel caught the bubbles as they floated up. Their expansion under heat, added to normal swelling due to diminishing hydrostatic pressure, created five times the power required

to turn the screw, and the balance supplied motive force.

Joseph had two fellow referees. The older was none other than Charles, the physicist and pilot of the hydrogen balloon, whose name was now attached to the law relating temperature to the variations of pressure and volume in an enclosed gas. The second was Gaspard Riche de Prony, director of the civil engineering school, the Ecole des Ponts et Chaussées. Joseph's name is not on their report. It was signed and presented instead by Lazare Carnot,[61] whom the permanent secretary appointed when Joseph suffered a stroke of apoplexy at dinner with his colleagues following a meeting of the Institute in April 1809. He retired, first to Lyons and then to Annonay, hoping to regain speech and health, and died on 26 June 1810 taking the waters at Balaruc-les-Bains, near Montpellier.[62]

That it should have been Carnot who prepared the report on the Cagniard de Latour engine is generally agreed to have been of much significance in the future development of thermodynamics. The analysis from which that branch of physics derives was the work of his son, Sadi Carnot, in the famous treatise of 1824 that applied Lazare Carnot's science of machines to the theory of heat, *Réflexions sur la puissance motrice du feu*.[63] Two central elements in Sadi's argument were present in the Cagniard engine, the production of mechanical work by the free (or adiabatic) expansion of a heated gas, which notion Joseph did not have, and the reliance on air to transmit the expansive force of heat, which he certainly and expressly did.

Joseph was equally conversant with another air engine imagined and constructed a few years earlier. The brothers Nicéphore and Claude Niepce, the first of whom collaborated long afterwards with Louis Daguerre in the invention of photography, submitted an internal combustion motor to the Institute for its approval in 1806. The chamber consisted of a brass cylinder fitted with a piston. An intake pipe passed a draft of air and a puff of powdered coal mixed with resin across a pilot light, and the cylinder was exhausted automatically after each firing. Lyco-

J.ᵗʰ Mᵗᵉ Montgolfier,	Membre de la Légion d'Honneur,
de l'Institut de france, de plusieurs	autres sociétés savantes, du Bureau
Consultatif du Ministre pour	les Arts, Démonstrateur au Conservᵗ
les Arts-et-Métiers de Paris;	Inventeur de l'Aërostat, du
Bélier-hydraulique,	&c. &c. &c.
Né à Annonay, Département de	l'Ardèche, en 1740; Mort en 1810.

Non ebur neque Aureum	At fides et ingeni
	Benigna vena est

67. Joseph de Montgolfier in old age, with his inventions

pod powder burned more cleanly but made too expensive a fuel.[64] The "*pyréolophore*" had obvious features in common with the Montgolfier heat pump, of which the description remained sealed in the files of the former Academy of Science, and it stimulated Joseph to persevere in experiments with heat engines.

The experiments succeeded. Even while developing the enlarged model of the hydraulic ram intended for Marly, Joseph perfected what he called a *pyrobélier*, a fire-ram. Marc Seguin gave inklings but no details concerning this, his uncle's last invention.[65] It was patented posthumously in Britain in 1816 by Joseph's son, in collaboration with one Henry Dayme or d'Ayme. In 1817 those two further attempted to establish a system of steam navigation on the Rhône, a project which was taken over in 1825 by the firm that Marc Seguin had formed with his brothers.[66] The fire-ram was not the source of power for that venture, however, and we know about its genesis through another of the sealed notes confided to the Academy of Science. This one came from the hand of Nicolas Clément, the chemist and industrialist. It was dated 2 January 1816, slightly before Joseph *fils* registered the patent in London.[67] Among other considerations, Clément evidently wished to safeguard the priority of his late and honored partner in the principles underlying the fruition of a lifetime of thought.

For Joseph's quest for a machine that would tame the force released in firearms culminated in the fire-ram. According to Clément, Joseph had calculated the "*force motrice*" that a given quantity of charcoal yields when burned to produce steam and compared the amount to that imparted on firing to a twenty-four-pound cannonball of known velocity. The latter value, though only a fraction of the force generated by explosion of the gunpowder, was still much the larger. Clément surely slipped here in writing "*force motrice*" (the product of mass times acceleration) instead of "live force" (half the product of mass times the square of the velocity). But he may well have been right in saying that no one had yet made such a comparison, for contained in it is tacit recognition of the mechanical equivalent of heat.

Rapid combustion was the key to reducing the effect of firing a cannon to manageable proportions, and Joseph achieved it by passing air into the cylinder at high velocity under pressure. His fire-ram was thus not only an internal combustion motor. It was an injection motor with an alternating action, equipped with ingenious arrangements for charging the fuel and removing the ashes, and it burned either pulverized coal or powdered charcoal. And the best way to describe the operation of the fire-ram will be to reproduce the language of the patent (Fig. 68) as well as the drawing of the first of two slightly variant models that it covered.[68]

68.

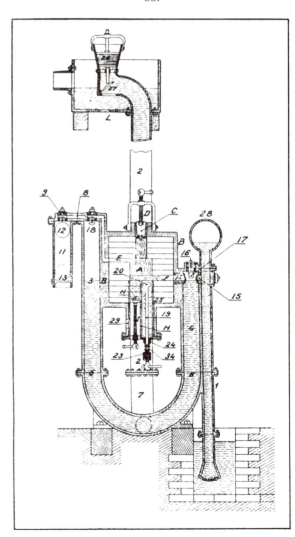

68. Joseph de Montgolfier's *Pyrobélier.* "The heated air proceeding through the valve 14 presses very suddenly and forcibly on the water in the chamber 4, and gives it a rapid motion through 6, 7, and the pipe 2. This motion continues after the expansive force of the air has ceased (from the increased space of the chamber which it occupies, and by the cooling or contracting of the air), and the motion of the moving water is sufficiently to increase the space so far as to produce a suction or aspiration within the whole machine; then as the atmospheric air finds the most free passage through the valve 9 into the air vessel 3, it will enter therein until the ball 12 strike[s] the valve 10 and stops it; the aspiration still continuing, it draws the water up the suction pipe 1 through the valve 15 into the water chamber 4, and in the same instant the column in the pipe 2 arrives at the top of the pipe, and a quantity of water flies out at the top into the reservoir L equal to the quantity drawn in, the water pouring into the water chamber 4 cools and contracts the air therein. The moving force of the column 2 being at length expended in overcoming its gravity, and in drawing in the air at 3 and the water at 4, it returns, that is, it descends in the pipe 2, and ascends in the chambers 3 and 4, and compresses the air contained therein until it will become equally elastic with the atmospheric air. The burned air in the water chamber 4 then lifts up the valve 16, and makes it escape until it is all gone, and the water then lifts up the float and shuts the valve 17. As the water cannot now rise any higher in the water chamber 4, the whole force of the returning column applies itself to compress the air just before drawn into the air chamber 3, and force it into the fire, and being thereby suddenly expanded it enters through the valve 14, and begins a third stroke, by expelling the water from the chamber 4 and making it mount up the pipe 2; the motion thus given to the water produces an aspiration, which first draws the air through 9 into the chamber 3, and then draws fresh water through 15 into the chamber 4, and in the same instant a portion of the water flies out at the top of the pipe 2. The moving force of the column 2 having expended itself, the column 2 returns, and the water returns into the 2 chambers 3 and 4; from the latter it expels by the valve 16 the remains of that air which has passed through the fire, and it draws the air contained in the air chamber 3 into the furnace to produce another stroke, and thus the action of the machine continues. It is to be observed that every time when the aspiration takes place the air will be drawn out of the furnace (or rarified therein), and the fire will be damped or burn very slowly until the fresh air is forced into the fire from the chamber C in a compressed state by the enterance of the water into the same. The fire then burns for a moment with great violence and heats the air, but it will be damped the next moment by the drawing away of the air when the aspiration takes place."

3. BRIDGES AND RAILWAYS

In 1824 the *Edinburgh Philosophical Journal* printed a letter that Marc Seguin had addressed to John Herschel on 11 December 1822. He wished to put before the Astronomical Society of London a new way of considering the effects of heat and of motion that his great-uncle Montgolfier had imparted to him in his youth. "The principle which he maintained was, that the *vis viva* could neither be created nor annihilated, and consequently, that the quantity of motion on the earth had a real and finite existence." Marc Seguin here imagined the structure of matter on a planetary model in which bodies consist of molecules revolving around one another under the influence of opposing forces of attraction and angular momentum. Change of state; collision; and thermal, electrical, and magnetic phenomena involve partition of the total quantity of motion between apparent loss in internal changes and observable displacements relative to other bodies.

Among general facts that thereby became explicable, in Marc Seguin's view, was the effect of steam engines. For if the cause were caloric, "it is not easy to see why we could not produce an indefinite number of oscillations with the quantity of caloric necessary to produce the first, if we could by any means whatever employ the low temperatures which are lost, to renew the effect." If, on the other hand, we suppose that a portion of the angular momentum of molecular rotation has been transformed into the rectilinear motion of the piston, then only "the quantity of motion, or caloric" that had not gone into producing the effect would remain.[69]

That passage is interesting for the mixture of speculative physics with sound practical instinct that it bespeaks in Marc Seguin and equally for the history of thermodynamics. The basic consideration, the inadmissibility of perpetual motion in the recycling of heat, is the same from which Sadi Carnot deduced the proposition that the effect of any heat engine is a function of the difference between the initial and final temperatures at which it operates.[70] Although Carnot's essay on the motive power of heat was also published in 1824, neither author knew anything about the other's work. Marc Seguin told Herschel that he had been thinking on these matters for some twenty years, but this fugitive letter was the only thing of his that had yet been printed.

At the time of writing, in December 1822, he had just completed the definitive draft of a proposal to the government to build a suspension bridge across the Rhône linking Tournon on the right bank with Tain on the left.[71] Its realization in 1824 and 1825 made his reputation along with the fortune of Seguin and Company. The printed prospectus characterizes their business as one "composed of five Seguin brothers, to whom their father, as respected as he was enlightened, afforded a sufficient education in Paris so that they might productively pursue the tastes they had formed under the influence of their uncle Montgolfier. . . ."[72] Complete with patriarch, Seguin Frères carried the pattern of the Montgolfier operation at Vidalon forward into the nineteenth century on a scale enlarged to the dimensions of industrial capitalism. The main differences were in tempo and financing. Seguin and Company raised money for successive ventures by floating shares on the Paris stock market and not through letters of credit discounted by a well-placed uncle.

The families had become related through the marriage of the Seguin father, Marc-François, with Etienne's and Joseph's niece, oldest daughter of the deceased Raymond Montgolfier, Pierre's original heir. His father before him, for whom our Marc was named, had come up country to Annonay from Dauphiny, where his people had settled widely. Their forebears, it was said, were of Egyptian Jewish stock, an ancestor having migrated from Alexandria in the 16th century. They had long since become Christians. Marc-François, indeed, seems to have belonged to some Catholic analogue of Freemasonry in Annonay. He was a draper and person of importance in commerce, exercising a moderating influence in the municipality throughout the Revolution. After 1820 he acquiesced in the urging of his sons that the future lay in converting their business from cloth and dyestuffs to civil engineering.[73]

In correspondence and also in his publications, Marc signed himself by the family name only, Seguin Aîné. Deferring to nothing except the memory of his uncle, and to no one except his father, Marc Seguin won deference from brothers, wives, and children as naturally as would some tribal potentate (Fig. 69). By his first wife, Augustine, a Duret cousin related to the Montgolfiers, he had thirteen children, only three of whom outlived him. By his second wife, also called Augustine, a Montgolfier cousin related to the Durets, he had six more, the last born in 1861 in his seventy-sixth year. Among the brothers, Camille was the businessman and administrator of the firm. Jules came closest to Marc Seguin himself in qualities of originality and daring. Perhaps for that reason, he was a maverick and eventually had to be hived off to work alone. Paul and Charles were virtually interchangeable parts in the management. In their enormous exchange of letters, all five leave the impression of great competence, bordering on the Promethean in Marc

69. Marc Seguin at about thirty years of age

Seguin. By way of further contrast with the 18th century, they do not leave the impression, as do Etienne de Montgolfier and his brothers, of a cultivated sensibility.

By all accounts, the departmental engineer, one R. de Plagniol, put into Marc Seguin's head the notion that opportunity awaited the entrepreneur who would improve transportation by replacing ferries with bridges, and that the crossing at Tournon was a good place to begin. Plagniol represented the Corps des Ponts et Chaussées, the public works administration, in the Ardèche, and he and Marc Seguin met often over Sunday dinners at the house of the latter's convivial cousin, Matthieu Duret, the doctor who left pen portraits of many members of the clan. Marc Seguin himself said that an article in the *Moniteur* of 8 December 1821 describing suspension bridges in the United States focused his thoughts on that form of construction, which was far more economical than stone arch bridges with piers to be built all across the riverbed.[74] Eight or ten suspension bridges then existed in America. The oldest, in southwestern Pennsylvania, dated back to 1796 and carried travelers on the road between Uniontown and Greensburg across Jacob's Creek, a tributary to the Youghiogheny. The most spectacular was a 244-foot single-span arch over the Merrimack above Newburyport in Massachusetts. In Britain a bridge over the Tweed at Berwick had opened in 1820. Telford, Brunel, Rennie, and others had projects in hand for the Mersey at Liverpool, for joining Anglesey with the mainland in Wales, and for extending a pier into the Firth of Forth in Scotland.[75]

Marc Seguin never explained how he hit on his distinctive contribution, which was to hang bridges from cables made of iron wire instead of from chains or linked bars of wrought iron, as was the British practice. It is possible that this idea may also have come from his reading of the *Moniteur*, however, for the article alludes to a bridge "en fil d'archal"—"brass wire," the first of its type, across the Schuylkill near Philadelphia. The planks constituting the roadway were laid on a network of "fils de fer"—"iron wire." In a draft of the preface to *Des ponts en fil de fer*,

published in 1824, Marc Seguin told how he had learned in this article that "des ponts suspendus à des fils de fer"—"suspension bridges of iron wire" existed in America. The phrase "à des fils de fer" is crossed out in the manuscript and does not appear in the printed text.[76]

More important than the origin of the idea is his having investigated its feasibility experimentally in a machine shop of the Seguin factory before going forward to a full-scale application. For this invention may be taken as one of those that marks the transition between technique and technology or between skill and science. He submitted the prospectus just mentioned both to the administration of the Ponts et Chaussées and to the judgment of the Academy of Science. The latter were impressed that he had already built two test models. But what mainly interested the referees—Prony, Fresnel, Molard, and Girard—was the series of experiments he reported on the resistance and elasticity of iron. The credibility of his design depended on the principle that the smaller the cross-section of wrought-iron rods or bars, the greater the ratio of tensile strength to weight. Working the metal, and specially drawing it out through the wire-mill, toughened the exterior layer into a kind of skin. Thus, the larger the surface was in proportion to bulk, the better. Marc Seguin ran twenty-four sets of measurements on wires of diameters varying from 0.25 to 6 millimeters. The breaking weight per square millimeter was eighty kilograms for the finest. The mean value for wires was sixty kilograms, whereas for rods 0.45 square millimeters in cross-section it was 40 kilograms, declining to twenty-one kilograms as the caliber increased toward 3 centimeters. The academic commissioners reviewed the engineering data that had been accumulated since the previous century when Musschenbroek had begun making systematic determinations of the strength of materials, and observed that "Our positive knowledge on this matter is thus increased by the work of M. Seguin."[77]

That was not his motivation, for as we shall see he undertook his experiments in order to defend his design against the criticism of an expert

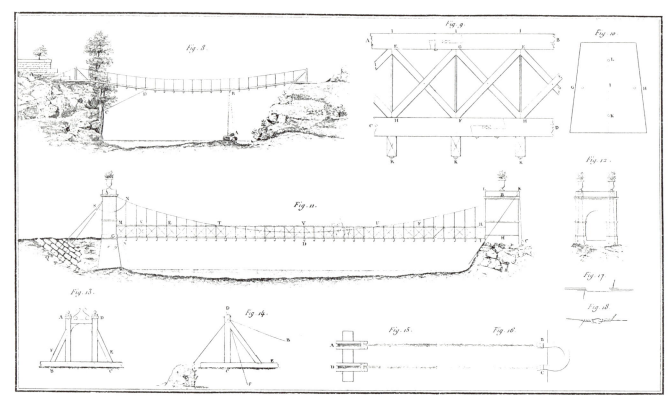

70. The bridge over the Cance (Fig. 8) and the bridge over the Galaure (Fig. 11) with detail of the latter

rather than with a view to increasing knowledge in general. His first model consisted of a foot-bridge, a "*passerelle*" across the Cance in the Seguin factory grounds at Saint-Marc, a little way upstream from Annonay. Marc Seguin completed it in March 1822, four months after having read about American suspension bridges. It was eighteen meters long and fifty centimeters wide and was supported on either side by cables stretched bank to bank, instead of over towers. Each cable consisted of forty-eight strands of iron wire 0.125 centimeters in diameter. The mayor of Annonay certified that he had observed eight adults weighing altogether 560 kilograms follow one another across the span at a distance of one meter with no apparent effect on its solidity. Right away the structure became one of the sights of the city, which to be sure has never had many, and a year or more later Marc Seguin said that, despite his warnings, people would crowd onto

his little bridge in numbers beyond the capacity he had calculated for it, without its showing any strain. Among the visitors were a pair of well-known scientists from Geneva, the botanist A. P. de Candolle and the physicist M. A. Pictet, who went out of their way to include Annonay in a tour of scientific and industrial points of interest. They described the structure for the benefit of the European public that read their newsy *Bibliothèque universelle*, reporting that the cost of the bridge had come to all of 50 francs (Fig. 70).[78]

Emboldened by that success, Seguin and Company lost no time in preparing an approach to government. Their proposal for a "Passerelle en fil de fer sur le Rhône entre Tain et Tournon" was ready by 25 March 1822. It was signed jointly by Marc Seguin and by Plagniol, who advised both on design and on the procedures of the Ponts et Chaussées. The promoters would undertake construction "at their risk and peril" in return for the right to collect tolls at half the rate currently charged by the ferry for a period of sixty years. They would be responsible for maintenance, and in 1882 would turn the structure over to the state in good condition.[79]

The width of the Rhône at the narrowest point was 178 meters, which distance would require a two-span bridge with a pier in mid-river, leaving a minimum clearance of seven meters above low water. As a first alternative, Seguin Frères were proposing a footbridge, though one with a width of 1.25 meters that could accommodate travelers on horseback. The walkway was to be suspended from two systems of ten iron cables on either side, each one composed of thirty two-millimeter strands. Wires and all other metal parts would be rust-proofed with a varnish of tar mixed with lampblack. The promoters gave the government a choice, however, Their calculations assured an ample margin of safety, and they were confident that a vehicular bridge could be constructed on the same principle if the authorities should prefer the more ambitious scheme. In that case, the width would be three meters and the cables composed of 800 instead of 600 wires in all. The estimates would be revised accordingly.[80]

Endorsed by the prefect of the Ardèche on 1 April, the proposal had then to come before the Conseil-Général des Ponts et Chaussées in Paris.[81] This body, composed of senior engineers in the service, was advisory, and in practice the Director General, a high officer of state, always abided by its recommendations. Louis Becquey, who held that post, referred the Seguin proposal to the judgment of Claude Navier, one of the leading representatives in the Corps of the new model of mechanical engineer. He had been trained mathematically at the Ecole Polytechnique and professionally in the Ecole des Ponts et Chaussées, the equivalent of a modern graduate school.

As bad luck would have it, Navier had just returned from the first of several missions to Britain, whither Becquey had sent him to inform himself about the suspension bridges already completed and those planned. He had himself begun work on the design of a chain bridge across the Seine on the site of the present Pont Alex-

andre III. His report to Becquey was accompanied by a *Mémoire sur les ponts suspendus*, published early the next year, in 1823.[82] The memoir is essentially a work of mathematics. Navier applied the brand-new technique of Fourier analysis to the perturbations that passage of a vehicle would produce in an idealized suspension bridge, and deduced the optimal proportions of length and mass for maximum stability. It is fair to surmise that in April 1822 Navier had never heard of Marc Seguin, and certain that his own position of chief engineer in the Corps was several echelons above that of Plagniol out in the provinces. In very short order, he recommended rejection of their proposal, coolly and briefly. Basing his dismissal on British precedent and calculation of moments of force, Navier concluded that wire cables would prove defective in tensile strength and in resistance to rust and fatigue. Besides that, the abutment on the left bank in Tain would lack an adequate margin of solidity, and the promoters had failed to show that their pier in mid-river would not interfere with navigation.[83]

Then it was, in the spring and summer of 1822, that Marc Seguin put in hand the systematic campaign of experimental determinations of the tensile strength of iron bars and wire that won the admiration of the Academy's commission a bit less than two years later. For, although the General Council accepted their referee's reservations, they were persuaded, as indeed was Navier, of the merit of suspension bridges in general, and also of the convenience to the public of spanning the Rhône at Tournon. The project was the more tempting in that it would cost the government nothing. Accordingly, Becquey conveyed the willingness of council to entertain a further proposal if it met the objections to the first. His colleagues also thought a vehicular bridge far preferable, and the prefect of the Ardèche was instructed to invite Seguin Frères to modify their design as they had themselves suggested.[84]

By 30 November 1822 Marc Seguin had the new proposal ready.[85] That he should have stuck to his guns in the form of iron cables is evidence of force of character no less than accuracy in experimental engineering, for as yet he and his brothers had nothing of a reputation to oppose to the rejection of their thinking by a leading engineer at the center of influence and power. Plagniol did point out that Marc Seguin was a nephew of the "celebrated Montgolfier" and a person to be taken seriously, but Plagniol himself lost his nerve and went over to Navier and chains, more perhaps for tactical than technical reasons.[86] Before proceeding to the Rhône, Marc Seguin also undertook a further model, larger than the tiny bridge across the Cance. This next one he designed with the express purpose of testing the applicability of his experimental findings along with the calculations that accompanied the theory. The account he printed to fortify his documentation in the eyes of the authorities makes a brochure of some fifteen pages.[87] It initiated a feature of his engineering that is interesting for itself and for its place in the evolution of technology. Thereafter, he accompanied all his constructions with publications explaining and justifying the designs and generalizing their potentiality (Fig. 71).

the width 1.65 meters. The four cables, a pair on both sides, were 2 centimeters in diameter, each consisting of thirty strands of iron wire. The walkway was suspended on vertical four-ply cords placed at intervals of one meter. Railings with diagonal struts provided both safety and rigidity. The towers rose 2.20 meters above the level of the bridge, which had a clearance of 5 meters over low water. Marc Seguin gave all the remaining specifications in detail in his brochure, calculating the forces from the weights and the resistances required of the abutments. He took care to draw on formulas derived by Navier in the work just mentioned as well as on the standard rules established by Coulomb (Fig. 70).

It remained to try the solidity. Marc Seguin traversed it first in company with three of his brothers. Even when they marched in step, they felt no tremor. Several horsemen next crossed without dismounting, even though three more prudent types were already on the bridge leading their steeds by the bridle. Another rider then dashed across at a gallop. Marc Seguin had un-

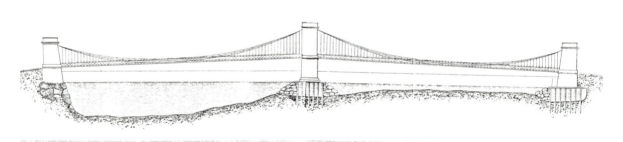

71. Profile of the Tain-to-Tournon bridge and of the bed of the Rhône, looking upstream. A rock formation provided a natural foundation for the abutment on the Tournon side (left). Foundations of piles had to be constructed for the abutment at Tain, as for the pier in mid-river

Marc Seguin built his second bridge across the mouth of the Galaure, a tributary that pours into the Rhône from the east at Saint-Vallier, about fifteen kilometers upstream from Tournon. Several landowners in the region clubbed together to underwrite the experiment, subscribing a sum of 4,000 francs. The length was 30 meters and

dertaken to build a structure that would support 5,000 kilograms. Joined to the weight of the bridge, such a burden would produce a traction of 17,000 kilograms in the cables pulling against the resistance of the abutments. The formal test consisted of loading the bridge with gravel, which laborers shoveled onto the walkway up to the amount of 4,500 kilograms. Onlookers cried that it was enough. The main investor was still not present, however, and Marc Seguin, full of confidence, walked out on the pebbles again with his brothers, inviting anyone who liked to join them. Fifteen people accepted the challenge, raising the total to 5,400 kilograms. Finally, the missing shareholder arrived. He wanted to know whether the structure would hold up under the traffic of as many as forty people at an ordinary walk. Workmen began clearing off the gravel. Before they could remove more than half of it, curious spectators crowded their way onto the span in such numbers that something like seventy people were trampling back and forth above the river. The total weight Marc Seguin estimated at 6,700 kilograms, a "terrible trial" that produced not the slightest crack in the masonry of the abutments left or right.

Navier had needed just two weeks in April 1822 to recommend rejection of the first Seguin proposal. Following submission of the second on 20 November 1822, almost a year elapsed before the General Council of the Ponts et Chaussées accepted it. Looking back in 1839 from the vantage point of the railway-builder he had meanwhile become, Marc Seguin considered that the authorities, far from being the obstructive bureaucrats they were conventionally imagined to be, had in fact acted in a highly responsible manner. In *De l'influence des chemins de fer*, he pointed out that the bridge at Tournon had an administrative importance at least as great as its architectural significance. It was the first concession in French history entitling private capital to invest in and exploit a public utility. So far-reaching a precedent could scarcely have been set other than deliberately.[88]

This time the Seguins requested the concession for a term of ninety-nine instead of sixty years, the justification being an increase in the outlay of capital to an estimated 190,000 francs in order to comply with the official preference for a vehicular bridge. The company felt bound to modify its original intention to halve the tolls paid at the ferry and asked to be allowed to charge the same rates: 10 centimes for a pedestrian with an additional 10 for a horse or mule and 5 for a steer, cow, calf, donkey, pig, sheep, or goat. A one-horse carriage would pass for 60 centimes, a two-horse for 1.20 francs, and a three-horse for 1.60 francs. The applicants also wished to take over the ferry and collect its tolls pending construction of the bridge in order to swell their flow of cash.[89]

In advancing these proposals, no less radical than the design itself, Marc Seguin now realized that he must do more than send papers through the proper channels to a distant committee in the capital. He must go there himself and become, in effect, a lobbyist. He must—though he did not put it this way—emulate not only his Uncle Joseph but also his Uncle Etienne, and make himself known to the people of importance who made the decisions. If that went well, he would then go on to Britain and see with his own eyes what the future might hold in industrial technology, for Seguin Frères and for France.

Marc Seguin arrived in Paris on 21 August 1823 for the first of many extended absences from home and family in the course of his industrial career. His letters and the replies during these intervals permit following developments almost day by day. Naturally, it was easier for him to be reflective in the successful retrospect of some fifteen years later than at the time. His latest letter had been more encouraging than the first, wrote his wife on 31 August, though he had not yet seen the "terrible Navier" (for whom Camille had provided him with a pack basket containing twenty-five bottles of red wine and five of white from the Hermitage vineyards terraced above Tain).[90] He called on others, among them the comte de Tournon and his great-aunt Adélaïde, Etienne's widow. She kept up well but was worried about her erratic daughter. Boissy d'Anglas, an elder statesman now and the most distinguished Ardèchois in the capital, introduced him to the duc d'Orléans, the future King Louis Philippe. More to the point, Boissy d'Anglas also arranged for him to read the memoir describing his experiments before the Academy of Science.[91]

He was to appear for that purpose at the Institute of France on 1 September. "I'm experiencing a feeling I haven't had for a long time," he confessed to Camille that morning, "the fear of having put myself forward in order, perhaps, to be dealt a setback."[92] In fact, he was well received, though the question of chains did come up in the discussion. At the close of the session he talked with Thenard, with Arago, and with Cuvier, all of whom were encouraging.[93] On other occasions, he conversed with Ampère, with Fresnel, and with Fourier.[94] "This sort of life in Paris is wearing me down," he wrote his father, "and the habit I've got into of thinking about scientific problems all by myself makes me a little awkward in the company of scientists who have always communicated with each other."[95] He was feeling the tension in his head, he wrote a few weeks later, and had put himself on a strict diet.[96]

On 6 September Navier did receive him, and he stayed two "long hours." To no purpose: "That man regards suspension bridges as his property which no one must touch."[97] After the failure of the interview, Marc Seguin could not be surprised when on 17 September Navier submitted a report on this, the second Seguin proposal, every bit as destructive as the earlier rebuff. Besides its failing to satisfy his own analytical formulas in point of resistance to the perturbation of heavy vehicles, Navier compared the characteristics unfavorably in all respects to those of his cynosure, the bridge at Berwick-on-Tweed.[98]

Marc Seguin refused to be cast down, however. Apparently, it was immediately after the disastrous conversation with Navier, who did not yet belong to the Academy of Science, that Marc Seguin took the precaution of submitting his proposal, with its experimental data in the form of a memoir, to the judgment of that body also. There it was received on 15 September.[99] Thanks probably to intercession by the scientists, he had been promised an opportunity to make his case in person before the General Council of the Ponts et Chaussées. Gaspard Riche de Prony may well have been his good angel here. Prony was an eminent older engineer, former director of the Ecole des Ponts et Chaussées, and the only member both of the jury that reported to the General Council and of the commission on his memoir named by the Academy.

The Pont de Tournon was to come before the Council on 30 September. Its first order of business was Navier's report. Thereupon, the Director General called in Marc Seguin. For over two hours he showed plans, exhibited tables summarizing the results of his experiments, and answered questions and objections. "I was heard with interest and spoke calmly," he wrote in a note to his father and all his brothers half an hour after emerging.[100] In fact, he swept all before him. Here is the critical passage from the jury's opinion, which was that

> An iron cable bridge over the Rhône between Tain and Tournon offers a fortunate occasion to try the experiment called for at no cost to the Treasury; and further that the similar constructions already executed by M[r]. Seguin l'aîné, . . . the experimental research that he has carried out on the subject of the resistance of iron, and the knowledge that his project bespeaks, independently of the considerations of fortune and reputation that he attaches to it—all this presents as great a probability of success as can reasonably be expected in the use of any new procedure.

Accordingly, the proposal was to be welcomed subject only to the stipulation that, on completion, the new bridge must undergo a series of tests, and the Council here specified them in detail, before being opened to the public.[101] The terms were better than he had dared hope, he wrote when the text of an agreement was communicated to him on 13 October.[102] In only two respects was he disappointed. Among his other efforts, he had been exerting himself to secure his design the award of a gold medal at an exposition in the Conservatoire des Arts et Métiers. All it won was the silver one, however. And, secondly, he failed to get a concession to collect ferry tolls in advance of construction.[103]

The great matter settled, he decided to go forward with the visit to England. If nothing else, he wrote his father, they could say to prospective shareholders that he had seen the British bridges with his own eyes.[104] He secured letters from his new scientific patrons introducing him to scientists in London, and also to John Rennie, and one from Boissy d'Anglas to "Lord d'Hastings," the last "Viceroi des Grandes Indes."[105] Rennie was well impressed, and handed him along to a Captain Brown of the Royal Navy.[106] Marc-Isambard Brunel also received him, and approved the design for wire cables. He visited Brighton and learned that suspension bridges were spreading rapidly. This first visit to England was not a success, however. Communicating with people was very difficult. Of those he met, only Brunel, an emigré, spoke French. In London, the theater was incomprehensible. "In general, I don't like this country," he wrote his father a few days after arriving. "I regard the English as very inferior to us in many respects, and altogether I prefer the State of France."[107]

He cut the visit short, therefore, and was back in Paris by late November, and soon thereafter at home in Annonay. The royal ordinance officially conceding Seguin and Company the right to build and operate the Tain-to-Tournon bridge issued from the Council of State on 22 January 1824.[108] Work began immediately. This is not the place to recount the history of its construction, however. That would require a book in itself. One could be written, for Marc Seguin and his brothers kept a detailed log of operations day by day. Few if any large works of civil engineering in its early stages were ever as well documented. The level of the river, the state of the weather, the price and supply of materials, the performance and pay of every workman, the obstacles encountered and the methods improvised for overcoming them—all that is recorded in the Livre du Pont, as is the near-catastrophe of a great flood in the spring of 1825, when debris swirling down on the crest carried away their service bridge and threatened the pier in midriver.[109]

In eighteen months the great job was finished. On 22 August 1825 all five Seguin brothers and a Montgolfier cousin foregathered to witness the tests in company with engineers of the Corps des Ponts et Chaussées and representatives of the department and of the municipalities of Tain and Tournon. A leveling line was affixed to the vertical cords on the upstream side. Segments of the roadway were then loaded with measured weights of gravel in order to determine the effect of various distributions on the funicular profile. Not to go into detail, the inspectors raised the total to an even spread of 69,150 kilograms including the weight of fifty-odd workers and onlookers. The span was then subjected to the additional stress of the jolting passage of two wagons, each pulled by a team of seven horses and weighing about 5,000 kilograms. The officials were entirely satisfied with the solidity both of bridge and abutments, and on 25 August the Tain-to-Tournon bridge was blessed by the bishop of Valence and ceremoniously opened to the public.[110]

Seguin and Company had not awaited its completion to enter on a contract for a second bridge, again across the Rhône, fourteen kilometers downstream at the next city of importance, Valence.[111] Construction and operation of suspension bridges thus became their main business. By 1840 the firm had built twenty-nine, and a balance sheet shows profits of 1,333,910.91 francs against losses of 214,336.33 for the previous six-year interval.[112] By the 1860s they had 186 bridges in service, in Italy and Spain as well as France. The original Tain-to-Tournon span survived until 1965 when the enlargement of oil tankers began to require higher clearance.

Readers may wish to know that in July 1824 the "terrible Navier" began construction of his chain bridge, which was to link the esplanade of the Invalides in Paris with the Champs Elysées. Work was virtually completed in September 1826, when a flash flood provoked by a burst sewer main undermined the foundations of the right bank and caused the tower to tilt slightly. On the insistence of the municipal authorities, who had opposed the project all along, the government ordered demolition of the entire structure before ever it entered into service, even though the damage could have easily been put right. Such at least was Navier's account, published for the record.[113]

Daniel Wilson, of the firm of Manby and Wilson, English contractors established in Paris, gave a different story. According to a letter he wrote to Thomas Telford, president of the Institution of Civil Engineers in London, Navier had miscalculated what would be required to resist the pull of the chains. When the scaffolding was taken down, their load augmented by their own weight caused the two towers to lean toward each other. The inclinations were perceptible. Had the scaffolding not been hastily restored and the chains removed, the structure would almost certainly have collapsed. Wilson supposed that the bridge would have to be abandoned. Already the cost was the equivalent of £ 50,000 to £ 60,000 although the materials had been ordered on the cheap.[114] It may have been even so. That a sewer of 1827 could have released enough water to endanger a sound structure seems implausible, the more so as the break was said to have occurred at Chaillot, which is a little downstream.

The Seguins too met with reverses in their next venture, which still involved transportation and the Rhône but never made a profit. We have already mentioned the project that Joseph de Montgolfier's son formed in 1817 to supersede horse-drawn barge traffic on the river with navigation under steam power. The notion was to install engines on board, not to run stern- or sidewheels, but to turn a capstan and haul the boats upstream by means of cables attached to a series of stanchions fixed at intervals of 800 meters along the towpath.[115] A member of the crew would advance the end of the mooring loop from post to post on horseback. When Seguin Frères absorbed what had proved a stillborn scheme in 1825, they enlarged the scale and proposed to put into service a barge-train of six or eight cargo vessels pulled behind the towboat, the *Remorqueur*, named for its function. Up ahead a small steamer, the *Voltigeur*, would carry the cable forward from one tethering to the next. The schedule called for twelve trips a year from Arles to Lyons, a distance of 275 kilometers as the river flows. Return shipments would ride the current downstream.

The new company was incorporated under the name of Seguin, Montgolfier & d'Ayme in May 1825 and capitalized by issuing 1,000 shares of stock at 500 francs each.[116] The identity of the shareholders is evidence of the reputation that

the bridge had won for the Seguins even before its completion. Scientists and engineers whom Marc Seguin had met in Paris are on the list: Arago, Gay-Lussac, Brisson, Thenard, Darcet, and Girard, the last of whom had been a member of the academic commission on *Des ponts en fil de fer*. Many titled names also appear, along with assorted Montgolfiers and Cansons. Nicolas Clément, the chemical manufacturer and Joseph's old associate, subscribed for fifteen shares. Sadi Carnot took two, and is identified in a note as "Carnot's son—has written on the theory of heat considered as motive force."[117] By now, therefore, Marc Seguin and he at least knew who the other was. The physicist J.-B. Biot was a shareholder, beginning an association through which his son, Edouard, got a start in engineering and soon became a member of the firm.[118]

Later in 1825 Paul Seguin surveyed the entire length of the towpath. In November Marc Seguin went to Britain again, in company with his brother Charles and Joseph's son. Their object, according to a letter of introduction, was to visit some of the "best manufacturing establishments; especially those where steam-engines, steamboats, and rail-ways are constructed."[119] Unlike the first, this second tour across the Channel was a great success for Marc Seguin. After returning he read a memoir on steam navigation before the Institute of France. The firm ordered two steam engines from Martineau in London, a large one for the *Remorqueur* and a small one for the *Voltigeur*. The boats themselves were constructed in Andance, a river town upstream from Tournon, and launched in the summer of 1826.

Thereafter, almost everything went wrong. When the steam engines arrived, they were a third heavier than called for and defective in several respects. The pair of English workmen sent to break them in turned surly and wanted to go home. Swirling currents along the banks made it impossible to handle the cable by satellite boat. The captain of the *Remorqueur* had to fall back on horses, and never extended service further south than Givors, a mere twenty-two kilometers below Lyons. Attempts to convert the *Voltigeur* into a packet boat failed after a few round trips carrying passengers and freight the thirty-two kilometers between Vienne and Lyons in April and, after repairs, again in August 1827. In order to breast the current, the engineer had to push the boiler so hard that the smokestack continually glowed red. Ever greedy for fuel, and with a crew of nine to support, the most she ever took in for a day's run was 157.25 francs.[120]

There was nothing for it but to cut the losses. The Seguin brothers were determined to justify the confidence of their shareholders, however, who were eventually compensated in shares of equivalent value in the next, and far more ambitious company that the house was already floating. Its object was construction of a railroad, the first in France, connecting Lyons with Saint-Etienne across the mountainous divide between the watersheds of the Rhône and of the Loire. In January 1828, before liquidation had quite been decided, one of the commissioners in the threatened bankruptcy held out hope to his fellow investors. In studying prospects for the railroad, he reported, Marc Seguin had imagined a new type of boiler. It would weigh only one-fifth what the disappointing monster from Martineau did, and it would produce 20 percent more steam.[121]

This "tubular boiler" was Marc Seguin's most interesting invention. He thought of it, evidently, at a time when he was preoccupied both with attempting to salvage the river hauling operation and with planning for the railway from Saint-Etienne to Lyons. Already, a new association, Seguin Frères & Edouard Biot, had been formed for the latter purpose. (Jules Seguin was not a member.) They won the concession from the government at a public adjudication on 27 March 1826, underbidding two competitors with an engagement to transport merchandise for a charge of 9.8 centimes per kilometer-ton. One of Marc Seguin's objects in England during the winter visit of 1825-1826 had been to estimate on the basis of British experience what that figure would need to be.[122] The Stockton and Darlington Railway, the first in Britain, had opened to the public less than a year before, in the spring of 1825. The experience was not extensive, therefore, and

native wit must have been an important factor in Marc Seguin's calculation.

The major factor in all these affairs was enterprise, multiplied by ingenuity. Just as the Seguins had launched into river navigation before completing the Tournon bridge, so now they moved into railroading before their boats were even built. Formally their relation with the shareholders of the Société de Chemin de Fer de Saint-Etienne à Lyons, who provided the capital, was that of contractors. In June 1827 Marc Seguin made a third trip across the Channel. His letter of introduction to Thomas Telford was that in which Daniel Wilson took occasion to mention the failure of Navier's Pont des Invalides while identifying Marc Seguin as author of the success at Tournon. "He is at present," Telford was further told, "occupied with the Rail Road from St. Etienne to Lyons, and goes to England for a few days to see if anything new and useful has lately been brought forward in that branch of engineering."[123] Marc Seguin may probably have already constructed his first, experimental locomotive, with the performance of which he was dissatisfied. A sketch by an employee survives (Fig. 72). After returning, he hit on the design of the tubular boiler, and on 13 December 1827 made application for a patent.[124]

As he saw it, the main problem was to improve the economy of heat transfer. How might a surface greater than that of the under half-cylinder of the boiler be exposed to the action of the fire in order to generate more steam from the same fuel? The patent declares the invention to be "A type of steam boiler on the principle of hot air circulating in separate tubes of small dimension."[125] Both the wording and the design make it clear that Marc Seguin's solution embodied two considerations emergent from his earlier thinking. On the one, that shortening the diameter increases the proportion of surface to volume, he had based his confidence in the tensile strength of cables of iron wire. The other operational feature realized a theme going back to his Uncle Joseph's heat pump and to the balloon. Motion may be obtained from the heat contained in the mixture of air with gaseous products of

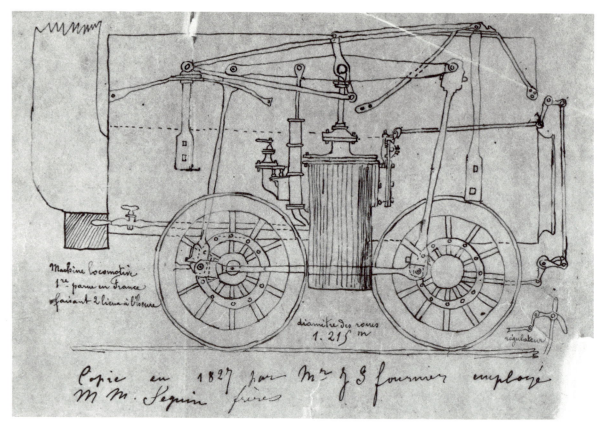

72. Employee's sketch of the tubular boiler

combustion. Instead of sending the smoke and exhaust straight up a stack, and throwing all their heat away with them, Marc Seguin passed the gases through a battery of forty-three four-centimeter copper tubes running lengthwise through the lower half of the boiler. They were thus immersed in the water that they helped turn into steam. Their combined surface came to 15.78 square meters in addition to the 2.56 square meters of the half-cylinder alone (Fig. 73). Other characteristics of Marc Seguin's locomotive will best be appreciated from the drawings (Fig. 74).[126]

The locomotive he constructed and put into service had two further features that formed the object of an additional patent application of 16 October 1829. Both were intended to improve the draft while permitting a lowering rather than a raising of the smokestack. Increasing its height, the normal recourse for obtaining a stronger draw, was precluded by the difficulty of the route the

railway would have to take. Surveys called for hollowing fourteen tunnels out of rocky and mountainous terrain. The first of the two devices Marc Seguin imagined for improving combustion was commonplace in its principle, which was to inject steam from the escape valve into the flue. The only originality was in the design of the pump (Fig. 75). The second expedient was truly singular, however. He mounted a pair of exhaust fans on the tender to suck air through the firebox and the tubes. They were rotated by means of a power takeoff from one wheel and equipped with a clutch so that the engineer could regulate the effect (Fig. 76). They could also be operated manually while the train was stationary.[127]

In England, meanwhile, the Stephensons were thinking along similar lines. Their Rocket won the famous contest against four competitors at the opening of the Liverpool and Manchester Railway on 1 October 1829. Robert Stephenson

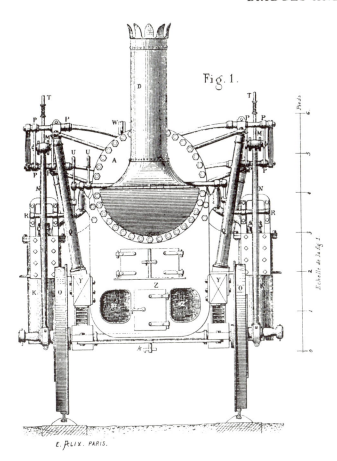

Fig. 1.

E. PLIX. PARIS.

73. The tubular boiler. Fig. 1, Front view; Fig. 2, End section; Fig. 3, Cross section

also employed steam injection and a tubular boiler, his being mounted at a steep angle to the vertical rather than horizontally. There appears to be no doubt that Marc Seguin had priority in the invention and Stephenson in the employment of their respective locomotives. The Rocket weighed 9 tons and the Seguin engine only 4.5 tons. Marc Seguin built it in 1827, and perfected it in 1830 and 1831. When the Saint-Etienne-to-Lyons Railway opened for business in 1832, it had two locomotives, that model and another ordered from the Stephensons. Nor did Marc Seguin build a second. He never said why he stopped. The operation of the fans proved cumbersome in practice, but the reason may more probably have been the difficulty and expense of obtaining good workmanship in steam engineering at that early stage in France.

The urbanity and judiciousness of Marc Seguin's *De l'influence des chemins de fer* might well mislead a casual reader into supposing that the work is drawn from reflections on the design and operation of a modern system like the spiderweb of main lines centered on Paris and radiating out

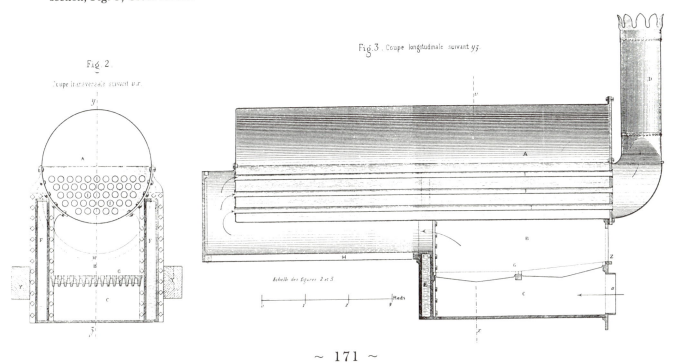

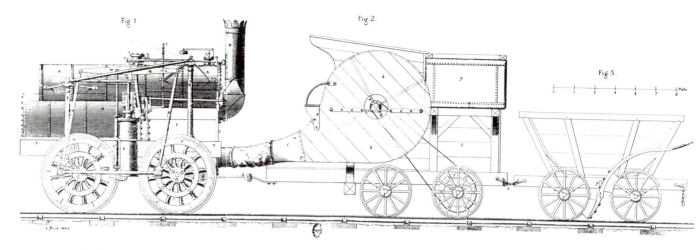

74. Marc Seguin's locomotive with tender and coal car. Fig. 1, The locomotive; Fig. 2, Ventilator mounted on the tender; Fig. 3, Freight car with coasting brake

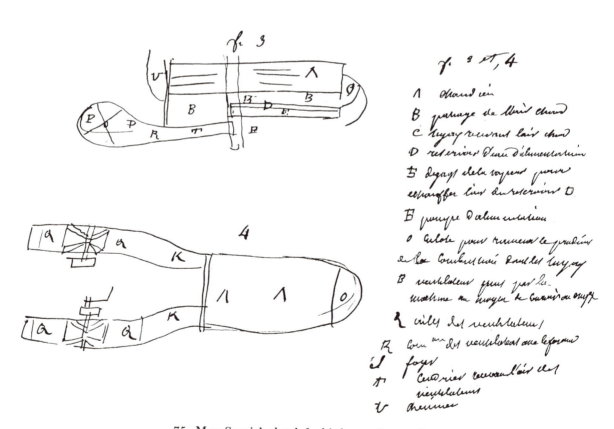

75. Marc Seguin's sketch for his locomotive ventilator

from the Gare Saint-Lazare, the Gare du Nord, the Gare de l'Est, and all the rest. The observations on the importance of transport for national wealth, on the integration of regional into worldwide commerce, on the types of raw material and merchandise to which delivery by rail was best suited, on the relation of investment to management (the railway builder "must take care ahead of time to make himself independent of the men whose capital he is expending"),[128] on the reconciliation of private enterprise with governmental regulation, on the acquisition of land for the right of way and the cupidity of property-owners, on the calculation of rates and the prospects for profitability, on the sometimes conflict-

ing and sometimes complementary needs of freight and passengers, and on the psychology of the latter ("It is noteworthy to what extent men taught the value of time by our civilization are eager to save it; impatient to arrive quickly at their destinations, they shut their eyes to danger, or dread it less than a delay")[129]—on all that, as well as on the engineering of the roadbed and the design and construction of track-work, locomotives, and rolling stock, Marc Seguin wrote in an assured voice that rings of extensive experience. In fact, his prescience is more impressive than his experience. In 1839, when his book was published, the railways in service in France covered 158 kilometers—the original 58 kilometers from Lyons

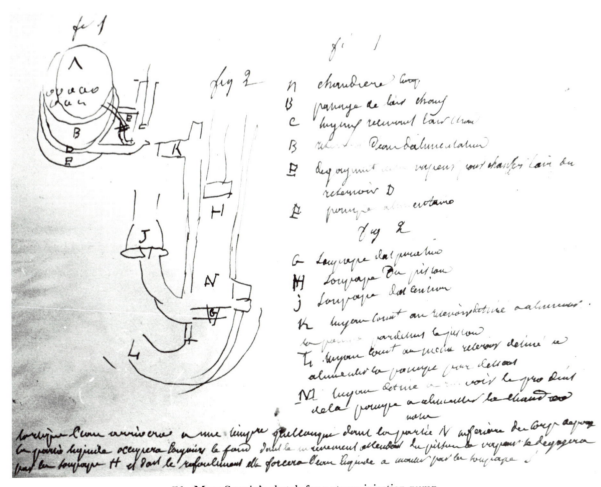

76. Marc Seguin's sketch for a steam injection pump

to Saint-Etienne, an extension of 70 kilometers from the latter city along the Loire to Roanne, a 14-kilometer spur from that stretch to Montbrison, and a 16-kilometer suburban line from Saint-Germain-en-Laye to Paris. His handful of hurrying passengers were being hurled along these distances at speeds approaching thirty miles an hour.

Besides its general qualities, the book is noteworthy for two specific features, one being the account, complete with charts, of the construction of the railway from Lyons to Saint-Etienne, and the other the chapter on the mechanical convertibility of heat. Work on the roadway began in September 1826, before Marc Seguin had invented his tubular boiler. Both the profile and detail of the terrain presented difficulties of a magnitude not yet confronted in Britain. Saint-Etienne lies at an altitude of 370 meters higher than the level of the Rhône, and the line had to climb the narrow and tortuous valley of the Gier. Marc Seguin divided the distance into three sections, each with its own foreman and work force. The first ran twenty kilometers from the site of the present Gare de Perrache in Lyons to Givors and required construction of a major bridge from the peninsular tip of the city to the right bank of the Rhône at its juncture with the Saône. An earlier span had been swept away after three years of resisting the combined currents. Marc Seguin was tempted to try a suspension bridge, but feared lest the vibrations be excessive.

At Givors the tracks turned away from the Rhône to mount toward Rive-de-Gier. In this second section, the average slope was six millimeters per meter over a distance of 16.3 kilometers. The third was even steeper, snaking up to Saint-Etienne with a pitch of thirteen millimeters per meter. Of the fourteen tunnels, the longest at Terre-Noire, the summit, ran 1,500 meters under the continental divide between the river systems of the Rhône and the higher Loire. Another was 900 meters long, and the total length of track underground came to 4,000 meters. At the start of an excavation, no one could foretell what conditions the drillers would encounter in

the strata to be pierced. Spongy formations had to be timbered, and both lateral and vertical ventilating shafts to be bored.

Marc Seguin was frank about what he learned from his mistakes and what they cost the shareholders. He had not at first appreciated the importance of keeping gradients to a minimum and had thought to save the cost of filling the roadbed in several bends along the Rhône by taking shortcuts over gentle rises. Not foreseeing the importance of passengers, he located the terminus at Saint-Etienne too far from town. But the most serious error was his initial estimate that curves would be negotiable if the radius was not less than 150 meters. Further visits to the Stockton and Darlington Railway, wherein the sharpest curves had a radius of 1,200 meters, and consultation with Stephenson, Rennie, and Brunel in London, persuaded him that 500 meters was the irreducible minimum. The survey had to be redone in several sectors, therefore. In order to eliminate eleven impossibly tight twists, the number of tunnels had to be increased from the original projection, which called for only three. On these accounts and many more, the most grievous being the extortion practiced by holdout landowners and certain local authorities, the initial estimate of 7,800,000 francs for capital requirements proved too small. In October 1831 a pair of visiting engineers, Albert Schlumberger and Emile Koechlin of Mulhouse, reported that expenditures over the previous five years had amounted to 10,000,000 and were expected to involve another 3,000,000. In fact, the final cost came to 15,350,000 before returns on the investment began to come in.[130]

When Schlumberger and Koechlin made their tour of the railway, the middle stretch from Givors to Rive-de-Gier was already open to traffic and competing with a canal along which horses hauled barges up and back through the gates of a series of twenty-nine locks. The entire line was in service a year later, in October 1832, limited at first to freight. The principal attraction for investors was the prospect of transporting coal from the mines of Rive-de-Gier and Saint-Etienne to Lyons and to other centers served by navigation on the Rhône and the Saône. On the return trip the cars would carry ore and pig iron from Burgundy to supply factories making small arms in Saint-Etienne and also sand for the glass industry in Rive-de-Gier.[131] Once again Marc Seguin's reader must beware lest a modern service be imagined. In the opening stages, the two locomotives served only to haul empty cars uphill (for the volume of the return traffic was far from balancing the delivery of coal). Trains of up to fifteen cars coasted downhill under gravity, a single brakeman slowing the descent. Horsepower supplemented locomotives until 1844. While Marc Seguin ran the railway, horses worked by night at first, and the track remained clear by day for the speeding locomotives.[132]

Institution of passenger service in June 1834 required modification of that policy, since passenger trains were all horse-drawn at the outset. A handbill, "Information for Travelers," sets forth the regulations and requests clients to register complaints about the service and to report any misconduct or infractions on the part of the conductors, whose job it was to assure their comfort and safety. Customers were at the same time asked to record "actions worthy of praise or reward." Conductors were always to be in uniform and to carry a trumpet they must blow in traversing the tunnels and lanterns to light the way. Should a locomotive or freight train approach on the opposite track, they must get out and lead their horses by the bridle lest the animals take fright and derail the carriages. It was forbidden to stop the train to retrieve unimportant effects like canes or hats that might fall out. Passengers were limited to baggage weighing fifteen kilograms, which they had to deliver to the conductor at check-in, together with such small carry-on luggage as would not inconvenience others. Smoking was strictly forbidden, except in the "impériale" (the term for the outside places in a stagecoach). Dogs might not be taken aboard unless a ticket was bought for them, in which case they were to be leashed to a seat near the conductor. No one might board or leave the train except at the stations in Lyons, Givors, Rive-de-Gier, Saint-Chamond, and Saint-Etienne, and at three additional stops along the way. The timetable called for five hours from Lyons to Saint-Etienne and four-and-a-half for the return journey.[133]

To turn to the theoretical aspect of Marc Seguin's book, what is now called the mechanical equivalent of heat occupies the seventh chapter. The term derives from the researches of James Prescott Joule, who measured its value experimentally four years later, in 1843, and gave a general statement in 1847.[134] The thrust of Marc Seguin's argument is a good deal less pointed. He mainly thought to explain the difference between the theoretical and the actual performance of steam engines on grounds of the incomplete convertibility of heat to motion. The discussion opens with the same consideration about the inadmissibility of perpetual motion that Marc Seguin had advanced in the letter sent to John Herschel back in 1822, and that he had evidently often had in mind throughout the intervening years of civil engineering. If it were true, as generally assumed, that all the heat imparted to steam could in principle be exploited in driving the piston, then an indefinite quantity of motion could be obtained by recycling a given quantity of heat at decreasing temperatures and lower pressures of the steam. Since that consequence was clearly absurd, he found it "more natural to suppose that a certain quantity of caloric disappears in the very act of producing force or mechanical power, and reciprocally." The mechanical work that a gas performs in expanding and cooling is thus "the measure and the expression of that lessening of heat."[135]

Much experimentation in recent years had been codified in the form of steam tables. Specifically, Marc Seguin cited F. M. Guyonneau de Pambour, author of *Théorie de la machine à vapeur*, who had communicated data to him privately.[136] In such compilations, what was known to every practitioner became evident numerically. The power obtainable from a given quantity of steam is greater the higher the temperature and the greater the pressure in the cylinder. Marc Seguin in his own discussion imagined a geometrical cylinder and piston, rather in the manner of Sadi Carnot. The quantity of steam is specified as the amount that exerts a pressure of two kilograms per square centimeter at 120° and one kilogram at 100°. Marc Seguin then calculated the work performed by the steam in expanding and raising the piston an amount corresponding to a sequence of 20° drops in temperature from 180° down to 80°, and he tabulated the results shown in Fig. 77.[137]

PRESSIONS en kilogrammes.	TEMPÉRATURES réelles.	EFFET produit en kilogrammes élevés à 1 mètre.	DIFFÉRENCES.	TEMPÉRATURES correspondantes à l'effet produit.	DIFFÉRENCES.
0,48	80°	7270		20°	
			657		1,80
1	100	6615		18,20	
			443		1,25
2	120	6170		16,97	
			390		1,07
3,61	140	5780		15,90	
			340		0,66
6,15	160	5540		15,24	
9,93	180				

77. Tabulation of mechanical equivalents of heat

The first column gives the pressure, the second the temperature, the third the work performed by the expenditure of heat through the drop indicated, and the fifth the increase in temperature that corresponds to compressing the gas by expending on it the same amount of work. The fourth and sixth columns give the increments of successive figures in the third and fifth respectively.

Marc Seguin nowhere stated a coefficient for the equivalence between heat and work that he thus illustrated. He used the term but once, and only in a passing remark. When steam escapes into the atmosphere, the reaction it exerts against the container, or the motion it imparts to the surrounding air, "form an equivalent to the loss of heat it undergoes."[138] Nevertheless (if we may venture to point out what he did not), dividing the figures for mechanical effect in the third column by the respective temperature differences in the fifth yields a quotient of approximately 363 in each instance. In 1841 Robert Mayer expressly calculated a value for the coefficient of equivalence that he published in 1842. The method was other than Marc Seguin's. It depended on the difference between the specific heats of gases at constant pressure and at constant volume. But the result was virtually identical, 365 kilogrammeters corresponding to 1,000 calories.

Not only did Marc Seguin omit giving that number, he nowhere explained how he arrived at the figures for temperature drop corresponding to mechanical effect listed in the fifth column, which he calls an "échelle fictive"—"fictitious scale."[139] What one wonders, therefore, is whether he constructed it by begging the question? Did he choose values so that the quotient would be constant, without ever writing the number down in his book? That seems the most probable rationale of what remains a pretty oblique argument. Only in 1847, eight years later, did Marc Seguin say that his purpose had been to calculate a value for the equivalence. The occasion was a note he wrote about Joule's work and sent to the Academy of Science claiming his own priority.[140]

All Marc Seguin said in his book in 1839 was that among the "great irregularities" of his table, the one uniform result appeared to be that the mechanical effect was always less than would be forecast from the degree of cooling, and that the deficit decreased with rising temperature and pressure. He compared the estimates obtained by his method with those yielded by procedures generally in use for five main classes of steam engine. His predictions ranged from 51.1 percent to 78.6 percent of the received values, and were in all cases much closer to results obtained in practice.[141]

On first arriving in London back in November 1823, lonely and battered from the campaign to win approval in Paris for his bridge, Marc Seguin wrote his father: "I've been toying with the idea of pushing ahead into a scientific career and taking a place among scientists, since I think it's indispensable in our position to have a name that is known."[142] Fifteen years later, having built his bridges, made the trains run, written his book on railways, and grown rich, he felt free to act on that ambition. He was now fifty-three years old, however, and it was too late. Physics had grown mathematical, and his repeated attempts to intrude by writing verbal and graphic treatises about the underlying unity of forces soon came to wear the appearance of an obsession.[143] The most signal of many chagrins must probably have been a snub that Sir John Herschel administered to the very ideas the English scientist had found worth printing forty years before when they both were young.[144]

The spectacle of an eminent engineer turning into a crank in retirement is neither very uncommon nor very instructive. Let us not display it, therefore. It is more agreeable to record the personal fulfillment of Marc Seguin's later years. His life rounded out the pattern of an extraordinary family in that, with variations appropriate to the 19th century, he became a patriarchal figure in the image of his great-grandfather, Pierre de Montgolfier.

In 1838 Marc Seguin married his second Augustine, namesake and niece of his first wife. His brother-in-law, Elie de Montgolfier, thereby became his father-in-law. The grandson of Augustin, and something of a fantast, Elie had purchased the lovely and remote abbey of Fontenay, the great Cistercian monastery founded by Saint Bernard in 1130 and nationalized during the Revolution. Under the inspiration of Charles Fourier, Elie installed a phalanstery in Fontenay, an industrial Utopia where a community of papermakers, printers, bookbinders, and writers produced all the components that go into the fabrication of social and cultural truths. The affair was a failure financially if not spiritually or aesthetically, and Marc Seguin bailed his relative out and bought the property. There he practiced his theories of education upon his children, contributed articles to the journal *Cosmos*, and arranged for translation of W. R. Grove, *The Correlation of Physical Forces*, adding a monograph of his own by way of appendix, and entertaining the author with his family throughout a long sojourn at Fontenay.[145] Grove was an English lawyer, as astute and marginal to mainline physics as Marc Seguin himself.

After twenty years in the fastnesses of Burgundy, Marc Seguin looked to end his days at home. In 1859 he bought the property of Varagnes just outside of Annonay. It is a house of heroic dimensions, with dependencies in which he installed a chapel, a greenhouse, an observatory, a laboratory of physics, and a library. All generations could be accommodated without strain or jostling. For children of all ages he built a working railway with a gauge of fifty centimeters, a locomotive to scale, and several cars to make the circuit of the front garden. The day started with the sound of a gong struck by a round from a vest-pocket cannon when a lens focused the first rays of the sun on the detonator. His last book, *Mémoire sur l'aviation, ou Navigation aérienne* (1866), gathered up the threads of his heritage and proposed a design for an airplane. Some thirty years later, Henri Fabre, inventor in 1910 of the first hydroplane, was often at Varagnes in company with two grandsons of Marc Seguin, Laurent and Augustin.[146] But somehow it seems better to end this history where it began, at Vidalon. In 1861 Marc Seguin bought back the paper mill from the Canson heirs and watched over its operation until his death in 1875.

SOURCES AND BIBLIOGRAPHY

EVEN A GRATEFUL HISTORIAN has difficulty in imagining that people who wrote down as much about what they were doing as did the Montgolfiers and the Seguins also had time to do it all, but so it was. Although access to family papers made it possible to write this book, I have not seen everything they left and am not conversant with the circumstances that produced the distribution of their papers that exists.

The starting point for any interest in their activities is a remarkable family history, Léon Rostaing, *La famille de Montgolfier, ses alliances, ses descendants* (Lyons: A. Rey, 1910). Rostaing was a relative. The name is one among the eight or ten encountered with such regularity in the forest of family trees that the configuration of the genealogy resembles a steady state with convergence balancing divergence. The others, besides Montgolfier and Seguin, are Béchetoille, Blachier, Canson, Chabert, Duret, Filhol, and Frachon. A second edition of the family history edited by Camille Rostaing, Léon's son, appeared in 1930, and a third by the latter's daughter, Madame André Chabert, in 1960. In the second and third editions, the lengthening of genealogy has displaced much of the history, and for that purpose the first is indispensable.

Documents that have since been dispersed were available to Léon Rostaing. The most important collection was located in the Château Colombier-le-Cardinal, a property that no longer exists. A careful calendar of the 1,596 individual documents was prepared in 1935 by Jean Frachon. This collection has survived and is conserved in the library of the Musée de l'Air, 91 boulevard Pereire, Paris XVIIᵉ. The library is open to qualified members of the public, though it is prudent to make an appointment in advance.

Another grouping, less extensive but still considerable, was divided into four lots two generations ago, and an inventory was made. It is through the good offices of Monsieur Charles de Montgolfier that I have been able to consult letters and documents deriving from three of these four divisions, those belonging to himself, to the late Madame Jean de Montgolfier (whose charm and kindness it is delightful to remember), and to Monsieur Régis de Montgolfier. In addition, the last-named has

papers deriving from their common ancestor, Jean-Pierre, the brother of Etienne and Joseph, which are not noted in the inventory.

Finally, an enormous volume of records of Seguin Frères, their business and their personal correspondence, belongs to Monsieur Stanislas Seguin, who is descended from Camille. Since the time several years ago when I went through this material in his house, he has placed it on deposit in the Archives départementales of the Ardèche in Privas, where it may be consulted with appropriate permission. Monsieur Maurice Daumas has made a very general classification of these papers, but there is as yet no inventory and nothing like an itemized listing.

The owners of these many documents, including the Musée de l'Air, allowed me to make photographs or photocopies of a large selection. I have worked mainly from these, and cite them in the notes by use of the following abbreviations:

MA Papers in the Musée de l'Air;
M Papers in one of the Montgolfier lots still in private hands;
RM Papers in the family archives of Monsieur Régis de Montgolfier;
SP Seguin Papers, deposited in Archives de l'Ardèche.

The numbering of the MA series refers to the classification made by Jean Frachon, which has been respected by the Musée de l'Air. The numbering of the M series is that of the inventory made when they were distributed into four lots. Only in rare instances are the Seguin papers yet grouped under any code permitting a ready identification. The collection of photographs and photocopies from which I have worked is now deposited in the Firestone Library of Princeton University, where it may be consulted as an adjunct to the Harold Fowler McCormick Collection of Aeronautica (below). With very few exceptions, copies of all the documents I have cited, together with many that I have not, will be found there. The exceptions are papers that are available in the Musée de l'Air, concerning minor matters. Photocopies of the respective inventories are also available.

An additional resource should be mentioned here. The records of the Montgolfier paper business are still preserved in the office of the factory at Vidalon. With the exception of a great register, the Grand Livre, too bulky to film, the Archives Nationales microfilmed much of this material because of its value as an unusually coherent and continuous set of sources for industrial history. Though I have not made much use of this material myself, it has served as the basis for a doctoral dissertation by Leonard Rosenband (below), and copies of nineteen reels of the Vidalon archive accompany the other Montgolfier material in Firestone Library. The collection in the Archives Nationales is called "Archives Canson-Montgolfier," and is numbered 131 MI, 53 AQ 1 through 53 AQ 270. Unfortunately, the numbering in the Inventory prepared by Jean Frachon has not been respected, though the inventory itself still exists.

The collection of aeronautica assembled by Harold Fowler McCormick, Princeton Class of 1896, was given to the library by Alexander Stillman. Maurice H. Smith, "Travel by Air before 1900," *Princeton University Library Chronicle* 27 (1966):143-47, gives a summary account of the holdings. (I am grateful to Mrs. Samuel H. Bryan, Jr., for calling this article to my attention.) They include iconography, documents, and printed materials. Among the documents are eight letters written by Etienne de Montgolfier to Desmarest. Two printed works have been specially valuable. The first item is the contemporary history of the earliest balloon experiments, Barthélemy Faujas de Saint-Fond, *Description des expériences de la machine aérostatique de MM de Montgolfier et de celles auxquelles cette découverte a donné lieu* (1783). It is bound together with a second volume, *Première suite de la description des expériences aérostatiques . . .* (1784). The second item in the McCormick Collection that has been specially useful is copy 278 of a privately printed volume, Comte de La Vaulx and Paul Tissandier, *Joseph et Etienne de Montgolfier* (Annonay, 1926). It consists of reproductions of portraits and contemporary prints together with facsimiles of certain documents from one or another of the collections of family papers mentioned above. The transcriptions are not always reliable.

The Richard Gimbel Collection is the major source of illustrative material. Colonel Gimbel presented the collection to the United States Air Force Academy, which houses it in the library on its campus at Colorado Springs. It is much larger than the McCormick Collection, or (I think) than any other on the history of aviation, and also consists of iconography, published works, and documents. In both collections, lighter-than-air craft occupy only a part of the whole coverage.

The Library of the Air Force Academy maintains a detailed catalogue of the Gimbel Collection, a copy of which may be consulted on microfilm in the library of the Air and Space Museum in Washington, D.C. That library also contains materials on the history of aviation, and there is an alcove in the museum illustrating the history of the balloon itself.

Bibliographical entries in the Index will guide readers to the authors of contemporary printed writings referred to in the Notes. Unless otherwise stated, the place of publication of all works in French was Paris.

Readers may also wish to consult certain secondary authorities. I have drawn my knowledge of the history of the paper industry largely from Leonard N. Rosenband, "Work and management in the Montgolfier paper mill, 1761-1804" (Ph.D. dissertation, Princeton University, 1980); and Marie-Hélène Reynaud, *Les moulins à papier d'Annonay à l'ère pré-industrielle: les Montgolfier et Vidalon* (Annonay: Editions du Vivarais, 1981).

The most sophisticated work on the pre-history of aviation is Jules Duhem, *Histoire des idées aéronautiques avant Montgolfier* (Paris: Sorlot, 1943). The book has been very little noticed, perhaps because of the date of publication, although the author was the son of the famous historian and philosopher of science, Pierre Duhem. I am indebted to my friend and colleague, Monsieur Maurice Daumas, both for my knowledge of it and for the gift of a copy.

The famous aviator, Charles Dollfuss, was a great patron and enthusiastic practitioner of the history of aviation. His lights were not entirely those of a professional historian, naturally enough, but the work on which he collaborated with Henri Bouché remains a classic: *Histoire de l'Aéronautique* (Paris: Editions Saint-Georges, 1932). Reference should also be made to Louis Figuier, *Les Aérostats* (Paris: Jouvet, 1822), the first full history.

A contemporary balloonist, with whom I have enjoyed a correspondence, has also written on the invention of the art: Paul Maravelas, "The Montgolfiers' moment in History," *Ballooning* (May-June 1981), pp. 59-63; and "Joseph Montgolfier: true ballooning pioneer," ibid. (September-October 1981), pp. 59-63.

One biography of Marc Seguin is worth consulting: P. E. Marchal and Laurent Seguin, *Marc Seguin (1786-1875), La naissance du premier chemin de fer français* (Lyons: Cuzin, 1957). On the specific matter of Joseph de Montgolfier and Marc Seguin on heat, there is a very valuable discussion in Pietro Redondi, *L'Accueil des idées de Sadi Carnot et la technologie française de 1820 à 1860* (Paris: Vrin, 1980).

GENEALOGICAL CHART

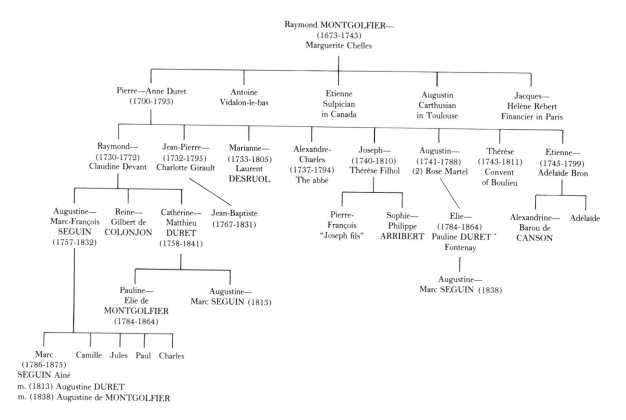

Raymond MONTGOLFIER—
(1673-1743)
Marguerite Chelles

Pierre—Anne Duret
(1700-1793)

Antoine
Vidalon-le-bas

Etienne
Sulpician
in Canada

Augustin
Carthusian
in Toulouse

Jacques—
Hélène Rébert
Financier in Paris

Raymond—
(1730-1772)
Claudine Devant

Jean-Pierre—
(1732-1795)
Charlotte Girault

Marianne—
(1733-1805)
Laurent
DESRUOL

Alexandre-
Charles
(1737-1794)
The abbé

Joseph—
(1740-1810)
Thérèse Filhol

Augustin—
(1741-1788)
(2) Rose Martel

Thérèse
(1743-1811)
Convent
of Boulieu

Etienne—
(1745-1799)
Adélaïde Bron

Augustine—
Marc-François
SEGUIN
(1757-1832)

Reine—
Gilbert de
COLONJON

Cathérine—
Matthieu
DURET
(1758-1841)

Jean-Baptiste
(1767-1831)

Pierre-
François
"Joseph fils"

Sophie—
Philippe
ARRIBERT

Elie—
(1784-1864)
Pauline DURET
Fontenay

Alexandrine—
Barou de
CANSON

Adélaïde

Pauline—
Elie de
MONTGOLFIER
(1784-1864)

Augustine—
Marc SEGUIN (1813)

Augustine—
Marc SEGUIN (1838)

Marc
(1786-1875)
SEGUIN Aîné
m. (1813) Augustine DURET
m. (1838) Augustine de MONTGOLFIER

Camille   Jules   Paul   Charles

NOTES

Chapter I

1. Abbé Alexandre-Charles Montgolfier to chanoine du Bourg, late August 1783, reproduced in André Foulon comte de La Vaulx and Paul Tissandier, *Joseph et Etienne de Montgolfier* (Annonay: privately printed, 1926), Plate XIII; see also an eyewitness account drafted for the *Journal de Paris* by a local lawyer, one Chomel, 30 July 1783 (MA XX, 1).

2. The draft of their petition is in Etienne's hand (M IV, 13). The entry in the minutes of the Etats particuliers du Vivarais for 5 June 1783 is reproduced in La Vaulx and Tissandier, Plate XVI.

3. On the local history and the Estates of Vivarais, see Jean Régné, *Histoire du Vivarais*, 3 vols. (Largentière [Ardèche]: Imprimerie Mazel, 1912-1945), 2 (1921): 352-96; Jean Charay, *Petite histoire politique et administrative du Vivarais* (Lyons: Imprimerie Audin, 1959), pp. 104-112.

4. M VIII, 3.

5. Nicolas Desmarest, "Mémoire sur l'état actuel des papéteries d'Annonay" (1779). Archives de l'Ardèche, series C-960.

6. For a discussion of the family history, Léon Rostaing, *La famille de Montgolfier* (Lyons: A. Rey, 1910), see the bibliographical essay. Three excellent doctoral dissertations discuss the businesses of the two families: Jean-Pierre Le Moine, "Les Johannot—famille protestante et papétière d'Annonay au XVIIIᵉ siècles" (Sorbonne, undated but c. 1975); Leonard N. Rosenband, "Work and management in the Montgolfier paper mill" (Princeton, 1980); and Marie-Hélène Reynaud, *Les moulins à papier d'Annonay à l'ère pré-industrielle, les Montgolfier et Vidalon* (Annonay: Editions du Vivarais, 1980).

7. Rostaing, *La famille de Montgolfier*, pp. 18-20, who reports the recollections written down by Marianne Desruol, Raymond's granddaughter and a sister of Etienne and Joseph.

8. The rules are printed ibid., pp. 508-511.

9. Adélaïde de Montgolfier, *Contes devenus histoire* (undated, but c. 1835), "La corbeille ailée," pp. 27-31.

10. Rostaing, *La famille de Montgolfier*, p. 75.

11. Ibid., pp. 75-76, note.

12. Pen portraits of Pierre and many of his children were left by Matthieu Duret, of the family of Pierre's wife, who himself married one of Pierre's granddaughters. The sketch of Pierre is specially vivid. M XI.

13. "Rules . . . in the Montgolfier paper factory," Article XIII; Rostaing, *La famille de Montgolfier*, pp. 510-11.

14. Ibid., p. 74.

15. Ibid., p. 83. The child was the son of Matthieu Duret (see note 12 above).

16. M XI. Rostaing devotes Chapter VIII to a biography of Joseph, *La famille de Montgolfier*, pp. 187-228.

17. M X.

18. Letters addressed by Boissy d'Anglas to Etienne from 1786 through 1791 are in the collection, MA XVI, 1-45. A typescript copy of many of these letters, made probably for Léon or Camille Rostaing, is in the Montgolfier papers. There are also letters from Ami Argand 1785-1798, M V, and MA XIII, 38-54.

19. On this tangled matter, see Rostaing, *La famille de Montgolfier*, pp. 145-56, together with Pierre's division of his estate (*partage des biens*) on 2 April 1793, just before his death, Archives Régis de Montgolfier.

20. Duret left a sketch of Marguerite-Thérèse, M XI; also Rostaing, *La famille de Montgolfier*, pp. 135-43; on the abbé, see pp. 129-34.

21. On Marianne, see pp. 126-28.

22. On Jean-Pierre, see Duret memoir, M XI.

23. Rostaing, *La famille de Montgolfier*, pp. 188, 461-68.

24. Ibid., pp. 197-98.

25. The first three volumes of Joseph Priestley, *Experiments and observations on different kinds of air*, were published in London in 1774, 1775, and 1777.

26. Duret memoir on Joseph Montgolfier, M XI.

27. MA VIII.

28. Joseph to Etienne Montgolfier, 16 May 1783, MA VIII, 1.

29. Joseph to Etienne Montgolfier, 10 October 1783, MA IX, 6.

30. Duret to Madame de Soras 12 June 1837. M XI. Madame de Soras was Etienne's granddaughter.

31. Rostaing, *La famille de Montgolfier*, pp. 192-95.

32. Joseph Galien, *L'art de naviger dans les airs, amuse-ment physique et géométrique* (Avignon, 1755).

33. J.-M. Degérando, "Notice sur . . . Joseph Mont-golfier," *Bulletin de la Société d'encouragement pour l'industrie nationale* 13 (1814):91-108.

34. Jean-Pierre to Etienne Montgolfier, 12 July 1783. MA VIII, 2.

35. Degérando, "Notice sur . . . Joseph Montgolfier," p. 107.

36. Quoted in Rostaing, *La famille de Montgolfier*, pp. 88-89.

37. The Diderot plates are reproduced in C. C. Gillispie, *A Diderot Pictorial Encyclopedia of Trades and Industry*, 2 vols. (New York: Dover, 1959), 2: Plates 359-68.

38. Bacalan to Pierre Montgolfier, February 1769, in Rostaing, *La famille de Montgolfier*, p. 88.

39. On the career and volcanological writings of Des-marest, see Kenneth L. Taylor, "Desmarest," *Dictionary of Scientific Biography*.

40. "Premier mémoire sur les principales manipulations, qui sont en usage dans les papéteries de Hollande," *Mémoires de l'Académie Royale des Sciences pour l'année 1771* (1774), pp. 335-64; "Second mémoire sur la papéterie . . ." *Mémoires de l'Académie Royale des Sciences pour l'année 1774* (1778), pp. 599-687. Both memoirs were also printed and paginated separately.

41. On the corps of manufacturing inspectors, see C. C. Gillispie, *Science and Polity in France at the End of the Old Regime* (Princeton: Princeton University Press, 1980), pp. 425-27.

42. Etienne Montgolfier to Nicolas Desmarest, undated but evidently February 1780. McCormick Collection, which contains eight autograph letters from Etienne to Desmarest.

43. Desmarest, "Mémoire sur l'état actuel des papéteries d'Annonay" (1779). Archives de l'Ardèche (Privas), series C-960.

44. Desmarest, "Second mémoire sur la papéterie . . . ," p. 88.

45. Ibid.

46. Jean-Pierre Montgolfier to Rome (syndic-général . . . des trois états . . . de Languedoc), 7 January 1780; Rome to De la Chadenède (subdelegate of the intendant of Languedoc at Vienne), 19 January 1780; Pierre Montgolfier certificate, 3 February 1780. These documents are in the Archives de l'Ardèche, series C-143.

47. Matthieu et Pierre-Louis Johannot à Nosseigneurs des Etats de Languedoc, undated printed remonstrance, c. 1781; Antoine-François Montgolfier à Nosseigneurs des Etats de Languedoc (1780), Archives de l'Ardèche, series C-143.

48. Etienne Montgolfier à Nosseigneurs des Etats, petition undated, but 1783 or 1784. Archives de l'Ardèche, series C-143.

49. Ibid.; Also Desmarest, article "Papéteries," *Encyclopédie méthodique*, Vol. 5, *Arts et métiers mécaniques* (1788), pp. 463-592.

50. On Augustin, see Rostaing, *La famille de Montgolfier*, pp. 327-40.

51. Rosenband, "Work and management in the Montgolfier paper mill."

52. Etienne Montgolfier to Desmarest, 16 December 1782. La Vaulx and Tissandier, Plates VI, VII.

53. Desmarest to Etienne Montgolfier, ibid., p. 27.

54. MA III, 9.

55. The "Mémoire sur les machines aérostatiques" is undated, but clearly pertains to the period in 1786 or 1787 when Etienne was hoping to elicit support from the government to salvage a transport balloon (MA, II, 8). See below, Chapter 4, Section 1.

56. M VI, 2, 3.

57. Abbé Alexandre Montgolfier to chanoine du Bourg, late August 1783, Plate XIII in La Vaulx and Tissandier.

58. Adélaïde de Montgolfier, *Contes devenus histoire*, pp. 37-39.

59. Rostaing, *La famille de Montgolfier*, pp. 260-61.

60. Letter cited in note 57 above. Jean-Pierre to Etienne Montgolfier, 12 July 1783, MA VIII, 2.

CHAPTER II

1. "Affiches, Annonces, et Avis divers," *Feuille Hebdomadaire*, no. 28, 10 July 1783, p. 112. The paragraph is headed, "Extrait d'une lettre d'Annonay, du 21 juin, 1783." In a postscript to a letter from the abbé Alexandre to Etienne of 21 July (MA, VIII, 12), Jean-Pierre alludes to this communication as "la lettre de M^r d'Abrieu de Paris," and attributes it to the resentment of the Johannots over their humiliation in a lawsuit they had brought against Joseph in Lyons over an alleged indebtedness. It is unclear whether d'Abrieu wrote the letter, or merely communicated passages from a letter he had received from Annonay. In the latter case, the actual author might well have been Johannot himself.

2. *Journal de Paris*, 27 July 1783, pp. 861-62.

3. D'Ormesson to Condorcet, 28 June 1783, reproduced in La Vaulx and Tissandier (1926), p. 34, Plate XXI.

4. "Rapport . . . sur la machine aérostatique inventée par MM. de Montgolfier," *Histoire de l'Académie Royale des*

Sciences pour l'année 1783 (1786), pp. 5-24, presented on 23 December 1783. We shall be discussing the report in due course. It should be noted here, however, that following its formal presentation by the secretary (Leroy), Desmarest took the floor to read passages from Etienne's letters to him recounting the early experiments dating back to 1782 (La Vaulx and Tissandier [1926], p. 39) and that the commission recorded their existence ("Rapport," p. 12).

5. Condorcet to d'Ormesson, 19 July 1783, La Vaulx and Tissandier, p. 35.

6. The abbé, Jean-Pierre, and Joseph to Etienne, 22 Sept. 1783 (MA VIII, 46).

7. See, for example, Joseph to Etienne, 18 August 1783 (MA VIII, 23).

8. For an account of the experiment synthesizing water, which Lavoisier carried out jointly with Laplace, see Henry Guerlac, "Lavoisier," *Dictionary of Scientific Biography*.

9. Paris, 1783. A second volume followed, describing the flights late in 1783 and early in 1784: *Première suite de la description des expériences aérostatiques . . .* The two are often found bound together, and will be cited as *Description* and *Suite*.

10. Faujas, *Description*, pp. 8-9; La Vaulx and Tissandier, pp. 35-36.

11. *Recherches sur les volcans éteints du Vivarais et Velay* (1778).

12. Joseph to Etienne, 6 August 1783 (MA VIII, 15).

13. Arthur Young, the English agricultural writer, spoke appreciatively of a visit to Faujas in his property near Montélimar: the "liveliness, vivacity, *phlogiston* of his character, do not run into pertness, foppery or affectation." *Travels in France*, 2 vols. (Dublin, 1793), 1: 358-59.

14. On Charles, see the article on him by J. B. Gough, *Dictionary of Scientific Biography*; Robert Chapeix, *Savants méconnus* (1966), pp. 1-52. The Fourier *éloge* is in the *Mémoires de l'Académie des Sciences de l'Institut de France*, series 2, 8 (1829), pp. lxxiii-lxxxviii. The Bontemps memorandum, 30 March 1827, is in the dossier of Charles in the Archives of the Academy of Science, Institut de France. Charles never published anything other than referees' reports, which appear in the *Procès-verbaux de la première classe de l'Institut de France 1795-1835*, 10 vols. (Hendaye, 1910-1922). He was librarian of the Institute at the time of his death, and his papers were placed in its Bibliothèque in 1870. Manuscript notes for his course in 1783-1784 are preserved there, MSS. 2104. A longhand memorandum in his dossier at the Academy by Ernest Maindron,

dated 7 March 1870, points out that Charles is often confused with two homonyms, a minor mathematician "Charles le géomètre" elected to the Academy in May 1785, and one Hyacinthe Charles, author of several memoirs on the quadrature of the circle in the 1770s.

15. My account of the preparations for the first Charles balloon depends on Faujas, *Description*, pp. 7-20.

16. "Lettre de M. de Meusnier . . . sur la force d'ascension du Ballon parti du Champ de Mars, sur la marche qu'il a tenue après avoir percé la nue, sur la hauteur à laquelle l'air inflammable a pu réagir contre son enveloppe, suivie de recherches sur les degrés de pesanteur des différentes couches de l'atmosphère, &c.," Faujas, *Description*, pp. 49-162. On the career of Meusnier, see Gaston Darboux, "Notice historique sur le Général Meusnier," *Mémoires de l'Académie des Sciences de l'Institut de France*, series 2, 51 (1910):i-xxxviii, followed by a reprinting of Meusnier's relevant writings, "Mémoires et travaux relatifs à l'aérostation," ibid., pp. 3-128. The "Lettre" above here occupies pp. 7-56. On Monge, see René Taton, *L'Oeuvre scientifique de Gaspard Monge* (PUF, 1951); and on Meusnier and the Monge entourage, C. C. Gillispie, *Science and Polity in France at the End of the Old Regime* (Princeton: Princeton University Press, 1980), pp. 509-48.

17. Meusnier, "Lettre . . ." in Faujas, *Description*, p. 49.

18. "Calculs sur les ballons aérostatiques faits par feu M. Leonhard Euler . . . ," *Mémoires de l'Académie Royale des Sciences, . . . pour l'Année* 1781 (1784), pp. 264-68.

19. Meusnier, "Lettre . . ." in Faujas, *Description*.

20. *Journal de Paris*, 29 August 1783 (MA V, 5). See also a memorandum headed "Réponse aux plaintes de MM Robert contre les souscripteurs de l'expérience faite au Champ de Mars" (MA V, 7).

21. "Lettre à M. Faujas de Saint-Fond, Faujas, *Description* . . . , pp. 197-200.

22. Etienne to Joseph, 20 December 1783 (M I, 22).

23. MA VIII, 12.

24. MA VIII, 13.

25. MA VIII, 14.

26. Joseph to Etienne, 6 August 1783 (MA VIII, 15).

27. "On pouvait aussi tenter cetter décomposition avec de la craye—à cause de la double affinité, la base du sel marin estant très amoureuse de l'air fixe contenu dans la craye." Joseph to Etienne, 10 August 1783 (MA VIII, 18). At the behest of the government (advised by Lavoisier), the Academy of Science had set a prize in 1781 for the best method of preparing soda from salt derived from sea water. The award was scheduled for November 1783, though in the event no en-

tries were deemed worthy. The process that did succeed after many vicissitudes was invented by Nicolas Leblanc and patented in 1791. Leblanc converted sodium chloride into sodium sulphate with sulfuric acid, and then fused the sulfate with charcoal and chalk (carbon and calcium carbonate) to yield sodium carbonate. John G. Smith, *The origins and early development of the heavy chemical industry in France* (Oxford: Clarendon Press, 1979), pp. 191-215.

28. Joseph to Etienne, 4 September 1783 (MA VIII, 32); reproduced in La Vaulx and Tissandier, pp. 51-52, Plates XXXVI-XXXVII.
29. Faujas, "Expérience . . . faite par M. de Montgolfier, le 12 Septembre 1783 . . . ," *Description*, pp. 29-36.
30. Joseph to Etienne, undated but evidently after the 4 September letter (note 26, MA VIII, 25).
31. Etienne to Joseph, 6 September 1783 (MA VII, 1).
32. Faujas, *Description*, p. 32.
33. The *procès-verbal* is reproduced in La Vaulx and Tissandier, pp. 38-39, Plate XXV.
34. Etienne to Joseph, 13 September 1783 (MA VII, 2).
35. The abbé and Jean-Pierre to Etienne, 25 August 1783 (MA VIII, 28).
36. Joseph to Etienne, undated but early September 1783 (MA VIII, 25).
37. Jean-Pierre to Etienne, 30 August 1783 (MA VIII, 30).
38. The abbé to Etienne, 4 September 1783 (MA VIII, 32).
39. Faujas, "Expérience faite par M. de Montgolfier à Versailles le 19 septembre 1783 . . . ," *Description*, pp. 36-48.
40. La Vaulx and Tissandier printed a facsimile, pp. 41-43, Plate XXVI. The original is in (M I, 1 *bis*). A copy in the handwriting of Jean-Pierre is in MA VII, 3.
41. Faujas, *Description*, pp. 44-48, and for the Pilatre offer, the latter to Faujas, 28 September 1783, ibid., p. 284. A month previously, on 30 August, Pilatre presented a collection of model animals in plaster of Paris to the Academy of Science. At the same time, he proposed himself as candidate to fly in the "machine de M. Montgolfier." The minutes of the Academy note that he was to be thanked for his zeal, and his offer was to be declined. Procès-verbaux de l'Académie Royale des Sciences, 30 August 1783, fol. 194-95. The register is preserved in the Archives of the Academy.
42. For Pilatre's account of himself, see Tournon de la Chappelle, ed., *La vie et les écrits de Pilatre de Rozier écrits par lui-même et publiés par M. T**** (1786). Cf. W. A. Smeaton, "Jean-François Pilâtre de Rozier, the first astronaut," *Annals of Science* 11 (1955):257-67; Arthur Birembaut, "W. A. Smeaton, 'Jean-François Pilâtre (sic) de Rozier,' " *Archives internationales d'histoire des sciences* 11 (1958):100-101. For the Musée see Smeaton, "The early years of the Lycée and the Lycée des Arts, I: The Lycée of the rue de Valois," *Annals of Science* 11 (1955):257-67.
43. Tournon de la Chappelle, *La vie*, p. 48.
44. Pilatre de Rozier, "Extrait d'un mémoire contenant une suite d'expériences sur les gaz," in Tournon de la Chappelle, *La vie*, pp. 110-45. That work also prints Pilatre's other essays.
45. For the reports of the Academy, see Procès-verbaux de l'Académie Royale des Sciences, 13 December 1780, 24 February 1781, 18 June 1783, and 5 May 1784, Archives de l'Académie des Sciences, Institut de France. The description of the respirator is printed in Tournon de la Chappelle, *La vie*, pp. 146-48.
46. Etienne to Joseph, letter misdated 8 October 1783 (see below note 59 and above note 26). Another, and perhaps stronger reason for placing Etienne's experiment earlier than the 15th is that the latter date would hardly have permitted the news to reach Annonay in time to provoke the reverberations in the letters cited in notes 47, 49, and 50 below, beginning with the letter of the 18th from the abbé. The sentence from the academic commission is cited from the "Rapport" cited in note 4 above.
47. Adélaïde appended this response to a postscript she had already added to a letter to Etienne from the abbé, 18 October 1783. (MA IX, 10).
48. Faujas, *Description*, pp. 268-76.
49. The abbé to Etienne, 22 October 1783 (MA IX, 12).
50. Jean-Pierre to Etienne, 22 October 1783 (MA IX, 11).
51. Etienne to Pierre, 30 October 1783 (MA I, 12).
52. Faujas, *Description*, pp. 268-76; *Suite*, p. 56.
53. Faujas, p. 270; *Journal de Paris*, 11 October 1783.
54. MA XV, 1.
55. Faujas, *Description*, pp. 272-73.
56. "Lettre de M. Giroud de Villette aux auteurs du Journal de Paris le 28 octobre 1783," reprinted in Faujas, *Description*, pp. 279-80.
57. Réveillon to Etienne, 21 November 1783 (MA XII, 9); Etienne to Joseph, undated but late December 1783 or early January 1784 (MA I, 36).
58. Faujas, *Description*, pp. 266-67. See also the letter Etienne wrote to Faujas, 20 October 1783, printed ibid., pp. 277-78, in which Etienne points out that the effect of the wind on the 17th had been to depress the

balloon by a load equivalent to an added weight of 350 or 400 pounds, and that the success of the 19th was due more to the absence of wind than to his having further lightened the gallery. He wished Faujas to incorporate these considerations in the account the latter intended for the *Journal de Paris*.

59. MA VII, 6. The original of this letter was given by Adélaïde to Geoffroy Saint-Hilaire. Several copies in different hands are identical in phrasing, and there is some mistake about the date, which is given as 8 8ᵇʳᵉ 1783. The dating must be wrong, unless what Etienne is describing is his own, hitherto unreported experiment. That seems highly improbable, however, since the description matches that of Faujas for the 19th. The mistake may have been the copyist's, or possibly Etienne's. Long exposure to the correspondence makes one feel that there may have been a depressive side to Etienne's enthusiasms. If so, that might be consistent with what otherwise seems out of character, for he was careless in dating his letters, frequently omitting to do so altogether, much to the abbé's annoyance.

60. Etienne to the abbé or Jean-Pierre, undated, but late September or early October 1783 (MA I, 2).

61. Joseph to Etienne, evidently 25 September 1783 though misdated 25 July 1783 (MA VIII, 7).

62. The abbé to Etienne, 20 September 1783 (MA VIII, 44); 29 September 1783 (MA VIII, 49).

63. Jean-Pierre to Etienne, 24 September 1783 (MA VIII, 47).

64. The abbé to Etienne, 16 October 1783 (MA IX, 8); 18 October (MA IX, 9); Etienne to the abbé or Jean-Pierre, 23 October (MA I, 9); Jean-Pierre and the abbé to Etienne, 30 October (MA IX, 18, 20); Jean-Pierre to Etienne, 8 and 13 November 1783 (MA IX, 24, 25). See also Léon Rostaing, *La famille de Montgolfier* (Lyons: A. Rey, 1910), pp. 148-56, and below, Chapter IV, Section 4, note 63.

65. Jean-Pierre to Etienne, 24 September 1783 (MA VIII, 47).

66. The abbé to Etienne, 6 October 1783 (MA IX, 3).

67. The abbé to Etienne, 11 October 1783 (MA IX, 7).

68. The abbé to Etienne, 16 October 1783 (MA IX, 8).

69. Etienne to Pierre, 8 October 1783 (MA I, 5).

70. Etienne to the abbé or to Jean-Pierre, 14 October 1783 (MA VII, 26, No. 5).

71. Etienne had occasional exchanges with Meusnier and also with Lavoisier (Etienne to Joseph, 2 October 1783, MA VII, 4). On the toy balloons, see Faujas, "Expériences faites avec de petits ballons en peau de baudruche," *Description*, pp. 22-29.

72. The copy in the Archives of the Académie des Sciences in Paris is entitled, "Mémoire au sujet des machines aérostatiques par M. Montgolfier de l'Académie de Lyon." It is in the dossier for the session of 15 November. It differs only in a few phrases from the copy preserved in the library of the Académie des Sciences, des Belles-Lettres et des Arts de Lyon, where it is numbered Recueil 232, with the title "Mémoire sur les expériences aérostatiques lu par Mʳ Montgolfier le 25 novembre 1783." Faujas printed a version in which there are variants, *Suite*, pp. 98-112. I understand from Paul Maravelas that a separately printed version also exists under the imprint "Lejay," and that there is a copy in the Munich Staatsbibliothek.

73. Faujas, *Suite*, pp. 12-13; The invitation to stage the flight in the garden of the Chateau de la Muette was conveyed to Faujas on 20 October 1783 (Faujas to Etienne, 21 October 1783, MA XV, 14).

74. Ibid., p. 35. *Journal de Paris*, 19 November 1783.

75. Faujas, *Suite*, p. 15.

76. Ibid., pp. 19-22. On behalf of the court, the signatories were the duc de Polignac, the duc de Guines, the comte de Polastran, the comte de Vaudreuil, and the chevalier d'Hunaud; and on behalf of the Academy of Science, Franklin, Faujas de Saint-Fond, Delisle, and Leroy. There is also a manuscript copy, MA XI.

77. "Lettre de M. le marquis d'Arlandes, major d'Infanterie, à M. Faujas de Saint-Fond," 28 November 1783, in Faujas, *Suite*, pp. 23-30. The quotations in the ensuing paragraphs are from d'Arlandes, as is the narrative. D'Arlandes also read a report of the flight before the Academy of Science (Procès-verbaux de l'Académie des Sciences, 28 November 1783, fol. 212).

78. Etienne to unidentified official, 22 November 1783 (MA VII, 26, No. 21).

79. *Journal de Paris*, 19 November 1783.

80. Faujas, "Manière de produire l'air inflammable en grand . . . ," pp. 232-35; "Méthode expéditive pour remplir un globe de 30 pieds de diamètre, à l'air inflammable . . . ," 236-39, in *Suite*.

81. Meusnier, "Calcul des différentes élévations auxquelles a du parvenir le globe . . . lancé du Jardin des Tuileries . . . ," *Journal de Paris*, 25 December 1783, reprinted Faujas, *Suite*, pp. 56-66. A footnote records that the gas in the Champ de Mars balloon was only four times lighter than air, whereas the gas in the Tuileries experiment was about four-and-a-quarter times lighter.

82. Above, Chapter II, Section 2.

83. *Journal de Paris*, 28 and 29 November 1783.

84. My account of the departure and of the flight derives from the minute drawn up by Charles himself, printed

in Faujas, *Suite*, pp. 48-55, and from Louis-Sebastien Mercier, *Tableau de Paris*, 12 vols., rev. ed. (Amsterdam, 1783-1789) 10:95-97, chap. 801, "Le premier Décembre 1783." Mercier is excellent on the temper of the crowd.

85. Printed in Faujas, *Suite*, p. 46.

<h2 style="text-align:center">CHAPTER III</h2>

1. "Rapport fait à l'Académie des Sciences sur la machine aérostatique, inventée par MM de Montgolfier," *Histoire de l'Académie Royale des Sciences pour l'année 1783* (1786), pp. 5-27.

2. Ibid., p. 23; For the texts of the 15 November memoir, see Chapter II, note 72.

3. "Rapport" cited note 1, p. 25.

4. Procès-verbaux de l'Académie des Sciences, 23 December 1783, fol. 235-36; see also C. E. Perrin, "Lavoisier, Monge, and the synthesis of water," *British journal for the history of science* 6 (1973):424-28.

5. Meusnier, "Mémoire sur l'équilibre des machines aérostatiques . . . ," *Observations sur la physique* 25, pt. 2 (July 1784):39-69. (This is the periodical often called "Rozier's Journal" after the founder.) The piece was reprinted by Darboux, "Mémoires et travaux de Meusnier relatifs à l'aérostation, *loc. cit.*, note 4, 61-91.

6. "Calcul des différentes élévations auxquelles a dû parvenir le globe . . . des Tuileries . . . ," *Journal de Paris*, 29 December 1783, reprinted in Darboux, "Mémoires," pp. 57-59. Procès-verbaux de l'Académie des Sciences, 3 and 6 December 1783.

7. "Rapport" cited in note 1, p. 27; Procès-verbaux de l'Académie des Sciences, 10 December 1783.

8. Procès-verbaux de l'Académie des Sciences, 13 December 1783.

9. The letters patent are printed in Léon Rostaing, *La famille de Montgolfier* (Lyon: A. Rey, 1910), pp. 317-18.

10. Jean-Pierre to Etienne, 29 December 1783 (MA IX, 48), and on the accident see Argand to Etienne, 29 November 1783, (MA XIII, 40).

11. The abbé to Etienne, 1 December 1783 (MA IX, 33).

12. The abbé to Etienne, 18 December 1783 (MA IX, 38).

13. Joseph to Etienne, 18 December 1783 (MA IX, 39).

14. Etienne to Joseph, 20 December 1783 (M I, 22).

15. Postscript by Adélaïde with letter from Augustin to Etienne, 27 December 1783 (MA IX 45).

16. The abbé to Etienne, 28 December 1783 (MA IX, 47).

17. Etienne to Joseph, 25 December 1783 (M I, 24); the abbé to Etienne, 31 December 1783 (MA IX, 50).

18. Joseph to Etienne, 18 August 1783 (MA VIII, 23).

19. Joseph to Etienne, 4 September 1783, La Vaulx and Tissandier, pp. 51-52.

20. Etienne to Joseph, 13 September 1783 (MA VII, 2).

21. Joseph to Etienne, 10 October 1783 (MA IX, 6); Faujas, *Suite*, pp. 67-68.

22. Joseph to Etienne, 25 September 1783 (MA VIII, 7). This letter is misdated 25 July.

23. Joseph to Etienne, 10 October 1783 (MA IX, 6).

24. Joseph to Etienne, 25 September 1783 (MA VIII, 7).

25. Joseph to Etienne, 18 December 1783 (MA IX, 39).

26. Joseph to Etienne, 18 December 1783 (MA IX, 48), partially reprinted in La Vaulx and Tissandier, pp. 53-54, who misread the text to compose each team "d'un chef, d'un prostitut [instead of "substitut"], de 3 volontaires, et d'un homme de paine [sic]." I have not figured out what the last-named was—"homme de peigne" perhaps? (*Peigne* = comb.)

27. Augustin to Etienne, 27 December 1783 (MA IX, 45).

28. The abbé to Jean-Pierre, 28 December 1783 (MA IX, 48).

29. Augustin to Etienne, 27 December 1783 (MA IX, 45); the abbé to Etienne, 31 December 1783 (MA IX, 50). Etienne's letter to Joseph commending Pilatre (25 December 1783) contains similar reservations, which Etienne may well have imparted to Pilatre (M I, 24).

30. The abbé to Jean-Pierre, 28 December 1783 (MA IX, 47); Joseph to Etienne, 28 December 1783 (MA IX, 46).

31. The abbé to Etienne, 9 January 1784 (MA X, 11).

32. Joseph to Etienne, 16 January 1784 (MA X, 18).

33. Augustin to Etienne, 27 December 1783 (MA IX, 45).

34. The abbé and Joseph to Etienne, undated but evidently 11 or 12 January 1784 (MA X, 16).

35. Fleurieu de la Tourette to Faujas de Saint-Fond, 20 January 1784, in *Suite*, pp. 80-83.

36. Accounts of the preparations will be found in the letter cited in note 35, and in accompanying contributions to Faujas, *Suite*: Mathon de La Cour (directeur de l'Académie des Sciences de Lyon), 23 January 1784, pp. 84-97, and a circumspect summary by Pilatre de Rozier, pp. 77-79. The best account is the letter written by the abbé to Etienne, 20-22 January 1784 (MA

X, 20), partially and inaccurately reprinted in La Vaulx and Tissandier, pp. 56-57.

37. The letter is the last cited above, note 36. Its printed excerpt gives "préparer" for "réparer le peu de succès" in the sentence just quoted. Together with the account of Mathon de La Cour (note 36), the abbé's letter to Etienne, begun on the 20th and completed on the 22nd January, also gives the fullest description of the flight itself.

38. Etienne to the abbé, 19 January 1784 (M I, 33).

39. The abbé to Etienne, 24 January 1784 (MA X, 26).

40. Etienne to the abbé and Joseph, 26 January 1784 (M I, 37).

41. Etienne to the abbé, 19 January 1784 (M I, 33); Etienne to Jean-Pierre, 20 March 1784 (M I, 52).

42. Marie-Hélène Reynaud, *Les moulins à papier d'Annonay à l'ère pré-industrielle* (Annonay: Editions du Vivarais, 1981), pp. 116-21; Leonard N. Rosenband, "Work and management in the Montgolfier paper mill" (Ph.D. diss., Princeton, 1980), pp. 87-88, 183-95.

43. The remonstrances are in the Archives de l'Ardèche, Series C-143.

44. "Mémoire sur l'état actuel des papéteries d'Annonay" (1779), Archives de l'Ardèche, Series C-960; Desmarest to Etienne, 12 December 1780, excerpted in Reynaud, *Les moulins à papier*, p. 119.

45. Joseph to Etienne, undated but February or March 1784 (MA X, 36). Also 4 February 1784 (MA X, 32); Rostaing, *La famille de Montgolfier*, pp. 192-95.

46. Etienne to Joseph, 4 March 1784 (M I, 49); Etienne to Desmarest, 22 June 1784 (McCormick Collection); Reynaud, *Les moulins à papier*, p. 127.

47. On Malesherbes, see C. C. Gillespie, *Science and Polity in France at the End of the Old Regime* (Princeton: Princeton University Press, 1980), p. 11; exchanges between Malesherbes, Boissy d'Anglas, and Etienne (MA XIV, 1-29). A series of letters from Boissy d'Anglas to Etienne (MA XVI) runs from 1783 until Etienne's death in 1799.

48. D'Antraigues to Etienne, April 1784 (MA XVII, 6). A series of over 100 letters from d'Antraigues occupies the series MA XVII.

49. Etienne to Desmarest, 22 June 1784 (McCormick Collection).

50. Printed in Rostaing, *La famille de Montgolfier*, p. 326, and in facsimile in Reynaud, *Les moulins à papier*, p. 269.

51. On Etienne's aspirations for Vidalon, see his letter to the abbé or Jean-Pierre on constituting an "attelier des états," M I, 51; his petition to the archbishop of Narbonne, August 1784, M IV, 11; the memoir of

Rome, provincial syndic in Montpellier, headed "Mr de Montgolfier papéterie erigée en Manuftre Royale," 9 August 1784, Archives de l'Ardèche, series C-143; Reynaud, *Les moulins à papier* pp. 126-29.

52. Joseph to Etienne, 5 February 1784, MA X, 32 (on "l'inperatrisse de rusie," the "prainse Potosky mynistre de Polognie," etc.; Scattered references allude to a printing of his "Discours . . . sur l'aërostat" before the Academy of Lyons in late March. I have not been able to find a copy, but I think it must refer to the 15 November memoir (Chap. 2, note 72). There is a report of it in the family papers of Monsieur Régis de Montgolfier.

53. Argand to Etienne, 23 April, 1784 (MA XIII, 11); the abbé to Etienne, May 1784 (MA XI, 38).

54. De Brantes to Joseph, 7 April 1784 (MA XV, 33).

55. Joseph to Etienne, 24 March 1784 (MA III, 5). Fourteen years later C.-A. Prieur de la Côte-d'Or found a copy of what is evidently this letter among the papers of Meusnier, and printed it in *Annales de chimie* 31 (30 Messidor *an* 7, 18 July 1798):269-73.

56. In printing the above letter, Prieur thought to inform the public that Joseph, the inventor of balloons, was also the inventor of the parachute. After it appeared, he received a memorandum from LeNormand, by now a professor of physics and chemistry at the *Ecole Centrale* of the department of Tarn, setting forth his own claims, and enclosing a copy of a memoir he had sent to the Academy of Lyons in 1784. Prieur printed this document in a later issue, "Reclamation relative à l'invention des parachutes," *Annales de chimie* 36 (30 Vendémiaire *an* 9, 22 October 1801):94-99.

57. Pierre Bertholon, *Des avantages que la physique et les arts qui en dependent peuvent retirer des globes aérostatiques* (Montpellier, 1784).

58. Jules Duhem, *Histoire des idées aéronautiques avant Montgolfier* (Paris: Sorlot, 1943), Chap. 7, pp. 236-64, discusses the parachute. A letter from the abbé to Etienne, 19 March 1784, mentions Joseph's visit earlier that month to Montpellier (MA XI, 6).

59. Garnerin's accounts of his own exploits are in the Archives nationales, AD VIII, 42.

60. "Memoire sur l'utilité des aérostats," undated but written in 1786 or 1787 (MA II, 3), fol. 9-10.

61. Etienne to Adélaïde de Montgolfier, 8 April 1784 (MA VII, 8).

62. Memoir cited note 60, fol. 10.

63. Etienne to the abbé, 17 February 1784 (M I, 43).

64. We do not have the exact date, but Etienne mentioned the award in a letter to his father of 16 January 1784 (M I, 30).

65. The accounts are summarized in MA IV, 1. Evidently, Réveillon made no charge for overhead, and there are no charges for his time, for Etienne's, or for the services of other principals. Readers may be interested in comparing the out-of-pocket expenses incurred for the various machines. I have indicated the cost of labor in parenthesis. The remainder went for cloth, thread, paper, paint, cordage, etc.

(1) Réveillon balloon	(222/6/8)	1,442/15/8
(2) Versailles balloon	(271/12/6)	2,418/18/6
Expenses common to (1) and (2)		682/0/0
(3) La Muette balloon	(235/8/5)	2,035/19/3
Total		6,579/13/5

Etienne's last balloon, the "Marie-Antoinette," launched on 23 June with Pilatre in command, had cost 6,551/8/6 (1,580/9/0 in labor) by mid-May. Construction was largely completed by the end of April. Evidently, therefore, Etienne succeeded in staying within his budget.

66. Joseph to Etienne, 5 February 1784 (MA X, 32).

67. Etienne to Joseph, undated but between 15 and 31 December 1783 (M I, 36).

68. Joseph to Etienne, 9 January 1784 (MA X, 10).

69. "Mémoire sur les expériences aérostatiques lu par Mr Montgolfier le 25 novembre 1783." For location, see Chapter II, note 72.

70. The caution about cross-Channel flights is in the letter cited in note 68.

71. Meusnier read his memoir to the Academy on 14 January 1784 (Procès-verbaux de l'Académie des Sciences), but apparently no copy has survived. His finding is stated in the memoir by Etienne cited in note 72.

72. Printed in Faujas, *Suite*, pp. 287-95.

73. Daniel Bernoulli, "Recherches sur la manière la plus avantageuse de suppléer à l'action du vent sur les grands vaisseaux," submitted to the Académie Royale des Sciences de Paris in competition for a prize set in 1753, and published (1769) in the series, *Pièces qui ont remporté les prix de l'Académie Royale des Sciences*.

74. Faujas, *Suite*, pp. 287-95. A draft in Etienne's hand is in MA III, 4 and undated, though we know from a letter to the abbé of 24 February that he had by then completed the calculations (M I, 46). Many work sheets containing calculations and rough jottings survive in M VI, 1-3 and M IX, 12, 13. Faujas also printed the report of the academic commission, *Suite*, pp. 296-301;

the original was copied into the Procès-verbaux de l'Académie Royale des Sciences, 13 March 1784, fol. 47-49.

75. M VI, 1-4; also Etienne to Castries, undated but March 1784 (MA VII, 16).

76. Etienne to Jean-Pierre, 17 January 1784 (M I, 32).

77. Etienne paid full tribute to Réveillon's loyalty in the account he wrote of these events a few years later, probably 1786. "Mémoire sur l'utilité des aérostats" (MA II, 3).

78. Ibid.; cf. Réveillon to Etienne, 17 June 1784 (MA XII, 15).

79. M IV, 1 and 2; MA VII, 16.

80. Réveillon to Etienne, 24 June 1784 (MA XII, 16); Argand to Etienne, 19 July 1784 (MA XIII, 42); d'Antraigues to Etienne, 21 June 1784 (MA XVII, 30).

81. Réveillon to Etienne, 17 June 1784 (MA XII 15).

82. La Vaulx and Tissandier, p. 65 (Plate LIV).

83. Letter cited note 81.

84. Dampierre to Etienne, 20 July 1784 (MA XV, 29).

85. Réveillon to Etienne, 24 June 1784 (MA XII, 16).

86. Pilatre de Rozier to Etienne, 30 July 1784 (MA XV, 10).

87. Réveillon to Etienne, 26 June 1784 (MA XII, 17).

88. Letter cited note 87; and De la Roche to Etienne, 27 July 1784 (MA XX, 38).

89. Réveillon to Etienne, 12 August 1784 (MA XII, 19).

90. Pilatre to Etienne 30 July 1784 (MA XV, 10). This letter was printed in La Vaulx and Tissandier, pp. 66-67, Plates LVI-LVII. Other references are to letters of 30 October, 27 November, 13 December 1783, and to an undated invitation in February or March 1784 (MA XV, 2, 3, 4, 7).

91. Etienne to Calonne, 1 July 1784 (M IV, 1); cf. Etienne to Castries, undated but several days later (M IV, 8).

92. Etienne to Castries, 1 July 1784 (M IV, 2); also 23 August 1784 (M IV, 3); Etienne, "Sur l'utilité des aérostats" (MA II, 3).

93. De la Roche to Etienne, 6 October 1784 (MA XX, 39).

CHAPTER IV

1. On the life and exploits of Blanchard, see Edouard Pelay, *Notes sur Pierre Blanchard* (Rouen, 1901) and Léon Coutil, *Jean-Pierre Blanchard, Physicien-Aéronaute* (Evreux, 1911).

2. Letter to the editors of the *Journal de Paris*, reprinted in Faujas, *Suite*, pp. 165-68.

3. The apparatus is described in Faujas, *Suite*, pp. 232-39.

4. "Expérience faite à Paris, . . . par M. Blanchard," Faujas, *Suite*, pp. 161-64; cf. Charles Dollfuss and Henri Bouché, *Histoire de l'Aéronautique* (Paris: Editions Saint-Georges, 1932), p. 24.

5. Etienne to the abbé (or perhaps to Jean-Pierre), 4 March 1784 (M I, 49).

6. MA XV, 34, 35, 36.

7. The library of the Air and Space Museum in Washington, D.C., has a scrapbook of early aeronautica assembled by William Upcott. There is a good contemporary account of the Miollan and Janinet fiasco in folio 153. The call number is ftl/620/A1V65/RB/NASM.

8. Réveillon to Etienne, 17 July 1784 (MA XII, 18).

9. Meusnier to Etienne, 27 July 1784 (MA XIII, 56).

10. Miollan to Etienne, 6 December 1786 (MA XV, 30).

11. Etienne to Miollan, undated (MA XV, 31).

12. On the background, see C. C. Gillispie, *Science and Polity in France at the End of the Old Regime* (Princeton: Princeton University Press, 1980), chap. 7, sec. 3, pp. 506-548.

13. Lavoisier reported the research with Laplace in "Mémoire dans lequel on a pour objet de prouver que l'eau n'est point une substance simple . . . ," *Mémoires de l'Académie Royale des Sciences . . . année 1781* (1784). He published an extract in the December 1783 issue of *Observations sur la physique* (often called "Rozier's journal" after the founder), pp. 452-54. The memoir is reprinted in the *Oeuvres de Lavoisier* 2 (1862), pp. 360-73. For the place of this research in Lavoisier's career, see Henry Guerlac, "Lavoisier," *Dictionary of Scientific Biography*; and for the relation to the work of Cavendish and Monge, see C. E. Perrin, "Lavoisier, Monge and the synthesis of water, a case of pure coincidence?" *British journal for the history of science* 6 (1973):424-28.

14. Gaston Darboux, "Notice historique sur le général Meusnier," *Mémoires de l'Académie des Sciences de l'Institut de France*, series 2, 51 (1910):xiv.

15. Ibid., pp. xv-xvi. Approval of the request by the minister of war himself, the maréchal de Ségur, is recorded in the procès-verbaux of the Academy of Science, 19 May 1784, fol. 119.

16. Meusnier and Lavoisier, "Mémoire où l'on prouve par la décomposition de l'eau, que ce fluide n'est point une substance simple . . . ," *Mémoires de l'Académie*

Royal des Sciences . . . année 1781 (1784), pp. 269-83; reprinted in *Oeuvres de Lavoisier* 2, pp. 360-73.

17. "Développement des dernières expériences sur la décomposition et la recomposition de l'eau," *Oeuvres de Lavoisier* 5 (1892), pp. 320-34. For some reason this paper was not published in the *Mémoires* of the Academy but only in the ephemeral *Journal polytipe*, 26 February 1786. Meusnier gave a description of his gasometers in "Description d'un appareil propre à manoeuvrer différentes espèces d'air . . . ," *Mémoires de l'Académie Royale des Sciences . . . année 1782* (1785), pp. 466-74; also *Oeuvres de Lavoisier* 2, pp. 432-40. The apparatus has survived and is on display in the museum of the Conservatoire des Arts et Métiers in Paris. Lavoisier's record of the experiments may be examined in his laboratory register, which is preserved in the archives of the Academy of Science. Meusnier's notes have found their way after many vicissitudes to the library of Cornell University. On the large-scale experiments, see Maurice Daumas, *Lavoisier, théoricien et expérimentateur* (1955), pp. 143-49, supplemented by Daumas and Denis Duveen, "Lavoisier's relatively unknown large-scale decomposition and synthesis of water, February 27 and 28, 1785," *Chymia* 5 (1959):113-29.

18. Meusnier, "Sur l'équilibre des machines aérostatiques . . . ," *Observations sur la physique, sur l'histoire naturelle, et sur les arts* 25, Pt. 2 (July 1784):44. The paper is reprinted in Gaston Darboux, ed., "Mémoires et travaux de Meusnier relatifs à l'aérostation," *Mémoires de l'Académie des Sciences de l'Institut de France*, series 2, 51 (1910):3-128. On this work of Meusnier, see also J. S. Voyer, "Histoire de l'aérostation: (1) Les lois de Meusnier," *Revue du génie militaire* 23 (1902):421-30; (2) "La ballonet de Meusnier," ibid., pp. 521-32; (3) "Le Général Meusnier et les ballons dirigeables," ibid., 24 (1902):135-56; and H. L. Malécot, *Ballons à ballonets, dits sphériques modernes. . . . Théorie de Meusnier, 1783-1909* (1910).

19. Archives de l'Académie des Sciences, Pli cacheté no. 236.

20. Procès-verbaux de l'Académie des Sciences, Archives de l'Académie, 12 June 1784, fol. 149.

21. Meusnier, "Sur l'équilibre des machines aérostatiques . . . ," p. 39.

22. Meusnier to Etienne de Montgolfier, 27 July 1784 (MA XIII, 56).

23. Meusnier, "Sur l'équilibre des machines aérostatiques . . . ," pp. 48-69.

24. It is probable that these considerations formed the topic of a memoir he read before the Academy of Sci-

ence in February 1784, of which no text remains (Procès-verbaux, 11 and 18 February 1784).

25. Meusnier, "Mémoire sur l'équilibre," p. 68. In these calculations, Meusnier assumed an atmospheric pressure of 28 inches of mercury, a temperature of 10° R, and a supply of hydrogen one-sixth the density of air.

26. The Robert brothers published an account of the Saint-Cloud flight in the *Journal de Paris* for 19 July 1784, reprinted in Malécot, *Ballons à ballonets*, pp. 21-24; cf. Meusnier to Etienne de Montgolfier, 27 July 1784 (MA XIII, 56).

27. Malécot, *Ballons à ballonets*, pp. 25-31, reprints correspondence published in the *Journal de Paris*, 20 and 21 September and 4 November 1784.

28. Printed in Darboux, "Mémoires et travaux de Meusnier," pp. 93-96.

29. Procès-verbaux de l'Académie des Sciences, 14 January 1784; cf., above, Chapter III, note 72.

30. The results of these experiments are tabulated in the Atlas Meusnier compiled to accompany the "Mémoire et devis du projet d'une machine aérostatique," which he later appended to his "Précis," and which is printed in Darboux, "Mémoires et travaux de Meusnier," pp. 97-128. On the Atlas, see below, note 32. On H.-L. Duhamel du Monceau and his *Traité de la fabrique des manoeuvres pour les vaisseaux; ou l'art de la corderie perfectionné* (1747), see Gillispie, *Science and Polity*, pp. 340-44.

31. Meusnier gives this formula for determining the metacenter without derivation or justification in the "Mémoire et devis" cited in note 30 (p. 111). A hundred years later an engineer called Caquot gave a derivation that I find convincing and follow (Voyer [3] "Le Général Meusnier," pp. 138-45). Voyer's diagrams are helpful.

32. Gaston Darboux assembled a folio volume of copies to accompany the separate printing (1910) of his "Mémoires et travaux de Meusnier." It is in the Bibliothèque nationale (fol. 529). The plates we reproduce are from a different set of copies, an album prepared for Gaston Tissandier in 1886 and now in the Library of Congress, TL617.M46. On the history of Meusnier's papers, see F. Letonné, "Le général Meusnier et ses idées sur la navigation aérienne," *Revue du génie militaire* 2 (1888):247-58.

33. Pilatre to Etienne, 8 October 1784 (MA XV, 12).

34. Above, Chapter III, note 93.

35. Procès-verbaux, Académie des Sciences, 5 May 1784, fol. 111-12.

36. Ibid., 12 June 1784, fol. 148.

37. Above, Chapter II, note 9. The *privilège* accorded

by the Academy to *Suite*, vol. 2, was dated 28 May 1784, pp. 365-66.

38. The full title is *L'Art de voyager dans les airs, ou les ballons, contenant les moyens de faire les globes aérostatiques suivant la méthode de MM de Montgolfier, et suivant les procédés de MM Charles et Robert*, and the passage cited appears on pp. 74-75. No bookseller is mentioned. The work is to be had "chez les libraires qui vendent les nouveautés." The copy I have seen belongs to the family of Madame Christine Picard, whose kindness brought it to my attention. A note pencilled on the flyleaf says "1ere édition, attribué à Piroux." The only Piroux listed in the catalogue of the Bibliothèque nationale who could qualify is identified as "architecte-juré." In 1791 he published a memoir on salt and salt-works in Lorraine, which won a prize from the Academy of Nancy, and an earlier work, incongruously enough, on fire protection, *Moyens de préserver les édifices d'incendie et d'empêcher les progrès des flammes* (Strasbourg, 1782).

39. Pilatre to Etienne, 8 October 1784 (MA XV, 12).

40. See, for example, the anonymous pamphlet attributed to Jean-Paul Marat, *Lettre de l'observateur Bon-Sens à M de *** sur la fatale catastrophe des infortunés Platre [sic] de Rosier & Romain* (1785), BN 8 Ln27, 16320. On my doubts about Marat's authorship, see Gillispie, *Science and Polity*, p. 319.

41. John Jeffries, *A narrative of the two aerial voyages of Doctor Jeffries with Mons. Blanchard, with meteorological observations and remarks* (London, 1786).

42. Réveillon to Etienne, 22 March 1785 (MA XII, 22); also Réveillon to Etienne, 8 June 1785 (MA XII, 23).

43. W. A. Smeaton, "Pilâtre de Rozier," *Annals of Science* 11 (1955):349-55; Charles Cabanès, "La mort d'Icare," *La Nature*, No. 2991 (15 December 1936), pp. 530-33.

44. Procès-verbaux de l'Académie des Sciences, 18 June 1785, fol. 129.

45. Argand to H. B. de Saussure, 29 October 1785, cited in a calendar of Argand's letters in the Bibliothèque publique et universitaire de Genève. The calendar is a fragmentary typescript in the family archives of Régis de Montgolfier. The same letter is cited and quoted more briefly in Michael Schrøder, *The Argand Burner* (Odense, Denmark: Odense University Press, 1969), pp. 48, 51.

46. Etienne to Boissy d'Anglas, 15 January 1787, Gimbel Collection, U.S. Air Force Academy.

47. MA II, 3. Though intended for publication, the memoir was never printed.

48. His phrase is "l'âme du monde policé." Ibid., fol. 17.

49. MA II, 5.

50. Pache to Etienne, 23 September 1785 (MA XIV, 76).

51. Boissy d'Anglas to Etienne, 9 January 1786 (MA XVI, 2).

52. Calonne to Etienne, 23 March 1786, printed in La Vaulx and Tissandier, 62; we know about the remaining conditions from the copy of a letter of 25 August 1787 from Villedeuil, then controller general, to Malesherbes, summarizing what he found in the files. It accompanies a letter from Boissy d'Anglas to Etienne, dated only 1787 (MA XVI, 5).

53. Memorandum, 3 February 1787 (MA III, 87).

54. Boissy d'Anglas to Etienne, 2 and 11 September 1787 (MA XVI, 6 and 7).

55. Rostaing, *La famille de Montgolfier*, pp. 300-301.

56. Marie-Hélène Reynaud, *Les moulins à papier d'Annonay à l'ère pré-industrielle* (Annonay: Editions du Vivarais, 1981), pp. 236-37, gives graphs showing the figures.

57. Family archives of M. Régis de Montgolfier; cf. Reynaud, *Les moulins à papier*, pp. 177-80.

58. Rome to Intendant of Commerce, 9 August 1784 (Archives départementales de l'Ardèche, series C-143). Etienne's letter to the archbishop of Narbonne (August 1784) is in M IV, 11. For Etienne's aspirations in detail, see a review of the state of the art he composed in 1781 or 1782, "Mémoire du Sr Montgolfier fabricant et propriétaire d'une papéterie à Annonay" (Archives nationales, F^{12} 1477).

59. Boissy d'Anglas to Etienne, 12 July 1787 (MA XVI, 3).

60. Réveillon to Etienne, 8 June 1785 (MA XII, 23).

61. The journal of Victor Dupont's journey is in the library of the Hagley Mills Foundation, Wilmington, Delaware (du Pont de Nemours papers, W3-3530). I owe my knowledge of this document, and of that cited next in note 62, to Leonard Rosenband.

62. Emric David, "Mon voyage de 1787" (Bibliothèque de l'Arsenal, Paris, MS 5947).

63. On the title and the Colonjon affair, see Reynaud, *Les moulins à papier*, pp. 32-35; Rostaing, *La famille de Montgolfier*, pp. 152-57; and correspondence between Jean-Pierre and Etienne (Archives familiales de M. Régis de Montgolfier, cited hereafter as RM).

64. Boissy d'Anglas to Etienne, 5 May 1789 (MA XVI, 11).

65. Boissy d'Anglas to Etienne, August 1789 (MA XVI, 18).

66. Boissy d'Anglas to Etienne, letter cited in note 64.

67. Registre des Procès-verbaux des séances du directoire du département de l'Ardèche, Archives départementales, Privas.

68. Etienne to the abbé, undated but evidently April 1790 (M VIII, 5).

69. Jean-Pierre to Etienne, with enclosure from the abbé, 14 April 1790 (RM). For Etienne's service on the organizational committee for the department, see Boissy d'Anglas to Etienne, 9 March 1790 (MA XVI, 21).

70. Etienne de Montgolfier, Mémoire à l'Assemblée Nationale, 1 December 1790, with a covering note to Boissy d'Anglas, 2 December 1790 (M VII, 1); for further detail, see Rostaing, *La famille de Montgolfier*, pp. 246-47, where a variant version is printed.

71. S.-J. de Boufflers, *Rapport . . . sur la propriété de nouvelles découvertes* (1791), BN Lb^{29} 1206. See also Boissy d'Anglas to Etienne, 14 January 1791 (MA XVI, 34).

72. Draft memoir, undated (M VII, 2).

73. Boissy d'Anglas to Etienne, under the heading "Dijon," 30 July. The year was probably 1791 (copy only, MA XVI, 39).

74. Charles Jolivet, *La Révolution dans l'Ardèche* (1930).

75. Rostaing, *La famille de Montgolfier*, pp. 244-45.

76. Reynaud, *Les moulins à papier*, pp. 181, 239-41.

77. RM. Excerpts from the correspondence are printed in Rostaing, *La famille de Montgolfier*, pp. 166-70.

78. Jean-Pierre to Etienne, 17 August and 21 August 1792 (RM).

79. Jean-Baptiste to Etienne, 22 August 1792 (RM).

80. Jean-Pierre to Etienne, 16 April 1792 (RM).

81. Etienne to Jean-Pierre, October 1792 (RM).

82. Jean-Pierre to Etienne, 13 November 1792 (RM).

83. Jean-Pierre to Etienne, 27 August 1792 (RM).

84. Etienne to Jean-Pierre, 27 December 1792 (RM).

85. Etienne to Jean-Baptiste, 29 January 1793 (RM).

86. "Boissy d'Anglas," *Dictionnaire de Biographie Française*.

87. Louis Pierquin, *Mémoires sur Pache* (Charleville, 1910); C.-F.-D. Dumouriez, *Correspondance avec Pache . . . Ministre de la Guerre* (1793). The Pache-Meusnier-Monge connection will figure in a work in preparation by myself; for the background, see Gillispie, *Science and Polity*, pp. 527-28.

88. Darboux, "Mémoires et travaux de Meusnier."

89. "D'Antraigues," *Dictionnaire de Biographie Française*.

90. "Flessells," *Dictionnaire de Biographie Française*.

91. On the Réveillon affair, see Charles-Louis Chassin, *Les électeurs et les cahiers de Paris en 1789, documents recueillis, mis en ordre, et annotés*, 4 vols. (1888-1889), 3:49-143. See also the following pamphlets, *Lettre au*

roi . . . (BN Lb³⁹ 1618); *Exposé justificatif par le sieur Heriot* (Bn Lb³⁹ 1619); *Acte patriotique de trois électeurs* (BN Lb³⁹ 1620); *Jugement prévotal* . . . [on Gilbert and Pourat] (BN Lb³⁹ 1628).

92. André Gardebois, *Meudon avant et pendant la Révolution: les municipalités* (Condé-sur-Noireau: Corlet, 1976), p. 144. For the initial decree of the Committee of Public Safety concerning military observation balloons, see *Recueil des actes du Comité de Salut Public*, ed. A. Aulard, 20 vols. (1889-1910), 8:672-73, 24 November 1793. Development of the project may be followed in later measures through the index entry for "aérostats."

93. Etienne to Desmarest, 20 Pluviose *an 2* (8 February 1794), McCormick Collection.

94. The draft is a manuscript of eight folios (M VII, 4); see also Etienne to Jean-Baptiste, 12 Fructidor *an 3* (29 August 1795; RM).

95. Rostaing, *La famille de Montgolfier*, pp. 335-39.

96. Ibid., pp. 132-33, 337-38; Jean-Pierre to Etienne 30 August 1792 (RM).

97. Rostaing, *La famille de Montgolfier*, p. 175.

98. Reynaud, *Les moulins à papier*, pp. 39-41; Rostaing, *La famille de Montgolfier*, pp. 179-84.

99. Rostaing, *La famille de Montgolfier*, pp. 183-84.

100. Ibid., 250-53.

101. On the history of this device, see Michael Schrøder, *The Argand Burner, Its Origin and Development in France and England, 1780-1800* (Odense, Denmark: Odense University Press, 1968). Schrøder has used Argand's papers, which I have not seen, in the Bibliothèque de l'Université de Genève, along with much other contemporary material.

102. Above, Chapter III, Section 3.

103. Argand to Etienne, 13 September 1785 (MA XIII, 45).

104. Argand to Etienne, 21 November 1783 (MA, XIII, 39).

105. Argand to Etienne, 6 Pluviose *an 2* (26 January 1794) (MA XIII 50).

106. *Idem.*

107. Argand to Etienne, 3 Frimaire *an 3* (23 November 1794) (MA XIII, 51).

Chapter V

1. *De l'influence des chemins de fer et de l'art de les tracer et de les construire* (Paris, 1839), p. 389, where Marc Seguin tabulated a series of measurements that yield an average value of 363 meter-kilograms for the mechanical equivalent of a loss of temperature of 1° Centigrade by the adiabatic expansion of steam.

2. Ibid., p. xvi.

3. Duret to Madame de Soras, 12 June 1837 (M XI). Madame de Soras was Etienne's granddaughter.

4. Joseph to Etienne, 10 October 1783 (MA IX, 6).

5. Above, Chapter III, Section 3.

6. Joseph to Etienne, 18 August 1783 (MA VIII, 23).

7. This is the memoir, cited in Chapter II, note 72, that Etienne also read before the Paris Academy on 15 November 1783.

8. Joseph to Etienne, 16 May 1783 (MA VIII, 1).

9. MA III, 71.

10. Letter cited note 6 above.

11. Letter cited note 4 above.

12. Joseph to Etienne, 9 January 1784 (MA X, 10); Jean-Pierre to Etienne, 3 April 1784 (MA XI 14); Joseph to Etienne, 23 April 1784 (MA XI, 23 and 24).

13. Jean-Pierre to Etienne, 29 December 1783 (MA IX, 48).

14. Joseph to Etienne, 12 May 1784 (MA IX, 36).

15. Procès-verbaux de l'Académie Royale des Sciences, volume 103, 9 June 1784, fol. 147. The *pli cacheté* is numbered 235.

16. *Comptes-rendus hebdomadaires des séances de l'Académie des Sciences* 202 (9 March 1936):791-93.

17. Joseph's memoir was reprinted, with commentary, by C. Cabanes, "Joseph de Montgolfier, inventeur du moteur à combustion interne," *La Nature* 64 (1936):364-68. Cabanes reconstituted the diagram, which I have taken the liberty of adapting slightly. I have also lettered the parts.

18. Letter cited note 14, printed in part by Cabanes.

19. Joseph to Etienne, undated (MA XI, 54).

20. Joseph de Montgolfier, "Du bélier hydraulique, et de son utilité," *Bulletin de la Société d'Encouragement pour l'Industrie Nationale* 4 (*an 13*, 1805):171-81. For a complementary account by an anonymous observer, see "Nouvelles expériences sur le bélier hydraulique de Montgolfier," *Journal des mines* 18 (*an 13*, 1805):19-24. Joseph had already published two earlier accounts of his ram in this latter journal, "Note sur le bélier hydraulique, et sur la manière d'en calculer les effets," *Journal des mines* 13 (*an 11*, 1803):42-51; and "Sur le bélier hydraulique," ibid. 15 (*an 12*, 1804):23-37.

21. "Du bélier hydraulique, et de son utilité," *Bulletin de la Société d'Encouragement* 4 (1805):175.

22. Ibid., p. 172.

23. Institut de France, *Procès-verbaux des Séances de l'Académie des Sciences* 1 (1910):235, 26 Messidor *an* 5 (14 July 1797). No text survives in the archives of the Academy, but it is virtually certain that he submitted the same memoir to the government in application for a patent (note 24 below). See also Argand to Etienne, 2 Thermidor *an* 5 (21 July 1797; M V, 4).

24. The patent application, complete with drawings and accompanying documents, is preserved at the Institut National de la Propriété Industrielle, 26 *bis*, rue de Leningrad. The title is "Machine nommée Bélier Hydraulique dont l'effet est d'élever les eaux de rivière au moyen de leur pente naturelle, sans pompes ni roues, ni d'autres machines proprement dites." The number 94, originally assigned, is no longer used by the Institute, which catalogues the early brevets by the date, in this case 13 Brumaire *an* 6 (3 November 1797). The application was later published, though without supporting documents, in the collection, *Description des machines et procédés spécifiés dans les brevets d'invention, de perfection, et d'importation dont la durée est expirée . . .*, ed. M(onsieur) Christian, 4 (1820), No. 300, 245-66. The date here given is 26 May 1798, which is that of a modification proposed by the Montgolfier brothers and Argand.

25. Argand to Etienne, 4 Fructidor *an* 5 (21 August 1797; M V, 1).

26. Charles Bossut, *Traité théorique et expérimental d'hydrodynamique*, 2 vols. (1786-1787). On his career, see Gillispie, *Science and Polity*, pp. 512-20.

27. Argand to Etienne, letter cited note 25.

28. Patent application, cited note 24.

29. Argand to Etienne, 14 Fructidor *an* 5 (31 August 1797); Arribert to Etienne, dated only "*samedy*," but written at about the same time (RM).

30. C. C. Gillispie with A. P. Youschkevitch, *Lazare Carnot Savant* (Princeton: Princeton University Press, 1971).

31. Léon Rostaing, *La famille de Montgolfier*, 2nd ed. (Lyons, 1910), pp. 207-208.

32. Note 24 above.

33. Arribert to Etienne, 16 Vendémiaire *an* 5 (7 October 1797; RM).

34. Arribert to Etienne, undated (RM).

35. Argand to Etienne, 6 Frimaire *an* 6 (26 November 1797; M V, 5).

36. Joseph to Etienne, 13 or 14 Thermidor *an* 5 (31 July or 1 August 1797; M V, 1).

37. Joseph to Etienne, 28 Fructidor *an* 5 (14 September 1797; M II, 2).

38. Argand to Etienne, 6 Frimaire *an* 6 (26 November 1797; M V, 5).

39. Letter cited note 37.

40. Joseph to Etienne, 6 Vendémiaire *an* 6 (27 September 1797; M II, 3).

41. The draft is rough and undated (M IX, 13). The family handlist mistakenly attributes it to Joseph.

42. Joseph's descriptions of both these variations are in M IX.

43. MA XXIII, 6.

44. Above note 24.

45. Institut de France, *Procès-verbaux des séances de l'Académie des Sciences* 1 (26 Frimaire *an* 6, 16 December 1797):318. See also the petition Joseph sent to the Minister of the Interior in Ventose *an* 6 (February 1798; M IX, 7).

46. Institut de France, *Procès-verbaux* 1 (1 Prairial *an* 6, 20 May 1798):396.

47. Ibid., 1, 415-18.

48. Archives RM.

49. Argand to Etienne, 9 Priarial *an* 6 (28 May 1798; M V, 8); and 27 Brumaire *an* 7 (18 November 1798; MA XIII, 54).

50. Arribert to Etienne, 10 January 1798 (RM).

51. Joseph to Etienne, 5 Brumaire *an* 6 (26 October 1797; M II, 8), quoted in Rostaing, *La famille de Montgolfier*, p. 216.

52. The foundation and early history of the Conservatoire des Arts et Métiers are treated in an excellent thesis, presented to the Ecole des Hautes Etudes en Sciences Sociales (1981) and still unpublished: Dominique de Place, "L'incitation au progrès technique et industriel en France de la fin de l'Ancien Régime à la Restauration, vue à travers les archives du Conservatoire des Arts et Métiers." The author is a member of the staff in the Centre de Documentation d'Histoire des Sciences in the Conservatoire.

53. The archives of the Conservatoire des Arts et Métiers (B-13) contain a manuscript "Mémoire sur la possibilité de substituer le Bélier hydraulique à l'ancienne Machine de Marly." It is undated but evidently composed in 1807, for it identifies the author as Joseph Montgolfier *membre de l'Institut* (his election occurred on 16 February 1807). The draft was then revised and expanded for publication under the same title in *Bulletin de la Société pour l'Encouragement de l'Industrie Nationale* 7 (1808):117-24; and *Suite*, pp. 136-52. The same memoir was also published in *Journal de l'Ecole polytechnique* 7 (1808):289-318. It is to be noted that Joseph had sent Matthew Boulton a description of a perfected model of the Bélier. A copy of the letter,

undated, was made by Charles Cabanes in 1937 for Jean Frachon, then director of the factory at Vidalon (RM).

54. A minute dated 9 July 1807 is signed by Champagny (the minister) and attested by Degérando for the Bureau des arts et manufactures, which was in the 2nd Division of the Ministry (RM). The report on the tests by the Bureau Consultatif des Arts et Manufactures (apparently the same body) appears in its minutes of 18 December 1810. It is signed by Thenard, Molard, Bardet, and Thoard (?). Archives du Conservatoire des Arts et Métiers, B-13.

55. RM.

56. J.-J.-H. Bottée and J.-R.-D.-A. Riffault, *Traité de l'art de fabriquer la poudre à canon . . .*, 2 vols. (1811), 1:237.

57. Joseph-Marie Socquet, *Essai sur le calorique, ou recherches sur les causes physiques et chimiques des phénomènes que présentent les corps soumis à l'action du fluide igné* (*an* 9, 1801). I am indebted to Pietro Redondi for calling this book to my attention. He points out that it is probably the first work in French to reckon with the views of Benjamin Thompson, Count Rumford, the leading exponent of the mechanical theory of heat.

58. See the minute of the Conseil d'Etat of 30 October 1806 granting the privilege of exploitation to Sieurs Montgolfier, Desormes et Clément, printed by Charles Cabanes, "Joseph Montgolfier, inventeur du moteur à combustion interne," *La Nature* 64 (1936):252-55; see also John Graham Smith, *The origins and development of the heavy chemical industry in France* (Oxford, 1979), p. 259.

59. Institut de France, *Procès-verbaux*, 1 Ventose *an* 9, 2:311; 16 February 1807, 3:501.

60. Ibid., 13 March 1809, 4:175.

61. Ibid., 8 May 1809, 4:200-202.

62. Rostaing, *La famille de Montgolfier*, pp. 220-21.

63. The modern critical edition of the text was edited by Robert Fox (1978). On the Cagniard engine, see T. S. Kuhn, "Sadi Carnot and the Cagnard Engine," *Isis* 52 (1961):567-74, and C. C. Gillispie (with A. P. Youschkevitch), *Lazare Carnot Savant*, pp. 28-29.

64. Institut de France, *Procès-verbaux*, 15 December 1806, 3:465-67. See also Pietro Redondi, *L'accueil des idées de Sadi Carnot* (Vrin, 1980), pp. 34-39.

65. Rostaing, *La famille de Montgolfier*, p. 209.

66. Below, note 116.

67. The Clément text was delivered to the Institute on 2 January 1816. It is reproduced in part in the paper of Charles Cabanes cited in note 58 and more fully in Redondi, *Sadi Carnot*, pp. 42-43.

68. The patent was enrolled on 14 September 1816 under the title "Machinery for obtaining and applying motive power," and was assigned the number 3995. The specifications and drawings were published in 1858 in the series, *Letters patent . . . and specifications of letters patent for inventions*, ed. Bennet Woodcroft (London, 1858). The series covers patents granted between 1 March 1617 and 1 October 1852. I am indebted to James Secord for searching out these documents for me in the Science Museum in Kensington, and for arranging to have them photographed.

69. "Observations on the effects of Heat and of Motion," *Edinburgh Philosophical Journal* 10 (1824):280-83.

70. Sadi Carnot, *Réflexions sur la puissance motrice du feu* (1824), critical edition ed. Robert Fox (Vrin, 1978).

71. Marc Seguin, "Mémoire sur un pont en fil de fer à établir entre Tain et Tournon," 30 November 1822 (SP).

72. Marc Seguin, *Des ponts en fil de fer* (1824), footnote to preface.

73. Rostaing, *La famille de Montgolfier*, pp. 397-400.

74. "Description d'une passerelle en fil de fer sur le Rhône entre Tain et Tournon," 25 March 1822 (SP). The article in *Moniteur universel*, 8 December 1821, pp. 1651-52, is a review of a book on the American system of internal navigation, Joseph-L.-E. Cordier, *Histoire de la navigation intérieure, comprenant la navigation intérieure des Etats-Unis d'Amérique*. I have been unable to find a copy, but there are some indications that the American part is a translation of a work by John Phillips.

75. The most complete contemporary listing is C.-L.-M.-H. Navier, *Mémoire sur les ponts suspendus* (1824).

76. SP.

77. Institut de France, *Procès-verbaux de l'Académie des Sciences* (26 January 1824), 8:11-12.

78. "Description d'une passerelle" (cited note 74), fol. 2; Marc Auguste Pictet, "Notice sur un pont en fil de fer près Annonay," *Bibliothèque universelle* 21 (7ème année, 1822):123-41. The mayor's certificate was dated 24 March 1822 (SP). Cf. work cited note 4, *Des ponts en fil de fer*, p. 10.

79. The financial conditions were specified in a covering letter on behalf of Seguin & Cie only, 28 March 1822 (SP).

80. "Description d'une passerelle" (cited note 74).

81. For the procedures of this body, essentially unchanged since the 18th century, see Charles Coulston

Gillispie, *Science and Polity in France at the End of the Old Regime* (Princeton: Princeton University Press, 1980), pp. 492-93.

82. C.-L.-M.-H. Navier, *Rapport à Monsieur Becquey . . . et Mémoire sur les ponts suspendus* (1823).

83. "Rapport de Mr Navier, Ingénieur en chef de Paris, sur le Pont de Tournon," 20 April 1822 (SP).

84. Becquey to the Prefect of the Ardèche, 13 September 1822 (SP).

85. Two drafts of this document exist in the Seguin papers, one entitled "Description d'un pont en fil de fer à établir entre Tain et Tournon" and the other "Mémoire sur un pont en fil de fer." They contain specifications in complete engineering detail and an estimate of costs (SP).

86. Memoir of 6 January 1823; Rapport, undated but November 1822 (SP).

87. *Description d'un pont en fil de fer*, undated but published late in 1823 or early in 1824 chez Bachelier in Paris. This brochure is not to be confused with *Des ponts en fil de fer* (1824), the work cited in note 72, which is about suspension bridges in general and contains the record of his experiments on iron wire.

88. Marc Seguin, *Sur l'influence des chemins de fer* (1839), pp. 52-53.

89. Seguin & Cie to Directeur-Général des Ponts et Chaussées, 30 November 1822 (SP).

90. Augustine Seguin to Marc Seguin 31 August 1823 (SP). She addressed him as "Mon cher Seguin" or "Mon cher ami," in a series of tender and touching letters, and often signed herself Seguin Duret.

91. Marc Seguin to Camille Seguin, 29 August 1823 (SP).

92. The same to the same, 1 September 1823 (SP).

93. Marc Seguin to Messieurs Seguin & Cie, 6 September 1823 (SP).

94. Marc Seguin to Camille Seguin, undated (SP).

95. Marc Seguin to his father, 22 September 1823 (SP).

96. Marc Seguin to Seguin & Cie, undated "le mercredi" (SP).

97. Letter cited note 93.

98. "Observations et Avis de l'Ingenieur en chef . . . sur le projet du pont suspendu présenté par MM. Seguin . . . ," 17 September 1823 (SP).

99. Institut de France, *Procès-verbaux de l'Académie des Sciences* (15 September 1783), 7:539.

100. Marc Seguin to Messieurs Seguin & Cie, 30 September 1823 (SP).

101. Avis du Conseil-Général des Ponts et Chaussées, 30 September 1783 (SP).

102. Marc Seguin à Messieurs Seguin, undated "le mercredi" (SP).

103. The same to the same, undated "vendredi" (SP).

104. Marc Seguin to his father, 17 October 1823 (SP).

105. Marc Seguin to Camille Seguin, mid-October 1783 (SP).

106. John Rennie to Captain Brown, 10 November 1783 (SP).

107. Marc Seguin to his father, 31 October 1783 (SP).

108. Copie de l'Ordonnance du Roi du 22 janvier 1824 (SP).

109. SP.

110. "Résumé des expériences faites le 22 août 1825 pour s'assurer de la solidité du pont suspendu à fil de fer . . . entre Tain et Tournon . . . " (SP).

111. Seguin & Cie to Directeur Général des Ponts et Chaussées, 29 November 1824 (SP).

112. "Etat des affaires faites par Mrs Seguin Frères, pendant la durée de la pacte de famille (6 8bre 1834 au 1er mai 1840)" (SP).

113. Navier, *Mémoire sur les ponts suspendus, deuxième édition, augmentée d'une notice sur le pont des Invalides* (1830).

114. Daniel Wilson to Thomas Telford, 9 June 1827, in a letter introducing Marc Seguin to the latter (SP).

115. *Notice de MM Montgolfier et d'Ayme sur la Remonte du Rhône des bateaux chargés . . .*, a prospectus addressed to the Directeur-Général des Ponts et Chaussées, and acknowledged on 30 June 1817 (SP).

116. A form letter accompanying the prospectus is dated 28 May 1825. The full designation was *Société en commandité de MM. SEGUIN, MONTGOLFIER, D'AYME ET COMPAGNIE, pour remplacer les chevaux de hallage employés à la remonte du Rhône, par des machines à feu.* This prospectus and other documents are in SP 88 and 89.

117. A ledger giving the names of the shareholders with the number of shares and accompanying annotations is in SP 88.

118. An interesting exchange of letters with Biot in 1825 and 1826 concerns this affair (SP).

119. From a letter of 17 December 1825, written in Edinburgh by a Frenchman with perfectly idiomatic English to someone in "your fine and ever-thriving metropolis of trade and industry," no doubt Manchester or Birmingham. The signature is difficult: Chevalier Mavelest(?). The recipient was evidently author of the General Report of Scotland, whatever that was.

120. The captain's log is in SP 109/7.

121. *Rapport de M. Richard-Lioud, . . . commissaire de l'entreprise Seguin, Montgolfier, d'Ayme et Comp^e. pour le halage sur le Rhône, par la vapeur à points fixes* (13 January 1828) (SP).

122. An administrative memoir by Marc Seguin gives an account of the foundation of the company, *Mémoire par M. Seguin Aîné, . . . l'un des administrateurs de la compagnie du chemin de fer de Saint-Etienne à Lyon, sur les droits respectifs de capital et d'industrie* (undated).

123. Letter cited in note 114.

124. Messieurs Seguin, ingénieurs civils, Petition "Au Roi," 13 December 1829 (SP 101/Ber).

125. The patent is recorded under the name Seguin et Cie, 22 February 1828, Institut National de la Propriété Industrielle.

126. The best account, with detailed specifications, was published by two industrialists of Mulhouse, Albert Schlumberger and Emile Koechlin, who visited Lyons and Saint-Etienne in 1831 and prepared a report for the Société industrielle de Mulhouse: *Description de la première locomotive avec chaudière tubulaire construite par M. SEGUIN, Aîné, pour le chemin de fer de Lyon à Saint-Etienne en 1828*. The report was read on 23 October 1831, and separately printed in Lyons in 1889. The copy in the Bibliothèque nationale has the *cote* 4° V, Pièce 2957.

127. The application is addressed to the minister of the interior, 16 October 1829 (SP 101/Ber), and the patent was registered 25 March 1830 (Institut National de la Propriété Industrielle). On 6 November 1829, Charles Seguin, then resident in London, also applied for a British patent (SP).

128. Marc Seguin, *De l'influence des chemins de fer, et de l'art de les tracer et de les construire* (1839), p. 46.

129. Ibid., p. 11.

130. Ibid., Chapter III, Section III, pp. 116-27, together with plans and charts in the appendix, for the account of the construction. The before and after picture of the costs may be obtained by comparing two reports to the shareholders, *Compte rendu aux actionnaires du chemin de fer de Saint-Etienne à Lyon, par MM Seguin frères et E. Biot, Gérants* (1826) in the B.N., and *Compagnie du chemin de fer de Saint-Etienne à Lyon, Extrait de la situation . . . 1836* (SP). The Schlumberger and Koechlin report, *Description de la première locomotive avec chaudière tubulaire*, is a cardinal source. It was read before the Société industrielle de Mulhouse on 31 October 1831, and separately printed in Lyons in 1889. See note 126.

131. *Compte rendu aux actionnaires . . . par MM Seguin Frères et E. Biot* (1826).

132. Seguin, *De l'influence des chemins de fer*, p. 377.

133. "Avis aux Voyageurs" (SP).

134. The formulation of the mechanical equivalent of heat independently by Mayer and Joule is a very well known episode. See the articles on Mayer by R. S. Turner and on Joule by L. Rosenfeld, *Dictionary of Scientific Biography*.

135. Seguin, *De l'influence des chemins de fer*, pp. 382-84.

136. Ibid., p. 384; the first edition of the work by F.-M. Guyonneau de Pambour, had the title *Traité théorique et pratique des machines locomotives* (1835); the second, *Théorie de la machine à vapeur* (1839) is rather a revision than a new work.

137. Seguin, *De l'influence des chemins de fer*, p. 389.

138. Ibid., p. 395.

139. Ibid., p. 390.

140. Marc Seguin, "Note à l'appui de l'opinion émise par M. Joule sur l'identité du mouvement et du calorique," published in *Cosmos* (8 May 1853), and reprinted in P. E. Marchal and Laurent Seguin, *Marc Seguin*, pp. 134-37. For Joule's opinion of the significance of the work of both Marc Seguin and Mayer, see his "Note on the history of the dynamical theory of heat," *Philosophical Magazine* 4th ser., 24 (August 1862), pp. 121-23. An exchange between Joule and Marc Seguin in 1862 is reprinted in Marchal and Seguin, *Marc Seguin*, annexe VI, 209-211.

141. Marc Seguin, *De l'influence des chemins de fer*, pp. 393-94.

142. Marc Seguin to his father, 11 November 1823 (SP).

143. Readers may be interested in the main titles: *Considérations sur les phénomènes naturels rapportés à l'attraction newtonienne* (1851); *Considérations sur les causes de la cohésion envisagées comme une des conséquences de l'attraction newtonienne* (1855); *Mémoire sur un nouveau Système de Moteur fonctionnant toujours avec la même vapeur, à laquelle on restitue, à chaque coup de piston, la chaleur qu'elle a perdue en produisant l'effet mécanique* (1857); *Mémoire sur l'origine et la propagation de la force* (1857); *Considérations sur les lois qui président à l'accomplissement des phénomènes naturels . . .* (1861); *Mémoire sur les causes et sur les effets de la chaleur, de la lumière, et de l'électricité* (1865); *Réflections sur l'hypothèse de Laplace relative à l'origine et à la formation du système planétaire* (1867).

144. Cf. note 69 above. The Herschel letters at the Royal Society of London contain an appeal from Marc Seguin dated 10 June 1861 (Vol. 17, letter 184) recalling their one-time common interests and requesting Her-

schel's intercession in having him elected a correspondent of the Royal Society. That never came about. In the draft of a reply (letter 185), Herschel noted that what Marc Seguin had evoked with retrospective appreciation were "some very crude and inadequate notions of mine in 1824, . . . so crude indeed that, cited in 1861, I am at a loss to understand what meaning I might then attach to them." Herschel then compli-

mented Marc Seguin on the success of his bridges.

145. *Corrélation des forces physiques, par W. R. Grove, Esq., Q. C., traduite par l'abbé Moigno, sur la 3ème édition anglaise, avec des notes par M. SEGUIN AÎNÉ* (1856).

146. Henri Fabre, *J'ai vu naître l'aviation* (Grenoble: Guirimand, 1980). The author attended the seventieth anniversary celebration of his invention in his hundredth year at Le Bourget in 1980.

LIST OF ILLUSTRATIONS

20. The improved hydrogen generator. Faujas credits this device to the first Blanchard flight (see Chapter IV, Section 1), but the Meusnier account, and iconographic sources, make it appear that Blanchard's suppliers adapted the arrangement from Charles and Robert. From Faujas, *Suite*, p. 232, Plate IV.

21. The Charles-Robert ascent, looking toward the château des Tuileries. Gimbel Collection 1128 A.

22. The Charles-Robert ascent, looking toward the garden of the Tuileries. Gimbel Collection 1120.

23. The Charles-Robert flight as seen from the left bank of the Seine. Gimbel Collection 1141.

24. The duc de Chartres and the duc de Fitz-James arrive to witness the Charles-Robert landing. Gimbel Collection 1140.

25. Charles takes off solo from Nesle. Gimbel Collection 1152 A.

26. Aircraft constructed in 1783. Gimbel Collection 1286.

27. Flight paths over Paris. Gimbel Collection 1212.

28. Joseph de Montgolfier's specifications for a gondola for the *Flesselles*. Letter to Etienne, 18 December 1783. From the Musée de l'Air (IX, 39).

29. The design of the *Flesselles*. Gimbel Collection 1082.

30. Launching the *Flesselles*. Gimbel Collection 1083.

31. The *Flesselles* airborne. Gimbel Collection 1078.

32. The *Flesselles* at its zenith. Gimbel Collection 1079.

33. The de Brantes balloon with Argand Burner. Gimbel Collection 1084.

34. Sketch for the parachute. The postscript of a letter from marquis de Brantes to Joseph de Montgolfier, 7 April 1784, Musée de l'Air (XV, 33).

35. André Garnerin descending by parachute over Paris. Gimbel Collection 2000.

36. Design and calculation for propelling a balloon, in the hand of Etienne de Montgolfier. Montgolfier family papers.

37. Sketch for a cargo balloon by Etienne de Montgolfier. Montgolfier family papers.

38. Madame Blanchard rising above Turin in 1812. Gimbel Collection 1819.

39. Blanchard's first balloon, launched from the Champ de Mars, 2 March 1784. McCormick Collection 27.

40. A caricature lampooning the Miollan-Janinet fiasco in the Luxembourg garden, 11 July 1784. Gimbel Collection 1187.

41. The Meusnier memoir on stabilization of altitude. From *Observations sur la physique* 25 (July 1784):36.

42. The Saint-Cloud experiment of an egg-shaped balloon with stabilizer, 15 July 1784. Gimbel Collection 1157.

43. The Roberts' long-distance flight, Paris to Béthune, 19 September 1784. Gimbel Collection 1158.

44. The diagrams are from Voyer, "Histoire de l'aérostation," cited Chapter IV, note 18.

45-53. The Meusnier Atlas. A selection of ten of the sixteen plates, together with the table of weights pertaining to one of the assemblies illustrated, the landing gear. The plates omitted have less mechanical or pictorial interest. They are the 1st, 2nd, and 3rd, top and side views of the gondola; the 12th, a top view of the tent to shelter the dirigible on the ground; and the 15th and 16th, architectural elevations of the hangar. Reproduced from the copy in the Library of Congress.

54. Table of Weights, Landing Gear of the Meusnier dirigible. The section reproduced appears on pp. 104 and 105 of Gaston Darboux, "Mémoires et travaux de Meusnier relatifs à l'aérostation," cited in Chapter IV, note 18. The table has been assembled onto one sheet for reproduction.

55. John Jeffries, M.D. Reproduced from John Jeffries, *A narrative of the two aerial voyages of Doctor Jeffries with Mons. Blanchard* (London, 1786).

56. A German print, headed "Unglückliche Luftreise des Herrn Pilastre de Rozier." Gimbel Collection 2168.

57-58. Itineraries for a cargo balloon, in the hand of Etienne de Montgolfier. Montgolfier family papers.

59. Balloon observation at the Battle of Fleurus, an Austrian view. Gimbel Collection 2025.

60. Drawing by the author of experimental model of Joseph de Montgolfier's heat pump.

61. Drawing of Joseph de Montgolfier's heat pump, as described in the *pli cacheté* deposited in the Academy of Science. Adapted from "Schema reconstituant le mécanisme de la pompe à feu de Joseph de Montgolfier," in Charles Cabanes, "Joseph de Montgolfier, inventeur du moteur à combustion interne," *La Nature*, No. 2975 (15 April 1936), p. 364.

62. The hydraulic ram, 1805 model. Reproduced from *Bulletin de la Société d'Encouragement pour l'Industrie Nationale* 4 (1805):Plate XVII. Princeton University Library.

63. The basic hydraulic ram. Drawing from the appli-

cation for a patent, 3 November 1797. *Institut National de la Propriété Industrielle*, 26 *bis*, rue de Leningrad, Paris VIIIᵉ.

64. The hydraulic ram with air reservoir. Same source as 63.

65. A hydraulic ram to be installed on shipboard for pumping out the hold. From a manuscript in the Musée de l'Air (XXIII, 6).

66. The hydraulic ram, 1807 model, intended to replace the Machine de Marly. Reproduced from *Bulletin de la Société d'Encouragement pour l'Industrie Nationale* 7 (1808):Plate XLVIII. Princeton University Library.

67. Joseph de Montgolfier in old age, with his inventions. Gimbel Collection 1836.

68. Joseph de Montgolfier's *Pyrobélier*, from the posthumous British patent, 1816, No. 3995. Reproduced in the Science Museum, Kensington.

69. Marc Seguin at about thirty years of age. Bibliothèque municipale d'Annonay, courtesy of Mlle. H. Frachon.

70. Suspension bridges over the Cance and the Galaure, Plate 2 of Marc Seguin, *Des ponts en fil de fer*, 2nd ed. (1826).

71. Profile of the Tain-to-Tournon bridge and the riv-erbed. Plate 1 of Marc Seguin, *Des ponts en fil de fer*, 2nd ed. (1826).

72. Employee's sketch of the tubular boiler. Seguin Papers, Archives de l'Ardèche, reproduced in Archives du Rhône.

73. The tubular boiler. End-view and front and cross-section. Reproduced from Albert Schlumberger and Emile Koechlin, *Description de la première locomotive avec chaudière tubulaire construite par M. SEGUIN, Aîné, pour le chemin de fer de Lyon à Saint-Etienne en 1828* (Lyons, 1889). Bibliothèque Nationale 4° V, Pièce 2957, Plate II.

74. The locomotive, with tender and coal car, Plate I of the work cited for Fig. 73.

75. Marc Seguin's sketch for his locomotive ventilator. Reproduced from the Seguin Papers, Archives de l'Ardèche.

76. Marc Seguin's sketch for a steam injection pump. Reproduced from the Seguin Papers, Archives de l'Ardèche.

77. Tabulation of mechanical equivalents of heat. Reproduced from Marc Seguin, *De l'influence des chemins de fer et de l'art de les tracer et de les construire* (1839), p. 389.

INDEX

The index is designed to guide the reader to bibliographical citations in the notes as well as to the people and subjects treated in the text. The materials of major importance are discussed in the section "Sources and Bibliography," pp. 178-79. Italicized page and note numbers in the listing below refer to other contemporary and secondary works entered under the name of the author.

Library of Congress Cataloging in Publication Data

Gillispie, Charles Coulston.
   The Montgolfier brothers and the invention of aviation, 1783-1784.

   Bibliography: p.
   Includes index.
   1. Montgolfier, Joseph-Michel, 1740-1810. 2. Montgolfier, Jacques-Etienne, 1745-1799. 3.
Seguin, Marc, 1786-1875. 4. Aeronautics—History. 5. Balloonists—France—Biography.
I. Title.
TL617.M66G48 1983   629.13′0092′2 [B]   82-61363
ISBN 0-691-08321-5

Charles Coulston Gillispie is Dayton-Stockton Professor of European History at Princeton University and Directeur d'Etudes Associé in the Ecole des Hautes Etudes en Sciences Sociales. While writing this book, he occupied the chair of history of science established in Paris by the Fondation de France. Among his many works are *The Edge of Objectivity: An Essay in the History of Scientific Ideas*; *Lazare Carnot, Savant*; and *Science and Polity in France at the End of the Old Regime* (Princeton, 1960, 1971, and 1980).